Best wishes
To

Grantland Johnson

Bill Hudcourt

3/31/09

# CHANGING METROPOLITAN AMERICA

## PLANNING FOR A SUSTAINABLE FUTURE

**WILLIAM H. HUDNUT III**

Urban Land Institute

ULI–the Urban Land Institute
1025 Thomas Jefferson Street, N.W.
Suite 500 West
Washington, D.C. 20007-5201

**Library of Congress Cataloging-in-Publication Data**

Hudnut, William H., 1932–

  Changing metropolitan America : planning for a sustainable future / William H. Hudnut III.

    p. cm.

  ISBN 978-0-87420-100-0

 1.  Urban planning—United States. 2.  City planning—Environmental aspects—United States. 3.  Sustainable development—United States.  I. Urban Land Institute. II. Title.

HT167.H827 2008

307.1'2160973—dc22

                                  2008038481

10  9  8  7  6  5  4  3  2 1
Printed in the United States of America.

**Also by William H. Hudnut III**

*Minister/Mayor*

*The Hudnut Years in Indianapolis, 1976-1991*

*Cities on the Rebound: A Vision for Urban America*

*Halfway to Everywhere: A Portrait of America's First-Tier Suburbs*

**Mixed Sources**

Product group from well-managed forests, controlled sources and recycled wood or fiber

www.fsc.org  Cert no. BV-COC-070702
© 1996 Forest Stewardship Council

FSC

# About ULI–the Urban Land Institute

The mission of the Urban Land Institute is to provide leadership in the responsible use of land and in creating and sustaining thriving communities worldwide. ULI is committed to

- Bringing together leaders from across the fields of real estate and land use policy to exchange best practices and serve community needs;
- Fostering collaboration within and beyond ULI's membership through mentoring, dialogue, and problem solving;
- Exploring issues of urbanization, conservation, regeneration, land use, capital formation, and sustainable development;
- Advancing land use policies and design practices that respect the uniqueness of both built and natural environments;
- Sharing knowledge through education, applied research, publishing, and electronic media; and
- Sustaining a diverse global network of local practice and advisory efforts that address current and future challenges.

Established in 1936, the Institute today has more than 40,000 members worldwide, representing the entire spectrum of the land use and development disciplines. ULI relies heavily on the experience of its members. It is through member involvement and information resources that ULI has been able to set standards of excellence in development practice. The Institute has long been recognized as one of the world's most respected and widely quoted sources of objective information on urban planning, growth, and development.

## Project Staff

**Rachelle L. Levitt**
Executive Vice President
Global Information Group
Publisher

**Dean Schwanke**
Senior Vice President
Publications and Awards

**Nancy H. Stewart**
Director, Book Program
Managing Editor

**Julie Stern**
**Sandra F. Chizinsky**
Manuscript Editors

**Betsy VanBuskirk**
Creative Director

**Tanya Owens Nuchols**
Book/Cover Designer, AURAS Design

**Craig Chapman**
Director, Publishing Operations

## About the Author

William H. Hudnut III, senior resident fellow, occupies the Urban Land Institute/Joseph C. Canizaro Chair for Public Policy at the Urban Land Institute, a nonprofit research and education organization dedicated to providing responsible leadership in the use of land.

A former congressman and four-term mayor of Indianapolis, Hudnut established a national reputation by spearheading the revitalization of downtown Indianapolis, including the formation of a public/private partnership that led to Indianapolis's emergence during the 1980s as a major entrepreneurial American city. After stepping down as mayor of Indianapolis, Hudnut held posts at the Kennedy School of Government at Harvard; the Hudson Institute, in Indianapolis; and the Civic Federation, in Chicago, before assuming his current position with ULI in 1996. He recently completed six years of service on the town council in Chevy Chase, Maryland, where he served as mayor for two years.

Hudnut is past president of the National League of Cities and the Indiana Association of Cities and Towns. He is the recipient of many awards, including Princeton University's highest alumni honor, the Woodrow Wilson Award for public service; the Rosa Parks Award from the American Association for Affirmative Action; and the Distinguished Public Service Award from the Indiana Association of Cities and Towns. In 1988, Hudnut was named the Nation's Best Mayor by *City and State* magazine. A graduate of Princeton University and Union Theological Seminary, he has received honorary degrees from 13 colleges and universities.

# CONTENTS

**Preface  Why We Need to Act Now**                                    **vii**

**1 The Forces Changing the Shape of Metropolitan America**              **1**
Consider Demographics **3**
Consider Housing **8**
Consider Energy **10**
Consider Transportation and Infrastructure **11**
Consider Sustainability **14**
Consider Governance **16**
Dreams Transformed **18**

**2  The Ever–Changing, Ever–Evolving Metropolitan Form**               **23**
The Changing Suburban Scene **27**
The Changing Downtown Scene **31**
The Emergence of Exurbs **33**
Shaping New Development **37**

**3  Where It All Begins: Government, Governance, and Regionalism**      **41**
The Federal Government's Role **42**
The State Government's Role **45**
Thinking and Acting Regionally **46**
The Role of Voluntary Regional Organizations **48**
The Role of Metropolitan Planning Organizations **49**
The Role of Regional Service Providers **52**
Megaregions and the Future of Metropolitan America **53**
Toward Wider Horizons **57**

**4  The Best Transportation Solution Is Being There**                  **61**
From Wagon Wheel to Spiderweb **61**
The Result: A Congestion Crisis **66**
A Different Approach **68**
Finding the Funding **86**
The Futility of an Open–Ended System **94**

**5  Infrastructure: The Backbone of the Global Economy**              **101**
What Is Infrastructure? **103**
The Infrastructure Deficit **104**
What Can We Do? **107**
Who Benefits? Who Pays? **113**
User Fees **115**
Public/Private Partnerships **116**
Privatization **117**
Will the Money Be There? **119**
An Idea Whose Time Has Come **121**

## 6 Get a CLUE: Climate, Land Use, and Energy                127

The Rising Cost of Energy **128**
Global Warming **129**
What Does This Mean for How We Design Our Future? **131**
The Impacts of Global Warming on Investment and Insurance **139**
How Can We Grow Smarter to Conserve Energy and Reduce Global Warming **140**
Wake Up, America **147**

## 7 The Challenge for Housing: Stop Driving 'Til You Qualify                155

The Housing Market in Historical Perspective **157**
Our Fundamental Housing Problem **160**
What Can Be Done? **163**
An Impossible Possibility? **176**

## 8 Building Better Communities through Retail                179

De-Malling the Mall **181**
Convenience and Experience **184**
The Urbanizing of Suburbia **185**
Big-Box Transformations **187**
Modern Retail Centers **188**
Urban Neighborhoods: The Forgotten Frontier **189**
Creating Real Places **194**

## 9 Green Is Neither Red nor Blue                197

What Can We Do? **201**
The Benefits of Going Green **213**
Green Is Here to Stay **215**

## 10 Leadership Creates Positive Change                219

Leadership Is Passionately Engaged **220**
Leadership Requires Vision **222**
Leadership Sees the Big Picture **223**
Leadership Takes Prudent Risks **225**
Leadership Collaborates **226**
Leadership Perseveres **228**
Leadership Discerns Signs of the Times **229**
Leadership Makes a Visible Difference **233**
Leadership Communicates Believable Hope **237**
Leading the Way **238**

## Related ULI Publications                241

# Why We Need to Act Now

Today we're at a critical inflection point in
human history where we can transition
to a sustainable future, or we can crash,
in ways that would hurt billions of people.

—CHARLOTTE KAHN, THE BOSTON FOUNDATION

**SOME PROPHESY** a coming apocalypse, be it unsustainable development, global warming, or infrastructure collapse. Others forecast a slow and steady deterioration in our quality of life. Some worry about the disastrous results of continuing with "business as usual." Others don't seem to be bothered at all. But the need for a call to arms is more urgent now than it has ever been. Why? Because America's cities and metropolitan areas are changing, and will continue to change, in ways that are having serious impacts on our lifestyles and quality of life. Consider the following factors:

- The pursuit of helter-skelter, low-density development farther and farther away from the center city.
- The transformation of metropolitan America into a sprawling constellation of interdependent jurisdictions—regions, rather than cities or states—that, in the new globalized economy, compete with each other at home and abroad.
- A growing imbalance between the location of jobs and the location of housing, and a shortage of adequate and affordable workforce housing.
- An ever-increasing dependence on cars.
- An "infrastructure deficit": a gap between what is being spent and what needs to be spent to keep our infrastructure in good repair.
- The convergence of two external forces—global warming and peak oil.

What do these changes mean for America's cities and metropolitan areas? Just this:

▸ Continued sprawl is unsustainable: in the interests of conserving energy, preserving natural resources, and addressing the jobs-housing imbalance, we must find new ways to accommodate growth.

▸ Traditional jurisdictional boundaries have become obsolete; to cope with problems at a regional scale, we need regional mechanisms.

▸ To cut down on the number of workers who must "drive 'till they qualify," affordable housing must be constructed closer to the workplace.

▸ To reduce the number of vehicle-miles Americans travel, land use patterns must become more compact.

▸ Without some type of "Marshall Plan" to repair and upgrade our nation's infrastructure, our bridges and roads, our airports and seaports, will continue to deteriorate under the burden of increased usage.

▸ To bring our lifestyles in line with the high cost of energy and the threat of global warming, Americans will have to use transit more—and cars and trucks less—and live "greener" lives.

In short, our country and its leaders need to wake up to the silent crises we are facing.

What can be done about these issues? What are the implications of an ever-changing, ever-evolving metropolitan form for the way we plan, use, and develop the land, our most precious resource?

The mission of the Urban Land Institute (ULI) is to propose answers to questions like these by providing "leadership in the responsible use of land and in creating and sustaining thriving communities worldwide." ULI is an education and research organization, some 40,000 members strong, that has been a leader in land use best practices and policies for more than 70 years. The Institute is committed to exploring issues of urbanization, conservation, regeneration, land use, capital formation, and sustainable development. My colleagues and I hear about the challenges, frustrations, and hopes raised by an emerging new metropolitan form. All of us, and ULI as an organization, are focusing more and more on three "superpriority" issues related to this changing form—infrastructure, sustainability, and housing—that are having a critical impact on our quality of life today, and that will continue to affect future generations.

I offer here some compelling reasons to plan for a sustainable America, coupled with some suggestions for accomplishing that goal. The vast changes that have occurred in our nation and our world since World War II—and that we are still experiencing today—require us to leave business as usual behind and to begin planning for the future in new ways. I do not intend to criticize what's gone on before. What's done is done. The past is prologue. But there *is* a better way.

This book focuses primarily on land development issues, and does not address matters that lie beyond ULI's areas of expertise, such as education and health care. *Due to a changed—and still changing—metropolitan form, responsible land use today requires a new paradigm for planning and development.* That is the main point of this book.

The new paradigm will assume many guises and involve several shifts: from energy consumption to conservation; from sprawling to more compact and transit-oriented development; from shopping at outlying malls to more urbanized retail; from expensive and expansive suburban housing to affordable housing closer to work; from reliance on taxes to creative, market-oriented ways to finance infrastructure needs; from local thinking and acting to regional collaboration; from separating land and transportation planning to combining them; from capacity to sustainability; and from a culture of "me" to a culture of "we." American metropolitan areas are making this transition. They are changing, and our task is not only to discern the changing paradigms, but to encourage and reinforce them. Business as usual is not a sustainable option.

I hope that developers, public officials, urban planners, and others interested in better stewardship of the finite resource we call "the land" will find the thoughts presented here to be provocative and illuminating. I am writing to suggest that through careful planning and smart development and redevelopment practices, we incorporate suburbia, exurbia, public spaces, urban neighborhoods, and downtowns into regional complexes. Doing so will enable us to achieve a better quality of life for all Americans, and will enable the United States to become a leader in dealing with the grave and profound issues raised here. My colleagues and I worry that the consequences of failing to adjust to the changes discussed here will be dire, and that our quality of life will deteriorate. We sincerely believe that a failure to disengage from business as usual will push our society unwittingly toward an unsustainable future.

In Chapters 1 and 2, I examine changes in the metropolitan form, their causes, and their implications for land use. Following this, I endeavor to make a case for the following:

▸ Traditional jurisdictional boundaries—most of which were formed in the 19th century—have become obsolete. Scant political will exists for changing city and county lines. Creating new layers of governmental bureaucracy is neither desirable nor feasible. But it is both possible and necessary to devise regional forms of collaboration and governance that will make land use planning more holistic and give it more teeth (Chapter 3).

▸ The current disconnect between transportation and land use planning requires a new approach, to accommodate the "spiderweb" configuration of today's metro areas and to reduce the number of vehicle-miles traveled (Chapter 4).

▸ Infrastructure investments have been underfunded for decades. If America's bridges, highways, sewers, and rail transport network are to keep pace with population growth—and if their inevitable deterioration with age is to be counteracted—we must find new ways to finance infrastructure (Chapter 5).

▸ Higher energy prices and global warming pose a threat to our car-oriented culture; in response, we must plan for more compact, greener communities (Chapter 6).

▸ High housing prices and a growing gap between housing prices and incomes are preventing many Americans from becoming homeowners. Despite the 2007–2008 downturn in the housing market, workforce housing remains an issue that must be addressed (Chapter 7).

▸ Retail has changed, becoming at once more urban and more polarized between "value" and "experience." How retail fits into a sustainable future is a subject planners and developers cannot ignore (Chapter 8).

▸ A growing sense of urgency about the need to protect the environment and conserve open space—as well as water and energy resources—requires a more steadfast ethic of conservation, and a number of changes in development practice (Chapter 9).

▸ Finally, visionary, innovative, and responsible leadership in the use of the land is needed to create sustainable metro areas (Chapter 10).

It is time to think anew and act anew, outside the old box, about how we Americans use the land. And that means updating the American Dream. As Martin Luther King. Jr. said (speaking in 1967, on the subject of ending the Vietnam War),

> *We are now faced with the fact that tomorrow is today. We are confronted with the fierce urgency of now. In this unfolding conundrum of life and history there is such a thing as being too late. . . . We may cry out desperately for time to pause in her passage, but time is deaf to every plea and rushes on. Over the bleached bones and jumbled residue of numerous civilizations are written the pathetic words: "Too late."*

Land use is the arena in which the issues discussed here come together. If we wait even a few years to change our ways; to make smarter choices; to craft a new, sustainable system of land use planning that will enable U.S. metro areas to compete effectively in the global economy, we could very well be too late. The time to change is now.

I would like to thank my six senior resident fellow colleagues at ULI—Michael Beyard, Steve Blank, Robert Dunphy, John McIlwain, Ed McMahon, and Tom Murphy—for their assistance in this project. I also appreciate the valuable guidance of Rachelle Levitt, ULI executive vice president/global information, who read every page of the manuscript and made many helpful suggestions. Maureen McAvey, ULI executive vice president/initiatives, helped coordinate the fellows' efforts on this project. The technical support of research associates Melissa Floca and Carl Koelbel, and of ULI summer intern Stephanie McCray, made a significant contribution to this project. Thanks also go to administrative graphics coordinator Karrie Underwood, administrative manager Clara Meesarapu, ULI information specialists Joan Campbell and Rick Davis, and ULI's director/book program and editorial, Nancy Stewart. Special thanks go to Julie Stern and Sandra Chizinsky, who edited the manuscript.

William H. Hudnut III
Senior Resident Fellow
ULI/Joseph C. Canizaro Chair for Public Policy
ULI–the Urban Land Institute
Washington, D.C.
August 2008

# CHAPTER 1

# The Forces Changing the Shape of Metropolitan America

The suburbs lured millions of Americans into thinking they had found the new repository of American virtues. Half a century after Levittown, that dream is coming apart at the seams. —HERBERT MUSCHAMP

*Since the 1950s, many forces have changed the way Americans live and work. The traditional American Dream of homeownership, equality of opportunity, and upward mobility still resonates strongly in the nation's psyche, but demographic, social, and environmental factors are creating a demand for more dreams—in other words, for more choices. The new realities of the morphing metropolitan form require new thinking on the part of developers, planners, public officials, and citizens about land use, transportation, housing, retailing, infrastructure, and regional cooperation. Before considering strategies for dealing with these new realities, it is important to examine them briefly.*

**THE SHAPE OF METROPOLITAN AMERICA** has changed dramatically over the past 50 years. The years after World War II brought the baby boom and the birth of television, air conditioning, interstate highways, and production housing. Americans moved off the nation's farms, out of its central cities, and into the suburbs: in the first decade after the war, 9 million people moved to the suburbs, and the suburban growth rate was ten times that of central cities.[1] (Today, roughly half the U.S. population—150 million people—live in the suburbs.)[2]

By the mid-20th century, the American Dream consisted of a stay-at-home mom; a dad who commuted to a job downtown; two kids; a new house in the suburbs with a long-term, fixed-rate mortgage insured by the Federal Housing Administration; a green lawn; good public schools; a shiny new car in the garage; nearby shopping; cheap gasoline; and open roads. Popular television programs—*Ozzie and Harriet, Leave It to Beaver, Father Knows Best,* and others—offered an idealized portrait of the American family of the 1950s and early 1960s, both reflecting and reinforcing the traditional American Dream.

Today, however, married couples with school-aged children represent less than 25 percent of all U.S. households, while the numbers of retirees, empty nesters, immigrants, and unrelated singles living in the same household are increasing. The open road is clogged with traffic, the era of cheap oil is long past, and a single-family suburban house is no longer everyone's ideal.

In the 1980s and 1990s, television shows like *Cheers, Seinfeld,* and *Friends* became as popular with gen-Xers and Millennials as *Ozzie and Harriet* had been with previous generations. But the placid idyll of Ozzie and Harriet's single-family home was often replaced by an apartment, the bucolic suburban setting by the fast-paced life and cool urbanity of the city, and the nuclear family by unmarried, childless men and women. (In an interesting trend, 21st-century American culture seems to be shifting away from the individualism of the 1980s and 1990s, toward more concern for community values and the common good.)

The Cleaver family would never have dreamed of living downtown—the sort of place from which upwardly mobile families like theirs wanted to escape. Nor would Harriet Nelson ever have contemplated working outside the home. Mid-20th-century suburbanites lived in a predominantly white, male-oriented society, never giving a thought to social or ethnic diversity: between federal lending rules and local exclusionary zoning, immigrants, minorities, and the poor were effectively screened out of the suburbs. The Interstate Highway System had just been built, and the nation's infrastructure was in great shape. Suburban families spent their free time shopping at new regional malls, relaxing in their backyards, and watching movies at the local drive-in. DVDs, iPods, BlackBerry devices, e-mail, SUVs, and ATMs would have seemed more strange to these families than Martian spaceships. Mid-20th-century suburbanites could scarcely see beyond their neighbors' fences, much less to the suburban edge; nor could they envision the need for regional approaches to problems that cut across jurisdictional lines.

Responding to new demographic, social, and environmental realities requires new thinking about land use planning, transportation, housing, infrastructure, and regional cooperation. The old models do not fit the new realities. The task before us is to create places that work for all of us—places that, whether in cities, suburbs, or exurbs, are "worthy of our affection," to borrow a delightful phrase from James Howard Kunstler.[3] In every corner of the metropolitan region, developers, builders, planners, architects, investors, and public officials will need to create places that are well planned, connected, environmentally friendly, culturally and spiritually alive, and sustainable. Those who plan and construct the built environment cannot—and ought not—stand by watching and just let things happen. "Business as usual" cannot be allowed to push America unwittingly into an unsustainable future.

What path *should* metropolitan America take? There is no one easy answer, no single model for metropolitan success. Indeed, numerous metro areas are already making headway in dealing with change and are finding a wide range of solutions to the problems they face. To list just a few examples, metropolitan Denver is expanding its transit system; Salt Lake City and central Texas are developing regional visioning processes and seeking ways to implement their visions; Seattle, Washington, and Mariemont and Shaker Heights, Ohio, are adopting strategies to preserve their environmental, natural, and historic resources; Lakewood, Colorado, and Winter Park, Florida, are creating new urban villages out of moribund malls; and Arlington County, Virginia, and Montgomery County, Maryland, are reshaping the suburban form and struggling to provide affordable housing for their region's workforce. But much work remains to be done, and that work must include a fundamental shift in how people think about the future of metropolitan areas and how we as a society cope with deep drivers of change.

Making that shift will require expanding the traditional American Dream. Of course, this dream has always been something of a myth in any case, a hybrid of fact and fiction. Americans were told that if they were honest, and if they worked hard, practiced thrift, and persevered, they could achieve better lives for themselves and their families. And the symbol of achievement, of course, was a nice place in the suburbs, where no hint existed of the smoldering problems of urban America. Although for the poor and for most minorities, this version of the American Dream was never a reality, it has stuck in the American mind for decades as the ideal toward which all should strive. But things have changed. As Jim Cullen writes in *The American Dream: A Short History of an Idea that Shaped a Nation,* "Beyond an abstract belief in possibility, there is no *one* American Dream. Instead, there are many American Dreams, their appeal simultaneously resting on their variety and their specificity."[4]

The dawn of the 21st century has witnessed radical changes from the middle of the 20th; the rest of the chapter takes a closer look at some of these changes.

## Consider Demographics

Perhaps the most important agent of change is demographics. As many have said, demography is destiny. Demographic trends show that population growth is inevitable; the only question is where and how growth will occur. Between 1950 and 2007, the U.S. population doubled, from 150 to 300 million people.[5] More than 32 million people were added in the 1990s alone—and the generation born during that decade will rival the baby boomers in size and importance. The 300-millionth American was born on October 17, 2006, and the 400-million mark is expected to be reached around 2043. During the intervening years, the homebuilding industry anticipates that the United States will need 100 billion square feet (9.3 billion square meters) of new residential space.[6] Arthur C. Nelson, director of the Metropolitan Institute at Virginia Polytechnic University, projects that the U.S. population will double—that is, add another 200 million people—by the end of the century.[7]

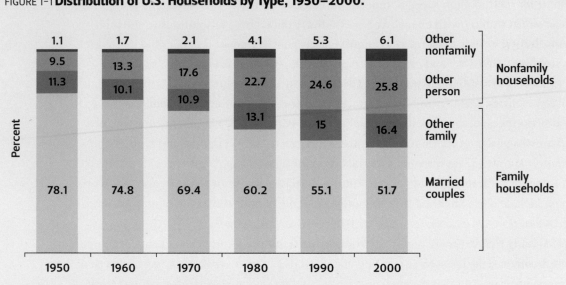

FIGURE 1-1 **Distribution of U.S. Households by Type, 1950–2000.**

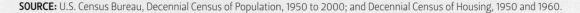

**SOURCE:** U.S. Census Bureau, Decennial Census of Population, 1950 to 2000; and Decennial Census of Housing, 1950 and 1960.

In addition to physically squeezing metropolitan .areas, such rapid growth creates psychological pressure to cope with rapid change—and that change is literally occurring *where we live.* The U.S. growth rate exceeds that of many developing nations. While this population boom has fueled our economy, it has also caused growing pains.

Pressure to accommodate growth is concentrated in a horseshoe-shaped area that encompasses major metropolitan regions in the South, the Southwest, and the West. Although some growth is concentrated along the eastern seaboard, the populations of New England and the Midwest are growing more slowly. Most rural areas are losing population, except those located along the coasts, around resort areas, and near protected areas such as national parks. As of 2000, more than half the U.S. population lived in the 39 metropolitan regions with populations of 1 million or more, and one-third lived in regions with populations over 5 million.[8]

The U.S. population also is changing rapidly in terms of family structure, household size, ethnicity, age, and expectations. The kinds of families popularized by *Ozzie and Harriet* and *Leave It to Beaver* have become a quaint memory. More than 75 percent of U.S. households today do *not* include children under 18. And, according to Nelson, single-member households will account for 34 percent of the coming population growth, which will increase demand for condominiums and townhouses situated near urban centers, and for detached homes on smaller lots.[9] Although families with children will continue to grow in terms of absolute numbers, by 2025, the number of single-person households will approximately equal that of households with children.[10] The Census Bureau estimates that among men who have less than four years of college, about 18 percent of those aged 40 to 44, and 22 percent of those aged 35 to 39, have never married; 25 years ago, the comparable figures were 6 and 8 percent, respectively.[11] High divorce rates, longer life expectancy, and smaller family size are other factors contributing to the changing household picture.

While the United States has a younger population than Russia, Japan, and most European countries, the aging of the baby boomers and growing life expectancies are increasing the demand for active senior living and assisted-living housing formats. As time goes on, and the 80 million people born between 1946 and 1964 head into their retirement years, the suburbs will morph into "silverburbs." Suburban areas can expect a "silver tsunami"—a doubling of their over-65 populations: between 2008 and 2030, it is estimated that the number of U.S. seniors will increase by 35 million, with the over-65 cohort of the population expanding in every state and the District of Columbia.[12]

Among baby boomers and older Americans, the style of aging is changing dramatically. Today's older Americans are not willing to be put out to pasture; they want to stay in shape, enjoy good times, and continue to walk, bike, and hike. Many of those over 65 are continuing to work—whether by choice or by need—well into their 70s, 80s, and even 90s. Most do not want to be seen as "old" or to live in age-segregated places, so words like "retirement" and "senior" are disappearing from developers' lexicons; instead, developers' marketing materials emphasize phrases like "active adult," "fitness," "lifestyles," and "country-club living." Active-adult developments already

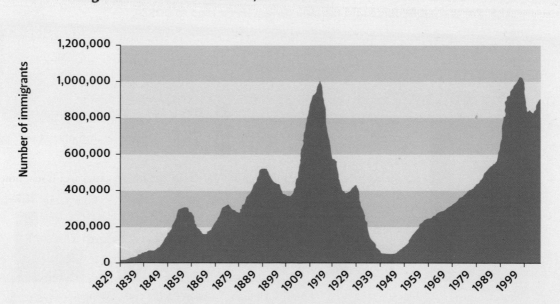

FIGURE 1-2 **Immigration in the United States, 1829–2006.**

**SOURCE:** U.S. Department of Homeland Security, Office of Immigration Statistics, *2006 Yearbook of Immigration Statistics,* Table 1, "Persons Obtaining Legal Permanent Resident Status: FY 1820–2006."

represent a hot market; communities for active 55-plus adults—with golf courses, swimming pools, clubhouses, and other amenities—are springing up in far-flung locales, while many cities, towns, and suburbs are beginning to address and plan for the changing needs of older Americans who want to age in place.[13]

Immigration has also altered the face of America, a country that has traditionally welcomed newcomers to its shores. The U.S. population is much more diverse than it was in the 1950s—in fact, America is well on its way to becoming a majority-minority nation. The challenge is to learn how to handle this diversity and embrace it as a core strength. This will not be easy. A massive new study by Harvard University political scientist Robert Putnam (author of *Bowling Alone*), based on detailed interviews of nearly 30,000 people across America, has concluded that "the greater the diversity in a community, the fewer people vote and the less they volunteer, the less they give to charity and work on community projects. . . . Virtually all measures of civic health are lower in more diverse settings."[14]

Irrespective of arguments and policy differences on the subject of illegal aliens, the fact is that immigration is changing metropolitan areas. An estimated 10 million immigrants arrived during the 1990s alone, and a million or so continue to arrive each year. Without immigrants, cities such as Dallas (which grew by 18 percent), and New York (which grew by more than 9 percent) would have expanded only slightly or even lost population during the 1990s.

While the number of foreign-born citizens appears large, immigrants actually make up a lower percentage of the population today than they did at the turn of the 20th

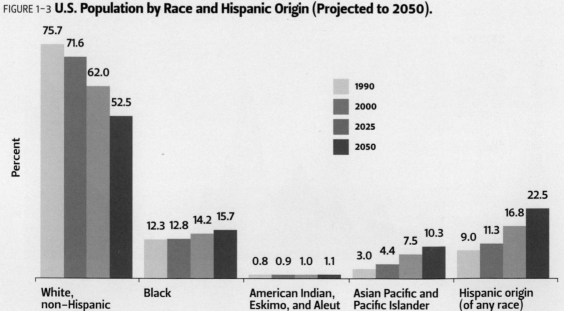

FIGURE 1-3 **U.S. Population by Race and Hispanic Origin (Projected to 2050).**

**SOURCE**: U.S. Census Bureau, "Population Projections of the U.S. by Age, Sex, and Hispanic Origin: 1993–2050," Current Population Reports, Middle Series Projections, Series P25-1104, 2008.

century (see Figure 1–4). In 1910, almost 15 percent of the U.S. population was foreign born, a figure that is closer to 11 percent today. Between 1950 and 1980, however, foreign–born residents represented only 6 percent of the total population.[15] What is different about today's immigrants is their countries of origin; earlier immigrants came primarily from Europe, whereas today's immigrants are more likely to arrive from Latin America or Asia (see Figure 1–5).

The nation's immigrant population has a proportionally larger group between the ages of 18 and 64 (69.8 percent) than the native-born population (51.2 percent).[16] The immigrant population is also growing faster, with Hispanics leading the way. Between 2005 and 2015, the number of households headed by Hispanics will grow by 5.2 million, while all other minority households combined will grow by 4.8 million, and non-Hispanic whites by 4.7 million.[17] The Hispanic population constitutes 14 percent of the population, surpassing African Americans (12 percent) and Asians (4.4 percent).[18] It is predicted that half of America's population growth to 2030 and beyond will be attributable to immigrants or to their children and grandchildren, the majority of whom will be from Latin America, Mexico, and South America.[19]

Immigrants share traditional American values: hard work, family, and religious faith. They boost the economies of the metro areas where they live, creating their own retail markets. As immigrants second- and third-generation children assume more of the customs of the American middle class, they are forming more cohesive political blocks and are beginning to have an increasing impact on local politics.

FIGURE 1–4 **Foreign–Born Share of the U.S. Population, 1900–2000.**

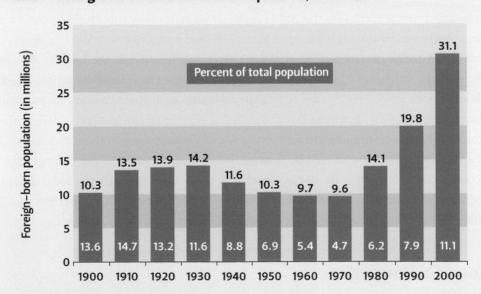

**SOURCE**: Audrey Singer, "The New U.S. Demographics," presentation to the Funders Network on Population, Reproductive Health and Rights, November 10, 2003.

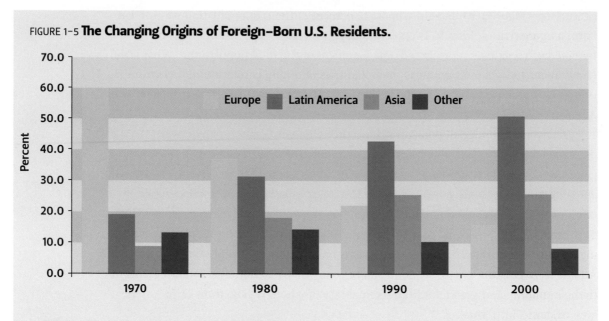

FIGURE 1–5 **The Changing Origins of Foreign–Born U.S. Residents.**

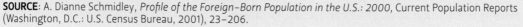

SOURCE: A. Dianne Schmidley, *Profile of the Foreign-Born Population in the U.S.: 2000,* Current Population Reports (Washington, D.C.: U.S. Census Bureau, 2001), 23–206.

Immigrant populations, once concentrated in big "gateway" cities, are moving to smaller cities and suburbs across the country, changing communities from Maine to California. The Somali community in Lewiston, Maine, and the Hmong community in Minneapolis–St. Paul have brought new faces, foods, and fashions to what were once "white bread" towns. Today, more than one in four suburban households are minority or foreign born: according to the 2000 census, 27 percent of the suburban population in large metropolitan areas is made up of minorities; and a majority of Asian Americans, half of all Latinos, and 39 percent of African Americans now live in the suburbs. Across the country, bilingual education programs for the more than 2 million school-aged children with limited proficiency in English are being conducted at a cost that runs into the billions of dollars. Journalist David Brooks has chronicled the increasing differentiation of suburbs—from those attracting new Korean immigrants, to those popular with Hasidic Jews, to those occupied by Guatemalans.[20] Today's suburbs are no longer the "cookie-cutter" 'burbs of the 1950s. Developing and redeveloping them—today and in the future—will require sophisticated knowledge of their populations' preferences for cultural attractions, retail and other commercial facilities, and housing types.

## Consider Housing

Since 2006, the housing market has taken a sharp downturn. The value of mortgage-backed securities has slumped. Credit has tightened. Extravagant consumer spending, coupled with heavy debt loads, has put many families in a financial bind. Housing prices have dropped, effectively decreasing the value of owners' equity.[21] Escalating interest rates on mortgages taken out when times were good—and housing values looked as if they would rise forever—are now making it difficult, if not impossible, for many Americans to meet their payments. Predatory mortgage lending is costing Americans more than $9.1 billion each year.[22] U.S. home foreclosures are up 60 percent (which figures out to about one foreclosure for every 134 homes).[23] America is teetering on the brink of recession.

Today's economic difficulties have exacerbated the problems of millions of working families who have been unable to find adequate, affordable housing. Not only have escalating housing prices outpaced growth in household incomes, but even in the current slowing market, where housing prices are beginning to drop, the combination of the credit crisis and an economic downturn is still keeping families from owning homes.

Some 5.2 million working families spend more than half their income on housing and/or live in severely inadequate housing conditions, and thus have "critical housing needs."[24] That number represents a 73 percent increase in less than ten years. Like many of their middle-class counterparts, these lower-income families are being squeezed. In the Washington, D.C., metro area, for example, the central city is losing affordable housing—little wonder, when the median sales price of a single-family home was $415,000 in 2005, and the average rent $1,321 per month. In search of housing they can afford, the folks who hold the city together—construction workers, schoolteachers, firefighters, domestic employees, janitors, sales associates, mechanics, and municipal employees—are forced to "drive until they qualify": this portion of the workforce can obtain affordable housing only by moving farther and farther away from the workplace. So sprawl continues: between 2000 and 2005, for example, outer-ring suburbs captured 65 percent of the population growth in the Washington, D.C., region, up from 49 percent in the 1990s.[25]

Rapid population growth is fueling major new housing construction not only within cities, but also at the urban fringe, putting intense pressure on the outer edges of developed suburbs. Continued sprawl will require radical changes in the way rural communities respond to rapid growth, and in the ways developers design subdivisions. Development on the outer edges of metro areas need not follow the same low-density patterns that have characterized suburbanization since World War II: there *are* other, more sustainable ways to accommodate a growing population.

The gradual aging of the baby boomers and the maturing of generations X and Y will create strong demand for a wide variety of housing, including condominiums, townhouses, apartments, duplexes, lofts, live/work arrangements, and active-adult communities—to say

FIGURE 1-6 **Percent Growth in Foreign–Born Populations, Selected Cities, 1990–2000.**

| Established Gateways | | Emerging Gateways | |
|---|---|---|---|
| Chicago | 61 | Atlanta | 262 |
| Los Angeles | 19 | Charlotte | 315 |
| Miami | 31 | Fort Worth–Arlington | 131 |
| New York | 37 | Las Vegas | 248 |
| San Diego | 41 | Orlando | 140 |
| San Francisco | 26 | Salt Lake City | 174 |

**SOURCE:** Robert Suro and Audrey Singer, *Latino Growth in Metropolitan America: Changing Patterns, New Locations,* Brookings Institution Survey Series (Washington, D.C.: Brookings Institution, July 2002).

nothing of the traditional single-family suburban home. The young, the middle-aged, and the aging will all want more options in every area of life—including housing, shopping, work, and entertainment. This changing market makes for a much more complicated metropolitan picture, to which wise developers will respond.

## Consider Energy

The postwar American Dream of a house in the suburbs was predicated on the availability of inexpensive energy, but the era of cheap oil is over: by the late winter of 2008, the price of oil had risen to $110 a barrel. The dream also arose before the 1970s, when domestic oil production peaked, and before China and India had developed automobile cultures and insatiable appetites for oil. If gas prices increase to $8 or $10 a gallon ($2.00 or $2.67 a liter)—as is already the case in Europe—or if we appear to be running out of gas, as was the case in 1973, we could be in a world of hurt, and many of our "drive everywhere, for everything" habits would have to change.

Rising oil prices are already forcing Americans to spend a lot more for gas, which means that families are being forced to allocate a larger percentage of their budgets to transportation—and, possibly, to rethink family travel patterns. The dependence of "Hydrocarbon Man" on fossil fuels has had a huge impact on the way we construct our built environment—both by encouraging sprawl and by fostering inefficient building practices. Unless we wean ourselves from the idea that fossil fuels will always be cheap and readily available, we are headed in a dangerous direction. The emerging "green building" boom reflects recognition of this fact. In addition, alternative and renewable energy sources are already being discovered and harnessed, and new, more efficient technologies are being developed. Nonetheless, our transition away from an oil-based economy will probably be difficult.

Overall, the need to conserve energy does not appear to have sunk in with many Americans; although SUV sales have declined while hybrid sales have soared, most people have not yet altered their driving habits. When oil production and energy prices reach a tipping point, with the former dropping and the latter rising, Americans will be in for a rude awakening. They will realize that their good fortune in having access to inexpensive energy has expired, and that this shift has serious implications for our quality and style of life, for the built environment, for land use and transportation planning, and for housing and infrastructure.

Furthermore, global warming has troubling implications for land use. Global warming, which has been brought about by the burning of fossil fuels and the consequent emission of greenhouse gases such as carbon dioxide, methane, and nitrous oxide, is indeed "an inconvenient truth," as Al Gore says. It will require us to change our habits or face the destruction of our environment and our way of life, to say nothing of the health and well-being of the entire planet. This means decreasing our dependence on the automobile; increasing the practicality of walking, cycling, and public transit as alternatives to driving; developing more compactly; discovering and harnessing clean, renewable forms of fuel such as wind, water, waves, solar and, yes, even nuclear power; disciplining ourselves with a stronger ethic of conservation; and building with an eye toward sustainability. None of these things were contemplated during the era of Ozzie and Harriet.

## Consider Transportation and Infrastructure

Our love of cars and our limited investment in public infrastructure have brought us relentless congestion, traffic accidents, and daily frustration. Between 1960 and 2000, transportation spending as a percentage of total household expenditures grew from less than 12 percent to 16 percent, with low-income households spending a disproportionately larger amount of their income on transportation than higher-income ones.

According to Gregg Easterbrook, author of *The Progress Paradox: How Life Gets Better While People Feel Worse*, during the past 30 years, the U.S. population grew by 40 percent, while the number of registered vehicles increased by nearly 100 percent. In the same period, the number of vehicle-miles traveled (VMT) increased by 143 percent, while road capacity rose by only 6 percent. Easterbrook also notes that only 1 percent of all U.S. trips occur on public transit.[26] In 1994, the percentage of urban passenger-miles traveled on transit was one-tenth of what it had been in 1945.[27]

While jobs have followed residents out to the suburbs, transit has been slow to respond. For most suburbanites, transit is simply not an option. Our roads are clogged

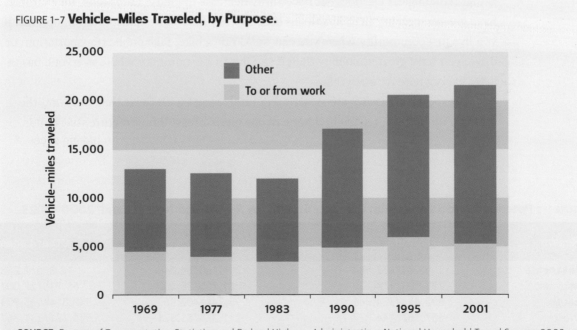

FIGURE 1-7 **Vehicle–Miles Traveled, by Purpose.**

**SOURCE:** Bureau of Transportation Statistics and Federal Highway Administration, National Household Travel Survey, 2003.

FIGURE 1-8 **Potential Cost Savings with Controlled Growth, 2000–2025 (Billions of $).**

| Region | Uncontrolled Growth | Controlled Growth | Total Savings | Percent Savings |
|---|---|---|---|---|
| Northeast | 691 | 636 | 54 | 7.9 |
| Midwest | 968 | 917 | 52 | 5.4 |
| South | 2,473 | 2,303 | 170 | 6.9 |
| West | 2,243 | 2,100 | 144 | 6.4 |
| Total | 6,375 | 5,955 | 420 | 6.6 |

**SOURCE:** R.W. Burchell et al., *Cost of Sprawl—2000* (Washington, D.C.: National Academy Press, 2002), 12.

not only by people driving to and from work, but also by those who are carrying out the tasks of daily life—shopping, taking children to and from school and activities, visiting friends, and so forth. These nonwork trips make up about three-quarters of today's traffic—and for most of them, the car is the only option.[28] In 2004, the University of California at Berkeley claimed that Americans spend 101 minutes a day in their cars, and that between 1990 and 2000, the proportion of workers who commuted 30 minutes or more a day had increased from 20 to 34 percent.[29] In our car-dominated culture, mobility has been democratized, but at a high price.

More compact development and more transportation options would lower transportation costs, freeing up funds for housing and other essentials. The question is whether, in the long run, Americans will be able to live with reduced levels of *automobile* mobility, compared with what they have become accustomed to. The key point here is that reducing car use does not necessarily decrease mobility; Europeans, for example, have greater mobility than Americans because they have more transportation options. If you live in a community where you can walk, ride a bike, take public transportation, or drive, you have greater mobility than if you live in a community where everyone has to drive everywhere for everything.

Transportation issues are inextricably intertwined with those that surround the nation's infrastructure, the backbone of our metro areas. Infrastructure that builds

FIGURE 1-9 **Potential Land Savings with Compact Growth, by Region and Type of Land, 2000–2025.**

| Region | Agricultural Land | Environmentally Fragile Lands | Other Lands |
|---|---|---|---|
| Northeast | 55,807/22,584 | 209,160/84,644 | 17,886/7,238 |
| Midwest | 283,503/114,730 | 89,205/36,100 | 66,735/27,007 |
| South | 802,464/324,746 | 995,742/402,962 | 340,814/137,923 |
| West | 357,862/144,822 | 211,328/85,521 | 571,721/231,367 |
| Total | 1,499,636/606,881 | 1,505,434/609,228 | 997,156/403,535 |

Acres/Hectares

**SOURCE:** R.W. Burchell et al., *Cost of Sprawl—2000* (Washington, D.C.: National Academy Press, 2002), 8.

vibrant, sustainable communities and connects them to the greater region and the nation can enhance economic competitiveness and quality of life. But our transportation system and our development patterns are at odds: our roads and highways have been designed for radial development around a central city, rather than for the spiderweb of low-density metropolitan development that is typical today.

Low-density, leapfrog development—and the resulting dispersal of population— leads to rapid consumption of rural and resource-rich lands and to escalating infrastructure costs: from 1950 to 1990, urbanized land grew almost four times as fast as the urban population; since 1950, land has been developed at more than twice the rate of population growth.[30] Sprawl generates demand not only for new roadways, but also for new schools, new sewers, new water treatment facilities, and new bridges. And as more infrastructure is built, higher gasoline taxes and property taxes follow. For example, we are warned that in South Carolina, "if sprawl continues unchecked, statewide infrastructure costs for the period 1995 to 2015 are projected to be more than $56 billion, or $750 per citizen per year for these twenty years."[31] Higher densities might help address the infrastructure shortage because, as many studies have found, development costs are higher in metro areas with low-density development patterns than in dense, clustered communities.[32] As figures 1-8 and 1-9 illustrate, controlled-growth scenarios yield lower aggregate property development costs, and compact-growth scenarios could save thousands of acres of land.

The infrastructure crisis is an issue that politicians prefer to avoid because the costs of fixing our streets, bridges, sewer and water systems, highways, dams, rail and transit systems, and public buildings are astronomical. (The American Society of Civil Engineers estimates the cost at 1.6 trillion.)[33] The breakdown of the levee system in New Orleans during Hurricane Katrina illustrates the need to focus on aging infrastructure. A visit to almost any first-tier U.S. suburb reveals infrastructure in serious need of repair. The key questions are, How do we balance the need to build new infrastructure with the need to maintain existing infrastructure? What new infrastructure should be built? Where should it be located? How do we pay for it? And most important, do Americans and their leaders have the political will to address these issues?

| Total Lands | Equivalent |
| --- | --- |
| 282,853/114,467 | Larger than New York City |
| 439,443/177,836 | Larger than the island of Oahu, in Hawaii |
| 2,139,020/865,631 | About the size of Yellowstone National Park |
| 1,140,911/461,710 | Over one-and-a-half times the size of Rhode Island |
| 4,002,226/1,619,643 | 85 percent of New Jersey |

## Consider Sustainability

Climate change is one of the most important and complex long-term challenges ever faced by communities throughout the world, and one that has tremendous implications for land use. While this challenge is global in scope, the actions needed to address it must be taken at every level of governance and the economy. Communities and regions must identify ways to adapt, and to mitigate existing trends with bold and transformational solutions. To ensure a sustainable America—one that can be enjoyed by future generations as well as those living today—we must take action now to reduce and manage greenhouse gas emissions, promote accessibility and a greater range of transportation options, and conserve natural resources by using land wisely.

The natural beauty of our country holds an important place in the American identity, but the pursuit of the traditional American Dream is at odds with environmental conservation. Sprawl has increased our infrastructure needs, ravaged habitat, and consumed green space at the rate of 206 acres (83 hectares) an hour.[34] Environmental degradation is waking us up to the threats of air, water, and land pollution, all of which result from the way we treat our natural resources. Green space can—and should—provide a framework for growth, but it cannot do so if it has already been paved over or plowed under. Between 1982 and 1997, the U.S. population increased 17 percent, while urbanized land use increased 47 percent. The figures are even more stark for the Midwest (7 percent versus 32 percent) and the Northeast (7 percent and 39 percent). Between 1992 and 1997, land was converted to urbanized use at a rate of 2.2 million acres (890,308 hectares) a year, 1.5 times the rate during the previous ten-year period.[35] Since 1982, the number of farms in the United States has decreased by 17 percent.[36] According to the Alliance for the Chesapeake Bay, 53,000 acres (21,448 hectares) of the bay's watershed—an astounding acre (0.4 hectares) every ten minutes—are developed each year.[37] The trend has been accelerating in California, where one-sixth of all developed land was developed between 1990 and 2004—and, if current trends continue, an additional 2 million acres (809,371 hectares) will be developed by 2050.[38]

Planners and developers who care about our country's excessive absorption of land for urban use would do well to reconnect planning with nature and make a conservation ethic the norm. Little thought was given to the preservation of green space in the postwar years. Most Americans did not begin to "think green" until near the end of the 20th century. Today, a new interest in environmental conservation and a growing commitment to walking, biking, running, and other outdoor activities have galvanized the desire for more recreational space and parklike settings. Green spaces must be part of the new American Dream.

Green space is not the only natural resource that we need to preserve. Water conservation is a growing global imperative. A recent study by the United Nations Food and Agricultural Organization and the Consultative Group on International Agricultural Research concludes that the worldwide need for water could double in 50 years. Since 1950, the number of acres of irrigated land worldwide has tripled. While the report

FIGURE 1-10 **Sources of Newly Developed Land (000s of Acres/Hectares).**

| Time Span | Cropland | Pastureland | Rangeland | Forest Land | All Other Land Uses | Total |
|---|---|---|---|---|---|---|
| 1982–1992 (ten years) | 3,900/1,578 | 2,270/918 | 1,950/789 | 5,600/2,266 | 360/146 | 14,080/5,698 |
| 1992–1997 (five years) | 2,880/1,165 | 1,930/781 | 1,270/514 | 4,740/1,918 | 470/190 | 11,290/4,569 |
| 1997–2001 (four years) | 1,830/741 | 1,470/595 | 1,210/490 | 4,150/1,679 | 280/113 | 8,940/3,618 |

**SOURCE:** Natural Resources Conservation Service, *Urbanization and Development of Rural Land*, 2001 National Resources Inventory (July 2003).

focuses more on Africa and Asia than on Europe and the Americas, its central point, according to the *New York Times,* is that "countries confronting severe water shortages cannot simply employ the same strategies for increasing food production that have had dramatic success over the past half-century."[39] One researcher wrote, "We can't just keep expanding the land used."[40] Why? Because this process cannot be sustained forever; eventually, we will run out of land. The situation is not as dire in the United States as it is in developing countries, but climate experts nonetheless predict that global warming will increase the severity of droughts, both here and around the world.

Sustainability is clearly a vital issue in land use practices as well. Growth will continue to take place on the fringes of our metro areas; there's no question about it. As noted earlier, the issue is not whether growth will occur but how and where. The challenge is to "grow smart"—to create better suburbs and stronger cities, rather than to permit new subdivisions to be built without attempting to reduce our dependence on the automobile or to develop pedestrian-friendly environments. As a new century unfolds, loss of green space, coupled with unlimited, low-density, leapfrog development on the periphery of our metro areas, raises a question: Is sprawl sustainable? And if not, where should we focus our effort and energy? What if we started by rebuilding the old before building the new? More compact development that relies on existing infrastructure makes eminent sense as a strategy for the future. There is little doubt that higher-density, well-designed development will be an essential element in sustaining our projected growth as a nation.

In his work on "the restoration economy," Storm Cunningham, executive director of the Revitalization Institute, points out that we have entered "the re-century."[41] This is a time when rebuilding is as important as new building, which emphatically was not the case 50 years ago. Much of our built environment is wearing out, as a visit to many first-tier suburbs makes readily apparent. Public policy ought to encourage—more than it has in the past—reconstruction, redevelopment, reinvestment, and reinvention.

The greenest building is one that has already been built. Renovating an older building—transforming it into a comfortable work or living space—requires a lot less energy than building an entirely new structure. Far too often, greenfield development has been favored at the expense of established areas, while opportunities to rebuild healthy older communities have been ignored. This pattern must be reversed so that we can make more efficient use of existing structures and infrastructure, while preserving green space and other natural resources for future generations.

Cunningham advances the thesis that within ten years, restorative work—that is, bringing something back to a state of health (not to its original state, necessarily)—will account for more than 50 percent of all expenditures in the United States and Europe, more than new development and maintenance/conservation combined. He believes that the shift from new development to redevelopment "is germinating a gargantuan new category of business opportunities that will dominate the rest of the 21st century."[42]

There is support for Cunningham's perspective. Consider the following:

▸ According to a survey undertaken in 2006 by the American Institute of Architects, 34 percent of 17,589 firms across the country reported that their work involved residential rehab rather than new construction.[43]

▸ According to the Joint Center for Housing Studies at Harvard University, over 20 million homeowners a year are undertaking modest to major improvements to their homes. In 2005, homeowners spent $280 billion on improvements and $424 billion on new construction, and the center predicts that by 2015, Americans will be spending almost as much on remodeling ($402 billion) as on new construction ($453 billion).[44]

▸ In New York City in the past five years, renovation of existing office space has outpaced construction of new space by a factor of two. Specifically, according to Mitch Rudin, President and CEO of the NY Tristate Region for CBRichardEllis, of the 127 million square feet (11,798,687 square meters) of office space that has been leased in Manhattan since January 1, 2004, only about 6 percent is in new buildings; the rest is in stock built before 2000—which suggests that a great deal of that space had been renovated and retrofitted.[45] Manhattan's inventory is getting older, and in this city or any other, there can be no doubt that refitting and re-renting older space represents a significant new market niche for developers. Moreover, the cost of adapting existing buildings and making them greener is lower than the cost of building from scratch.

## Consider Governance

The proliferation of multiple nodes of development in metropolitan regions and the rise of "edgeless" cities have challenged traditional modes of governance and rendered many 19th-century jurisdictional boundaries and forms of governance obsolete. America needs 21st-century governmental structures to address its 21st-century problems and issues. Unfortunately, most metropolitan areas are burdened by governmental systems that were created to address the issues and problems of the 19th century. Our fragmented systems of local governance do not adequately serve the needs of a broadened metropolitan form. Regional issues such as air and water pollution, land consumption, economic development, transportation planning, and affordable housing cross jurisdictional boundaries and thus require regional responses.

From the founding of the republic until the early 20th century, all but a few of America's urbanized areas contained only one major city, within the boundaries of which all metropolitan growth and development occurred. Jobs, housing, shopping, culture, entertainment, and urban infrastructure were all concentrated within the city. Local governance was handled locally by a single jurisdiction that comprehensively managed, coordinated, and paid for public services and infrastructure as the city grew.

Beginning with the construction of the streetcar suburbs of the late 19th century, however, this efficient and comprehensive way of managing urban growth began to disintegrate. For the first time, people who worked and shopped in an urbanized area began to live outside the city limits, in separate jurisdictions. America's suburbs were born. Stores followed their customers to the suburbs, first coalescing around suburban commuter-rail stations and downtowns, then moving to the shopping centers that developed around freeway interchanges in the 1950s. These areas formed the nuclei of new business centers that soon became appealing locations for employers, who were no longer tied to the original downtowns.

This dispersal of housing, shopping, and jobs—followed by entertainment and cultural facilities—resulted in a new American metropolitan form. While our cities were originally urban solar systems with dependent neighborhoods revolving around a single downtown sun, today's American cities are urban constellations characterized by many different commercial centers, of varying sizes, each of which is surrounded by residential neighborhoods that also take many different forms. Although these constellations are still connected by the interactivity of metropolitan life and a complex, web-shaped transportation network, they have become increasingly self-sufficient, and are often separated by income and race.

In this new metropolitan universe, the old downtown is often the largest, most diverse, and most important sun in the constellation, but it is not the only one. The most successful suburbs—the so-called edge cities—have become suns themselves, competing with and sometimes eclipsing a city's original downtown.[46] And the proliferation of low-density suburbs, malls, and office parks has perpetuated the development of edgeless cities, which are accessible only by car, and are now competing with the more traditional suburbs.

The new, multicentered metropolitan form is reflected in governance. Our nation's 50 states contain more than 3,000 counties and 35,000 other units of local government. If we add in school districts and special service districts of one sort or another, the number of political entities balloons to almost 90,000. Such fragmentation has developed over the decades as America has grown; it is neither desirable nor efficient.

Some cities and counties have consolidated either in whole or in part, while others have experienced abortive initiatives to do so. Most have never considered such a project, preferring to color inside the predefined lines. Changing entrenched governmental structures is difficult because elected officials are reluctant to give up turf and citizens are likely to resist change, particularly when urban/suburban splits reflect racial, ethnic, or class differences. People like grass-roots government that is close to them, not mega-government that seems to rob them of their autonomy. Furthermore, the Internet fosters virtual networking and increased local decision making, which runs counter to big government structures.

Nonetheless, cooperation across jurisdictional lines is not impossible to achieve. Throughout the country, new mechanisms have been put in place to consolidate certain local services and serve more than one municipality; examples include regional parks authorities, crime labs, and waste disposal and treatment plants; entities that oversee land use and transportation planning; and economic development organizations that market entire metro areas. A new global/regional/neighborhood paradigm could be developed that supersedes the old federal/state/local one. Thinking and acting regionally does not necessarily mean "big government." But it *does* imply cooperation—either mandated by higher levels of government or forged voluntarily by local communities.

In today's global economy, businesses compete region-to-region across the world; our competitors are Singapore, Beijing, Tokyo, London, Dubai, and Bangalore. We have discovered, with author Thomas Friedman, that the world is flat, and that we can be in instantaneous electronic touch with almost anyone, anywhere.[47] Regional cooperation is therefore essential to advance economic development.

## Dreams Transformed

"We are living through one of those great historical times of transformation and redefinition," says Senator Chuck Hagel (R-NE).[48] The American Dream of yesteryear no longer reflects how Americans live today—or the ways they will want and need to live in the future. It's time to expand the dream: to make it plural. Adapting to the new realities of

FIGURE 1-11 **Old versus New Metropolitan Forms.**

| Old Metropolitan Form | New Metropolitan Form |
|---|---|
| Downtown as primary commercial center | Multiple commercial centers |
| Transportation "hub and spoke" | Transportation spiderweb |
| Sense of community/connectivity | Sense of separation/fragmentation |
| Coordinated local decision making | Balkanized local decision making |
| Cheap land and affordable housing | Housing out of reach for many working families |
| Easy commutes, extensive transit | Congested commutes, limited transit |
| Suburbs close to downtown | Suburbs distant and disconnected from downtown and from each other |
| Transit dependent | Automobile dependent |
| Nuclear families living in single-family houses | Wider range of households (singles, childless couples, nonfamily groups) and housing types (apartments, condos, townhouses) |

life in our country and the new dreams of Americans will require new planning policies and development strategies that can guide our continuing effort to build successful and sustainable communities within the ever-changing, ever-evolving metropolitan form.

**ENDNOTES**

1 See Kenneth T. Jackson, *Crabgrass Frontier: The Suburbanization of the United States* (New York: Oxford University Press, 1985), 238.

2 Robert E. Lang, director, Metropolitan Institute, Virginia Tech University, Arts and Economic Development Symposium speech, Overland Park, Kansas, March 4, 2008.

3 James Howard Kunstler, "Home from Nowhere," *The Atlantic* 278, no. 3 (1996): 43–66.

4 Jim Cullen, *The American Dream: A Short History of an Idea That Shaped a Nation* (New York: Oxford University Press, 2003), 7.

5 U.S. Census Bureau, "2000 Census of Population and Housing, Population and Area: 1790 to 2000," Table 1; U.S. Census Bureau, Population Estimates Program (2007), T1.

6 John Caulfield, "This Way," *Builder* (September 2007): 133.

7 Arthur C. Nelson, "Leadership in a New Era," *Journal of the American Planning Association* 72, no. 4 (2006): 393–407.

8 U.S. Census Bureau, "Population Change and Distribution: 1990 to 2000," Census 2000 Brief (April 2001).

9 Caulfield, "This Way," 133.

10 Christopher B. Leinberger, "The Next Slum," *The Atlantic* (March 2008): 74; available at www.theatlantic.com/doc/200803/subprime. In 2025, there will be about 4 million more households with children than there were in 2000.

11 Eduardo Porter and Michelle O'Donnell, "More Men Facing Middle Age with No Degree and No Wife," *New York Times*, August 6, 2006, 1, 22.

12 Haya El Nasser, "Cities Revisit Needs of the Elderly," and "Cities Brace for the Elderly," *USAToday*, May 14, 2007, 1A, 3A.

13 See, for example, Annie Gowen, "Brave New Boomers," *Washington Post*, September 16, 2007, A1; and Allan Lengel, "Nothing Old About It," *Washington Post*, November 24, 2007, F1.

14 Michael Jonas, "The Downside of Diversity," *Boston Globe*, August 5, 2007, D1.

15 Audrey Singer, "The New U.S. Demographics," presentation to the Funders Network on Population, Reproductive Health and Rights, November 10, 2003.

16 U.S. Census Bureau, "Profile of the Foreign-Born Population in the United States: 2000" (2001), 27.

17 M. Leanne Lachman and Deborah L. Brett, *Global Demographics 2008: Shaping Real Estate's Future* (Washington, D.C.: ULI–the Urban Land Institute, 2008), 84.

18 U.S. Census Bureau, "S0201: Selected Population Profile in the United States," 2006 American Community Survey.

19 Lachman and Brett, *Global Demographics*, 83.

20 David Brooks, *On Paradise Drive: How We Live Now (and Always Have) in the Future Tense* (New York: Simon & Schuster, 2004).

21 Between March 2007 and March 2008, housing prices dropped 8 percent; some analysts hold, however, that the decline is probably bringing prices back in line with their actual value, after astronomical increases.

22 Cherie Duvall, "NLC Supports Efforts to Strengthen Housing Finance System," *Nation's Cities Weekly,* March 10, 2008, 1, 8. See also Neil Irwin, "Why the Downturn Had to Happen," *Washington Post,* March 14, 2008, D1, D3.

23 Irwin, "Downturn."

24 Maya Brennan and Barbara J. Lipman, "The Housing Landscape for America's Working Families, 2007," Center for Housing Policy, 10; www.nhc.org/pdf/pub_landscape2007_08_07.pdf. According to the U.S. Census, households with critical housing needs have one or more of the following problems: housing lacks a complete kitchen; housing lacks complete plumbing; housing is overcrowded (more than 1.01 persons per room), housing cost burden is severe (household pays more than 50 percent of its income toward housing). See U.S. Department of Housing and Urban Development, Comprehensive Housing Affordability Strategy, 2000 Census, Special Tabulation Data.

25 Fannie Mae Foundation, "Housing in the Nation's Capital 2006."

26 Gregg Easterbrook, *The Progress Paradox: How Life Gets Better While People Feel Worse* (New York: Random House, 2003), 91–92.

27 Pietro S. Nivola, *Laws of the Landscape: How Policies Shape Cities in Europe and America* (Washington, D.C.: Brookings Institution Press, 1999), 15.

28 Bureau of Transportation Statistics and Federal Highway Administration, National Household Travel Survey, 2003.

29 Cited in Richard Louv, *Last Child in the Woods: Saving Our Children from Nature-Deficit Disorder* (Chapel Hill, N.C.: Algonquin Books of Chapel Hill, 2006), 119.

30 David Rusk, *Inside Game Outside Game: Winning Strategies for Saving Urban America* (Washington, D.C.: Brookings Institution Press, 1999), 344–346.

31 Robert Burchell, Anthony Downs, Barbara McCann, and Sahan Mukherji, *Sprawl Costs: Economic Impacts of Unchecked Development* (Washington, D.C.: Island Press, 2005), 4.

32 See, for example, Burchell et al., *Sprawl Costs.*

33 American Society of Civil Engineers (ASCE), *2005 Report Card for America's Infrastructure* (Washington, D.C., and Reston, Virginia: ASCE, 2005); available at www.asce.org/reportcard/2005/index.cfm.

34 Natural Resources Conservation Service, *Urbanization and Development of Rural Land,* 2001 National Resources Inventory (July 2003); available at www.nrcs.usda.gov/technical/NRI/2001/urban.pdf.

35 Natural Resources Conservation Service, *Urbanization and Development of Rural Land,* 2001 National Resources Inventory (July 2003), cited in Mark A. Benedict and Edward T. McMahon, *Green Infrastructure: Linking Landscapes and Communities* (Washington, D.C.: Island Press, 2006), 5–7.

36 Nigel Key and Michael J. Roberts, "Measures of Trends in Farm Size Tell Differing Stories," *Amber Waves* (November 2007); available at www.ers.usda.gov/AmberWaves/November07/DataFeature/. The figure refers to farms of 50 to 1,000 acres (20 to 405 hectares); the number of farms smaller than 50 acres increased by roughly the same percentage. The number of farms larger than 1,000 acres increased by 14 percent.

37 As quoted in Louv, *Last Child in the Woods,* 30.

38 American Farmland Trust, "Paving Paradise: A New Perspective on California Farmland Conversion," November 2007; www.farmland.org/programs/states/ca/Feature%20Stories/PavingParadise.asp.

39 Celia W. Dugger, "Need for Water Could Double in the Next 50 Years, U.N. Study Finds," *New York Times,* August 22, 2006, A12.

40 Ibid.

41  Storm Cunningham, *The Restoration Economy: The Greatest New Growth Frontier* (San Francisco: Berrett-Koheler, 2002).

42  Ibid., 5, 7, 8.

43  The survey also reported that smaller firms did more work in the remodeling sector, and that larger firms were more likely to undertake new construction. American Institute of Architects (AIA), *2006 AIA Firm Survey* (Washington, D.C.: AIA), 33–35.

44  Joint Center for Housing Studies, "Foundations for Future Growth in the Remodeling Industry," 2007, 5; www.jchs.harvard.edu/publications/remodeling/remodeling2007/r07-1.pdf.

45  Mitch Rudin, telephone conversation with author, August 7, 2008.

46  Joel Garreau, *Edge City: Life on the New Frontier* (New York: Anchor Books, Doubleday, 1991).

47  Thomas L. Friedman, *The World Is Flat* (New York: Farrar, Straus, and Giroux, 2005).

48  Quoted in Juliet Eilperin, "A Bold Plan for National Security," *Princeton Alumni Weekly*, October 25, 2006; available at www.princeton.edu/~paw/archive_new/PAW06-07/03-1025/notebook.html#Notebook4.

# CHAPTER 2

# The Ever-Changing, Ever-Evolving Metropolitan Form

The best cure for destructive sprawl is to build cities
people don't want to abandon, places where they can
live healthy, fulfilling lives in densities that don't devour
our landscapes, pave our wilderness and pollute our
water sheds, air and wildlife. —ROBERT F. KENNEDY JR.

*No urban community is static: each is an organism that either grows or dies. Since World War II, our metro areas have metastasized, with most new development taking place on the ever-evolving urban fringe. For some decades, this pattern led to a degree of disinvestment in core cities and close-in suburbs. Although many urban downtowns, residential neighborhoods, and first-tier suburbs are making a comeback, a good deal of stress is still evident. And as unplanned growth continues, second- and third-tier suburbs and emerging exurbs are experiencing growing pains. This chapter takes a brief look at the evolving suburbs, downtowns, and exurbs that have so radically changed the metropolitan form.*

**THE RETURN OF MILLIONS OF SOLDIERS** and sailors after World War II caused a huge spike in suburban homebuilding—which, in turn, accelerated the deconcentration of housing in America. Most Americans bought into an American Dream that linked property ownership to success and civic virtue. Homeownership and automobile ownership, undergirded by rising affluence, became cornerstones of post–World War II society.

FIGURE 2-1 **U.S. Homeownership, 1930–2000.**

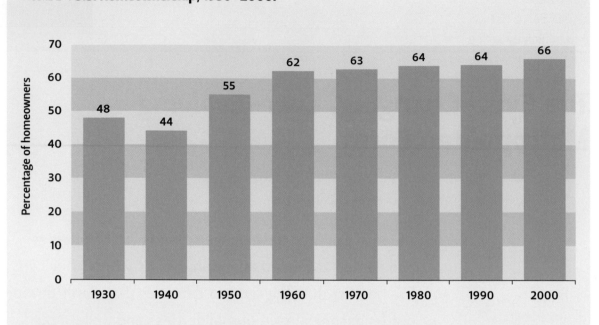

SOURCE: U.S. Census Bureau, "Homeownership," Historical Census of Housing Tables, Census of Housing; www.census.gov/hhes/www/housing/census/historic/owner.html.

The National Housing Act of 1949 called for "a decent home and a suitable living environment for every American family." It also authorized slum clearance and redevelopment. Responsibility for public low-cost housing for low-income households fell to the federal government. The private sector would build suburbia.

Between 1946 and 1951, the foundations of 15.8 million houses were laid. The 1.692 million single-family housing starts in 1950 turned out to be an all-time high. The mass production of single-family homes by the Henry Fords of housing provided further impetus for urban decentralization and the universalization of suburbia. Levitt and Sons (Abraham, William, and Arthur) started the production-homebuilding craze with the development of 17,400 one-and-a-half-story dwellings on a 4,000-acre (1,619-hectare) Long Island potato patch. The 750-square-foot (70-square-meter) Levittown model featured two bedrooms, one bath, and no garage—and cost about $7,990. Originally, these homes rented for $60 per month; they were subsequently sold for a downpayment of only $400.[1] Levittown's success was replicated across the country in the form of low-density, architecturally homogeneous, and eminently affordable housing.

The huge growth in homebuilding was accompanied—indeed stimulated—by a tremendous increase in highway building, which culminated, in the mid-1950s, with the beginning of the 42,000-mile (67,592-kilometer) Interstate Highway System. (Although interstates represent only 1 percent of U.S. highway miles, they carry 24 percent of all traffic and 41 percent of travel by large trucks.)[2] Streetcars and trolleys disappeared, and automobile ownership rose dramatically. The number of cars on the road escalated from just under 26 million in 1945 to more than 52 million by 1955, 97 million by 1972, and 136 million by 2005—plus 103 million trucks.[3]

The security represented by a suburban home and the mobility represented by a family car became the backdrop for Ozzie and Harriet's life in what has been called "the sitcom suburb."[4] These suburbs were featured in books like William Whyte's *The Organization Man* and Kenneth Jackson's *Crabgrass Frontier*.[5] In *The City in History*, the historian and critic Lewis Mumford was unmincing in his characterization of the postwar suburbs:

> *A multitude of uniform, unidentifiable houses, lined up inflexibly, at uniform distances, on uniform roads, in a treeless communal waste, inhabited by people of the same class, the same income, the same age group, witnessing the same television performances, eating the same tasteless prefabricated foods, from the same freezers, conforming in every outward respect to a common mold, manufactured in the central metropolis.*[6]

Of course, what critics like Mumford missed, or chose to ignore, was the strong desire of middle-class people in the 1950s to have their own home—to realize the American Dream.

Although television shows like *Ozzie and Harriet, Leave It to Beaver, and Father Knows Best* presented "typical" households of the postwar period, such families were probably in the minority. According to the 1960 U.S. Census, 32.3 percent of the total population lived in central cities; 21.1 percent in what the census called "the urban fringe" (which was probably where Ozzie and Harriet lived); 16.4 percent in "other urban" areas; and 30.1 percent in rural and farming areas. Slicing and dicing the census figures by income, 6.2 million American households had a single breadwinner and were made up of a husband, a wife, and two children under 18; of that number, the Ozzie and Harriet types (whose incomes would have been between $15,000 and $25,000) numbered 192,000, while there were 2,919,900 million households with incomes under $6,000.[7]

The poor and very poor were housed in federally subsidized public housing, invariably in inner-city locations. Lower-income families lived in the city or in first-tier suburbs, as did immigrants and minorities, because they were effectively screened out of suburbia by exclusionary zoning, or by covenants and regulations drafted by homeowners' associations. There is ample historical evidence that large-lot zoning, minimum building-size regulations, and prohibitions against apartments were popular tools for segregating out those Americans who had lower incomes or were the wrong color or nationality.[8] It is revealing that in the 1960s, a defender of four-acre- (1.6-hectare-) lot minimums in Greenwich, Connecticut, said that large-lot zoning is "just economics. It's like going into Tiffany and demanding a ring for $12.50. Tiffany doesn't have rings for $12.50. Well, Greenwich is like Tiffany." In the same spirit, a New Jersey legislator said that large-lot zoning was a way of making sure "that you can't buy a Cadillac at

Chevrolet prices."[9] In search of "a better place to live," middle-income Americans kept moving farther out from the central city, while some pushed all the way to what has become known as "exurbia."

The suburbs evolved through a series of phases—from the railroad and streetcar suburbs of the 19th century; to the automobile suburbs of the years after World War I; to the bedroom suburbs of the years after World War II, when mass-produced, cookie-cutter "Levittowns" popped up to meet the needs of 16 million returning GIs. During the first several decades after World War II, the man of the house still commuted to the central city; but by 1965, "enclave suburbs" had appeared: self-sufficient places where people lived *and* worked *and* shopped—in huge regional shopping malls. Gradually, suburbs became more economically complex and more diverse, while the older core cities emptied out. But by the 1990s, yet another set of shifts had begun: exurban development gained speed, and central cities began to undergo a resurgence. At this point, some of the wealthy decided to stay in the city, either in grand old family homes or in new, high-end condos or apartments. Others chose the grandeur and luxury of exclusive suburban enclaves occupied by 3,000- to 5,000-square-foot (279- to 465-square-meter) "McMansions." These ever-larger homes, with their "two-story entrance halls, great rooms, three- or four-car garages, huge kitchens, spa-sized bathrooms, his-and-hers room-sized master closets, media rooms, fitness centers, home offices, high-tech security systems, and perhaps even an *au pair* suite"—have been called the "American Dream Extreme."[10]

A 1999 survey of consumer attitudes conducted by the National Association of Home Builders (NAHB) came up with a figure that ought not to surprise anyone who is steeped in the American Dream: 88 percent of respondents said that they preferred to live in a single-family home, and adamantly opposed the idea of living in or near higher-density single-family homes, townhouses, or multifamily rental apartments.[11] Although household size has declined over the years, the median size of new homes increased every year between 1974 and early 2007, from 1,755 to 2,302 square feet (163 to 214 square meters). After the first quarter of 2007, this number began slipping (to 2,241 square feet [208 square meters] in the second quarter)—a possible indication of things to come.[12] Members of some market segments are buying townhouses and smaller houses on smaller lots, but even with the current slump, a substantial share of the homebuyers' market continues to buy large houses in greenfield locations.[13]

Decades of decreasing densities in America's metropolitan areas are a clear reflection of this preference. By the turn of the 21st century, densities were substantially lower in most metro areas than they had been in the 1950s.[14] Lower densities plus population growth equals more sprawl and greater consumption of land. According to research conducted by noted urbanologist and former mayor of Albuquerque David Rusk, between 1950 and 2000, America's total urbanized population increased by 121 percent, while total urbanized land area (square miles) increased by 305 percent. In the suburbs, the figures were 384 percent and 511 percent, respectively. Thus, urban and suburban densities (people per square mile) decreased by 45 percent and 21 percent, respectively.[15]

## The Changing Suburban Scene

The dramatic changes that have occurred in America's suburbs since the 1950s have taken on two faces: one bleak, one hopeful. On the bleak side, as more and more Americans have migrated from urban to suburban settings, poverty has moved with them. The suburban poor now outnumber their urban counterparts by at least 1 million, although in 2005, the poverty rate in large cities (18.8 percent) was twice as high as in the suburbs.[16] Other metropolitan problems—including traffic congestion, aging infra-structure, and social pathologies (drugs, crime, and so forth)—also have seeped into the suburbs, and beyond.

Ever-expanding suburbs have gobbled up green space, natural habitats, and open space. Suburban residents complain about long commutes and congestion, and often oppose new developments on the grounds that they will create more traffic jams, destroy more green space, or simply be nuisances. In the words of Lend Lease Real Estate Investments, "Most of all, suburbanites are tired of traffic—the congestion, the pollution, and the hectic and unfulfilling lifestyle it promotes."[17]

FIGURE 2–2 **Urban and Suburban Populations, 1950–2000.**

| | 1950 | 2000 | Total Change, 1950—2000 | Percent Change, 1950—2000 |
|---|---|---|---|---|
| **Central cities and suburban areas combined** | | | | |
| Urbanized population | 69,268,854 | 152,890,470 | 83,621,616 | 121 |
| Urbanized land area (square miles/square kilometers) | 12,850/33,281 | 52,090/134,912 | 39,240/101,631 | 305 |
| Population density (people per square mile/per square kilometer) | 5,391/2,081 | 2,935/1,133 | -2,455/-948 | -46 |
| **Central cities** | | | | |
| Urbanized population | 51,389,148 | 66,344,621 | 14,955,473 | 29 |
| Urbanized land area (square miles/square kilometers) | 7,017/18,174 | 16,436/42,569 | 9,419/24,395 | 134 |
| Population density (people per square mile/per square kilometer) | 7,324/2,828 | 4,037/1,559 | -3,287/-1,269 | -45 |
| **Suburban areas** | | | | |
| Urbanized population | 17,879,706 | 86,545,849 | 68,666,143 | 384 |
| Urbanized land area (square miles/square kilometers) | 5,833/15,107 | 35,654/92,343 | 29,821/77,236 | 511 |
| Population density (people per square mile/per square kilometer) | 3,065/1,183 | 2,427/937 | -638/-246 | -21 |

**SOURCE:** U.S. Census Bureau data, as analyzed by David Rusk.

**NOTE:** The analysis is based on a comparison of 157 urbanized areas.

The financial crisis of 2007–2008 has not helped matters. Triggered by overextension of debt, lax loan policies, and a downturn in home values—a record 10.7 percent in 2007[18]—the crisis has meant that up to 15 million homeowners owe more on their mortgages than their homes are worth.[19] As of early July 2008, foreclosures nationwide totaled over 1.2 million.[20]

Furthermore, as the suburbs age and as the taste for downtown living increases, some urban experts are expecting newer fringe suburbs to turn into "slumburbs." According to Christopher Leinberger, a Brookings Institution fellow and the director of the graduate real estate program at the University of Michigan, there are "reasons to believe [that] . . . many low-density suburbs and McMansion subdivisions, including some that are lovely and affluent today, may become what inner cities became in the 1960s and 70s—slums characterized by poverty, crime, and decay." He voices this pessimistic prediction in an article in *The Atlantic,* in which he boldly asserts that "fundamental changes in American life may turn today's McMansions into tomorrow's tenements."[21] Leinberger notes that "over the last few decades, we've structurally over-invested in fringe real estate"—a fancy way of saying that new suburbs are overbuilt. His observations are based on Arthur C. Nelson's forecast that by 2025, there will be "a likely surplus of 22 million large-lot homes (houses built on a sixth of an acre [0.68 hectares] or more)."[22] That's 40 percent of the large-lot homes in existence today, according to Leinberger. When asked if edge cities are turning into slums, Richard Florida, author of *Cities and the Creative Class,* says, "they are already well on their way. The knowledge workers can't afford the time cost, they can't afford the commuting time."[23]

Let's contrast this dim view of the suburban future with a more hopeful one. America's suburbs are no longer mere bedroom communities, as they were in the 20th century. They have evolved into more complex and complete places. The majority of suburbanites no longer work in downtowns; their workplaces are scattered throughout low-density suburban regions.[24] As they have gained more jobs, suburbs have also become more attractive places to live, work, and play. Cultural amenities—performing arts centers, symphony halls, museums, and the like—have followed the population to the suburbs, as have educational and medical facilities and commercial centers. The success of Strathmore Hall, in Bethesda, Maryland, outside Washington, D.C., and the world-class performing arts center planned for Carmel, Indiana, just north of Indianapolis, attest to such a migration.

Near Providence, Rhode Island, the suburban city of Pawtucket is experiencing its biggest building boom in 40 years, thanks in no small measure to its ten-year-old arts and entertainment initiative, which has served as an economic engine to bring new vitality to the city. The district encompasses 60 streets and 23 old textile mill sites, many of which were vacant for decades but are now being renovated by artists and creative-sector companies. Overall, some 2.5 million square feet (232,258 square meters) of space in historic mills and commercial properties has been saved or restored, or will be converted to new uses as live/work space. In one instance, 25,000 square feet

(2,323 square meters) of dead space at the former Rhode Island Cardboard Company was transformed into 13 live/work spaces and studios. Herb Weiss, the city's economic and cultural affairs officer, says that this initiative has enhanced the quality of life in the community, created new jobs, and yielded secondary effects that include new restaurants and more tourists. He calls the arts and entertainment initiative a "fantastic, low-cost marketing tool."[25]

In the arena of suburban development, a new emphasis has emerged on saving open space by clustering housing, mixing land uses, and implementing zoning policies that set apart green space as inviolate. Smart growth policies that focus on pedestrian friendliness, town centers, conservation of open space, more choices in housing products, appealing streetscapes, mixed uses, and more compact development have had a substantial impact on suburban planning and development.

A new interest in connectivity has also appeared. According to Peter Calthorpe, president of Calthorpe Associates, in Berkeley, California, and William Fulton, president of Solimar Research Group, Inc., in Ventura, California, "The once segregated places of the suburbs are beginning to be connected by strategic mixed-use projects on infill and redevelopment sites. A network of centers that are urban in the best sense of the word is beginning to overlay and transform the suburban landscape."[26] To slow traffic and increase pedestrian safety and comfort in new communities, planners are replacing culs-de-sac with more urban street patterns that feature shorter blocks, lots of intersections, and narrower, sidewalk-lined streets.[27] The challenge for existing suburbs is to forge such connections. Weaving together the variegated pieces of the metropolitan mosaic, new communities, as well as existing suburbs, will create more livable and sustainable suburban settings. This can be achieved "through a comprehensively managed, multimodal transit network that combines a variety of transit options such as commuter rail, light rail, buses, trolleys, bikeways, walkable streets, ridesharing, and on-demand vanpools."[28]

Compact development has become attractive because developable land is becoming scarce; to ensure that enough will be available for development tomorrow, it makes sense to build more compactly today.[29] Compact development does *not* mean overcrowding, building high rises, or warehousing people in barracks-style public-housing projects. In contrast to the currently prevailing pattern of low-density development, well-designed compact development can provide a variety of housing choices, preserve open space, support economic vitality and transit, and create more livable, walkable, bikeable communities. Research has shown that every time a neighborhood doubles in compactness, the number of vehicle trips residents make is reduced by 20 to 30 percent, resulting in less pollution, less traffic congestion, and more transportation options.[30] Compact development comes in many forms: in clusters around open spaces, in higher densities around transit stops, in multifamily development, in mixed-use development, in master-planned communities, and in traditional neighborhoods with a mix of housing types and land uses.

It is a hopeful sign that parts of our suburbs have become ideal locations for new types of redevelopment in the 21st century. Many of the nation's first-tier suburbs—located contiguous to central cities and built, for the most part, immediately after World War II—are suffering from declining tax bases, poor schools, growing poverty, crumbling infrastructure, fiscal stress, outdated housing, and resegregation. These communities, where one-fifth of America lives, were based primarily on a manufacturing economy, and have had difficulty making the transition to the postindustrial era. For example, between 1970 and 2000, in Dundalk, Maryland—a community just east of Baltimore—the poverty rate doubled; the over-65 population tripled; and, as General Motors and Bethlehem Steel phased out their Dundalk plants, two out of every three manufacturing jobs disappeared.[31]

However, with tax incentives; zoning changes; better public transit; and county, state, and federal aid, reinvestment in first-tier suburbs, which lie halfway between downtown and the more affluent second- and third-tier suburbs, can overcome their incipient decline. Shaker Heights and Mariemont, Ohio, have held the line against decay through scrupulous adherence to architectural standards. Englewood, Colorado, has capitalized on a light-rail transit stop to stimulate redevelopment. The creation of a tax increment financing district in Gates, New York, a suburb on the western edge of Rochester, led to the construction of a new industrial park and helped Gates recover from the closing of a giant Eastman Kodak facility. With the hope of attracting investors, the Michigan Suburbs Alliance is working with communities to streamline zoning rules and the redevelopment process. In short, prospects in many first-tier suburbs are looking up. With their location and their established—albeit aging—housing stock, they represent significant market opportunities.

In addition, functionally obsolete suburban malls and office parks are being redeveloped as urban villages; as walkable, mixed-use town centers; and as mixed-use campuses with higher densities, larger building footprints, structured parking, on-site support services, fitness centers, daycare facilities, conference centers, hotels, multifamily housing, and even assisted living facilities.[32] The conversion of the old Villa Italia mall in Lakewood, Colorado, into a magnificent urban village, Belmar, attests to the possibility for renewal on a large scale. With some 7 percent of the country's 2,400 shopping centers containing more than 400,000 square feet (37,161 square meters) of leasable space now considered "dead," and many more (12 percent) dying, the redevelopment of suburban shopping malls offers an unparalleled opportunity.[33] These greyfields can become goldfields. As William Fulton has succinctly put it, "The future of America lies in dead malls."[34]

Former Milwaukee mayor John Norquist, who now serves as president of the Congress for New Urbanism, believes that we may be witnessing "the evolution of the American dream toward a far healthier, more ecological vision." Noting that "thirty percent of the housing stock that will exist in 2030 hasn't been built yet," he sees opportunities in the near future for the development of more urbanized, walkable suburbs.[35]

As noted earlier, 88 percent of respondents to a 1999 NAHB survey would rather live in a single-family home, and have no desire live in or near higher-density residential developments. One can easily imagine that for these families, suburban life constitutes the realization of the American Dream. According to a more recent survey, conducted in 2007,[36] this number has dropped to 68 percent, even though many observers think the number hovers around 80 percent. Whatever the exact number is, well over half of the surveyed group prefers the suburbs, in spite of the traffic congestion and other frustrations they have to endure. And they have every right to be there.

## The Changing Downtown Scene

As is well known, the ever-widening gyre of suburban development had a serious unintended consequence: the central cities began to empty out. Middle-class whites moved in droves to the economically and racially homogeneous suburbs, leaving the poor and minorities behind. Between 1950 and 1960, central cities averaged an 11 percent increase in population, whereas the suburbs grew by an astounding 49 percent.[37] By 1970, for the first time in our nation's history, more than half the population lived outside of central cities, and the central cities began a decline from which they did not begin to recover until the 1990s.[38]

Central cities have experienced a considerable rebound in the past two decades, both in terms of population growth and desirability. As Leinberger puts it, "people are being drawn to the convenience and culture of walkable urban neighborhoods. . . . Over the next 20 years, developers will likely produce many, many millions of new and newly renovated town houses, condos, and small-lot houses in and around both new and traditional downtowns."[39] Three demographic cohorts seem to be expressing a preference for the amenities of downtown living: "singles" (the young, laptop-toting ex-suburbanites who are looking for more excitement and connectedness in their lives than the places where they grew up seem to offer); "mingles" (couples, either married or unmarried, as well as gay men and women, artists, software makers, craftspeople, and business and professional people); and "jingles" (the happy empty nesters who want to leave the big house in the suburbs and move to where cultural and entertainment opportunities are abundant).

While a strong trend cannot yet be discerned, there are signs that the decline that hit central cities in the 1970s and 1980s may be yielding to an imperfect renaissance. According to a study that followed 45 sample downtowns from 1970 to 2000, downtown populations grew by 10 percent during the 1990s—a significant increase that came in the wake of 20 years of decline; downtown homeownership rates more than doubled (to 22 percent) during those 30 years; and downtowns in general boasted a higher percentage of both young adults and college-educated residents than the nation's cities and suburbs.[40]

The experiences of several central cities are informative. In 45 downtowns analyzed by Eugenie L. Birch, of the University of Pennsylvania, during the 1990s, the number of downtown households increased by 13 percent; homeownership rates reached 22 percent; racial diversity increased; and the percentage of 45- to 60-year-olds increased; throughout the decade, however, the percentage of families with children remained stable, at 10 percent. In Philadelphia, the central city population jumped 11 percent between 2000 and 2005; by 2007, 97 downtown residential projects that will accommodate 18,000 new people were on the drawing board, although the amount of downtown office space remains the same as it was in 1990.[41] In Chicago, after decades of decline, the downtown population grew by 39.4 percent between 1970 and 2000, and the percentage of homeowners increased by 1,583 percent during the same period.[42] Many of these new urban dwellers came from the suburbs and sought housing in and near downtown, taking advantage of the cultural activities, shopping, and other amenities the city has to offer. In Manhattan, older commercial space is being converted to residential condominiums at a rapid rate. Thirty floors of

FIGURE 2-3 **Changes in Downtown Population, Selected Cities by Region.**

| Northeast | Percent Change, 1970–1990 | Percent Change, 1990–2000 | Midwest | Percent Change, 1970–1990 | Percent Change, 1990–2000 |
|---|---|---|---|---|---|
| Baltimore | -17.51 | 5.10 | Chicago | 7.27 | 30.00 |
| Boston | -2.68 | 4.70 | Cincinnati | 10.54 | -16.90 |
| Lower Manhattan | 39.63 | 15.60 | Cleveland | -20.02 | 32.20 |
| Midtown Manhattan | 22.49 | 3.30 | Columbus, Ohio | -52.59 | 0.60 |
| Philadelphia | -6.50 | 4.90 | Des Moines | -32.50 | 0.30 |
| Pittsburgh | -31.17 | 26.10 | Detroit | -44.13 | -3.30 |
| Washington, D.C. | -13.63 | 4.00 | Indianapolis | -45.65 | 20.20 |
| **Total, Northeast** | **4.61** | **7.40** | Milwaukee | -11.99 | 13.10 |
| South | | | Minneapolis | 2.24 | -16.60 |
| Atlanta | -17.60 | 26.10 | St. Louis | -60.03 | -17.50 |
| Austin | -22.68 | -0.70 | **Total, Midwest** | **-25.15** | **7.70** |
| Charlotte | -30.03 | -0.70 | West | | |
| Chattanooga | -29.53 | 7.40 | Albuquerque | -28.45 | 45.20 |
| Columbus, Georgia | -31.39 | -24.40 | Boise | -28.78 | 5.50 |
| Dallas | -36.53 | 24.10 | Colorado Springs | -38.39 | 48.00 |
| Jackson | -33.96 | -3.10 | Denver | -10.45 | 51.40 |
| Lafayette | -8.64 | 21.00 | Los Angeles | 53.64 | 5.70 |
| Lexington | -22.82 | -6.10 | Mesa | -15.83 | -10.70 |
| Memphis | -15.57 | 6.40 | Phoenix | -18.73 | -9.10 |
| Miami | -42.17 | 31.60 | Portland | 14.93 | 35.40 |
| New Orleans | -30.74 | 22.30 | Salt Lake City | -20.89 | 23.10 |
| Norfolk | 63.25 | 20.50 | San Diego | 48.78 | 16.10 |
| Orlando | -33.04 | -11.60 | San Francisco | -5.98 | 32.30 |
| San Antonio | -23.78 | -1.90 | Seattle | 4.89 | 76.90 |
| Shreveport | -38.80 | 17.50 | **Total, West** | **7.80** | **24.60** |
| **Total, South** | **-28.90** | **8.80** | Aggregate total | -10.47 | 10.40 |

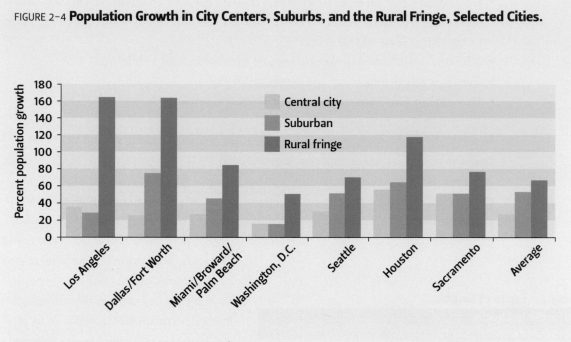

FIGURE 2-4 **Population Growth in City Centers, Suburbs, and the Rural Fringe, Selected Cities.**

**SOURCE:** Robert Dunphy, *Metropolitan Mobility* (Washington, D.C.: ULI–the Urban Land Institute, forthcoming).

the Woolworth Building are being turned into condos; 326 new condo units now fill the House of Morgan; and the number of people living in the area below the World Trade Center has doubled since 2001, from 15,000 to 30,000.[43] In short, evidence suggests that, as Birch puts it, "the impetus for downtown residential living has continued and is broadening."[44]

## The Emergence of Exurbs

As the line demarcating rural and suburban America has become increasingly blurred, exurbs—neither fully rural nor fully suburban—have emerged as the places that lie between the two. Exurbs result from the outward migration of urban and suburban residents who are in pursuit of lower-density development, from the formation of edge cities (other knots of settlement on the urban periphery), and from regional economic decentralization. Furthermore, the advent of new technologies has made it possible, through telecommuting, to enjoy urban and suburban conveniences without living in an urban or suburban area. Many different types of exurbs—ranging from affordable-housing havens for middle-class families to "favored quarters" for high-income residents—have emerged across America.

As defined by Tom Daniels in *When City and Country Collide,* exurbs tend to have certain characteristics; they

▶ Are located ten to 50 miles (16 to 80 kilometers) from an urban center with a population of approximately 500,000 people, or five to 30 miles (eight to 48 kilometers) from a city with at least 50,000 people

▶ Offer one-way, home-to-work commute times of at least 25 minutes

▶ Contain a mix of long-term and newer residents

▶ Are home to active but declining agriculture and forestry.[45]

In addition, the typical exurban census tract has many more acres of land per home than the national average for a typical tract.

There's no question that exurbs represent the fast-growing communities on the metropolitan fringe[46]—the area where 80 percent of new development is likely to occur in the coming years.[47] According to Alan Berube et al., between 1990 and 2005, exurbs grew more than twice as fast as their respective metropolitan areas overall; in the 1990s alone, the population of exurbs increased by 31 percent.[48] Nationwide, 245 counties have at least one-fifth of their residents living in exurban areas.[49] All told, as of the 2000 census, some 6 percent of the population (10.8 million people) lived in the exurbs of large metropolitan areas.[50]

Berube et al. note that exurban residents are disproportionately white, middle-income homeowners, and commuters.[51] Two communities—Orange Shoals, in Cherokee County, Georgia, and Coffee Creek Center, in Chesterton, Indiana—illustrate the attractive qualities of successful exurbs. Orange Shoals is 25 miles (40 kilometers) south of downtown Atlanta, in a favored quarter where regional growth is occurring.[52] A good example of compact development on a greenfield site, Orange Shoals has been developed with conservation and green infrastructure in mind. The 400-acre (162-hectare) property, nestled in the foothills of the Appalachian Mountains, features 317 detached homes, with a gross density of 0.8 homes per acre (1.9 per hectare); one-quarter of the site is designated as preserved forest. The homes

FIGURE 2-5 **Types of Exurbs.**

| Affordable Exurbs | |
|---|---|
| **Metro Area** | **Exurb** |
| Boston | Strafford County, New Hampshire |
| Dallas | Henderson and Hunt counties |
| New York | Dutchess County, New York; Pike County, Pennsylvania |
| Philadelphia | Cecil County, Maryland |
| Portland | Yamhill County |
| **Recreational Exurbs** | |
| **Metro Area** | **Exurb** |
| Austin | Burnet and Blanco counties (Texas Hill Country) |
| Denver | Park and Gilpin counties (Rocky Mountains) |
| Providence | Washington, Rhode Island (Narragansett Bay and Rhode Island Sound) |
| Seattle | Island County (Puget Sound) |
| Stockton | Calaveras County (Sierra Nevada foothills) |
| **Favored-Quarter Exurbs** | |
| **Metro Area** | **Exurb** |
| Baltimore | Carroll County |
| Cleveland | Geauga County |
| Detroit | Livingston County |
| Hartford | Tolland County |
| New Orleans | St. Tammany Parish |
| Richmond | Goochland County |

**SOURCE:** Alan Berube, Audrey Singer, Jill H. Wilson, and William H. Frey, "Finding Exurbia: America's Fast-Growing Communities at the Metropolitan Fringe," Brookings Institution, Living Cities Census Series, October 2006, 30–31; www.brookings.edu/~/media/Files/rc/reports/2006/10metropolitanpolicy_berube/20061017_exurbia.pdf.

range in size from 2,500 to 4,000 square feet (232 to 371 square meters), and are buffered from each other by an integrated greenbelt of woods and trails. In an area that is rapidly becoming suburbanized, Orange Shoals has a rural, low-density, secluded feel.

Coffee Creek Center, 45 miles (72 kilometers) southeast of Chicago,[53] is an exurb consciously designed to counteract sprawling, low-density, car-dependent bedroom communities and to preserve and nurture natural systems instead of displacing them.

FIGURE 2-6 **Supercommuter and Early–Riser Exurbs, 2000.**

| Supercommuter Exurbs[1] | | | | |
| --- | --- | --- | --- | --- |
| County | Associated Metro Area | Total Number of Commuters | Number of Workers with a Commute of 60+ Minutes | Percentage of Supercommuters |
| Park, Colorado | Denver, Colorado | 7,110 | 2,344 | 33 |
| Pike, Pennsylvania | New York, New York-New Jersey-Connecticut-Pennsylvania | 18,643 | 5,712 | 31 |
| Warren, Virginia | Washington, D.C.-Virginia-Maryland-West Virginia | 14,994 | 4,346 | 29 |
| San Jocinto, Texas | Houston, Texas | 7,891 | 2,156 | 27 |
| Charles, Maryland | Washington, D.C.-Virginia-Maryland-West Virginia | 60,032 | 15,225 | 25 |
| Calvert, Maryland | Washington, D.C.-Virginia-Maryland-West Virginia | 36,187 | 9,127 | 25 |
| Amelia, Virginia | Richmond, Virginia | 5,326 | 1,334 | 25 |
| Van Zandt, Texas | Dallas, Texas | 18,759 | 4,675 | 25 |
| Elbert, Colorado | Denver, Colorado | 9,863 | 2,429 | 25 |
| Culpeper, Virginia | Washington, D.C.-Virginia-Maryland-West Virginia | 15,469 | 3,804 | 25 |

| Early-Riser Exurbs[2] | | | | |
| --- | --- | --- | --- | --- |
| County | Associated Metro Area | Total Number of Commuters | Number of Workers Departing Before 6 A.M. | Percentage of Early Risers |
| Crawford, Indiana | Louisville, Kentucky-Indiana | 4,377 | 1,234 | 28 |
| Juniata, Pennsylvania | Harrisburg, Pennsylvania | 9,915 | 2,733 | 28 |
| Nye, New York | Las Vegas, Nevada | 11,660 | 3,211 | 28 |
| Washington, Missouri | St. Louis, Missouri-Illinois | 8,331 | 2,260 | 27 |
| Warren, Virginia | Washington, D.C.-Virginia-Maryland-West Virginia | 14,994 | 4,050 | 27 |
| Liberty, Texas | Houston, Texas | 25,409 | 6,525 | 26 |
| San Jacinto, Texas | Houston, Texas | 7,891 | 2,003 | 25 |
| Bibb, Alabama | Birmingham, Alabama | 7,754 | 1,923 | 25 |
| East Feliciana, Louisiana | Baton Rouge, Louisiana | 7,280 | 1,784 | 25 |
| Breckinridge, Kentucky | Louisville, Kentucky-Indiana | 7,518 | 1,805 | 24 |

**1** Supercommuter exurbs are those whose residents commute at least 60 minutes to work.
**2** Early-riser exurbs are those whose residents depart for work before 6 a.m.

The community's master plan calls for a series of compact, mixed-use, pedestrian-oriented neighborhoods where homes, workplaces, and retail centers "sit lightly on the land." It is an environmentally sensitive community defined by compact, urbanlike densities, streets that are made for walking, extensive bicycle paths, restored native ecosystems and habitats, advanced energy systems, and walkable destinations. A visit to this 675-acre (273-hectare) master-planned community reveals a variety of residential building types—live/work units, townhouses, attached and detached homes, apartments—as well as mixed-use buildings, brick-paved walking trails, reconstructed wetlands, public spaces, and public parks. Ten percent of the homes qualify as affordable housing. Coffee Creek Center contains all the important elements of a well-designed exurb: street connections, walkability, relatively high densities—at buildout, 3,000 residential units of varying sizes and types on less than 20 acres (8 hectares)—open and recreational space, commercial and retail space, civic and public facilities, and proximity to two major regional arteries.

Considered as a whole, exurbs ought not to create an antithesis between the edge and downtown. Instead, they invite synthesis—that is, "better connectivity within all these areas so the entire region functions more efficiently," as ULI chairman Todd Mansfield, who also is chairman and CEO of Crosland, a Charlotte, North Carolina–based real estate company, puts it. Mansfield points out that 52 percent of the jobs in large metro areas are located more than ten miles (16 kilometers) from downtown, while only 17 percent are downtown; he goes on to note that

> these outer areas tend to have very little access to transit, leaving people with no choice but to constantly drive between suburbs for work and errands. And too often, housing is still far too isolated from retail and commercial uses. This disconnect between how these areas are being built and how they should be built has serious economic, social, and environmental implications.[54]

It seems inevitable, given the country's growing population, that exurbs represent the shape of things to come. The escalating price of oil and gasoline, however, is becoming an increasingly important factor in this equation. A recent *New York Times* article puts the case most trenchantly: "The economics of American suburban life are under assault as skyrocketing energy prices inflate the costs of reaching, heating and cooling homes on the distant edges of metropolitan areas."[55] If (or, rather, when) the price of oil rises above $150 a barrel and gas climbs above $5 a gallon ($1.30 a liter), what impact will the increasing costs have on land development on the fringe? It stands to reason that energy costs will slow growth. It's one thing to spend a lot of time driving; it's another entirely when doing so puts a huge dent in one's pocketbook. People will look for smaller, more fuel-efficient cars and for smaller houses that are closer to work and to more compact communities. The appeal of large homes on substantial acreage out on the fringe will wane, and the price of suburban and exurban dwellings will fall. Chances are that these price trends will not reverse: the market will shift from exurbia to less distant locations for home and work, and the inevitability of exurban growth will become less clear.

Political and corporate leaders will have to learn to read these tea leaves. It will be prudent to devise strategies that handle future metropolitan growth through more compact, fiscally efficient land use patterns, connected by transportation linkages. (These strategies are often found in master-planned communities.) Otherwise, land will not be conserved, and fringe development will falter. As a 2006 Brookings Institution report warns, "low-density 'build-out' could fuel rapid growth farther out in the region, creating even more severe economic and environmental challenges."[56] To say nothing of the possibility that such development might miss the market!

## Shaping New Development

The ever-evolving metropolitan form should raise many questions in the minds of planners, policy makers, developers, and citizens. Are current patterns of growth sustainable? For example, if the land development patterns of the past half-century persist, will traffic come to a standstill? Will today's suburbs become tomorrow's slums? Will green space continue to be devoured at a rapid rate? Will housing continue to be unaffordable for the many workers who hold our country together? Does the American Dream need to be redefined in order to improve our quality of life in the coming decades? Most important, are there strategies that could be used to reverse or mitigate the centrifugal forces shaping American life today?

At a recent meeting for Delaware state executives of the Governors' Institute on Community Design, a project of Smart Growth America, ULI/Charles Fraser senior resident fellow for sustainable development Ed McMahon pointedly asked, "Do you want the character of Delaware to shape new development, or do you want new development to shape the character of Delaware?"[57] The goal of the remaining chapters is to show how the character of our communities can shape new development, rather than the other way around.

**ENDNOTES**

1   Kenneth T. Jackson, *Crabgrass Frontier: The Suburbanization of the United States* (New York: Oxford University Press, 1985), 233–235.

2   U.S. Department of Transportation, Federal Highway Administration, and Federal Transit Administration, "2006 Status of the Nation's Highways, Bridges, and Transit: Conditions and Performance"; www.fhwa.dot.gov/policy/2006cpr/pdfs.htm.

3   Paul Knox, "Schlock and Awe: The American Dream Bought and Sold," *The American Interest* (March–April 2007): 60; Federal Highway Administration data.

4   For a fuller treatment of this topic, see Jackson, *Crabgrass Frontier;* and William H. Hudnut III, *Halfway to Everywhere* (Washington, D.C.: ULI–the Urban Land Institute, 2003). The phrase *sitcom suburb* is from Knox, "Schlock and Awe."

5   William H. Whyte Jr., *The Organization Man* (New York: Simon & Shuster, 1956); Jackson, *Crabgrass Frontier.*

6   Lewis Mumford, *The City in History: Its Origins, Its Transformations, and Its Prospects* (New York: Harcourt, Brace & World, 1961), 486.

7   U.S. Census Bureau, "Part 1, United States Summary," in *Characteristics of the Population,* vol. 1 of *Census of Population: 1961* (U.S. Department of Commerce, U.S. Bureau of the Census, 1964).

8   See, for example, Dennis R. Judd and Todd Swanstrom, *City Politics: Private Power & Public Policy* (New York: Harper Collins, 1994), Ch. 9.

9   Quoted in Judd and Swanstrom, *City Politics,* 227.

10   Knox, "Schlock and Awe," 65. See also Judd and Swanstrom, *City Politics,* Ch. 8.

11   National Association of Home Builders (NAHB), *Smart Growth* (Washington, D.C.: NAHB, 1999), 3.

12   Kelly Evans, "Size of New Home Starts Shrinking," *Wall Street Journal Online,* September 18, 2007; available at http://finance.yahoo.com/real-estate/article/103528/Size-of-New-Homes-Starts-Shrinking.

13   Adrienne Schmitz, *The New Shape of Suburbia* (Washington, D.C.: ULI–the Urban Land Institute, 2003), 5.

14   David Rusk, private correspondence with author.

15   Schmitz, *Suburbia,* 33.

16   Alan Berube and Elizabeth Kneebone, "Two Steps Back: City and Suburban Poverty Trends, 1999–2005," Brookings Institution, Living Cities Census Series, December 2006, 1; www.brookings.edu/metro/pubs/20061205_citysuburban.pdf.

17   Schmitz, *Suburbia,* 16.

18   Rex Nutting, "Home Prices Fall a Record 10.7% in Past Year," MarketWatch.com, March 25, 2008.

19  James Surowiecki, "Home Economics," *New Yorker,* March 10, 2008, 62; available at www.newyorker.com/talk/financial/2008/03/10/080310ta_talk_surowiecki.

20  Foreclosure Data, "Listings: Real Estate Foreclosure Homes Listings," April 1, 2008; www.foreclosuredata.com.

21  Christopher B. Leinberger, "The Next Slum," *The Atlantic,* March 2008, 74; available at www.theatlantic.com/doc/200803/subprime.

22  Ibid.

23  Quoted in Carol Lloyd, "Mortgage Crisis Is Creating New 'Slumburbs,'" *San Francisco Chronicle,* March 16, 2008; available at www.sfgate.com/cgi-bin/article.cgi?f=/c/a/2008/03/16/BU7NVIT2O.DTL&type=printable.

24  Schmitz, *Suburbia,* 10.

25  Herb Weiss, economic and cultural affairs officer, Pawtucket, Rhode Island, "Pawtucket's Arts and Entertainment Initiative," and "Arts Districts Cost-Effective Way to Enhance Economy" (white papers).

26  Peter Calthorpe and William Fulton, *The Regional City: Planning for the End of Sprawl* (Washington, D.C., and Covelo, California: Island Press, 2001), 198.

27  Schmitz, *Suburbia,* 35.

28  Ibid., 45.

29  NAHB, "Mixed Use and Compact Development Introduction"; www.nahb.org/generic.aspx?genericContentID=16945.

30  Local Government Commission, "Compact Development for More Livable Communities"; www.lgc.org/freepub/PDF/Land_Use/focus/compact_development.pdf.

31  Ryan Blitstein, "Addressing the Silent Crisis of Declining Suburbs," February 28, 2008; http://ryanblitstein.wordpress.com/category/miller-mccunecom/.

32  Schmitz, *Suburbia,* 40.

33  Ibid., 41.

34  William Fulton, speech presented at the Brookings Institution, Washington, D.C., March 13, 2001.

35  Lloyd, "Slumburbs."

36  NAHB, Consumer Preferences Survey 2007–2008 (NAHB Economics Group, 2008).

37  Eugenie L. Birch, "Who Lives Downtown?" Brookings Institution, Living Cities Census Series, November 2005; www.brookings.edu/~/media/Files/rc/reports/2005/11downtown redevelopment_birch/20051115_Birch.pdf.

38  Ibid.

39  Leinberger, "The Next Slum?" 74.

40  See Birch, "Who Lives Downtown."

41  Alan Ehrenhalt, "Extreme Makeover," *Governing* (July 2006): 29.

42  Birch, "Who Lives Downtown?" 5, 9.

43  Ehrenhalt, "Extreme Makeover," 29.

44  Birch, "Who Lives Downtown?" 16.

45  Tom Daniels, *When City and Country Collide* (Washington, D.C.: Island Press, 1999).

46  See Alan Berube, Audrey Singer, Jill H. Wilson, and William H. Frey, "Finding Exurbia: America's Fast-Growing Communities at the Metropolitan Fringe," Brookings Institution, Living Cities Census Series, October 2006; www.brookings.edu/~/media/Files/rc/reports/2006/10metropolitanpolicy_berube/20061017_exurbia.pdf.

47  See, for example, Trisha Riggs, "A Man with a Master Plan," *Urban Land* (September 2007): 157.

48  See Berube et al., "Finding Exurbia."

49  Ibid., 26.

50  Ibid.

51  Ibid.

52  Schmitz, *Suburbia,* 164–171.

53  Jo Allen Gause et al., *Great Planned Communities* (Washington, D.C.: ULI-the Urban Land Institute, 2002), 124ff.

54  Todd Mansfield, speech to Nashville ULI District Council, June 2007.

55  Peter S. Goodman, "Fuel Prices Shift Math for Life in Far Suburbs," *New York Times,* June 25, 2008.

56  Berube et al., "Finding Exurbia," 32.

57  As quoted in *The SGA Newsletter*, Issue 61, July 18, 2007.

# CHAPTER 3

# Where It All Begins: Government, Governance, and Regionalism

## To think intelligently of the future is to think regionally.

—JOHN GARDNER

*Expanding development has rendered 19th-century jurisdictional boundaries obsolete. For the most part, these lines cannot be changed; entrenched political interests and the public's desire for local control stand in the way. However, thinking and acting regionally—either voluntarily or on a mandatory basis—has come into vogue as a strategy for dealing with the changed metropolitan form. Americans no longer live and work in cities and suburbs; instead, we find ourselves—whether we are conscious of it or not—operating within regional economic units that need multijurisdictional governance. As urbanologist and syndicated columnist Neal Peirce has written, "Far too many of America's metro regions have been sleepwalking into the 21st century, only mistily aware of how severely global economic competition and climate change may hit them. Or if aware, so splintered politically they're dangerously slow to respond."[1]*

**BACK IN THE 1950s,** when Ozzie and Harriet or the Cleavers thought about their neighbors, their vision probably stopped in the neighborhood. They would not have had much occasion to think in terms of an entire metropolitan area, because the old metropolitan form basically had two poles: city and suburb, downtown and the community in which one lived. The suburbs, with their single-family dwellings, constituted both a real and a symbolic rejection of urban life. Those who fled the cities for the suburbs were drawn by the mystique of open space, superior services and convenience, better schools, a healthier environment, and a homogeneous community. The suburbs were their cocoon.

Even in the 1950s, however, some leaders had a broader vision, as evidenced by the fact that the 1956 Interstate Highway Act mandated regional transportation planning and required that each regional metropolitan district in the country create a metropolitan planning organization (MPO). These organizations brought together local officials from different jurisdictions within a region and required them to develop regional transportation plans. With the federal mandate came standardized construction methods and signage, requirements for matching local funding, and contentious location issues.

Although technological advances have drastically changed the communication and transportation infrastructure on which we rely, our local governance structure—a 19th-century model predicated on decentralization, local control, and uniform land use and zoning—has remained fundamentally the same. This system has led to turf battles and balkanization of governance. As cities have spread out, nodes of independent development and edgeless cities have engulfed the landscape, rendering the old heliocentric city—with its center of business and industry surrounded by rings of bedroom suburbs—obsolete, and consigning that particular urban model to the proverbial dustbin of history. The spiderweb configuration of the new metropolitan form has replaced that of the spoked wheel.

Any effort to address the changing metropolitan form has to begin with one irreducible fact: America is no longer made up merely of cities and suburbs; it consists of regional economic units that need multijurisdictional governance. Today, most Americans dwell and work within a metropolitan region that contains multiple governmental jurisdictions. These communities are closely intertwined, connected by transportation networks, economic interests, and a common commuter shed, where people basically read the same papers, listen to the same radio stations, and root for the same sports teams.

A region has common needs, such as clean air and clean water, jobs, affordable housing, transportation choices, and a healthy economy. These issues do not stop at city limits or county lines. There can be no strong city in a weak region, no strong region with weak cities. Katy Sorenson, a member of the Miami-Dade Board of County Commissioners, states the case well for her region: "Today, most of the big challenges we are dealing with are regional and cannot be solved by one local jurisdiction acting alone. In southeast Florida, setting aside turfs for a common goal—the restoration of the Everglades—will be key to our future prosperity and quality of life."[2] Nathaniel P. Reed, former assistant secretary of the U.S. Department of the Interior, frames the challenge this way: "If we don't take the gigantic step and make regionalism work, 40 years from now, we will look back and wish we had."[3]

## The Federal Government's Role

To make coordinated land use and transportation planning among a region's municipalities a reality, higher levels of government need to be brought into play—in ways that support, rather than undermine, local efforts. In Fairfax County, Virginia, for example, federal policies have allowed transportation to drive land use, scattering employees to the region's outer edges and, in effect, counteracting local efforts to concentrate growth near public transit and the urban core. "I continue to be amazed by the shortsightedness of the federal government," says Fairfax County supervisor T. Dana Kauffman. Decisions that will shape regional commuting and development patterns for years are made with little local input. "Whatever they do is 'here and now,'" Kauffman continues. "They seem to have no interest in trying to plan for the rational development of a sustainable community. I suppose if they had the chance to relocate to the moon, they would."[4]

Federal programs have long been criticized for policies such as the following, which seem to aid and abet sprawl:

- Federal funding for roads and highways, which fostered the steady slide in urban transit use that has occurred since World War II, when transit accounted for approximately 35 percent of passenger-miles traveled in urban areas
- Federal tax policies—subsidies for mortgages, the deductibility of property taxes, and the capital gains treatment of housing—all of which have encouraged people to build second and third homes and to discard older homes to build newer ones farther out
- Low federal taxes on gasoline, which have facilitated our reliance on the automobile as the preferred mode of travel
- Federal funding for new sewer systems on the urban periphery, which draws new development to the greenfield areas served by those systems
- Federal policies that award transportation funding to states according to increases in vehicle miles traveled (VMT), fuel use, and lane miles.

In 1998, the National Academy of Public administration declared that each of these factors helps "to drive industrial, commercial, and residential development toward low-density suburban areas."[5] And as David Rusk has observed, "the federal government provides about forty times more support for suburban-oriented, middle-income homeownership than it does for largely city-based, lower-income rental housing."[6] Yet each of these long-standing federal policies is popular among and defended by powerful interests, and will not disappear anytime soon. The highway lobby fiercely protects highway money at the expense of transit dollars, for example, while the public opposes raising gas taxes and supports the continued deductibility of mortgage interest. Political will is needed to enact policies that reinforce more compact development.

The U.S. Constitution contains no mention of cities or counties, much less regions. Because the Constitution defines the federal government only in terms of its relationship to the states, it might be tempting to conclude that the federal government has no role in fostering effective regional problem solving in areas such as land use and transportation planning. Nonetheless, the federal government can and should use its muscle—that is, its funding powers—to mandate regional planning. The Safe, Accountable, Flexible, and Efficient Transportation Equity Act of 2003 (SAFETEA) authorized innumerable programs and $247 billion in expenditures on highway, safety, and public transportation projects and programs. While SAFETEA is heavily weighted toward the states, it does require regional planning as a precondition for receiving federal monies. It will be updated with the anticipated reauthorization in 2009 of its successor legislation—the Safe, Accountable, Flexible, and Efficient Transportation Equity Act: A Legacy for Users of 2005 (SAFETEA-LU)—which is expected to allocate approximately $300 billion for highway, transit, and transportation safety projects. To address the new regional realities, our country needs to cast aside the old federal, state, local paradigm and replace it with a new global, regional, neighborhood one—because, as a general rule, MPOs propose but cannot dispose.

What can the federal government do to strengthen a regional approach to planning? It can fine regions that do not comply with the requirements of the Clean Air Act and the Clean Water Act. Through the U.S. Environmental Protection Agency (EPA), it can bring suit against municipalities that do not meet clean water requirements and can require construction of regional sewer and water systems that meet federal mandates. In the 13-county Atlanta metro area, for example, nonattainment of Clean Air Act standards led to an EPA interdiction on further road building—and prompted the state to establish the Georgia Regional Transportation Authority (GRTA) and to give it substantial powers over taxation, bonding, and transportation planning. According to its Web site, GRTA is focusing on "the role of land use and regional development goals in the transportation project selection process."[7] The authority also reviews the impact of projects such as new subdivisions, office parks, and shopping centers on the region's transportation network and identifies strategies to limit negative effects.[8]

To establish national goals and objectives for ensuring climate stability—that is, for reducing greenhouse gas (GHG) emissions by reducing VMT—the feds can also shift the emphasis in federal transportation legislation from planning procedures to outcomes. According to Reid Ewing et al., new legislation could create an Energy Conservation, Congestion Mitigation, and Clean Air Act Bonus program, as proposed in the original ISTEA bill that was passed by the Senate in 1991.[9] States that show a 10 percent or greater decrease in VMT per person would be rewarded with increased funding, while those that demonstrated a 10 percent or greater growth in VMT would be penalized through reductions in funding. A state could require its MPO regions to comply with federal goals for reductions in VMT.

One brilliant new idea has come from the MetroPolicy initiative, a new effort of the Brookings Institution: the feds should provide incentive grants to state and local governments to "entice" metropolitan areas and their leaders into designing and implementing "truly integrated transportation, land use, housing, and economic development plans aimed at promoting quality regional place-making and environmental sustainability."[10] Brookings calls the idea "a national Sustainability Challenge." Instead of using fines and other "sticks," the feds would offer a big "carrot," in the form of a huge block grant, to regions that undertake metropolitanwide collaboration on sustainability issues, such as reductions in GHG emissions and carbon footprints. Where would the money come from? How about phased-out federal earmarks and miscellaneous grant programs?

## The State Government's Role

Partnerships between states and their cities also are important, because cities are the creatures of the states—"the mere tenants at will of the legislature," as Dillon's rule phrases it.[11] And yet, to a large extent, cities determine a state's destiny, so it behooves state legislatures to overcome their traditional antiurban bias and work closely with their cities and metro areas. This is not the place to explore the intricacies of state/city partnerships in areas like community development, economic and workforce development, education, transportation, housing, environment, and so on. But it *is* the place to say emphatically that if state legislatures want to exercise their authority, they can and should require local governments to think and act regionally.

As the following examples indicate, some states have taken admirably strong steps to promote regional thinking and action.

▸ In the 1970s, Oregon established the nation's first and only elected regional (and nonpartisan) government, today known simply as Metro, to serve the 25 cities and three counties in the Portland metro area. Metro was founded because Oregonians saw the need to deal with issues—such as infrastructure and growth management—that cut across jurisdictional lines. According to its Web site, the Metro Council "provides leadership from a regional perspective, reflects an ongoing, innovative planning orientation, and focuses on issues that cross local boundaries and require collaborative solutions."[12] Metro owns and operates the Oregon Zoo, the Oregon Convention Center, the Portland Center for the Performing Arts, and the Portland Metropolitan Exposition Center. Metro provides a forum where business and community leaders, elected officials, planners, scientists, and residents can come together to talk about the region's future. Metro manages the region's urban growth boundary, and handles transportation planning, waste disposal, recycling, preservation of natural areas, and habitat restoration—a pretty full regional plate!

▸ After Oregon, the most salient example of sound regional cooperation at the state level is the Twin Cities fiscal disparity program. The state of Minnesota enacted this tax-base-sharing program for the Minneapolis–St. Paul metro area in 1971, although court challenges delayed its implementation until 1975. The program, which is administered by the governor-appointed Met Council, has the following goals: (1) to provide an equitable way for local governments to share revenues produced by new growth without removing any of the resources that local governments already had and (2) to promote more orderly regional development. The region's 88 municipalities and seven counties agreed to put 40 percent of all increases in property tax revenues generated by new industrial and commercial development into an areawide pool, to be dispersed among participating municipalities according to a complex formula based on fiscal capacity and population. In other words, the region's "haves" are helping its "have nots." If a municipality's fiscal capacity falls below the metropolitan average, its share of revenues goes up; if a municipality's fiscal capacity is above the average, its share goes down. Elsewhere in the nation, many municipalities spend a significant amount of revenue competing for development with other municipalities in the region in order to widen their tax base. The Twin Cities' agreement prevents such competition, to a large degree, and allows the region to look more holistically at land use decisions.

▶ Oregon and Washington require all municipalities and counties to develop comprehensive growth management and land use plans, and California requires a regional council of government (COG) to be involved in the development of regional housing goals and allocations for each jurisdiction. However, the COGs lack the authority to require compliance with their recommendations.

▶ The California Senate, under the leadership of state senator Darrell Steinberg, is tackling the connections between land use and GHG emissions by working up a bill (SB 375) that would require the state's 18 MPOs to show that their future planning scenarios will lower VMT and thereby reduce carbon emissions. Says Steinberg: "Air quality, traffic congestion, and carbon know no artificial boundaries. These issues must be tackled regionally." The bill provides incentives for regions to consider the impact of land use on climate change.[13]

▶ Tennessee law requires each "planned growth area" of a county to devise a 20-year growth projection, which will be adjusted every three years.[14] Territory "that is reasonably compact yet sufficiently large to accommodate residential and nonresidential growth" must be identified in order to delineate planned growth areas in each county. In 1998, when the law was passed, city planner Bill Terry, of Goodlettsville, Tennessee, summarized it this way: "This bill essentially says that counties and cities are to consider the issue of urban sprawl in their planning. They need to look at and address the impact of urban growth on agricultural land, on forest land and on communities."[15]

▶ In 1969, the Indiana state legislature passed the UNIGOV (Unified Government) law, which authorized the merger of Indianapolis and Marion County. This represented a step forward in regional governance, incorporating some 300,000 people and 300 square miles (777 square kilometers) of territory into the new arrangement. The benefits of this consolidation have been tremendous: a widened tax base, greater efficiency, more focused city/county leadership under a strong-mayor system of government, and a stronger sense of connectedness and cohesion in the community, since every registered voter can cast a ballot for the mayor and the four at-large city council members.

▶ Maryland requires every city and town to have a comprehensive plan that, among other things, protects the Chesapeake Bay.

In short, when it comes to regional thinking and action, where there is a state will, there is a state way.

## Thinking and Acting Regionally

American governance is excessively fragmented: we have too many jurisdictions, special districts, authorities, and commissions. What are the unintended consequences of this fragmentation?

▸ Insane competition among local jurisdictions for tax base

▸ Little coherent planning—even though, in this age of polycentric development, problems spill across jurisdictional lines

▸ Damage to our ability to cooperate regionally—which, in turn, undermines our capacity to compete globally.

A new paradigm—global, regional, and neighborhood—is needed to replace the old "federal, state, local" paradigm. Efforts to think and act regionally are being driven by three factors: a desire for greater governmental efficiency, the need to create a stronger competitive advantage, and the recognition that, in the 21st century, "regions are the ideal geographical unit to respond to intensifying global forces."[16] Regions represent one facet of the "death of distance" that characterizes life in this era of globalization. It would be fatuous to talk about the Washington, D.C., metro region in terms of a Fairfax County economy, a Bethesda economy, a Prince George's County economy, or a District of Columbia economy. All these areas constitute one regional economy, one "city-state" (as in ancient Greece), one commuter shed, one air shed, one labor market, one housing market, one media market. The region's airports, universities, sports and cultural venues, restaurants, and public buildings belong to the region, not to a specific city or other subarea within the region. The same holds for the region's problems. Traffic congestion, air pollution, crime, housing, economic competition, transportation and land use planning, and protection of the environment are regional problems, not local ones confined to one jurisdiction.

This is not meant to imply that efforts at collaboration across jurisdictional lines are not being made in metropolitan America. Although mandates for regional collaboration are rare, voluntary cooperation has sparked many encouraging efforts. Recognizing that they are part of a regional economy in which a benefit to one municipality benefits all, the city of Indianapolis and some neighboring municipalities hammered out a noncompete agreement that is designed to prevent bidding wars over new business and to keep the jurisdictions from cannibalizing each other's prospects.

The First Suburbs Coalition of Northeastern Ohio represents the interests of some 14 suburbs around Cleveland that have banded together voluntarily to pool resources, process grant applications, discuss solutions to common problems, share databases and GIS information, and present a united voice in approaching the state and national governments. The venerable Regional Plan Association (RPA) is another outstanding example of regionalism at work. Founded in the 1920s by farsighted business and professional leaders, the RPA does independent research, planning, and advocacy on regional issues affecting the 31-county tristate region of New York, New Jersey, and Connecticut.

In western New York, Chautauqua County and the city of Jamestown have worked out ways to divvy up and share, rather than duplicate, services. Indeed, across the country—from Valley Vision, in the Sacramento area; to the Metro Mayors Caucus, in Denver; to the North Metro I-35W Corridor Coalition, in the Twin Cities; to myregion.org, in the Orlando area; to Envision Utah, in Salt Lake City—communities have banded together to think and act on a regional basis.

One more example: in the wake of hurricanes Katrina and Rita, the Louisiana Speaks initiative developed a regional plan for the revitalization of south Louisiana, from the Texas border to the Mississippi border. Tens of thousands of citizens weighed in on a regional poll, indicating that they wanted more transit options; more economic development; better ways to reduce the risk from future storms; and a safer, stronger Louisiana. The plan, which contains more than 100 recommendations on how to manage risk, reinvest in communities, and create a regional transit system, is being discussed in public meetings throughout the region, and has been submitted to the Louisiana Recovery Authority for approval. This regional plan represents a more responsible and holistic approach to recovery and sustainability than it would have been possible for each parish, or each community along the Louisiana coast, to undertake alone.

As the examples in this section illustrate, municipal governments throughout the nation are exploring ways to overcome fragmentation, work together, and plan and act for the benefit of the entire region. They understand that "united we stand, divided we fall."

## The Role of Voluntary Regional Organizations

Voluntary organizations—including regional COGs, chambers of commerce, academic research programs, United Way organizations, and civic organizations—can also play an important role in promoting regional action.

A regional council of governments is a broad-based, voluntary public organization that provides local member governments with a forum for discussing matters of mutual interest; it may also provide various services, such as transportation planning. The first COGs were established in the 1920s; today there are 501 councils in 48 states (the number peaked at 669, in 1976). However because of dwindling federal support, councils have been absorbing their subregional councils or combining with adjoining regions. Two-thirds of COGs work in economic development; two-thirds serve as clearinghouses to review applications for state or federal funding; half conduct land use planning; half help allocate revolving federal and state loan funds for wastewater and drinking water facilities; one-third contract for services to the elderly; and one-third conduct regional transportation planning.

There are 205 regional chambers of commerce in the country. These nongovernmental organizations, which were designed to promote economic growth, often focus on attracting and retaining business for their area. About 80 percent of a community's growth comes from business retention.

Sixty-four U.S. universities have urban programs, research centers, think tanks, and/or institutes that deal with urban and regional issues. Georgia Tech's Center for Quality Growth & Regional Development (CQGRD) is undertaking substantial work on transportation planning in megaregions. For four decades, the Center for Urban Policy

Research, at Rutgers University, has been doing applied research on a range of issues, including affordable housing, land development and sprawl, transportation information systems, and environmental and infrastructure development impact analysis.

Some 1,500 regional United Way organizations serve metro areas nationwide, raising funds to address concerns such as homelessness, early-childhood education, and services for the mentally ill and medically underserved. Funds are raised regionally, the services are rendered regionally, and jurisdictional lines are irrelevant to the groups' work.

Regional civic organizations (RCOs) are independent, nonpartisan, open-membership organizations that study emerging regional challenges and encourage involvement. These groups have popped up in many places to give voice to citizens' regional concerns, and to support efforts to overcome balkanized thinking. Perhaps the best known and most influential RCO is the RPA, which has been addressing regional issues such as transportation, economic competitiveness, open space, and community design in the New York–New Jersey–Connecticut region for more than 85 years. To quote from the mission statement posted on the RPA's Web site, "We anticipate the challenges the region will face in the years to come, and we mobilize the region's civic, business, and government sectors to take action."[17]

Regional organizations of all kinds make significant contributions to the social, economic, and environmental needs of their areas. But because many jurisdictions do not want to give up any authority, and because elected officials often prefer the status quo to changes that might dilute their power, voluntary cooperation can only go so far. So it is instructive to look at other regional operations that are backed by the authority of law.

## The Role of Metropolitan Planning Organizations

MPOs are multijurisdictional entities, typically composed of local elected officials, state agency executives, and, sometimes, planning experts. While their responsibilities vary from state to state, much of their work involves transportation planning. For example, the Delaware Valley Regional Planning Commission (DVRPC) has covered the Greater Philadelphia and Chester areas, in Pennsylvania; and the Camden and Trenton areas, in New Jersey, for 40 years. Its goal is to provide "continuing, comprehensive and coordinated planning to shape a vision for the future growth of the Delaware Valley region."[18] In conjunction with the New Jersey and Pennsylvania departments of transportation, the DVRPC has overseen the preparation of the *Smart Transportation Guidebook,* which advances six principles: tailor solutions to the context; tailor the approach; plan all projects in collaboration with the community; plan for alternative transportation modes; use sound professional judgment; and scale the solution to the size of the problem. The book also provides guidelines for improving roadway systems, ranging from principal arterial highways owned by the state government to local roadways.

In spite of the good work that many MPOs like the DVRPC perform, America clearly needs stronger regional decision-making bodies to deal with growth. Florida recognizes this, and is addressing the issue through the Florida Transportation Plan (FTP). A 2007 report on transportation and land use states:

> *Increasingly, Florida's economy is functioning at a regional scale as development spreads out from city centers and metropolitan areas grow together. The FTP identifies regional-level coordination as critical to the process of making good decisions about transportation planning and programming. The FTP established a long-range objective that each region should develop a regional vision and action plan that integrates transportation, land use, economic, community, and environmental systems to guide transportation decision-making. . . . FDOT [the Florida Department of Transportation] and the Department of Community Affairs . . . have provided seed funding and in-kind support to a prototype regional visioning process in Central Florida, led by myregion.org in partnership with the Central Florida MPO Alliance, the East Central Florida RPC [Regional Planning Council], and the Orlando Regional Chamber of Commerce. This process is engaging county and city elected officials, business and civic leaders, and more than 10,000 citizens in a 15-month process to answer the question "How Shall We Grow?"*[19]

Florida has 26 MPOs—which, according to the report, "*may* have a key role in regional transportation and land use coordination as they help implement the 2005 Growth Management Act and the various FTP objectives related to coordination among local governments" [italics added]. The state also has 11 regional planning councils, which are "charged with serving as coordinating bodies to aid local governments in making decisions about growth and development that affect both local communities and the region as a whole" [italics added].[20] A careful parsing of the italicized words leads one to wonder how strong these organizations really are.

MPOs provide an opportunity for public officials to gather at the same table and talk about regional planning. All too frequently, however, these meetings are horse-trading sessions, focused narrowly on transportation projects within a region without regard to other land use issues. It may sound harsh, but the fact is that most MPOs do little more than develop a wish list of transportation projects that are agreed to by their members, and then sent as recommendations to a city council, a county council, or a state legislature. MPOs lack clout, have no taxing authority, and are not given the power to enforce the plans they recommend. In short, most MPOs have no teeth. Many of them do an excellent job within the parameters of their responsibilities, but those parameters are not sufficiently broad, and the responsibilities are not accompanied by sufficient authority. For example, the extremely professional and competent staff of the Sacramento COG/MPO (SACOG) worked long and hard on a strategy (known as the "blueprint") for regional transportation planning and submitted it to the six counties and 22 cities within its jurisdiction. Most entities adopted the recommended plan, but some did not, and without the state of California backing the recommendations through statute, SACOG had no power to require that the holdouts implement the plan.

One organization that provides a sharp contrast to the typical MPO is the San Diego Association of Governments (SANDAG)—one of the strongest regional agencies in the MPO business. SANDAG's primary function is to provide a regional framework for connecting land use to the area's transportation systems. The agency develops both a comprehensive land use plan (mandated, for this county only, by the state legislature) and a regional transportation plan to implement a long-range vision for buses, trolleys, rail, highways, major streets, bicycle travel, walking, the movement of goods, and airport services. According to executive director Gary Gallegos, SANDAG allocates millions of dollars each year in local, state, and federal funds for the region's transportation network.[21]

In November 2004, 67 percent of San Diego County voters approved a 40-year extension of TransNet, a local half-cent sales tax that funds local transportation projects. In San Diego's healthy economy, the bonds backed by this revenue source will generate $14 billion for public transit, highway, and local street and road improvements. SANDAG—with the approval of its board of elected officials—will allocate the monies according to its plans.[22]

In most communities, MPOs are sleeping giants. However, the following changes in either federal legislation or state requirements could significantly strengthen the leadership role of MPOs:

▶ Require that the voting membership of the MPO reflect the population of the metropolitan area. Currently, within an MPO, a county with 20,000 people has the same voting power as a county with 1 million people. Yet a county with a significantly larger population—or a major employment center—will obviously have more demand for transportation and other services than a smaller county.

▶ Elect the membership. All eligible voters in the metro area could participate. The elected members would come from the participating communities; the elected and appointed public officials who, under the current system, serve on the MPO board, would serve ex officio.

▶ When it comes to allocating funds, MPOs should be required to use a "fix it first" strategy. Given that transportation funds are limited, investments in new projects can hobble reinvestment in and maintenance of existing infrastructure. Some MPOs are investing as much as 60 percent of their annual allocation in new projects, when they should be using 80 percent of their allocation for maintenance. A fix it first policy creates a more thoughtful plan for allocating funds.

▶ Before allocating funds for new projects, MPOs should be required to assess the land use impact of proposed development. Land use is largely determined by transportation, sewers, and water. With current concerns about energy costs and sprawl, it is irresponsible not to take those factors into account. Density, environmental protection, brownfields, and other related issues all need to be part of the equation in determining where to invest transportation dollars.

▸ Give MPOs (or their equivalents, if a state creates a similar entity) actual authority to control zoning, allocate funds, issue bonds, levy taxes, and enforce federal and state regulations regarding air and water pollution.

▸ Require MPOs to focus on GHG emissions as a planning issue. They need to recognize that higher densities result in lower emissions (notwithstanding possible reductions in vehicle speeds), and to implement strategies that encourage compact development. Different growth scenarios yield different results for VMT and GHG emissions; when MPOs think about land use and transportation planning for new development, they need to consider these factors. It would help if the 2009 version of SAFETEA-LU were to include a provision mandating that MPOs' long-range plans and transportation improvement programs comply with results-based goals for climate stability.[23]

▸ Reduce the number of MPOs. In many areas—the continuous metropolitan regions of New York and south Florida, for example—multiple MPOs cover the same area. Moreover, MPOs and the regions they serve tend to operate in "myopic bubble worlds."[24] In its study of infrastructure needs, ULI recommends that federal mandates be put in place to require neighboring regions to link their planning efforts and to use a uniform approach to presenting information and benchmarking results.[25]

## The Role of Regional Service Providers

The number of special districts—including both single- and multiservice authorities—increased almost threefold during the past 60 years, from around 12,500 to more than

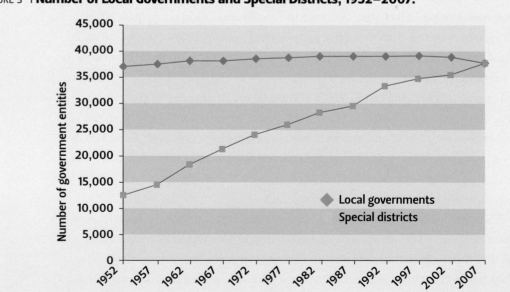

FIGURE 3-1 **Number of Local Governments and Special Districts, 1952–2007.**

**SOURCE:** U.S. Census Bureau, 2007 Census of Governments; www.census.gov/govs/www/index.html.

35,000 today. The proliferation of these quasi-independent governmental entities stems from the realization that localities can achieve economies of scale by providing regionwide public services, from water and sewer services to parks, transit, stadium and convention center management; libraries; schools; recycling; and public safety. Consider three examples:

▸ Cleveland Metroparks—born as the Cleveland Metropolitan Park District in 1912—is governed by a board of commissioners. Funded by a tax district that includes all of Cuyahoga County, plus Hinckley Township, in Medina County, the district receives its own dedicated revenue stream from a property tax that yields about two-thirds of its $94 million budget. The district manages seven golf courses, the Cleveland Zoo, and some 21,000 acres (8,498 hectares) of parkland that treasurer David Kuntz refers to as "Cleveland's emerald necklace."[26] People from the entire region enjoy the system's many amenities—from a bookstore to hayrides, hiking and biking trails, and a toboggan slide.

▸ In 1961, the state of Colorado formed the Metro Wastewater Reclamation District to transmit and treat wastewater in a 380-square-mile (984-square-kilometer) service area that includes more than 45 sanitation and water and sanitation districts. Today, the district serves some 1.5 million people in the Denver area, and treats about 130 million gallons (492,103,532 liters) of wastewater a day. The treated water is discharged into the South Platte River, where it makes up nearly 90 percent of the river for nine months of the year.[27] The district also conducts water-quality–related educational programs in public and private schools in its service area, reaching about 100 classrooms each year.

▸ In Pittsburgh, a 14-square-block downtown cultural district has replaced a former red light district, thanks to the support of the city and Allegheny County; investments made by the Howard Heinz Endowment; and other private and public support. Now a cultural mecca, the district is home to the city's symphony, ballet, opera, and theater organizations. There are almost 1,500 performances annually, which support a growing number of restaurants and galleries. Major-league football and baseball stadiums—as well as a new convention center—have been built adjacent to the district. The district itself, as well as its various cultural venues, is operationally supported by a regional asset tax, in the form of a one-half percent countywide sales tax, which generates about $75 million per year. The tax also supports parks and libraries, and was critical in the financing of the stadiums and convention center.

## Megaregions and the Future of Metropolitan America

A megaregion is an extended network of metropolitan centers and their surrounding areas. Megaregions often cross county and state lines, and are linked by transportation and communication networks as well as by geographic, environmental, economic, and social factors.

What counts as a megaregion depends on how the term is defined. According to Georgia Tech's CQGRD, there are six megaregions in the United States:

▸ The Northeast (the Washington-to-Boston corridor)

▸ The Piedmont-Atlantic megaregion (Atlanta-Charlotte-Birmingham)

▸ Southern California (Los Angeles to Tijuana)

▸ The Cascadia Ecolopolis (Seattle, Portland, and Vancouver)

▸ The Midwest (centered on Chicago, stretching northwest to Minneapolis, south to St. Louis, and east to Buffalo and Toronto)

▸ South Florida (the southern portion of the Florida peninsula and neighboring island nations).[28]

One also might add Texas (Houston to Dallas to Austin to San Antonio) and the San Francisco Bay Area, as well as a few others. In a 2007 article in *Planning* magazine, Robert Lang and Arthur C. Nelson, codirectors of the Metropolitan Institute at Virginia Tech, identified 20 emerging megaregions, which they call "megapolitans." These superregions account for only one-tenth of the nation's land area, but six out of every ten Americans (181 million people) live in them.[29]

Megaregions result from rapid population growth and the expansion of suburbia. The phenomenon of the megaregion suggests a need for a national framework for planning, and for public investment that is regional, farsighted, and based on cross-disciplinary analyses. The first century of our nation's growth was founded on Thomas

FIGURE 3-2 **Megapolitan America, September 2006.**

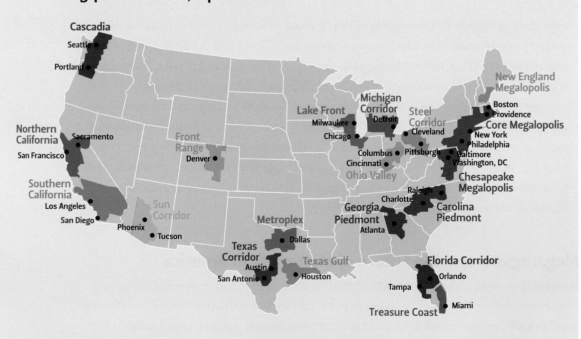

**SOURCE:** Robert E. Lang and Arthur C. Nelson, "America 2040: The Rise of the Megapolitans," *Planning* (January 6, 2007): 11.

Jefferson's national plan for westward expansion, and the second was stimulated by Theodore Roosevelt's vision of an improved and expanded energy and natural resource infrastructure that would support industrial expansion. Perhaps, as suggested by CQGRD, a third-century strategy should foster regional cooperation and confront the challenge of global competition. Such a strategy would assist megaregions to address the problems looming on the planning horizon, such as aging infrastructure, increased social inequity, strained ecosystems, and uneven and inequitable inter- and intra-regional growth patterns. Realistically, however, such huge planning and coordinating efforts are politically a long way off.

The Piedmont-Atlantic megaregion (PAM) offers a useful perspective on the kinds of problems that megaregions face. PAM encompasses the entire states of Alabama, Florida, Georgia, North Carolina, South Carolina, and Tennessee, and includes four core cities: Atlanta, Birmingham, Charlotte, and Raleigh. By 2050, the population of PAM will almost double, from 34 million to more than 57.2 million. In metro Atlanta, residents already drive about 31 miles (50 kilometers) per day, and the future holds the prospect of more cars, more congestion, and more air pollution for more people. Throughout the megaregion, infrastructure is aging, and pressure is mounting to fund new infrastructure to accommodate rapid population growth. The total square footage of the region's buildings (residential, commercial, and industrial space) is projected to increase 54 percent before 2030. Most counties in the region have high poverty rates (21 percent or greater). About 650,000 acres (263,045 hectares) of land are converted each year from undeveloped to developed uses, and the rate of urbanization exceeds population increases by some 20 percent. Investment in education falls below national rates. Many medium-sized cities and more rural areas are struggling to maintain fiscal solvency in the face of the transition from an industrial to an information-based economy. The region relies heavily on groundwater systems, and will struggle in the coming years to provide an adequate water supply. On top of all this, of course, is the fragmentation of governance structures—six states, 504 counties, 3,839 cities and towns—which impedes consensus and cooperation on regional issues.[30]

Of course, it is easier to describe a problem than to develop a strategy for addressing it. That will involve changing the way people think about the issues that megaregions face. No man, woman, city, or suburb is an island; we are all part of the mainland, which means we must recognize our interdependence. This is not easy. The human tendency is to conceptualize so locally—in ways that are geared to our neighborhood, our town, our city, or our suburb—that we miss the bigger picture.

Ground-breaking organizations—from Envision Utah to Envision Central Texas; from the Southern California Association of Governments, in California, to the RPA, in New York—are working on these issues, but the awareness that what affects our neighbors affects us all, and vice versa, comes slowly. Multinational corporations have grasped this reality, but many elected officials, frankly, have not. There are several reasons for this. First, state legislators, county commissioners or supervisors, and municipal officials are elected locally, and therefore tend to focus on the interests of their local constituencies. Second, because officials want to protect their own turf, they find it difficult to embrace change. Finally, it's all officials can do to manage their own communities; they have neither the time nor the resources necessary to attend to regional—let alone global—issues.

As time goes on, a new national framework for spatial planning and funding may evolve. This will constitute a huge public policy challenge for all levels of government: to plan spatially means to recognize that traditional jurisdictional boundaries have become obsolete. In our nation's third century of development, intelligent, forward-thinking planning will understand the new realities at a scale that is appropriate to the challenges and opportunities faced by megaregions. According to Georgia Tech's CQGRD, major public and private infrastructure investments, made in support of strong interjurisdictional networks, have strengthened transportation, communication, cultural, and economic connections among major cities and regions in Europe and Asia.[31] Similar investments by local, state, and federal levels of government could, and should, be made in the United States—because without doubt, our ability to collaborate regionally will determine our success in competing globally. Two areas where a national framework of spatial planning and funding might most appropriately be focused are rail transit and green infrastructure.

There is no question that America's rail infrastructure could be enhanced, but only if our elected leaders have the political fortitude to do so. Given the necessity of reducing Americans' dependence on their cars, one can only hope that rail infrastructure will once again become a federal priority. Although policy makers generally seem to regard investment in rail as a subsidy rather than a necessity, long-range thinkers certainly should be dreaming about connecting megaregions by rail, as has already been done between Boston and Washington. A southeastern high-speed rail corridor—with speeds in the 150 to 200 miles per hour (241 to 322 kilometers per hour) range—that would link major PAM cities to Washington, D.C., would be a noteworthy initiative. Such a project is now under study. "Whoever moves goods, information, currency, services and people most efficiently," observes Georgia state senator Sam Zamarripa, "will win."[32]

Ewing et al. agree that "it is time to get serious about a national high-speed passenger rail network."[33] They recommend the establishment of a new federal agency within the U.S. Department of Transportation that would be responsible for all nationally operated passenger systems, including both aviation and rail, to ensure intermodal integration. This, they suggest, "would strengthen central cities and subregional centers, further encouraging compact, infill development and discouraging sprawl."[34]

The establishment of "green infrastructure" to link places together in ecologically sustainable ways is another idea whose time has come, and that might be subject to planning on a megaregional basis. A network of open space, wildlife habitat, parks, bike trails, woodlands, and other natural areas would not only help protect clean air and water and natural ecological processes, but could also provide a framework for future development patterns.

A word of caution is in order. Many people are suspicious of big government. To them, words like *regional* and *megaregional* conjure up images of Big Brother. Consequently, the emphasis must be on collaborative *planning,* rather than on governance through some huge new megastructure. Render unto localities what is local, and unto regional entities what is regional. Suggesting a wider approach to planning is not the same as advocating megaregional government. While the planning should be issue and need specific, key questions in a larger dimension will arise. Who's in charge of a megaregion? How can a megaregional decision-making process be institutionalized when no political structure exists to accomplish such a goal? How can we get the right people to sit together at the table? Mayor Joe Riley, of Charleston, South Carolina, offered a general answer when he spoke at a conference on megaregions at Georgia Tech: "Put regional planning at the front of our community agendas. You've got to understand the totality of it, and being visionary helps."[35]

The Chattanooga-Atlanta Regional Collaborative, which is jointly supported by the Atlanta Regional Council and the Chattanooga Institute, is a powerful example of efforts to put planning at the top of the agenda. The collaborative has a vision: a high-speed rail link that would make it possible to travel between Chattanooga and Atlanta in 30 minutes. The hope is that the project will "leverage economic development, tourism, technology and education efforts" in the region; give people along the route access to nonauto transportation choices; and "preserve the region's natural, agricultural, historical and cultural assets."[36] Whether this innovative and audacious vision will be realized remains to be seen. But the effort is exceedingly worthwhile.

## Toward Wider Horizons

As Mayor Riley also said, "We are not comfortable with the future, but the rules have all changed, and we need to understand what the future will look like."[37] The future will depend, in no small part, on how we grow. Cities and counties have burst their seams; regions and megaregions are here to stay. America is a metropolitan nation, full of interwoven cities and suburbs. According to the Brookings Institution, the 100 largest U.S. metropolitan areas contain 65 percent of the nation's population and 68 percent of its jobs, so "the ability of our nation to meet the great economic, social and environmental imperatives of our time . . . rests largely on the health and vitality of our metropolitan areas."[38]

The difference between strong and weak metropolitan regions may very well lie in their growth strategies. Cooperating and working together to achieve regional goals, rather than infighting and quibbling about turf or who gets the credit, is thus a wise way to proceed, either voluntarily or through mandates. Successful regions will use special districts. They will also engage in comprehensive, cross-jurisdictional planning, relying on agencies that have the authority and funding to support their plans as new development occurs. Furthermore, they will invest in existing neighborhoods, public transportation, affordable housing, compact development, mixed land uses, energy efficiency, and green infrastructure. All of these issues will be explored in greater detail in the following chapters. For now, let the matter rest with former German chancellor Konrad Adenauer, who once said, "We all live under the same sky, but we don't all have the same horizon."

**ENDNOTES**

1  Neal Peirce, "Getting U.S. Regions Past Sleepwalking," *Washington Post* Writers Group, July 1, 2007.

2  ULI–the Urban Land Institute, *Building Florida's Future: State Strategies for Regional Cooperation* (Washington, D.C.: ULI–the Urban Land Institute, 2005), 12.

3  Ibid.

4  Alec MacGillis, "Federal Agencies' Outward Migration Irks Area Officials," *Washington Post*, October 31, 2006, 1.

5  National Academy of Public Administration (NAPA), *Building Stronger Communities and Regions: Can the Federal Government Help?* (Washington, D.C.: NAPA: March 1998), 17.

6  David Rusk, *Inside Game Outside Game: Winning Strategies for Saving Urban America* (Washington, D.C.: Brookings Institution Press, 1999), 89.

7  Georgia Regional Transportation Authority Web site, www.grta.org/.

8  Ibid.

9  Reid Ewing, Keith Bartholomew, Steve Winkelman, Jerry Walters, and Don Chen, *Growing Cooler: The Evidence on Urban Development and Climate Change* (Washington, D.C.: ULI–the Urban Land Institute, 2008), 132.

10  Brookings Metropolitan Policy Program, "Blueprint for American Prosperity: MetroPolicy for a MetroNation," June 2008, 3; www.brookings.edu/papers/2008/06_metropolicy_bradley.aspx.

11  Judge John F. Dillon, an Iowa magistrate, decreed in 1868 that the state may create or destroy, abridge or control, cities. The state "breathes into them the breath of life without which they cannot exist." See Dennis R. Judd, *The Politics of American Cities,* 3rd ed. (New York: HarperCollins, 1988), 40–41.

12  Portland Metro Council Web site, www.metro-region.org/.

13  Darrell Steinberg, "SB 375 Connects Land Use and AB 32 Implementation," *The Planning Report* (July 2007); available at www.planningreport.com/tpr/?module=displaystory&story_id=1257&format=html.

14  1998 Pub. Acts, c.1101, &7, eff. May 19, 1998.

15  Quoted in Renee Elder, *Nashville Tennessean,* June 4, 1998.

16  Boston Indicators Report, quoted in Peirce, "Sleepwalking."

17  Regional Plan Association mission statement; www.rpa.org.

18  DVRPC Web site, www.dvrpc.org/.

19  Office of Policy Planning, Florida Department of Transportation, and Center for Urban Policy Research, University of South Florida, "Trends and Conditions Report—2007,

Impact of Transportation: Transportation and Land Uses," October 2007, 7; www.dot.state.fl.us/planning/policy/trends/tc-report/landuse101107.pdf.

20 Ibid., 8.

21 Gary Gallegos, telephone conversation with author, April 14, 2008.

22 See "TransNet Keeps San Diego Moving"; www.sandag.org/index.asp?projectid=255& fuseaction=projects.detail.

23 Ewing et al., *Growing Cooler*, 131ff.

24 ULI–the Urban Land Institute and Ernst & Young, *Infrastructure 2008: A Competitive Advantage* (Washington, D.C.: ULI–the Urban Land Institute, 2008), 34.

25 Ibid., 34–35.

26 David Kuntz, telephone conversation with author, April 8, 2008.

27 Metro Wastewater Reclamation District Web site, www.metrowastewater.com/.

28 CQGRD, "Megaregions," 2006; www.cqgrd.gatech.edu/megaregions/.

29 Robert E. Lang and Arthur C. Nelson, "America 2040: The Rise of the Megapolitans," *Planning* (January 6, 2007): 7–12.

30 See CQGRD, "Emerging MegaRegions: Studying the Southeastern United States," January 2006; www.cqgrd.gatech.edu/PDFs/PAM_overview_1-30-06.pdf.

31 Ibid., 8.

32 Sam Zamarripa, remarks at the Megaregion Conference, Georgia Tech University, Atlanta, Georgia, January 30, 2006.

33 Ewing et al., *Growing Cooler*.

34 Ibid., 135.

35 Joe Riley, remarks at the Megaregion Conference, Georgia Tech University, Atlanta, Georgia, January 30, 2006.

36 Atlanta Regional Commission and the Chattanooga Institute, "Chattanooga–Atlanta Regional Collaborative: Linkage for the 21st Century" (PowerPoint presentation, 2008).

37 Ibid.

38 Alan Berube, "MetroNation: How U.S. Metropolitan Areas Fuel American Prosperity," Brookings Institution, 2007, 5; available at www.brookings.edu/~/media/Files/rc/reports/2007/1106_metronation_berube/MetroNationbp.pdf.

# CHAPTER 4

# The Best Transportation Solution Is Being There

The 20th century was about getting around. The 21st century will be about staying in a place worth staying in. —JAMES HOWARD KUNSTLER

*Chiefly because of the ever-expanding gyre of sprawling development, the spiderweb has become an apt metaphor for the new metropolitan form. Many strands of the web suffer from increasing congestion and lack of transit connections. Choices for travel should be expanded. Land use planning should drive development. The country needs to invest in transportation systems that connect more closely with regional metropolitan visions and plans. When public policy focuses on where the growth will go, roads and transit—in the right places—can follow.*

**THE POST—WORLD WAR II,** car-dependent suburbs created "a giant sucking sound" as people, tax base, and economic vitality left the cities. Spreading growth in new suburbs rendered obsolete the old transportation patterns, which had run from first-tier suburbs into the city and back out again. Land uses were driven by transportation policy, rather than the other way around. Much of the public understanding of transportation issues is still rooted in the mid-20th century. But today, we need development patterns that will reverse this process; we cannot make major transportation improvements simply by layering new roads and transit systems over existing ones.

## From Wagon Wheel to Spiderweb

During the 1950s and beyond, as the population moved to the suburbs, strong ties to downtown employment, shopping, and retail began to weaken. Although it was possible to live in the suburbs and use the city, enjoying the best of both worlds, once retailers discovered a substantial customer base in the suburbs, they followed. Shopping malls sprang up, often at the intersections of circumferential freeways on the upper-income side of town. Employers soon followed the malls, creating edge cities whose skylines gave the illusion of new downtowns. In reality, however, the components of these suburban downtowns were physically separate, and trips within them had to be made by car, rather than on foot or by transit.

At the same time that development patterns were changing, personal mobility was rapidly expanding. By 1960, car ownership had reached the middle class, with an average of one vehicle per family.[1] Between 1960 and 2000, the U.S. population increased by 102 million; the number of vehicles increased by 123 million. By 2006, there were roughly 1.75 vehicles per household,[2] and the number of vehicles is expanding faster than the number of licensed drivers.[3] Meanwhile, in the 1960s, almost 8 million Americans commuted by transit, compared with about 6 million in 2000.[4]

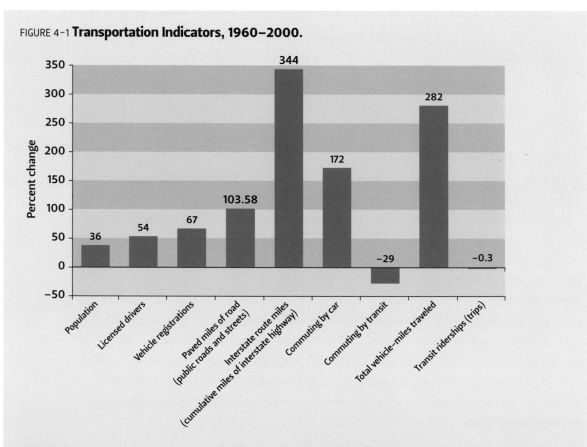

FIGURE 4-1 **Transportation Indicators, 1960–2000.**

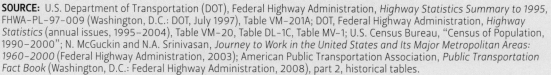

**SOURCE:** U.S. Department of Transportation (DOT), Federal Highway Administration, *Highway Statistics Summary to 1995*, FHWA-PL-97-009 (Washington, D.C.: DOT, July 1997), Table VM-201A; DOT, Federal Highway Administration, *Highway Statistics* (annual issues, 1995–2004), Table VM-20, Table DL-1C, Table MV-1; U.S. Census Bureau, "Census of Population, 1990–2000"; N. McGuckin and N.A. Srinivasan, *Journey to Work in the United States and Its Major Metropolitan Areas: 1960–2000* (Federal Highway Administration, 2003); American Public Transportation Association, *Public Transportation Fact Book* (Washington, D.C.: Federal Highway Administration, 2008), part 2, historical tables.

FIGURE 4-2 **The Evolving Metropolitan Form.**
Some metropolitan activity clusters are still centered in downtown and radiate outward along transit corridors. But in many of today's regions, nodes of development and activity are spread throughout the area.

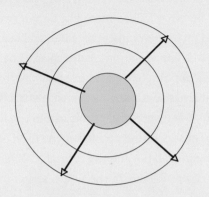

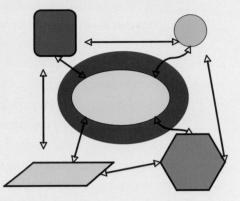

The radial city is changing.

Today's cities are multicentered.

The enormous expansion in private mobility has put intense pressure on public agencies responsible for expanding roads. Americans are wedded to their cars, and no divorce is likely. Leonard Forkas Jr., a partner in Milestone Communities, Inc., in Reston, Virginia, puts the issue this way: "In the fifties, sixties, and seventies, the car stood for freedom. Now, with commuting and congestion being what they are, the car stands for torture chamber."[5] Al Eisenberg, a former official in the U.S. Department of Transportation (DOT) and currently a member of the Virginia legislature, points out that "the car makes a wonderful servant but a terrible master."[6]

As more and more people lived, shopped, and worked in the suburbs, they lost their sense of connection to the old urban core. By 2000, 69 percent of suburban residents worked in the suburbs; only 25 percent worked in the central city.[7] As if the pudding needed proof, two members of Congress from the Chicago area—Rep. Mark Steven Kirk-R and Rep. Melissa Bean-D—initiated the formation of the Suburban Transportation Commission (STC), a new effort oriented toward Chicago's collar suburbs, predominantly those to the north. The STC is a pro bono, bipartisan advisory group, brought together "to facilitate the representation of the interests of their suburban constituencies and their efforts to ensure that these interests receive appropriate consideration as changes to Illinois's transportation funding structure are being evaluated."[8] Says Kirk: "Suburb-to-suburb commuting has increased 56 percent while traditional suburb-to-city commuting increased only 9 percent. Our transportation plans should set a priority on the needs of the new suburban majority where our economy is growing fastest."[9] The new metropolitan form, with its many nodes of development surrounding the central city, requires a richer network of connections between suburbs, so that residents can reach suburban destinations without going downtown.

As noted in earlier chapters, private development decisions transformed what was once a wagon wheel into a new spatial pattern—one that looked more like a spiderweb. Because mass transit works best when riders travel on high-volume routes into and out of a central location—that is, downtown—the spiderweb configuration creates special challenges: the new metropolitan form lacks the "mass" for mass transit. Moreover, suburban destinations typically offer free parking, making alternatives to driving even less attractive.

Like other critical components of public works, transportation suffers from too little money, too much politics, and lack of leadership in addressing problems. The level of neglect is reflected in the congestion that has spread well beyond the typical rush hour and to smaller cities unaccustomed to such big-city problems. In the 1990s, serious congestion cropped up in Minneapolis and St. Paul, ending the ability of Twin Cities residents to "think about traffic the way people in Arizona think about snow: as someone else's problem." Congestion has prompted a growing chorus among public officials and the public at large to do something. But politicians who run on an "I will cut congestion" platform often find, once they are elected, that this is a hard promise to keep. The challenge is to devise sustainable transportation policies that will assure residents that traffic issues are being addressed, and that improvements will keep pace with traffic growth and new development.

An increased emphasis on alternatives to driving will not eliminate roads and private vehicles as important elements of the transportation system. But it will direct

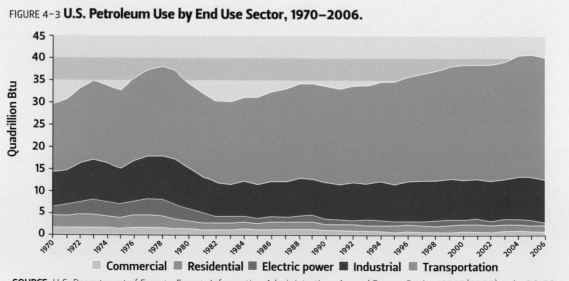

FIGURE 4-3 **U.S. Petroleum Use by End Use Sector, 1970–2006.**

**Commercial** ▪ **Residential** ▪ **Electric power** ▪ **Industrial** ▪ **Transportation**

**SOURCE:** U.S. Department of Energy, Energy Information Administration, *Annual Energy Review 2007* (2008), xxiv, 36, 38.

some growth to areas that are more compact, and where alternative forms of transportation—including walking, biking, and transit use—are more available. It will also reduce the number of vehicle-miles traveled (VMT). Thus, patterns that create more transportation options will reduce traffic growth and the need for new roads. Such a strategy has several advantages: first, the construction of new roads will be more closely aligned with growth and financing mechanisms, and will therefore involve greater participation from landowners and developers. Second, because some households will be able to get by with fewer cars, homeowners' transportation costs will decrease. Finally, since transportation consumes more oil than industrial, residential, commercial and electric power combined, the strategy will reduce the nation's dependence on oil.

Just as transit requires supportive development policies to be sustainable, a mix of new arterial roads and secondary streets is needed to serve suburban growth, provide access to nearby destinations, and avoid overloading main streets. Gordon Price, a former councilor from Vancouver, British Columbia, claims that "for most of this century, our auto-based transportation system has been built on this understanding: the Private Sector will produce the vehicles and the Public Sector will build the pathways."[10] Increasingly, Will Rogers's solution to congestion seems appropriate: the private sector should build the roads and the public sector should build the cars.

The way the country has been growing creates the problem. Since the 1950s, development patterns and burgeoning prosperity have added to the growth in VMT—not just for commuting, but for shopping, trips to school, and every other conceivable travel purpose. Much of the nation's growth has occurred in areas characterized by sprawling, low-density development—auto-oriented regions where the lack of other transporta-

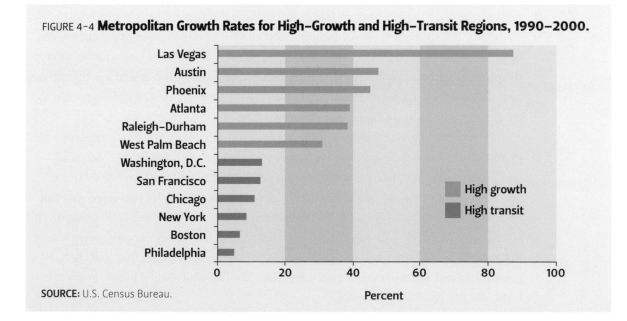

FIGURE 4-4 **Metropolitan Growth Rates for High-Growth and High-Transit Regions, 1990–2000.**

**SOURCE:** U.S. Census Bureau.

tion options forces people to drive more and more to meet their daily needs. Meanwhile, older regions like New York, Boston, Chicago, and Philadelphia, which offer the best public transportation options and provide many opportunities for shopping, dining, and work within a short walk or drive—are experiencing relatively slow growth.[11] The proliferation of low-density suburbs, malls, and office parks perpetuates an "edgeless city" model, in which new developments are accessible only by car.

## The Result: A Congestion Crisis

The transportation infrastructure demands imposed by sprawling suburbs create extra costs for new residents, reduce the residential base for maintaining the existing transportation infrastructure, require most new trips to be made by car, and generate growing levels of traffic congestion—all of which can threaten a region's future economic health. David Hartgen, of the University of North Carolina at Charlotte, states that traffic "congestion in North Carolina will more than double over the next 25 years. . . . [It] threatens the state's economic future." He cites a Reason Foundation report showing that by 2030, traffic delays will increase some 65 percent across the board in the United States. According to the same report, North Carolina "needs to spend $12.4 billion to clear congested urban roads and prepare for traffic growth in the next 25 years."[12] And what's true for North Carolina is undoubtedly true for most other states, as the secretary of the DOT warned in a 2006 report: "Congestion is one of the single largest threats to our economic prosperity and way of life."[13]

Highway expansion—once assumed to be the best solution to our traffic congestion problems—is now perceived to induce more congestion and development.[14] Brookings Institution senior fellow Anthony Downs is quite emphatic on this point: "Experience shows that if a road is part of a larger transportation network within a region, peak-hour congestion cannot be eliminated for long on a congested road by expanding that road's capacity. . . . This 'cure' is totally impractical and prohibitively expensive."[15] Therefore, the strategy of simply building new roads and widening existing ones needs to be supplemented. It is imperative that government coordinate transportation infrastructure investment with local land use plans, manage our traffic systems well, harness new technologies to control traffic, and impose stiffer user charges. If it does not do so, congestion will be exacerbated, not relieved.

The example of Interstate 270 in the Washington, D.C., metro area is instructive. During the 1980s and early 1990s, I-270 was widened between Frederick, Maryland, and Washington, D.C. But the additional roadway capacity only induced more traffic and more congestion—so much that an article in the *Washington Post* declared that the widening was a failure because it had induced even more traffic, effectively using up the added capacity.[16] Yes, planners had encouraged growth and development—particularly in the biotech industry—and channeled it to the I-270 corridor, and this concentrated growth has had a positive impact on the region. But the widening of I-270, in and of itself, did not reduce congestion.

# CAN WE MANAGE OUR WAY OUT OF CONGESTION?

The usual response to traffic congestion is to build, but a key—and often neglected—ingredient in solving transportation (and other infrastructure) problems is better management. What tools should we be using to manage congestion and protect our transportation infrastructure? Here are some suggestions:

1  **Traffic signal improvements.** Simply updating signal timing to reflect current traffic conditions can greatly reduce congestion. Yet most cities have cut back on the number of technicians available to make such adjustments.

2  **Intersection improvements.** Selective adjustments to traffic lanes can help traffic move more smoothly. One approach combines signalization, control of access, and intersection separations to create a continuous inter-regional route, referred to as a "super street" or "strategic arterial." Installation of ramp metering, already in use in many places, helps control gradual entry onto expressways, which in turn speeds traffic.

3  **Transit operations.** Rationalizing existing transit routes to match current travel patterns, and to allow for more convenient transfers, can improve convenience for users and reduce costs.

4  **Clearing accidents fast.** Studies show that up to 60 percent of highway congestion stems from disabled vehicles and accidents. Creating an incident management system to identify problem locations and respond quickly can produce dramatic time savings for travelers.

5  **TMAs and TROs.** Partnering with the business community to form a transportation management association (TMA) to encourage car pooling and transit use is a quick, cost-effective method of decreasing peak-period congestion. Local governments can also adopt trip reduction ordinances (TROs) to achieve the same result.

6  **HOV and HOT lanes.** High-occupancy vehicle (HOV) and high-occupancy toll (HOT) lanes provide exclusive passage for buses, carpools, or vanpools for all or part of the day. These lanes offer commuters an incentive to choose higher-occupancy forms of travel.

7  **Telecommuting.** One of the most effective methods of reducing congestion is to keep cars off the road in the first place. Telecommuting allows employees to be productive without wasting time in traffic and contributing to traffic congestion. "Parking cash-out" programs are another means of reducing the number of cars on the road: firms that supply free or discounted parking to employees simply convert that benefit to a stipend for those who shift to carpooling or transit.

8  **Car sharing.** Even people who do not own a car—whether by need or by choice—need to use one on occasion: to shop at a big-box store, take a pet to the veterinarian, or visit friends in the country, for example. Car-sharing programs allow members to rent cars on a short-term basis, providing mobility when needed while eliminating many of the costs of owning a car.

9  **Unbundling parking.** Requiring parking for all rental or condominium projects—and including the cost of that parking in rents or condo fees—increases the cost of housing, especially in high-cost markets that offer alternatives to automobile travel. Making parking optional for those who wish not to own a car can make some neighborhoods more affordable.

10  **Road pricing.** Economists complain that one of the reasons for congestion is that driving is underpriced, and that making driving more expensive could reduce congestion. This rationale, along with the need for increased funding, is causing many communities to consider charging tolls on what are now free roads, and/or assessing a fee for entering the downtown.

11  **Smart cars and smart highways.** Increasingly, intelligent transportation systems are being used to enable communication between vehicles and highways, providing drivers with information on road conditions and services. Electronic coordination of signal lights, and global positioning system equipment in vehicles can also help speed traffic flows. Perhaps future developments will allow a fully automated, "hands-off" ride.

**SOURCE:** Adapted from Robert Dunphy, *12 Tools for Improving Mobility and Managing Congestion* (ULI–the Urban Land Institute, 1991); and Anthony Downs, "Traffic: Why It's Getting Worse," Brookings Policy Brief Series #128, January 2004, 6–8; www.brookings.edu/papers/2004/01transportation_downs.aspx.

## A Different Approach

As things stand now, we are caught in a vicious cycle: we expand roads to reduce congestion, which attracts new development near the new road capacity, which further increases congestion, which necessitates even more road improvements. But what if local jurisdictions adopted a new approach—not a transportation plan, but a regional development strategy designed to regenerate existing communities and reinforce the existing transportation infrastructure? Such a strategy would connect transportation and land use planning, expand transportation choices, and help protect congestion-relief programs from constantly losing ground to continued sprawl.

Consider a couple of examples of this approach, which is commonly known as *concurrency.* Washington State's 1990 Growth Management Act introduced concurrency as "a way of more effectively linking land-use and infrastructure planning";[17] the overarching goal is to "ensure that development does not outpace the provision of infrastructure, particularly for transportation." According to a memo describing the program, the act focuses on "making land development more efficient, conserving rural land, and reducing urban sprawl." The transportation infrastructure that "a jurisdiction may examine to determine what might be required to serve new development can include roads, transit service and facilities, or other modes of travel, depending on the nature of the city/county in which the development will occur."

Similarly, in the high-growth state of Florida—where planners realized as early as the 1970s that the state was growing at the rate of about 1,000 new residents per day—land use planning programs have been enacted that address the changing metropolitan form by managing growth and overcoming inefficient land use patterns. Thus, Florida's concurrency principle states that "consistent with the public welfare . . . transportation facilities needed to serve new development shall be in place or under actual construction no more than 3 years after issuance by the local government of a certificate of occupancy or its functional equivalent."[18] In other words, local governments in Florida must analyze projected population increases and future public facility needs, then ensure that no further development occurs until infrastructure and other public services are adequate to address the impacts of new development. The key idea is that land use planning must precede the development of new roads and other infrastructure. Moreover, concurrency requirements implicitly suggest that new development pay its own way, so that urban residents are not taxed to support the development of sprawling suburbs. In practice, the primary focus is on whether local roads—both existing and new—are free of congestion. However, because the law does not cover private utilities—which can extend their services (if the public service commission approves) without regard to local comprehensive plans or to the impact on land use patterns—local control of growth is hampered.

As might be expected, concurrency has its critics. Robert Dunphy, ULI senior resident fellow for transportation and infrastructure, believes that it has too often been abused, halting growth where it might logically occur. In explaining why "road concurrency is not a workable policy," Anthony Downs cites two major flaws: first, "building more roads or expanding existing ones cannot prevent many major roads from becoming overloaded during peak periods"; second, "in a free country, limiting overall new development in a state is basically unconstitutional."[19] The drawbacks are real, so policy makers must find other ways to coordinate and balance urban development and the roads needed to serve it.

A variant of concurrency is used in Montgomery County, Maryland. Rockville Pike—an extremely busy artery lined with shopping centers and commercial buildings—is almost always congested. Yet Royce Hanson, director of the Montgomery County Department of Parks and Planning, does not believe that widening the pike is the answer. Instead, he sees better land use planning as a more appropriate response. "We are changing the paradigm from capacity to sustainability," comments Hanson, who believes that adding lane capacity and even facilitating greater speeds on the pike is "a losing proposition." Hanson continues:

> *Our great challenge now is to create not new development on raw land, because Mont-*
> *gomery County is pretty well built out, but at a livable density. What we need to do is*
> *to increase mixed-use density at key centers, which can reduce the carbon footprint of*
> *development; facilitate the use of transit, walking, and biking; and, if well designed with a*
> *good internal grid, actually reduce congestion. We will also need to improve operations on*
> *the road, especially use of bus lanes and queue jumping, etc. We have four of the nation's*
> *largest developers with key parcels along the Pike, and they seem interested in a more cre-*
> *ative approach to development than we have usually seen in the county. So I am hopeful that*
> *we can come up with a great plan that actually works.*[20]

## Better Development, Less Traffic, More Choices

Can different land use patterns reduce traffic congestion, or at least slow its growth? That question is increasingly being asked as part of regional planning activities. In a survey of 31 such efforts around the United States, Keith Bartholomew, of the University of Utah, found five regions where future growth scenarios demonstrated a 10 percent or greater reduction in traffic: Denver (10 percent); Minneapolis–St. Paul (12 percent); Portland, Oregon (13 percent); San Diego (14 percent); and Contra Costa County, California (17 percent). However, the median reduction was only 2 percent.[21] These modest results are caused partially by regional agencies' reluctance to stray too far from current trends. Only six of the regional planning efforts considered future densities that exceeded today's levels by more than 20 percent, and the median was only 11 percent. Growth scenarios that rely on raising density to reduce traffic are unlikely to have much appeal—to put it mildly.

In Los Angeles County, the most congested region in the United States, the population was 9.5 million as of 2000; as of 2050, it is expected to be 13 million.[22] How can the region best accommodate this growth, in ways that will not have horrifying effects on traffic, air quality, housing affordability, open space, and the economy? In 2002, building on the work of ULI's Los Angeles Reality Check program, the Southern California Association of Governments (SCAG), which serves as the federally designated metropolitan planning organization for transportation planning for six counties—Los Angeles, Orange, San Bernardino, Riverside, Ventura, and Imperial—attempted to answer this question by convening a series of 13 workshops attended by more than 1,300 participants.[23]

The result was a growth vision—now known as the "2% Strategy,"[24] because planners estimated that if growth were concentrated in just 2 percent of the land, 98 percent of the region could be spared the negative effects of uncontrolled growth. This vision emphasized mixed-used, infill, and transit-oriented development (TOD), generally in centers and corridors with available infrastructure.[25] Under this scenario, the region's projected transportation system performed much better than it would under a "business as usual" projection. Transit use, for example, was projected to be 44 percent higher under the 2% Strategy, and to continue growing. Daily driving was projected to be 5 percent lower per capita, and congestion 42 percent lower (although future congestion would still be worse than it is today).[26]

What metropolitan America needs is a growth strategy that will result in lower infrastructure costs, wider transportation choices, expanded transit ridership in the places that transit can most easily serve, and less driving. Such an approach would have four parts:

▸ Taking care of business—that is, maintaining and managing existing infrastructure
▸ Expanding in place, to minimize the need for new infrastructure
▸ Extending facilities to serve new growth
▸ Expanding transportation choices as a deliberate development strategy.

## Fix It First

Before we finance new infrastructure to serve a growing population, we should address current infrastructure needs. Granted, it's always more exciting to engage in a new venture than to take care of old business. Focusing on the new can help elected officials seem hip and future oriented; it can also increase their appeal to new (and often more influential) voters. But consistently favoring new development at the expense of established areas makes older areas even less attractive to new residents and businesses, and can lead to deterioration at the core while promoting sprawl at the fringe. This is the same pattern that led to many of the urban ills that developed after World War II. Healthy older communities need healthy infrastructure: streets, transit, school buildings, water and sewer facilities, and electricity. Public policy makers and utilities should carefully assess existing infrastructure and develop a program of improvements to bring them up to standard.

New York City's Department of Environmental Protection, for example, which monitors the water system, has discovered that a cracked 70-year-old drinking-water tunnel is leaking up to 36 million gallons (136,274,824 liters) a day; engineers estimate that the repair will cost $480 billion. Department commissioner Emily Lloyd says, "It is important to fix the leaks now because there is no way to tell how the system might deteriorate in the next 30 years."[27] After improvements are completed, an ongoing maintenance program should be developed to keep them operating efficiently.

Properly maintaining older water pipes, streets, and antiquated transit stations can also help make a community more welcoming. Jeffrey Slavin, mayor of Somerset, Maryland—a tiny, beautiful enclave just outside Washington, D.C.—understands this point well. Calling for a 20-year town budget that would include long-range plans for maintaining roads and streetlights, Slavin said, "We need to look at each part of the infrastructure and how long it's going to last."[28] The patient preservation and restoration of community infrastructure provides lasting value to older residential and commercial structures in established neighborhoods.

FIGURE 4-5 **A New Approach to Regional Growth.**

| Priority | Development Strategy | Transportation Strategy |
|----------|---------------------|------------------------|
| First | Infill, expand in place | Fix it first |
| Second | Extend growth to the fringe | Expand transportation choices |

Long-range transportation capital improvements often have to be jettisoned for lack of funds. In Boston, the need to fix old infrastructure runs up against the regional transit agency's $15 billion deficit. In 2007, the agency announced that it could not begin any of the expansions that had been planned because so much money was going to the operation and maintenance of existing infrastructure.[29] In some cases, a realistic assessment may reveal that once-great cities can no longer be maintained at their former scales, and that strategic downsizing is necessary. In Cleveland, for example, hopes were dashed for an expanded rail system along what was once the city's premier avenue because there are too few prospective riders; new plans call for a bus line. New Orleans, whacked by nature's fury and government incompetence, faces perhaps the most dire outlook of any large city, and is struggling with the reality that significant numbers of residents may not return, and that services can be delivered only to a community with a much smaller footprint.

Many jurisdictions are struggling to make room for tomorrow's growth in their capital budgets without shortchanging the infrastructure of today. In the older parts of metropolitan regions, the new rule should be "fix it first"—then worry about growth. ULI's Robert Dunphy frames the issue most aptly: "The best locations from a transportation perspective are those that are the hardest to develop. The worst locations are the easiest to develop. Why don't we make it easier to do infill and harder to do sprawl?" Such a reversal of current trends would not be adequate to serve growth in most regions, but it would help regions to refocus on areas that have already been developed, and would engage suburban leaders in broader regional infrastructure issues. Fix it first is essential, but not sufficient.

## Expand in Place

Once existing deficiencies are addressed, we must take advantage of existing capacity before adding new infrastructure—in other words, we must expand in place. Facilitating redevelopment in established areas reinforces opportunities for infill and economic development and complements efforts to expand transportation choices, because these areas typically contain connected pedestrian networks and more extensive public transportation. Targeting growth to areas with available infrastructure capacity leads to generally lower costs for extending infrastructure and will help make public utilities more affordable for all. This strategy also responds to the congestion crisis (described in greater detail later in this chapter) by expanding new development where multiple travel options already exist, rather than by trying to get suburbanites out of their cars through expensive transit extensions. It will also relieve pressure on newly developing areas.

In the San Francisco Bay Area, for example, the Bay Area Smart Vision proposal developed in 2003 by the Association of Bay Area Governments recommended that future development take place around major transit or in other infill locations in the urban core. The effects of this proposal would be to direct 25 percent of new households to the urban cores of San Francisco, Oakland, and San Jose—a substantial increase over the goal of 15 percent contained in previous plans—and to decrease the proportion of growth that will occur in the outer counties from 50 to 38 percent. According to Stuart Cohen, executive director of the Oakland-based Transportation and Land Use Coalition, the Transportation 2030 Plan adopted by the Oakland-based Metropolitan Transportation Commission (MTC) on February 23, 2005, "does an excellent job of articulating the complicated world of transportation policy and funding, and the emerging, more holistic philosophy of MTC in confronting these issues."[30] Providing better access to transit and walkable communities represents a sharp break from past policies in the Bay Area. The strategic implication of Bay Area policies is that regional transportation decisions can reinforce downtowns and inner-city neighborhoods.

## Encourage Redevelopment Downtown

The centrifugal forces of suburbanization need to be balanced by centripetal ones that bring people and tax base back to the metropolitan core. Certain transportation strategies—in particular, discouraging downtown driving and, where appropriate, improving public transit—can be used to accomplish this goal. Downtowns—the original transit-oriented locales—generally offer five travel choices: walking, cycling, taxis, public transit, and driving. Driving is a rational decision when it is faster, less expensive, and more convenient than other options. When it becomes slower, more expensive, and less convenient, people will consider another mode. Driving can be discouraged in many ways: by creating better access to transit, building bike paths, installing sidewalks, developing shuttle systems—and, yes, by increasing gas taxes and imposing a tax on carbon emissions.

Recent market trends have been very favorable for downtown housing, creating a substantial base for transit in transportation-rich cities such as Boston, Chicago, Denver, Los Angeles, San Diego, and Seattle.[31] Especially in locales where suburbanites are moving back downtown, there may be significant opportunities to improve transit, which would further encourage an inflow of residents and tax base. As Cathy Webre, executive director of the Downtown Development Authority in Lafayette, Louisiana, says: "Downtown is the original smart growth place."[32]

As downtown populations increase, parking will of course become an issue. In 2006, San Francisco eliminated minimum parking requirements for downtown, and required that parking be sold or leased separately from residential units. The previous requirement was estimated to have increased the price of housing by 20 percent per unit per space, whether residents wanted it or not.[33]

## Enhance Older Suburbs

As I noted five years ago, older suburbs are located "halfway to everywhere,"[34] and consequently typically offer good transit options, as well as short drives to both downtowns and close-in suburban centers. In some of them—including Hoboken, New Jersey, outside New York; the Chicago suburb of Winnetka; Bainbridge Island, outside Seattle; and Miami Beach—transit use by commuters is even higher than it is in nearby central cities. Increasing residential development may result in increased congestion, which will require especially sensitive enhancements to the road network, including better management of existing traffic signals and operations.

## Remake Suburban Business Districts

Many older suburbs need extensive remodeling to freshen up their retail offerings, increase the functionality of their office and industrial uses, improve vehicle and pedestrian connections, and add residential components. They are endangered by growing traffic congestion, a somewhat dated look, and competition from newer centers farther out. Moreover, they need to incorporate shared parking to create one-stop destinations that will free drivers to become pedestrians. Transforming previously car-oriented suburban business districts into more enjoyable pedestrian-oriented centers will be challenging because nearby residents and property owners who are pleased with the status quo are likely to raise opposition.

## Extend Transportation Alternatives to the Fringe

Even with the most aggressive targeting of growth to downtowns and older urban and residential neighborhoods, the preponderance of new growth will continue to occur where it always has—in formerly rural areas on the developing fringe. Creating transportation choices and greater long-term sustainability in these places requires a substantial rethinking of the historical suburban model. As syndicated urban columnist Neal Peirce wrote after attending a ULI workshop on the new metropolitan form, "The physical chessboard will be different. Unlike the traditional city-suburb-'exurb' pattern of the 1950–2000 period, the emerging 'megapolitan' regions show commuting patterns linking, 'daisy-chaining' and filling in once-empty spaces between formerly separate places as much as 100 miles [161 kilometers] apart."[35]

In an environment of multiple property owners and political jurisdictions, the challenge will be to forge more compact development, greater mixing of uses, pedestrian-friendly commercial districts, a variety of housing types, better transportation connections, and protection of valuable green infrastructure into a "daisy chain." While opportunities to create pedestrian-oriented places do exist, the prognosis for public transit seems much more limited as development decentralizes. Residents will be living farther from jobs, schools, shopping centers, houses of worship, and entertainment destinations, making it highly inconvenient to use public transit, while the costs of building and operating such services will be extremely high. Moreover, the cost of financing growth will fall more squarely on newly developing areas. Growing antitax sentiment will make it increasingly difficult to use traditional funding, especially regional transit and state transportation money, to extend the needed facilities. The options appear to be either much higher development fees or greater user pricing, especially for new highway corridors.

In the absence of aggressive policy intervention, growth at the suburban fringe will likely account for at least two-thirds of development in most regions, and maybe even more. An infrastructure program to serve such areas needs to be closely aligned with development policies that preserve strategic open spaces, create focused clusters of mixed-use development, identify appropriate density levels, and offer transportation options. Planning smart transportation at the fringe requires a more fine-grained and sensitive approach to development, one that will integrate needed public facilities with plans. One reason why transit averages "a measly 5.5 percent" of all commuting, notes ULI and Ernst & Young's *Infrastructure 2008: A Competitive Advantage,* is that land use planning assumes "continued growth patterns toward the suburban edge, where car-dependent lifestyles predominate out of necessity."[36] The report goes on to warn that "if regions fail to modify land use models to integrate with infrastructure plans, people will remain car bound." The answer lies in "developing residential communities in and around densifying suburban nodes and providing pedestrian access from neighborhoods to transit centers and retail districts."[37] Recommended land use development principles include the development of transit-ready communities, the use of multiple connections to enhance mobility and circulation, and the delivery of sustainable transportation choices.[38]

## Develop Transit-Ready Communities

Assuring locations for compact development and mixed-use centers will make it possible for transportation planners to identify potential locations for future transit routes (buses, subways, light rail, commuter rail) and for the supporting development that is required to make them work. In addition, creating pedestrian-friendly suburban places will produce attractive, walkable destinations—something most conventional suburbs lack. Of course, accomplishing this goal will require high densities. The experts tell us that "public transit works best where gross residential densities are above 4,200 persons per square mile [1,621 persons per square kilometer]."[39] Clustering high-density housing around transit stops—enabling commuters to walk to transit, and thus shift from their cars to buses or rail—will make public transit service more feasible in many areas.[40]

## Use Multiple Connections to Enhance Mobility and Circulation

Too many developers working in isolation on the urban fringe acquire a property that is adjacent to a main arterial road—often, off a freeway—and then build a subdivision in which all properties connect to the main road. As other developers follow suit and the new area is built out, the result is a series of disconnected subdivisions from which all trips—even those to an adjacent subdivision—involve travel on the main road. This development pattern overloads intersections with local traffic and requires circuitous trips for what should be relatively short journeys—so short that some of them could be made on foot, if pedestrian connections were there. A better approach to fringe development is to plan all such projects in advance, connecting commercial and community centers with secondary routes as development proceeds. Most importantly, transportation planners should make it clear that future connector streets will be built as new subdivisions open, regardless of opposition from older subdivisions.

## Deliver Sustainable Transportation Choices

To be sustainable, a range of transportation choices must be planned and built into new suburban development, rather than added later to a car-based community. Staged development of real estate and transportation facilities can ensure that a full range of options will be available to residents and that each will be adequately supported.

# Expand Transportation Choices

Americans love their cars and their 30-minute commutes. Most of us spend much of our lives traveling in 30-minute circles—from home to school to office to shopping to restaurants to playing fields to our friends' homes. In 2000, more than 87 percent of our commuting occurred in private vehicles, and 75 percent of us drove to work alone—even though by 2003, the average motorist experienced 47 hours of delay per year as a result of congestion, and even though each year, traffic congestion costs 3.7 billion hours of delay and wastes more than 2 billion gallons (7.5 billion liters) of fuel.[41] So if we agree that more choices are desirable, we must pose the question: Can a car-based culture shift toward other means of getting around?

## Walking and Biking

Gordon Price, a former member of the Vancouver (British Columbia) city council, points out that if traffic congestion is to be overcome, people need more options: "Ideally, people should have at least five choices—feet, bike, transit, taxi and vehicle—and the ability to mix and match them appropriately to the kind of trip and the circumstances faced. Of course, the provision of alternatives assumes a city designed around more than the car—and a citizenry comfortable with the choices."[42] While Price's ideal may not be attainable in most U.S. metro areas, it should certainly be possible to expand the current choices in the suburbs—which typically, amount to just one choice: driving. The most viable options to add are walking and cycling, which are often discussed in the same category, and transit. Each of these choices requires development patterns that differ from those of conventional suburbs.

Since the 1950s, many Americans have become more sedentary: sitting at a computer all day; commuting via car, trolley, subway, or bus; watching TV in the evenings; driving to shop or to keep appointments for the kids. Although the amount of time people spend exercising as a leisure-time activity has remained constant, what has dropped is the amount of exercise that people get in their daily routines. According to the Surgeon General of the United States, 60 percent of Americans do not engage in physical activity on a regular basis, and 25 percent engage in none.[43] The results are increasing obesity, more type 2 diabetes, less social interaction, higher risk of heart disease, and on and on. But Americans are becoming more conscious of the significant health benefits of regular physical activity, and of the fact that walkable places have a positive effect quality of life.[44] So why not create more walkable environments?

Walking and biking are inexpensive, healthy, and environmentally benign means of travel. Creating vibrant, mixed-use environments, with opportunities for walking and biking nearby, is a growing opportunity. When people find themselves in settings where shopping, dining, and even work are located close to each other, they walk or bike. Of course, in such settings it is especially important to provide a pedestrian- and bicycle-friendly environment, so people who want to walk or bike actually can.

Like walking, biking provides not only a means of getting around, but also a means of achieving health benefits and reducing air pollution. Owning, housing, and maintaining a bicycle is also much less expensive and consumes much less space than owning a car (or a second car)—an important consideration in many U.S. metro areas. All that metro areas need to do to encourage cycling is to provide more bikeways!

Bicycle-sharing programs, which were pioneered in Europe in the late 1960s and early 1970s, can encourage biking. Various programs—Amsterdam's white bicycle project; La Rochelle, France's *vélos jaunes* (yellow bikes) program; and, in the United States, the red and yellow bike projects in Madison, Wisconsin—offer free or inexpensive bicycles to anyone who wants to use them.[45] Paris's Vélib bike sharing system, introduced in July 2007, offers residents and tourists the use of 20,600 bicycles, which can be picked up and dropped off at any of 1,450 stations. In the system's first year, the bicycles were used for 27.5 million trips, many of them daily commutes. On average, they are used for 120,000 trips a day.[46] "These are city-transformative projects," says Eric

Britton, founder of the New Mobility Agenda, "and as such have surprisingly massive potential impacts in terms of mobility, environment, life quality, social equity, economic and planetary impacts that come with cost-effective zero—or at least very low—carbon transport for very large numbers of people, trips and places every day."[47]

The first bike-swapping program in a major U.S. city is in Washington, D.C., where a public/private venture called SmartBike DC began making bicycles available in ten central locations in May 2008. The District Department of Transportation has teamed up with advertiser Clear Channel Outdoor (which began sponsoring a similar program in Rennes, France, in 1998, and which has received exclusive advertising rights in Washington, D.C.'s, bus shelters) to provide the nation's first automated bike-share program. For a $40 annual membership fee, SmartBike users can check out three-speed bicycles for up to three hours at a time, simply by swiping their membership card. The program, which replicates Paris's Vélib system, is expected to eventually offer as many as 1,000 bicycles.[48]

What potential does walking have as part of daily travel? Pretty good potential, for the right trips—that is, those of a mile (1.6 kilometers) or less. In 2001, walking captured 43 percent of trips of one-half mile (0.8 kilometers) or less, while slightly more than half of those trips involved driving. For trips between one-half mile and a mile, the walking share dropped to 14 percent, and driving increased to 80 percent. For distances

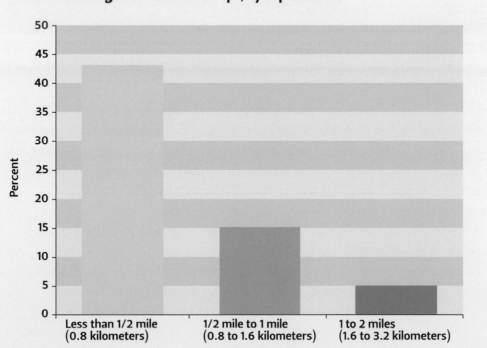

FIGURE 4-6 **Walking As a Share of All Trips, by Trip Distance.**

**SOURCE:** Nationwide Personal Transportation Survey data, analyzed by Paul Shimek, of the Massachusetts Institute of Technology.

greater than a mile, the amount of walking deteriorated quickly, to 5 percent of all trips of one to two miles (1.6 to 3.2 kilometers). The problem is that trips of less than one mile represent less than one out of every seven daily journeys.[49] But since trips of less than one mile are so infrequent, we need to create more opportunities—through urban design—for getting things done on short trips.

If one's destination is close, why not walk instead of drive? The American Podiatric Medical Association surveyed 500 U.S. cities, and a panel of experts used 14 criteria—including the number of pedestrian accidents and fatalities in relation to population; the number of parks and schools per square mile; and the percentage of people who walk to work, use mass transit, and walk for exercise—to determine which were the best and worst cities for walking.[50] The panel concluded that Cambridge, Massachusetts, is the nation's best walking city. Cambridge has more walking commuters than any other city, probably because it is a college town, home to Harvard and the Massachusetts Institute of Technology. The other top-ten walking cities (some naturally come to mind, while others are surprises) are, in order, New York, Ann Arbor, Chicago, Washington, San Francisco, Honolulu, Trenton, Boston, and Cincinnati.

Christopher Leinberger, of the Brookings Institution, has written of "the emerging reality of walkable urbanism."[51] He distinguishes between the walkable urbanism of many downtowns in the 1950s and the "drivable sub-urbanism" of 30 years later, and propounds the thesis that the sprawling patterns of development that created car-dependent suburbia need to be modified by walkable urbanism in suburbs, neighborhoods, and cities. He calls these walkable communities "another way of life, . . . the next American Dream . . . a built environment that provides choice, lines up with the new economy . . . and is more environmentally, fiscally, and economically sustainable."[52] Leinberger believes that the benefits of denser and more walkable communities are considerable:

▸ Fewer cars on the road and fewer hours spent in traffic jams—and, as a result, greater environmental sustainability, because of reductions in the number of cars required per household and the number of miles driven

▸ Building wealth through homeownership, rather than frittering away thousands of dollars a year on depreciating car values and auto maintenance

▸ Getting unintentional exercise while walking to the store or work

▸ A deeper sense of community, because of the social interactions that occur when people walk

▸ Greater energy efficiency and a smaller carbon footprint, because higher-density buildings use less energy for heating and cooling than stand-alone buildings.[53]

Leinberger foresees a surge in the market for more choice, including a growing demand for walkable urbanism, which appeals to a large segment of the market. Back in 2001, Joel Hirschhorn, of the National Governors' Association, predicted that about "one-third of Americans" would like to live in places that have "walkable streets and less dependence on cars," but lamented that "less than 1 percent of housing offers such mixed-use places."[54] This product type may be attractive to 33 percent or so of all buyers—but for decades, investors have directed capital mostly to the real estate products they understand and can trade in large quantities: namely, drivable, low-density, suburban development. The challenge facing developers who want to capitalize on this new trend is to prove, in the words of Pres Kabacoff, CEO of New Orleans–based HRI Properties, "that walkable communities are what buyers actually want."[55]

Walkable places have blossomed all over the American landscape. They have numerous common characteristics: linked streets; grid systems; pedestrian-friendly scale; reachable destinations interconnected by networks of safe, convenient, comfortable, and interesting sidewalks and paths; public spaces; a mix of land uses; walking trails and/or bike paths that connect homes with schools, shops, and workplaces; and development that is more compact than is typical in car-dependent, single-family-home suburbs.[56] According to ULI, one of the "best bets" for development in 2008 is to focus on mixed use and infill: "Fringe subdivisions without amenities lose appeal. Increasingly, people want 24-hour residential environments closer to where they work, . . . pedestrian-friendly layouts, offering varied living options—condo, single family, apartments—and service retail, including grocery stores, pharmacies, cleaners, and restaurants."[57]

The following communities are good examples of how walkable places have been created throughout the nation, in urban and suburban settings alike:

▶ In the early 1970s, Rockville, Maryland, demolished much of its downtown and replaced it with a large, unattractive megamall. The mall never performed up to expectations, and after several attempts were made to revive it, it was torn down. At that point, Rockville decided to restore its downtown. The new Rockville Town Center, which opened in 2007, brought back the city's original street grid and is a classic example of compact, walkable urbanism. The new development includes the city's main public library, a high-tech innovation center, a full-service grocery store, and dozens of new retail shops and restaurants. It also includes housing above retail and offices, and a new town square.

▶ Denver's historic Lower Downtown (LoDo) District is a 23-block area featuring generous sidewalks and a pedestrian scale. Its mixed-use built environment offers ground-floor retail with residences or offices above. No building is more than eight stories high. LoDo is connected to the city's original street grid and is within walking distance of Coors Field and the transportation hub at Union Station. Furthermore, it offers cultural attractions and enjoys a lively nightlife.

▶ Harbor Town, Tennessee—on Mud Island, in the shadow of downtown Memphis—is strongly oriented to pedestrians and features three walkable, interconnected neighborhoods and an accessible town center that includes a grocery store, a private neighborhood school, restaurants, and specialty retail.[58] Composed of a series of radial boulevards superimposed on a grid of short, narrow streets, with minimal building setbacks, Harbor Town is the product of developer Henry Turley's pedestrian-oriented planning.

▸ What was once a tired industrial district in downtown Indianapolis has been rede-veloped as the Massachusetts Avenue Arts District—a walkable, mixed-use, urban district with an emphasis on arts and performing arts venues. The area, which runs diagonally northeast from the city's business core, lies adjacent to the cultural trail and the greenways that connect all of downtown Indianapolis's cultural and historic neighborhoods, and has become a mecca for offices, residences, pubs, artists' lofts and studios, and eateries.

▸ Ladera Ranch, in Orange County, California, is an 8,100-residence development orga-nized around a hierarchy of community, village, and neighborhood planning concepts. Each of the six villages has its own core of social and recreational facilities, as well as open space and amenities—all linked to the village center and to the community's nonresidential districts by means of pedestrians paths.[59]

▸ What is now CityPlace, in West Palm Beach, Florida, used to be a motley collection of properties. Under the leadership of former mayor Nancy Graham, the city negoti-ated with more than 300 different parties, acquired the 70 acres (28 hectares) in 1996, and had the site converted into a mixed-use development made up of 580 residential units plus office buildings, retail offerings, and public space. An old church on the site was converted into a multipurpose venue. CityPlace's half-million square feet (46,452 square meters) of ground-level retail features different colors and textures as well as individually articulated designs, so the space does not have the cookie-cutter look often found in retail developments. The second level of one block features a movie theater and some late-night "fun" places. Parking garages are hidden in the center of one block. Adjacent to the project are the Kravitz Center for Performing Arts and an affordable-housing development. "What's significant," says Graham, "is we honored the street grid already there, rather than rebuilding an insulated, protected environ-ment, and made it all pedestrian-friendly."[60] At the traditional Thursday night gather-ing, which features entertainment and local artists displaying their work in and around CityPlace's restaurants and fountain, between 8,000 and 10,000 people typically show up to hang out, shop, and wine and dine. Special events attract up to 300,000 people. The civic plaza flows from an active space into one that is more passive, where visitors can enjoy a different, more quiet experience.

▸ In Uptown Dallas, immediately adjacent to downtown, high-density apartments that surround parking hidden in the middle of the block have "pioneered the revival of walkable urbanism in the Dallas metropolitan area."[61]

For walkable urban development to happen, habits will have to change, and the culture of the drivable suburb will have to be modified. Leinberger lists five steps that he believes we must take to implement walkable urbanism:

▸ Change zoning and land use regulations to make walkable urbanism legal, chiefly through overlay districts and form-based codes.

▶ Educate the financial community about walkable opportunities in the built environment.

▶ End "the subsidies favoring drivable suburbanism," and make sprawl pay its own way.

▶ Invest in the appropriate infrastructure, especially rail transit.

▶ Manage walkable urban districts closely, to guarantee that the complexity necessary for success actually develops.[62]

As these changes are instituted, and as we overcome our attachment to drivable communities—with their single-product focus, at-grade parking, and easy financing (and the legal mandates behind them)—walkable urbanism will become more prevalent.[63]

## Transit

Interestingly, support for public transit as a solution to traffic congestion seems to be quite high. A 2005 nationwide poll by ABC and the *Washington Post* showed that 42 percent of those surveyed thought transit improvements were an effective solution to traffic congestion. And ridership is up: in 2007, according to the American Public Transportation Association (APTA), 10.3 billion trips were taken on public transit (light rail, commuter rail, heavy rail, and buses): this is the highest number of trips in 50 years, and represents a 2.1 percent increase over 2006.[64] Nevertheless, the poll also showed that a mere 4 percent of respondents used transit to commute.[65] Apparently, most of those who say that they support transit—and most of those who vote for it—do not use it themselves. That's the transit conundrum: there is strong support for building more

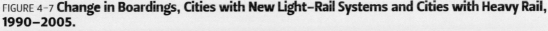

FIGURE 4-7 **Change in Boardings, Cities with New Light–Rail Systems and Cities with Heavy Rail, 1990–2005.**

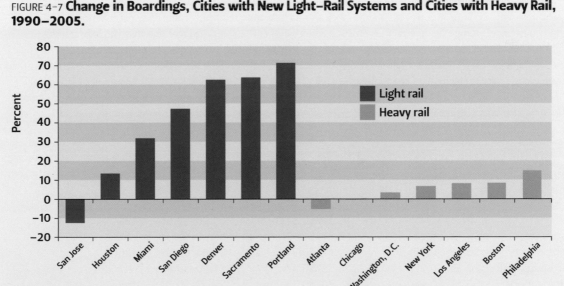

**SOURCE:** Wendell Cox, "21st Century Transportation: Expanding Mobility through Technology," presentation to the Transportation Issue Seminar, Sun Valley, Idaho, July 24, 1997, 1, 13–15; www.publicpurpose.com/21stcent.htm; and American Public Transportation Association, "APTA Ridership Reports Statistics—United States Light Rail Agencies Index," 2008; www.apta.com/research/stats/ridershp/riderep/indexlr.cfm.

transit, but not for riding it. As Robert Dunphy has put it, "The primary constituency for transit improvements is people who do not use public transit." Or, as the satirical newspaper *The Onion* puts it, "Take the bus; I'll be glad you did!"[66]

Given the support that, at least in surveys, is voiced for transit, why don't more people use it? Because it takes too long and, paradoxically, despite heavy subsidies, it may also cost too much. Nationally, commuting by transit typically takes twice as long as driving, and transit trips usually involve shorter distances.[67] Yet even the staunch conservative Paul Weyrich says that "dedicating federal and local funds for transit is both smart and responsible public policy."[68]

One way to encourage transit ridership is through TOD—defined in a 2008 APTA article as "mixed-use, walkable, location-efficient development that balances the need for sufficient density to support convenient transit service with the scale of the adjacent community."[69] TODs can be found all over the United States: from Evanston, Illinois, to Charlotte, North Carolina; from Oakland, California, to Atlanta, Georgia.

The TOD process requires a public/private partnership. The private sector brings capital as well as market research, design, and marketing expertise to the table. The public sector—which has both the regulatory power to control zoning and design, and the tools to grant meaningful entitlements and incentives, should help develop the long-

## THE REAL COSTS OF TRANSIT

One often hears that transit is less expensive than driving. It isn't, as the accompanying table illustrates.

Transit costs are determined by two factors: the cost of running the transit vehicle, and the number of riders. Light-rail vehicles, for example, cost almost twice as much to operate as buses, but they carry almost twice as many passengers longer distances. Thus, in 2004, the cost of carrying a passenger one mile (1.6 kilometers) on light rail was $0.56 ($0.38 per kilometer), about three-fourths the cost carrying a passenger on a bus ($0.73 [$0.45 per kilometer]). The costs per passenger on heavy rail (subway-type transit) and commuter rail (such as the Long Island Railroad) were even cheaper: $0.33 and $0.35 per mile ($0.20 and $0.22 per kilometer), respectively. Of course, that does not necessarily make the higher-capacity modes an economical choice in any given situation, since most transit corridors do not have sufficient riders to make this level of investment feasible.

### Comparative Transportation Costs per Passenger-Mile/per Kilometer, 2004

|  | Operating Costs (Direct) | Capital Costs (Indirect) | Total | Percentage of Costs Paid by User |
|---|---|---|---|---|
| Bus | $0.73/0.$45 | $0.17/$0.11 | $0.90/$0.56 | 28 |
| Heavy rail | $0.33/$0.20 | $0.27/$0.17 | $0.60/$0.37 | 61 |
| Light rail | $0.56/$0.38 | $1.47/$0.91 | $2.04/$1.27 | 26 |
| Commuter rail | $0.35/$0.22 | $0.75/$0.47 | $1.10/$0.68 | 47 |
| Driving alone | $0.13/$0.08 | $0.40/$0.25 | $0.53/$0.33 | 98 |
| Shared car* | $0.07/$0.04 | $0.20/$0.12 | $0.27/$0.17 | 98 |

**SOURCES:** Federal Transit Administration for bus and rail (past three years used for light rail, to balance capital); Bureau of Transportation Statistics for automobile travel (adjusted to account for other funding sources).

*Assumes two people share costs.

term vision and identify areas in which TOD should take place. The public sector is often criticized for murky, arbitrary, and time-consuming decision-making. To create a supportive environment for development, it must strive for transparency and predictability, and provide developers with assurance that any agreements made by one administration will be upheld by the next. Elected officials can help by not wavering in their support for the vision, by securing the necessary political support for a project, and by persuading the public of its value. Government also should encourage TOD by helping with land assembly; insisting on design excellence; supporting higher densities; and requiring sufficient amounts of parking, retail space, and vertical mixed uses. The public should also be involved in the creation of a vision for the TOD project, and in its design. Nonprofit groups often play advocacy and educational roles; they may also be conduits for funding.

In existing communities and on the suburban fringe, extending bus routes can bring transit closer to where people live. Nationwide, 50 percent of the population and 60 percent of workplaces are located within one-half mile (0.8 kilometers) of a bus route, whereas only 10 percent of the nation's population and workplaces are located within one-half mile of a rail station.[70]

There is an established market for transit, especially among people who do not have their own vehicle, whether by need or by choice. In 2001, two out of three bus riders and half of rail users did not have access to a car.[71] The two ways to increase the percentage of the population served by transit are to expand transit service and to increase the share of development in areas currently served by transit. The latter is obviously much easier, at least for transit agencies. Nationally, 80 percent of city residents reported that transit was available, and 22 percent actually used it regularly, meaning at least once a week. In the suburbs, however, only half of residents reported that transit was available, with a mere 6 percent using it at least weekly.[72] A survey in the San Francisco Bay area showed that residents living near Bay Area Rapid Transit stations were four times as likely to use public transit as other residents.[73]

People need to be able to access jobs in the suburbs by means of transit. Every spiderweb metropolitan form requires a rich network of connections: links between suburbs and other development nodes surrounding the central city are just as important as routes into and out of the city. It is encouraging to note that several metro areas are assuming the financial burden of establishing some of these connections. The following examples offer glimmers of hope that transit will eventually connect various parts of the spiderwebs in these regions.

▸ Phoenix voters have authorized funding for 27 additional miles (43 kilometers) of light-rail transit.
▸ In Austin, citizens have approved a transportation system focused on regional commuter rail.
▸ St. Louis has opened an eight-mile (13-kilometer), $678 million expansion of its light-rail transit line.

▶ Nashville and Albuquerque have opened commuter-rail lines.

▶ Kansas City voters have approved a three-eighths of a cent sales tax for a 27-mile (43-kilometer) light-rail system.

Even more significantly, in the Denver metro area, an alliance of mayors, environmentalists, and the chamber of commerce persuaded voters to approve, by a vote of 65 percent to 35 percent, a $4.7 billion initiative to build an additional 119 miles (192 kilometers) of light rail and commuter rail, with tracks and trains reaching as far as Boulder and the Denver International Airport. Columnist Neal Peirce believes that as this system, known as FasTracks, gets built during the next 20 years, it "could make a significant difference in the look, feel and mobility of one of America's fastest-growing, strategically located cities." Peirce points out that 51 of the 57 stations envisioned along FasTracks lines "are expected to pose major opportunities for TOD. . . . The variant to subdivisions marching along the Front Range of the Rockies may be compact new, transit-served communities in which people can live, work, dine or shop in town-like settings with significantly reduced auto needs." He cites an example: in Boulder, a used-car lot along a railroad spur will be transformed into a dense, affordable neighborhood.[74]

In Honolulu, at the end of December 2006, the city council, instead of opting to build more highways, gave its okay to a fixed-guideway system that would accommodate buses or light rail—"the best Christmas present one could have asked for," exulted mayor Mufi Hannemann. The cost—more than $5 billion—will be covered by federal grants, state and private development funds, and an excise tax increase. The route will traverse a long coastal area, running roughly parallel to highway H1 for 25 miles (40 kilometers)—from Kapolei, on the west, past Pearl Harbor and the Honolulu International Airport, then eastward into downtown Honolulu and out to the University of Hawaii and Waikiki. Honolulu architect David Miller says that building the infrastructure for this project is the city's front-and-center issue as 2008 unfolds.[75]

Unfortunately for transit, population trends are pushing metro areas in the wrong direction.[76] America's highest-growth regions—including Houston, Las Vegas, Los Angeles, Phoenix, San Antonio, San Diego, and San Jose—are still dominated by automobile use, while five of our leading walkable, transit-oriented cities— Philadelphia, Chicago, Boston, Washington, and San Francisco—have lost a combined total of 1.9 million people since 1950. This does not mean that transit should be deemphasized, even where its market is shrinking. It means that the faster-growing cities must grapple with their transportation futures, and must move away from driving and toward greater transit use. The examples cited earlier indicate that metro areas in many parts of our country are beginning to make a stronger commitment to transit. One of the challenges these areas face is how to make transit a reasonable alternative to driving. Commuters and other travelers will decide to leave their cars at home and take transit only if they view transit as an attractive, affordable, convenient, and reliable alternative.

Rail—including commuter rail, light rail, and subway systems—has been called "the rising star of metropolitan areas," even though rail systems are found in only about 30 American cities.[77] Railroads were eclipsed by cars, trucks, and airplanes during the 20th century, but they seem to be enjoying something of a comeback in the 21st. Since 2000, U.S. railroads have spent $10 billion on upgrading tracks, facilities, and equipment, and have budgeted another $12 billion for more of the same.[78] Freight-train haulers are tapping into the strong demand for moving container shipments from other places in the world around the United States. A coordinated federal program to formulate a national approach to freight hauling—one that would integrate rail and truck routes from seaports and airports, and would include state and local governments as well as the private sector—could relieve highway congestion and reduce carbon footprints.[79]

Once again, then, we come to the point that land use and transportation planning can—indeed, must—be connected in order to keep our metro areas sustainable. As is discussed in more detail in Chapter 10, visionary leaders in Arlington County, Virginia, put land use planning ahead of transportation planning back in the 1970s, when county government—with the intent of focusing higher-density development around the subway stations—insisted on routing the Metro line *through*, rather than around, the

## TRANSPORTATION AND PLACE MAKING: DOWNTOWN SILVER SPRING, MARYLAND

Transportation plays an important role in place making, whether in redeveloped older cities and suburbs or in new developments on the fringe. Location, access, parking, transit, and walkability all help determine how successful a place will be. Silver Spring, Maryland, offers a notable example of successful place making.

Downtown Silver Spring is a 24-acre (10-hectare), $322 million mixed-use infill and rehabilitation project in an inner-ring suburb of Washington, D.C. Anchored by restaurants, retail, offices, public spaces, cinemas, and an existing Metro station, it is the product of a public/private partnership between Montgomery County, Maryland, and three Washington, D.C.–area private developers: the Peterson Companies, Foulger-Pratt, and Argo Investment Company. After assembling the land and entering into two failed attempts to redevelop it, the county negotiated a joint development agreement with the new development team (known as PFA Silver Spring, LC) that resulted in the county's funding and operating two state-of-the-art parking garages containing more than 3,800 spaces (built on the county's behalf by PFA)—without which, according to Peterson president Jim Todd, the project would not have been feasible.

A civic building is in the works, and a historic 1930s theater has been renovated for the American Film Institute. The project consists of approximately 440,000 square feet (40,877 square meters) of retail space, 185,000 square feet (17,187 square meters) of office space, a hotel, multiple public parks, and 23 movie screens in two cinema complexes. Featuring a traditional urban grid oriented around two plazas and a town square, downtown Silver Spring will eventually include a 160-condo residential component.

The Silver Spring Metro station provides direct transit access to downtown Washington, D.C., in less than 20 minutes. The station is also a major bus terminal, with extensive bus routes serving communities beyond the rail service area. Downtown Silver Spring is one of the most accessible places in the metro area, by public transit as well as by car. Not only is transit use by nearby residents high, but the transit share among the area's workers is among the highest in the region.

**SOURCES:** "Downtown Silver Spring," *ULI Development Case Study* 35, no. 21 (2005); William H. Hudnut III, *Halfway to Everywhere* (Washington, D.C.: ULI–the Urban Land Institute, 2003), 146–148.

heart of the county. Consequently, 23 percent of Arlington residents—ten times the national average—commute by transit, and 6 percent of them walk to work.[80] In short, people who live in places that are shaped by transit tend to drive less, reducing their overall petroleum use and their carbon footprint. According to APTA, transit reduces U.S. travel by an estimated 102.2 billion VMT each year, which equaled 3.4 percent of the annual U.S. VMT in 2007; the direct petroleum savings attributable to public transportation is 1.4 billion gallons (5.3 billion liters) a year.[81] "If planners want to get people out of their cars onto public transportation, we need to make transit less expensive and driving more expensive," says Dunphy.[82] Meanwhile, people may be encouraged to take transit for other reasons: to avoid parking hassles, to reduce a community's carbon footprint, and, in some instances, to get to their destination faster.

## Finding the Funding

The American Association of State Highway and Transportation Officials (AASHTO) warned in a 2007 report that if the United States is to remain competitive in the world economy, "all levels of government" must make significant investments in renewing the nation's transportation system.[83] AASHTO estimates that necessary improvements to highways and bridges would cost $155.5 billion, and that transit improvements would cost is $31.4 billion. The report projects that in the next 50 years, "435 million people will be driving 400 million vehicles as much as 7 trillion miles [11.2 trillion kilometers] on the nation's highways."[84]

Meanwhile, as noted earlier, other countries are investing aggressively in their transportation systems to support their economic growth. India is building a 10,000-mile (16,093-kilometer) expressway system; Europe is spending billions of euros on high-speed rail and on highways, bridges, tunnels, and ports; and China is building a 53,000-mile (85,295-kilometer) national expressway system that, when completed in 2020, will rival our nation's 42,000-mile (67,592-kilometer) Interstate Highway System. While these nations are spending more and more on their transportation infrastructure, the United States is heading in the opposite direction.

The AASHTO report anticipates growing shortfalls between revenue and expenditures in the highway account of the Highway Trust Fund as the country heads into the future . . . unless, of course, a new bill is enacted by Congress that addresses this possibility. In commenting on AASHTO's report, the National Chamber Foundation of the U.S. Chamber of Commerce has pointed out that current revenue streams between 2006 and 2015 will fall short of what is needed to maintain our current transportation system by $0.5 trillion, and that the cost of improving the system in that same period of time, the *cumulative* shortfall—from all levels of government—is a whopping $1.1 trillion. To close the gap, the National Chamber Foundation recommends, for the short term (2006 to 2015), indexing federal and state motor fuel taxes, expanding the use of tolls and innovative financing tools, and increasing motor fuel taxes and other existing fees.[85]

The decline in federal highway dollars will enlarge the transportation infrastructure deficit, which should be a cause for concern, because our growth as a nation is going to necessitate more roads as well as more transportation in modes other than the car. Says Jerry Amante, mayor pro tem of Tustin, California, and a director of the Orange County Transportation Authority:

> *In Orange County, we're proud to build lanes, not trains. While buses, trains, monorails and subways seem like enticing transportation solutions in theory, they simply don't pencil out. Not in terms of true traffic relief for the vast majority of commuters and certainly not from a fiscal standpoint. Nationwide, spending on public transit has increased seven-fold since 1960. And what have those billions of dollars done for commuters? Not much. During that same period, the number of public transit users has dropped by 63 percent and today less than five percent of all Americans use public transportation. Orange County transportation leaders have a clear-eyed understanding that freeway widenings and arterial improvements provide real traffic relief.[86]*

The obvious truth in Amante's statement is that freeway widenings and other road improvements are necessary to assist in relieving congestion. Yet we must not lose sight of the fact that we still have to reduce the need for driving. Yes, new roads will be needed, but in many cases highway investments are not so much a response to growth and development as a cause of them.

Transportation funding faces problems that are similar to those associated with infrastructure financing in general, which will be discussed in the next chapter. Growing interest in relieving congestion should result in public support for transportation improvements. We must consider a broad range of traditional and nontraditional sources, because it is unlikely that any one revenue stream will be adequate. Traditional government sources of transportation finance, while declining as a share of the total, are still core components, as they not only represent substantial infusions of money into transportation improvement projects, but also leverage substantial investment from state and local governments and the private sector.

At a more mundane level, development fees have become important sources of transportation funding in some growing communities; and in many cases, local sales taxes dedicated to transportation—often approved by voters for specific projects—have become popular in California and elsewhere, as a means of replacing deteriorating state revenues.

## The Federal Role

The 2005 Safe, Accountable, Flexible, Efficient Transportation Equity Act: A Legacy for Users (SAFETEA-LU)—"the largest surface transportation investment in our Nation's history"[87]—provided $244.1 billion in funding for highways, highway safety, and public transportation; made it easier for the private sector to participate in highway infrastructure projects; gave states more flexibility to use road pricing to manage congestion; and created the potential for the establishment of state infrastructure banks. Yet when transportation funding at all levels of government is combined, it is still not adequate to maintain the condition of our current roads and transit. As noted earlier, many jurisdictions face difficulties in attempting to provide for tomorrow's growth in their capital budgets without shortchanging maintenance of existing infrastructure.

One answer to the question "How will we find the money?" could be to increase the gasoline tax, as the National Chamber Foundation recommended in 2005. Ken Orski, author of *Innovation NewsBriefs,* says that a one cent per gallon (0.26 cents per liter) tax increase would generate approximately $1.9 billion a year.[88] The tax revenues could be split between reinvesting in infrastructure and improving energy security. Dunphy points out that a modest increase in the federal gasoline tax—seven cents a gallon—would make us whole, meaning that we would have enough revenue to keep the Highway Trust Fund solvent and keep our roads in good repair. That level of increase would restore the purchasing power of the federal fuel tax (which is now 18.4 cents per gallon [4.8 cents per liter]) to the level that it had in 1993 (the last time the tax was increased). The average American pays $240 a year in fuel taxes—two cents per mile (1.2 cents per kilometer)—which does not seem like a huge amount. But as Dunphy points out, although such an increase would probably be affordable, politically, as of now, it is probably a "nonstarter."[89]

## The State Role

State government—which has responsibility for key highway routes and controls most highway funding, as well as often-significant levels of transit funding—can be an important ally for transportation improvements. Unfortunately, the state role does not always work out in a positive way. In Euclid, Ohio, for example, residents pay some $8.6 million in state gasoline taxes (22 cents per gallon [5.8 cents per liter]) according to former mayor Paul Oyaski, but receive only $760,000 back from the state for street maintenance.[90] Furthermore, the Ohio road-building program subsidizes low-density peripheral growth. Oyaski points to an interchange to the east of Euclid, in low-density Lake County, and calls it "a pellucid example of the type of sprawl-inducing project that is, plain and simple, irrational."[91] What Oyaski is really saying to the states is: "Stop subsidizing sprawl." ULI and Ernst & Young's *Infrastructure 2008: A Competitive Advantage* is very direct about this: "States must stop funding or subsidizing road and water projects that reward developers at suburban fringes and focus instead on improving and maintaining existing systems, which can more efficiently and economically serve people and businesses in more densely populated infill locations."[92] The report notes that although it may be easier and cheaper to build homes in suburban areas, the per-capita costs for infrastructure and maintenance are much higher.[93]

On a more positive note, many states have state transportation improvement programs (STIPs):[94]

▸ California's Infrastructure and Economic Development Bank created the Infrastructure Revolving Fund to provide low-interest loans to various infrastructure projects,
including highway and transit projects.

▸ Connecticut is planning a new train station in Madison, east of New Haven, and an
upgrade of another station in Westbrook. In late 2005, the state finished construction on new stations in Branford and Clinton as part of its STIP, which was designed
to improve overall rail transportation in the state and "up-and-over" facilities at the
station sites.

▸ In 2007, the Oregon Legislature created the Oregon Streetcar Project Fund, which
finances grants to municipalities to assist with the purchase of rail-based streetcars to
be used in public transit systems. The fund is financed by some $20 million in lottery-
backed revenue.

▸ In Pennsylvania, the Sound Land Use Implementation Plan developed by the state
department of transportation ties funding for transportation projects to responsible
land use. The principles outlined in the plan are designed to maximize the impact
of funds by focusing on maintenance and on a few key projects with high value-
to-price ratios. The plan also discourages sprawl by calling for the majority of funds
to be spent on maintaining facilities in established areas, instead of on new facilities
in greenfields.

## User Fees

Taxes are, in a sense, user fees. When you buy a gallon of gas, you pay a tax that is
essentially a fee on the use of public roads. Similarly, property taxes or sales taxes can
be used to back general-obligation or revenue bonds used to finance improvements to
highways and transit and bridges and airports. The same goes for license fees, license
plate fees, truck fees, some lottery proceeds, interest income, and tolls. Thus defined,
user fees represent the lion's share of transportation revenues, and are expected to do so
for at least 15 years.[95] Despite the loss in buying power of user fees such as the gas tax,
increases in user fees should be the foundation for a transportation plan.

## The Ballot Box

Local governments, frustrated by inaction at the state and federal levels, are increasingly going directly to the voters for support, and adopting local sales taxes to fund
transportation. As noted earlier, voters in Austin, Denver, Kansas City, and Phoenix
have authorized substantial new revenues from sales taxes and bond issues to build
new rail lines for commuters. Other localities have approved local taxes for a variety
of road and transit projects. This is especially true in California, where nine counties
have passed new tax measures, despite tough state rules that require a two-thirds
majority to approve such increases. In the Bay Area alone, new local option sales taxes
were approved in Marin and Sonoma counties, and extensions of existing taxes were
approved in Contra Costa and San Mateo counties. The monies will go for a range of
road and transit improvements.

## Parking Fees

Parking is a critical but often overlooked element of the transportation system. Expanded use of parking fees and meters could raise additional revenues for municipalities while reducing VMT. The suburban model that has ruled much of our thinking about transportation dictates that free parking must be available everywhere, generally on paved-surface parking areas around malls and shopping centers, office buildings, and homes. Unfortunately, this custom of paving over vast amounts of space consumes excessive land; it also reinforces the need to drive. Charging for parking just might do more to tame the car than the most ambitious transit improvements, by increasing the cost—and decreasing the attractiveness—of traveling by car.[96] A parking pricing strategy can take various forms:

▸ Fee increases (and, in some cases, decreases)
▸ Short-term versus long-term fee differentials
▸ Metered on-street parking
▸ Elimination or diminution of employer-subsidized parking
▸ Fee differentials for single-occupant versus high-occupancy vehicles (ridesharing)
▸ Park-and-ride fees.[97]

In 1990, the National Personal Transportation Study, a DOT survey of external costs, estimated that more than 95 percent of all commuter auto trips in the survey year involved free parking. And this old figure does not include the free parking that is often provided in suburban shopping centers, office complexes, apartment and condominium buildings, parks and recreational spots, schools, and places of worship. Donald Shoup, a professor at the University of California, Los Angeles, and author of *The High Cost of Free Parking,* estimates that paid parking accounts for no more than 4 percent of all parking, and possibly as little as 1 percent.[98] If, for example, a driver with a daily 30-mile (48-kilometer) round-trip commute who once was able to park for free had to pay $10 a day for parking, that would translate into an additional cost of $0.33 a mile ($0.20 per kilometer), a more than 60 percent jump in driving costs.

The often-high cost of downtown parking helps make transit more attractive. And increased demand for downtown transit helps to justify service improvements. This lesson could be applied to the broader metro area. By making drivers pay the fair market cost of parking throughout the metro area, governments, employers, managers of shopping malls and residential buildings, and others in the business of supplying free or subsidized parking could accomplish several important goals: encouraging greater use of transit; decreasing VMT; reducing some of their own business expenses; increasing their return on investment; and generating funds that could be used to expand transit throughout the metro area.

The federal government was once one of the worst offenders in this area. By providing free parking for many employees but not subsidizing transit use, it effectively encouraged people to drive rather than to take transit. But in November 1979, the feds began requiring federal employees to pay one-half the prevailing rates of commercial garages, which reduced the number of autos used for commuting by 1 to 10 percent in the central city, and by 2 to 4 percent in the suburbs.[99] In the Washington, D.C., area, the federal government subsidizes federal employees' use of transit and vanpools. Outside the Washington, D.C., area, qualified federal employees are permitted to set aside pretax income, up to an established limit; the federal government then uses those funds to purchase transit vouchers or passes for the employees.[100]

## Innovative Funding Strategies

The innovative funding strategies described in this section may depend on new technologies, but they are based on the same principle as old-fashioned tolls: that those who benefit from transportation improvements should pay for them. While helping to "tame the car," the strategies could also be used to fund transportation improvements—and could very well change how, when, and where people decide to drive.[101]

### Dynamic Pricing

In the words of columnist George Will, "The congestion crisis requires joining an old material—concrete—with new technologies."[102] Dynamic pricing is one of the answers. For years, restaurants and movie theaters have lowered their prices during off-peak hours to attract patrons. Dynamic pricing—which is already in use on Interstate 15, in southern California—uses a similar strategy. In high-volume intercity corridors, interconnected multijurisdictional networks of dedicated tollways using dynamic pricing could reduce congestion on interstate highways, enhance trucking productivity, and capture revenues from all who use the routes.

Like California, Florida is experimenting with dynamic pricing. According to transportation writer Ken Orski, Florida is inviting the private sector to help finance, build, and operate a 10.5-mile (17-kilometer) stretch of elevated toll lanes intended to relieve congestion in the busy I-595 corridor that connects I-75 with the Florida Turnpike and I-95 in Broward County. Orski notes that the busiest stretch of I-595 currently carries about 180,000 vehicles per day, and that volume is expected to rise to 300,000 by 2035. This is a $1.2 billion project; the state will pay $900 million and is asking the private sector to finance the remaining $300 million—as well as to build, operate, and maintain the facility. "But instead of letting out a toll concession wherein the private concessionaire would collect and pocket the toll revenue," Orski notes, "the state proposes to collect the tolls and pay the private builder-operator a fee based on the number of vehicles using the toll facility."[103] The contract has not yet been let.

### Congestion Zone Pricing

Congestion zone pricing involves charging a toll for entering certain parts of town or for using certain highways during peak hours. In 2003, according to the Texas Transportation Institute, American motorists in 85 urban areas squandered 3.7 billion hours and 2.3

billion gallons (8.7 billion liters) of gas while stuck in traffic, at a cost of $63 billion in wasted time and fuel.[104] Economists have long believed that the problem with traffic is that drivers pay the same amount regardless of whether they are traveling in congested conditions or in free-flowing ones, and that if they paid the full costs imposed on the traffic stream, fewer would travel and congestion would decline.

Despite widespread opposition, London now contains a large zone in its center—a zone that doubled in size in early 2007—in which vehicles are charged a fee of $15.60 a day to travel. Net revenues are expected to be $49 million to $78 million a year.[105] Observers believe that the program has significantly reduced traffic congestion, improved bus and taxi service, and generated substantial revenues. They anticipate that with growing public acceptance, the program will be expanded to other parts of London and other cities in the U.K. and elsewhere.[106] In London, authorities have set up 693 cameras at 137 sites to catch violators. According to Michael Beyard, senior resident fellow and ULI/Martin Bucksbaum chair for retail and entertainment, although many were concerned that retail sales in the zone would suffer, sales have actually increased since congestion pricing went into effect.[107] Similar experiments have succeeded in Stockholm and Singapore, and a few U.S. regions are considering trying out this strategy. The federal budget for fiscal 2008 sets aside $100 million for demonstration projects. Nevertheless, the political reality is that few American politicians would be interested in making motorists put up with what appears to be yet another tax—not to mention a gross inconvenience—in order to have the privilege of using the busiest streets.

New York City mayor Michael Bloomberg is an exception. He has boldly proposed a congestion pricing scheme for vehicles traveling between 86th Street and the Battery. Between 6 a.m. and 6 p.m., those traveling into or out of the congestion zone would pay a fee of $8 per car or $21 per truck. Taxis and livery cabs would be exempt, and those traveling only *within* the congestion zone would pay half price. The fees would be assessed electronically. According to the *New Yorker*, sitting in traffic costs $5 billion annually in lost time, and if other expenses like wasted fuel and lost revenue are toted up, the figure rises to $13 billion.[108] In a city where a car traveling along 42nd Street between 10 a.m. and 4 p.m. averages 4.7 miles (7.6 kilometers) per hour, the question, as Mayor Bloomberg says, is "not whether we want to pay but how do we want to pay."[109] Not unexpectedly, the proposal, which requires approval by the state legislature, has encountered vocal opposition.[110] Bloomberg's plan has been stalled in the New York State legislature since 2007, but perhaps it will be revived another day. (Reportedly, $153 million of the $354.5 million in federal financing that New York City was hoping to obtain if its congestion pricing scheme had been approved in 2008 went to Chicago, for the creation of a new bus-rapid-transit network and a variable-rate parking-meter system downtown.)[111]

## Vehicle-Miles-Traveled Pricing

Basically, VMT pricing programs charge travelers who use certain segments of roads or who travel during peak hours; they may also be implemented on a per-mile basis.

Robin Chase, the founder of Zipcar and now CEO of Meadows Networks, has floated this strategy as a means of funding transportation improvements while taming car use. She recommends abandoning all gas taxes and shifting to VMT pricing, using wireless technology to track VMT. Doing so would involve installing a small computer on board every vehicle, which would report the number of miles actually traveled; VMT would be the basis for a user charge that could also be adjusted to reflect peak and nonpeak hours, a vehicle's weight and footprint, and its greenhouse gas emissions. As ULI and Ernst & Young's *Infrastructure 2008* explains, "The idea is you pay more for traveling on congested roads during rush hour; driving heavier vehicles, which cause more road wear and tear; owning less fuel-efficient, higher emissions cars; and going longer distances."[112] Revenues would be divided among local, state, and federal levels of government.[113]

Chase isn't the only supporter of VMT pricing; Oregon has actually conducted an experiment with it. In 2001, the legislature established the Road User Fee Task Force—which, in turn, created a pilot program to test how information for a mileage-based tax, as opposed to a per-gallon tax, might be collected. One advantage of a mileage-based fee is that it does not erode as fuel efficiency improves. The pilot currently underway in Portland involves about 260 drivers and a handful of area service stations. The experiment is not about policy (that is, how to set pricing), but about the technology. One participant described the program this way:

> The system in the vehicle has two radios: one for GPS tracking, the other to relay to the central system at a service station while refueling. The driver can see how much mileage is being accumulated in each category on a dashboard display. A transponder on the pump gets the details to print on the receipt. A central transponder at the service station gathers the VMT data from the vehicle. The receipt shows you VMT tax for each category of mileage: outside the state, inside the state, inside the Metro area during rush hour.[114]

That was in 2007. Nothing much has happened since. The system seems to be viable, but there does not appear to be any political movement toward implementation, so no law has yet been passed to enact VMT pricing.

VMT pricing would be similar to the way we pay for other utilities. It would generate substantial revenues—quite possibly reducing the need to increase gas taxes, or eliminating them entirely. America may need to use both VMT pricing and dynamic pricing to fund its transportation infrastructure needs. Putting the "user pays" principle to work on the roads, which is being done already with tollbooths, "holds enormous promise," according to U.S. Secretary of Transportation Mary E. Peters (who does not favor a gas tax increase), for generating large amounts of revenue.[115]

## Shadow Tolling

Under another innovative financing method, the government would award a concession to a private contractor to design, build, finance, and operate a road (or road section) for an agreed-upon period of time. The annual fee paid by the government to the contractor would be based on traffic volume; no tolls would be collected from drivers, and there would be no visible tollbooth—hence the term *shadow tolling.* The U.K. adopted this method in 1997; it has also been used in several other European countries, most notably Portugal and Finland. In Canada, the provincial government of New Brunswick is preparing to introduce shadow tolling on the Fredericton-Moncton highway, but there are no examples of its use in America . . . yet.[116]

## The Futility of an Open-Ended System

Americans drive an awful lot. In 2006, total VMT on all public roads was 1.942 trillion miles (3.125 trillion kilometers).[117] And the majority of those trips did not involve commuting to or from work (see Figure 1-7).

As we Americans drive mile after mile after mile, we are vexed, in most metro areas, by traffic congestion, and worried about GHG emissions from all the cars and trucks on the road. In order to plan for a sustainable future in the spiderwebs of dispersed development, we will have to reinvent metropolitan America as a place that is less automobile dependent. Congressman Mark Steven Kirk (R-IL) stated the case well when he argued in favor of the federal transportation bill of 2004: "Updating our transportation infrastructure is critical to reducing highway gridlock and improving our environment."[118]

Leaving aside technological innovation and concentrating on the relationship between land use and transportation, this reinvention has a number of implications. First, our metro areas should offer a mix of transportation options, including light rail, commuter rail, buses, jitneys, shuttles, walking, and biking—and, of course, driving, on both major and minor roads; these options should be integrated into high-capacity multimodal facilities, and adequate parking should be provided. Second, land use planning should ensure that this mix of transportation options is accommodated, and that neighborhoods and communities are efficiently connected in the multinucleated, spiderweb regions in which we now live. To create sustainable transportation networks in 21st-century metropolitan regions, we need land use policy to drive transportation and development, not the other way around. One reason that downtown Vancouver is so attractive and pedestrian-friendly is that the local government requires all parking to be underground, does not allow any freeways, and refuses to authorize expansion of existing road capacity. Vancouver understands what Gordon Price calls "the futility of the open-ended system."[119] We cannot build our way out of congestion. Finally, mechanisms to fund our transportation system should include market-based options based on the principle that users pay. The strategies explored in the previous section, along with taxes and traditional fees, can help to fund, finance, design, and build the transportation improvements needed to keep America's 21st-century metro areas competitive. Similar approaches can be applied to the broader issues of our nation's infrastructure deficit, the subject of the next chapter.

**ENDNOTES**

1   Nancy McGuckin and Nanda Srinivasan, "Journey to Work Trends in the United States and Its Major Metropolitan Areas: 1960–2000," FHWA-EP-03-058 (Washington, D.C.: U.S. Department of Transportation, Federal Highway Administration, Office of Planning, 2003), xvi.

2   That is, roughly 195.79 million vehicles owned by 111.62 million households. U.S. Census Bureau, "2006 U.S. Community Survey."

3   U.S. Department of Energy, *Transportation Energy Data Book* (Washington, D.C., 2008), Ch. 8, Table 8.1.

4   U.S. Department of Transportation (DOT), *Journey to Work Trends, 1960–2000,* FHWA-EP-03-058 (Washington, D.C.: DOT, 2003), ch. 1, exhibit 1.1.

5   Leonard Forkas Jr., speech to ULI trustees, February 1, 2007.

6   Al Eisenberg, telephone conversation with author.

7   Alan E. Pisarski, *Commuting in America III: The Third National Report on Commuting Patterns and Trends* (Washington, D.C.: Transportation Research Board, 2006), 48.

8   "Representatives Bean, Kirk, Host Bipartisan Meeting to Address Suburban Transportation Issues," press release, April 10, 2007.

9   Jim Newton, "Bipartisan Panel Criticizes Mass Transit Spending," *Suburban Chicago News,* April 11, 2007.

10  Gordon Price, "A Local Politician's Guide To Urban Transportation" (unpublished paper, 2001).

11  For example, between 2000 and 2006, the New York region grew by almost 2.7 percent, whereas in the same period, the Dallas-Fort Worth area grew by 16.4 percent and the Houston area by 17.4 percent. See Les Christie, "The Fastest-Growing U.S. Cities," CNNMoney.com, June 28, 2007.

12  David Hartgen, news release, March 19, 2007.

13  Secretary of Transportation, "National Strategy to Reduce Congestion on America's Transportation Network," March 2007; www.fightgridlocknow.gov/docs/conginitooverview070301.htm.

14  See Anthony Downs, *Law of Peak-Hour Traffic Congestion* (Washington, D.C.: Brookings Institution, 1962); and "Traffic: Why It's Getting Worse," Brookings Institution Policy Brief #128, January 2004; www.brookings.edu/comm/policybriefs/pb128.pdf.

15  Downs, "Traffic," 4, 2.

16  "Widen the Roads, Drivers Will Come: MD's I-270 Offers a Lesson," *Washington Post,* January 4, 1999.

17  Mark E. Hallenbeck et al. and Washington State Transportation Research Center, "Options for Making Concurrency More Multimodal: Response to SHB 1565 (2005 Session)," report prepared for the Puget Sound Regional Council, December 2006, 5. Subsequent quotations in this paragraph are taken from the same source.

18  Florida Statute 163:3180, 1(c), quoted in Anthony Downs, "Why Florida's Concurrency Principle for Controlling New Development by Regulating Road Construction Does Not—and Cannot—Work Effectively," *Transportation Quarterly* (Winter 2003): 13–17, 2 (fn.).

19  Downs, "Florida's Concurrency Principle," 2.

20  Royce Hanson, e-mail communication with author.

21  Keith Bartholomew, "Land Use Transportation Scenario Planning: Promise and Reality," *Transportation* 34, no. 4 (July 2007): 397–412.

22  California Green Solutions, "California Growth Projections Are +25 Million by 2050~!" July 7, 2007; www.californiagreensolutions.com/cgi-bin/gt/tpl.h,content=625.

23  Southern California Association of Governments (SCAG) and Southern California Compass, *Growth Vision Report* (Los Angeles: SCAG, June 2004), 24. ULI Los Angeles, in partnership with the University of Southern California Lusk Center for Real Estate, conducted a visioning exercise in 2002 to raise awareness of the impending population increase forecast for the region. Close to 200 community leaders from the public, private, and not-for-profit sectors gathered to try to envision where to accommodate the growth projected for the Los Angeles region. The outcome of the exercise was a series of growth models presenting alternative visions for how Los Angeles might accommodate new residents.

24  More technically, the SCAG 2% Compass Blueprint program.

25  *The 2% Strategy* (Los Angeles: SCAG, Fall 2007).

26  SCAG and Southern California Compass, *Growth Vision Report*, 46, 47.

27  Quoted in "US Water Pipelines Are Breaking," *New York Times*, April 8, 2008.

28  Audrey Dutton, "Somerset Elections Bring New Mayor . . . ," (Bethesda) *Gazette Community News*, April 9, 2008, A-8.

29  Philip Warburg and Carrie Russell, "Filling the Transportation Funding Gap," *Boston Globe*, September 21, 2007.

30  Metropolitan Transportation Commission, "Transportation 2030 Plan Charts New Course for the Bay Area: Vision Calls for 'HOT' Lanes and Transit-Oriented Development," *Transactions Online* (April–May 2005).

31  Eugenie L. Birch, "Who Lives Downtown?" Brookings Institution, Living Cities Census Series, November 2005; brookings.edu/~/media/Files/rc/reports/2005/11downtown redevelopment_birch/20051115_Birch.pdf.

32  Quoted in Smart Growth News, "More Residential Buildings Needed in Lafayette's Downtown, Architects Say," theadvertiser.com, February 4, 2006.

33  "San Francisco Cuts Parking Demand," *New Urban News* (September 2006).

34  William H. Hudnut III, *Halfway to Everywhere* (Washington, D.C.: ULI–the Urban Land Institute, 2003).

35  Neal Peirce, "How Do We Develop in a Radically Altered World?" syndicated column, December 17, 2006.

36  ULI–the Urban Land Institute and Ernst & Young, *Infrastructure 2008: A Global Perspective* (Washington, D.C.: ULI–the Urban Land Institute, 2008), 38.

37  Ibid.

38  Mary Beth Corrigan et al., *Ten Principles for Smart Growth on the Fringe* (Washington, D.C.: ULI–the Urban Land Institute, 2005).

39  Downs, "Traffic," 6, 7.

40  Ibid.

41  Neal Peirce, "As We Add Millions, How Do We Stay Mobile?" syndicated column, November 26, 2006; Downs, "Florida's Concurrency Principle," 13-17.

42  Price, "Local Politician's Guide."

43  Cited in Adrienne Schmitz and Jason Scully, *Creating Walkable Places: Compact Mixed-Use Solutions* (Washington, D.C.; ULI–the Urban Land Institute, 2006), 7.

44  See Schmitz and Scully, *Creating Walkable Places*.

45  Red bikes can be picked up and left anywhere in the city; for yellow bikes, users leave a deposit at a local bike shop, which is returned when the bike is returned.

46  Steven Erlanger, "A New Fashion Catches on in Paris: Cheap Bicycle Rentals," *New York Times*, July 13, 2008; available at www.nytimes.com/2008/07/13/world/europe/13paris.html?pagewanted=1&th&emc=th.

47  The World City Bike Collaborative: 2008/9; www.ecoplan.org/wtpp/citybike_index.htm.

48  Bernie Becker, "Bicycle-Sharing Program to Be First of Kind in U.S.," *New York Times*, April 27, 2008; available at www.nytimes.com/2008/04/27/us/27bikes.html?pagewanted=all.

49  Paul Shimek, Massachusetts Institute of Technology, unpublished analysis of 2001 database, Nationwide Personal Transportation Survey.

50  Wendy Bumgardner, "Best 10 Walking Cities for 2008"; About.com: Walking.

51  Christopher J. Leinberger, *The Option of Urbanism: Investing in a New American Dream* (Washington, D.C.: Island Press, 2008).

52  Ibid., 10–11.

53  Ibid., 10.

54  Quoted in a National Governors Association news release, "Sprawl Has a Solution, Says New NGA Report," July 24, 2001.

55  Information and quotations in this paragraph are taken from John Caulfield, "This Way," *Builder* (September 2007): 136.

56  For a more complete analysis, see Schmitz and Scully, *Creating Walkable Places.*

57  ULI–the Urban Land Institute and PricewaterhouseCoopers LLP, *Emerging Trends in Real Estate 2008* (Washington, D.C.: ULI–the Urban Land Institute, 2007), 14–15.

58  Jo Allen Gause et al., *Great Planned Communities* (Washington, D.C.: ULI–the Urban Land Institute, 2002), 79.

59  Adrienne Schmitz, *The New Shape of Suburbia: Trends in Residential Development* (Washington, D.C.: ULI–the Urban Land Institute, 2003), 206.

60  Nancy Graham, phone conversation with author, April 15, 2008.

61  Leinberger, *Urbanism,* 107.

62  Ibid., 151.

63  Ibid., 150–151.

64  Virginia Miller, "10.3 Billion Trips Taken . . . ," March 10, 2008; www.apta.com/media/releases/080310_ridership.cfm.

65  ABC News/*Time* magazine/*Washington Post* poll, "A Look Under the Hood of a Nation on Wheels," January 31, 2005; http://abcnews.go.com/images/Politics/973a2Traffic.pdf.

66  "Report: 98 Percent of U.S. Commuters Favor Public Transportation for Others," *The Onion*, November 29, 2000, 1; www.theonion.com/content/node/38644.

67  Robert Dunphy, conversation with author.

68  Paul Weyrich, "True Conservatives Should Back Metro Funding," *Washington Post,* November 12, 2006, B8.

69  Linda Bailey, Patricia L. Mokhtarian, and Andrew Little, "The Broader Connection between Public Transportation, Energy Conservation and Greenhouse Gas Reduction," February 2008, 7; www.apta.com/research/info/online/land_use.cfm.

70  Steven E. Polzin and Xuehao Chu, *Public Transit in America: Results from the 2001 National Household Travel Survey* (Tampa: Center for Urban Transportation Research, University of South Florida, 2005), 12–15.

71  U.S. Department of Transportation (DOT), Federal Highway Administration, *National Personal Transportation Study* (Washington, D.C.: DOT, 2001).

72  U.S. Census Bureau, Current Housing Reports, Series H150/50, American Housing Survey for the US: 2005 (Washington, D.C.: U.S. Government Printing Office, 2006).

73 Planning Section, Metropolitan Transportation Commission (MTC), "Characteristics of Rail and Ferry Station Area Residents in the San Francisco Bay Area: Evidence from the 2000 Bay Area Travel Survey" (Oakland, Calif.: MTC, 2006), 1.

74 Neal Peirce, "Voting on How We Grow," syndicated column, November 14, 2004.

75 David Miller, personal conversation with author, January 24, 2008.

76 Robert Dunphy, e-mail to author, April 21, 2008.

77 Schmitz, *Suburbia*, 21.

78 ULI–the Urban Land Institute and Ernst & Young, *Infrastructure 2008: A Global Perspective* (Washington, D.C.: ULI–the Urban Land Institute, 2008), 15; see also Daniel Machalaba, "New Era Dawns for Rail Building," *Wall Street Journal*, February 13, 2008.

79 Information in this paragraph is taken from ULI and Ernst & Young, *Infrastructure 2008*, 14–15.

80 Bailey, Mokhtarian, and Little, "Broader Connection," 7.

81 Ibid., 3.

82 Robert Dunphy, e-mail to author, April 17, 2008.

83 *AASHTO Journal*, March 9, 2007.

84 Ibid.

85 Ibid, vii.

86 Jerry Amante, "The Orange Grove: O.C. Prefers More Lanes to Trains," August 22, 2007; OCRegister.com.

87 U.S. Department of Transportation, Federal Highway Administration, Summary Information, SAFETEA-LU Web site, www.fhwa.dot.gov/safetealu/index.htm.

88 Ken Orski, "News from the Transportation Front," *Innovation NewsBriefs*, no. 19 (August 2007).

89 Robert Dunphy, personal communication.

90 Paul Oyaski, conversation with author, 2002.

91 Ibid.

92 ULI and Ernst & Young, *Infrastructure 2008*, 19.

93 Ibid.

94 The information for California, Connecticut, and Oregon is taken from state Web sites: www.ibank.ca.gov/; www.ct.gov/dotinfo/cwp/view.asp?A=2337&Q=302396; and www. oregon.gov/ODOT/HWY/STIP/. The information on Pennsylvania is from ULI–the Urban Land Institute, *Action Agenda for Infrastructure* (Washington, D.C.: ULI–the Urban Land Institute, January 2008).

95 Alan E. Pisarski, *Future Highway and Public Transportation Financing* (Washington, D.C.: National Chamber Foundation, 2005). See also Pisarski, *Future Highway and Public Transportation Financing: Phase I—Current Outlook and Short-Term Solutions* (Washington, D.C.: National Chamber Foundation, 2005); and Pisarski, *Future Highway and Public Transportation Financing: Phase II* (Washington, D.C.: National Chamber Foundation, 2005).

96 Erin Vaca and J. Richard Kuzmyak, "Parking Pricing and Fees," chapter 13 of Transit Cooperative Research Program, Report 95 (Washington, D.C.: Federal Transit Administration, 2005), 13-2.

97 Ibid.

98 Donald Shoup, *The High Cost of Free Parking* (Chicago: Planners Press, 2005).

99 Vaca and Kuzmyak, "Parking Pricing and Fees," 13-17.

100 See U.S. Department of Transportation, Federal Transit Administration, "Executive Order 13150: Federal Workforce Transportation—Frequently Asked Questions," www.fta.dot.gov/ about/about_FTA_4645.html.

101 ULI and Ernst & Young, *Infrastructure 2008*, 10.

102 George F. Will, "Fighting the Real Gridlock," *Washington Post*, March 11, 2007, B7.

103 Ken Orski, "'Shadow Tolling' Eyed for I-95 Express Lanes in Broward County," August 13, 2007; www.cascadiaprospectus.org/2007/08/shadow_tolling_eyed_for_browar.php; see also www.i-595.com/improve.aspx#revlanes.

104 David Shrank and Tim Lomax, *2005 Urban Mobility Report* (College Station, Tex.: Texas Transportation Institute, 2006).

105 "London Adds to Its Zone for Road Tolls," *New York Times*, February 18, 2007; www.nytimes. com/2007/02/18/world/europe/18london.html.

106 Todd Litman, *London Congestion Pricing: Implications for Other Cities* (Victoria, B.C.: Victoria Transport Policy Institute, January 10, 2006).

107 Michael Beyard, personal communication.

108 Elizabeth Kolbert, "Don't Drive, He Said," *New Yorker*, May 7, 2007, 23-24.

109 Ibid.

110 Ibid.

111 Jennifer Lee, "Chicago Gets New York's Congestion Money," CityRoom blog, *New York Times*, April 29, 2008; available at http://cityroom.blogs.nytimes.com/2008/04/29/ chicago-gets-new-yorks-congestion-money/.

112 ULI and Ernst & Young, *Infrastructure 2008: A Competitive Advantage* (Washington, D.C.: ULI-the Urban Land Institute, 2008), 10.

113 See Neal Peirce, "Selling Our Toll Roads: Good or Retrograde Idea?" April 8, 2007.

114 Chris Smith, "Piloting a VMT Tax," March 13, 2007; portlandtransport.com/ archives/2007/03/piloting_a_vmt_1.html.

115 Mary E. Peters, "The Folly of Higher Gas Taxes," *Washington Post*, August 25, 2007, A15.

116 American Association of State Highway and Transportation Officials, Innovative Finance for Surface Transportation.org, "Shadow Toll Agreements"; www.innovativefinance.org/ topics/finance_mechanisms/shallow_toll/shadowtolls.asp.

117 Office of Highway Policy Information, Federal Highway Administration, *Highway Statistics 2006*.

118 Quoted in "House Passes Federal Transportation Bill," part of a newsletter released by Congressman Mark Steven Kirk, April 2, 2004.

119 Gordon Price, telephone conversation with author, May 2, 2008.

# CHAPTER 5

# Infrastructure: The Backbone of the Global Economy

## Our infrastructure is falling apart.

—DOUGLAS H. PALMER, MAYOR, TRENTON, NEW JERSEY

*Two activities—building new infrastructure and maintaining existing stock—are necessary to support the evolving metropolitan form. Moreover, without up-to-date infrastructure, a country loses its competitive advantage. Good infrastructure fuels an economy and supports prosperity. But however necessary, infrastructure is very expensive. How will government and the private sector cover the costs? Money will not solve all of America's infrastructure problems, but they cannot be solved without it. Funds to cover the "infrastructure deficit"—the gap between what is being spent and what needs to be spent in order to keep infrastructure in good repair—can and should be raised: first, through an expanded public commitment at all levels of government to cease deferring maintenance; and second, through a market-oriented approach that taps into user-generated revenues.*

**IF THE COLLAPSE** of the New Orleans levees in late August 2005 and the burst steam pipes in Manhattan in July 2007 did not catch the attention of America, the collapse of the I-35W bridge in Minneapolis on August 1, 2007, and the flooding of New York City's subway system a week later certainly did. These incidents were a red flag that said "America, wake up! Stop deferring maintenance of your infrastructure. Pay close attention to it, and fix it while it still *can* be fixed. Don't wait until it has crumbled beyond repair, when the cost of replacing it will be even greater."

The United States is fast approaching a turning point in terms of its infrastructure. Much of the nation's transportation, water/sewer, and power infrastructure is reaching the end of its life span, and a burgeoning population and expansive sprawl are putting even greater strains on already weakened systems. Compounding the problem, funding for infrastructure maintenance and improvements is becoming increasingly difficult to secure because large costs are involved and political will is weak.

People tend to take things for granted until a crisis occurs. When we sip our coffee at the breakfast table, we don't stop to consider that producing a single cup of java requires 140 liters of water, and that it takes more than 1,000 drops of water to make one drop of coffee. We don't contemplate the hidden delivery system that brings us that coffee—the pipes that carried the water needed to irrigate the coffee plants, the ports and airports through which the coffee beans were transported, the roads and bridges over which the beans were trucked to market, the pipes that brought the water to fill the coffee machine in our home, the reservoir that the water came from, or the sewers that carried the wastewater used to clean the cups to some unknown treatment plant. Few people ever give a second thought to these infrastructure issues, as long as water continues to come out of the tap, a nearby bridge does not collapse, a neighboring dam or levee does not break, a sewer or storm drain does not back up into their basement, or a road that they use regularly does not disintegrate. But these are important issues—to which the sad circumstances surrounding New Orleans, New York City, and Minneapolis attest—and the sad truth is that, typically, infrastructure breakdowns must occur before politicians and voters respond to unmet needs.

America is built on infrastructure. In May 2007, ULI and Ernst & Young stated the case as follows:

> *Sound infrastructure forms the backbone that is critical to maintaining and enhancing regional economic growth, competitiveness, productivity, and quality of life. For businesses, infrastructure has the greatest influence on location after tax rates, the availability of an educated workforce, and low crime. Where time is money, moving people to and from jobs, facilitating deliveries and shipments, freedom from business interruptions like loss of power, and ample telecommunications capacity all enter the equation. Prime access to ports and airports along global pathways becomes more essential for expanding enterprise and profits. Congestion and transport bottlenecks, meanwhile, can threaten regional sustainability.[1]*

Some of our infrastructure is new and strong; consider, for example, the magnificent Sunshine Skyway Bridge over Tampa Bay. But, as we learned with the I-35W bridge collapse, some infrastructure is aging and unable to carry increasing loads, and the cost of maintaining it is growing. In a ULI/Ernst & Young survey of U.S. directors of planning for state departments of transportation published in May 2007, 83 percent of respondents did not believe that the nation's transportation infrastructure was capable of meeting the country's needs over the next ten years.[2] Fourteen percent of America's bridges are now deemed structurally deficient,[3] and some 33 percent of the nation's 78,000 dams are rated unsafe.[4] Meanwhile, decision makers yield to the temptation to build new projects rather than to invest in existing structures that need repair.

What's more, the costs of building new infrastructure place a hidden burden on housing—and, as discussed in the preceding chapter, traffic congestion threatens the quality of life in communities new and old. In New Jersey, for example, Rutgers University has estimated that by 2020, the new roads, sewers, schools, and other public facilities needed to serve sprawling development will cost the state $8 billion, which comes to about $15,000 to $20,000 per household.[5] At the same time, infrastructure in many established neighborhoods is being neglected, accelerating its deterioration, creating an impossible burden for developers who want to build in declining neighborhoods, and adding to the cost of rehabilitation. In Honolulu, for example, a sewer repair job took seven years, went through three contractors, and cost $58.5 million—$22.5 million more than initially projected.[6] The lesson from Honolulu is that you can spend so many dollars annually to maintain infrastructure, but if you fail to do so and later have to rehabilitate it, the costs are multiplied considerably.

## What Is Infrastructure?

Infrastructure is, literally, the foundation of our communities—the built structures such as sewers, roads, railroad tracks, airports, tunnels, seaports, dams, wastewater treatment facilities, levees, and bridges. *Webster's New World Dictionary* defines infrastructure as "the substructure or underlying foundation, especially the basic installations and facilities on which the continuance and growth of a community depends." The word came into common parlance in the United States in the 1980s, following the publication, in 1983, of *America in Ruins*, a landmark book that spoke of an "infrastructure crisis" that had been caused by decades of inadequate investment in and poor maintenance of what had been called "public works."[7] In 1983 and 1984, a bridge collapsed on the Connecticut Turnpike, and some highly visible water main and subway breakdowns occurred in New York City. In 1984, Congress established the National Council on Public Works Improvement, chaired by Senator Daniel Patrick Moynihan (D–NY). The council issued three reports on the nation's infrastructure, including recommendations on what to do about the problems that had been uncovered. But still the problems persist.

Infrastructure that builds vibrant, sustainable communities and connects them to the greater region and the nation enhances economic competitiveness and quality of life. Dale Anne Reiss, global and Americas director of real estate for Ernst & Young, says that infrastructure is "the backbone of the global economy": countries "depend on it to move people and goods expeditiously, efficiently, and safely."[8] The National Petroleum Council estimates that it will take some $20 trillion worldwide (that's $3,000 for every person on the planet today) in infrastructure improvements through 2030 just to keep up with energy demand.[9]

Today, the United States is suffering from an "infrastructure deficit" that has three dimensions. First, our infrastructure is deficient—in need of repair. Second, we are not spending as much as we should on infrastructure construction and maintenance. Third, we are spending money in the wrong places: sprawling development patterns require us to constantly build new infrastructure, while abandoning or neglecting what's already in place, but it costs more to service sprawl than it would to serve more compact, mixed-use communities. The bottom line is that inadequate investment in infrastructure constrains growth in metropolitan areas. For example, If traffic congestion is not relieved, the cost of doing business—including lost person-hours—goes up. And if capacity at a waste-water treatment facility is not enlarged, industrial, residential, or commercial growth may be curtailed.[10]

FIGURE 5-1 **2005 Report Card for America's Infrastructure.**

| | |
|---|---|
| Aviation | D+ |
| Bridges | C |
| Dams | D |
| Drinking water | D- |
| Energy (national power grid) | D |
| Hazardous waste | D |
| Navigable waterways | D- |
| Public parks | C- |
| Rail | C- |
| School facilities | D |
| Security | Incomplete |
| Solid Waste | C+ |
| Transit | D+ |
| Roads | D |
| Wastewater | D- |

**KEY: A = exceptional; B = good; C = mediocre; D = poor; F = failing**

**SOURCE:** American Society of Civil Engineers (ASCE), *2005 Report Card for America's Infrastructure* (Washington, D.C., and Reston, Virginia: ASCE, 2005), 2; www.asce.org/reportcard/2005/index.cfm.

## The Infrastructure Deficit

In a well-publicized 2005 report on the condition of America's infrastructure, the American Society of Civil Engineers (ASCE) gave it a grade of "D" overall, and estimated that some $1.6 trillion in further investment would be needed to bring conditions to acceptable levels before 2010. The report stated that the establishment of "a long-term development and maintenance plan must become a national priority."[11]

Fifteen categories—from roads to airports, waste-water, and drinking water—were evaluated on the basis of condition and performance, capacity versus need, and funding versus need. The society interviewed more than 2,000 engineers in preparing the report. The consensus was that the three top areas of concern were roads, bridges, and wastewater treatment facilities. This is what the report had to say about roads:

> *Poor road conditions cost U.S. motorists $54 billion a year in repairs and operating costs—$275 per motorist. Americans spend 3.5 billion hours a year stuck in traffic, at a cost of $63.2 billion a year to the economy. Total spending of $59.4 billion annually is well below the $94 billion needed annually to improve transportation infrastructure conditions nationally. . . . The nation continues to shortchange funding for needed transportation improvements.[12]*

In short, the report concluded that America is failing in its responsibility to address the nation's significant and troubling infrastructure deficit—the gap between what is being spent and what needs to be spent in order to keep infrastructure in good repair. Implicitly, the ASCE report also lays bare the utter failure of the federal government—which has woefully and inadequately funded infrastructure maintenance, operation, and construction—to pull its weight.

Because much of the country's 20th-century metropolitan infrastructure is reaching its capacity, new capacity will have to be added to meet 21st-century needs. The

2008 ULI/Ernst & Young infrastructure report states that "since the 1970s, the country has coasted, not planning or investing nearly enough."[13] Moreover, the federal government has "dramatically reduced its share of [infrastructure] spending, pushing more of the burden on cash-strapped states and local governments."[14] The local and state shares of funding have increased, while overall spending as a percentage of gross domestic product has decreased.

Chapter 4 emphasized that land use planning should precede efforts to increase capacity in transportation infrastructure. "Planners must decide where they want growth to occur, and then build the roads and put the transit and other infrastructure there," says ULI's Robert Dunphy.[15] Following this strategy will induce development where it makes the most sense.

Local officials understand the perils captured by Figure 5-2 all too well. Just five days before the Minneapolis tragedy, Douglas H. Palmer—mayor of Trenton, New Jersey, and president of the U.S. Conference of Mayors—said on National Public Radio, "Of course I know we have a responsibility to rebuild [Iraq's] infrastructure, but we need to take care of home as well, because this is important for our future generations."[16] And in testimony before Congress, Kathleen Novak, mayor of Northglenn, Colorado, and the first vice president of the National League of Cities, said that "current levels of federal spending . . . fall far short of the actual costs of maintaining and improving our nation's infrastructure, and the shortfall is too large for local governments to make up on our own."[17]

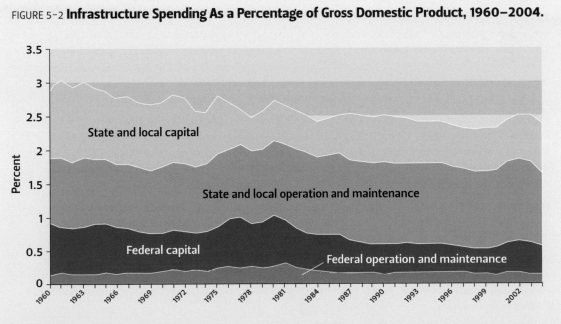

FIGURE 5-2 **Infrastructure Spending As a Percentage of Gross Domestic Product, 1960–2004.**

**SOURCE:** Congressional Budget Office, *Trends in Public Spending on Transportation and Water Infrastructure, 1956–2004* (August 2007).

# AN ACTION AGENDA FOR INFRASTRUCTURE

The Urban Land Institute recommends the following eight infrastructure principles, which it believes will help make America's communities, regions, and the nation appealing, competitive, and sustainable places in which to live, work, and play.

1 **Build a vision for the community.** Lead with a vision. No matter what their level of affluence, all communities deserve high-quality, well-maintained infrastructure and thoughtful civic design. Infrastructure investment should be informed by a long-range vision for quality of life. Encourage strong community participation in the visioning process. Build walkable communities with access to transit to reduce the overall cost of living, increase affordable housing, and create access to good jobs. Encourage strong community building.

2 **Invest strategically.** Decisions made about infrastructure must begin with land use objectives. Make strategic, performance-based, outcome-oriented investments that support a common regional agenda. Cooperate across jurisdictions to produce infrastructure that encourages population and economic growth. Consider conservation of scarce resources in all investment decisions. Set criteria.

3 **Fix and maintain first.** Repairing and maintaining existing infrastructure keeps communities healthy and competitive. Invest in existing infrastructure before building new infrastructure. Before undertaking repair, evaluate old infrastructure against current standards to make sure that good money does not follow bad. Ensure that all investments are performance based. Create a schedule for funding and maintenance, and stick to it.

4 **Reduce driving.** Current infrastructure patterns precipitated growth in urban travel that far exceeds population growth—resulting in congestion, pollution, greenhouse gas emissions, and driving costs. Reduce VMT by promoting projects that encourage bicycling, walking, and the use of public transit. Make drivers pay the full costs of driving. Foster development patterns that provide transportation choices in individual communities rather than merely discouraging travel through congestion charges and tolls. Build transit to serve existing towns before stretching out to sparsely populated areas.

5 **Couple land use decisions with water availability.** Merge land and water use planning, renegotiate regional water use agreements, and create shared portfolios of water solutions to sustain growth. Advocate for states to actively encourage conservation, find new sources of water, and share costs for desalinization and graywater treatment plants. Encourage state and regional agencies to coordinate water use, flood planning, and land use data.

6 **Break down government "silos."** Governments must integrate infrastructure investment and sustainable land use by mandating cooperation among agencies. Use a regional vision to speak in one voice. Unify capital budgets to coordinate spending. Pool program dollars across agencies. Ensure that standards across agencies are not in conflict. Screen and score infrastructure funding requests, from open space to sewers to schools, through a matrix that encourages smart land use and sustainable development.

7 **Pay up.** Infrastructure spending must support sustainable land use objectives, rather than promote sprawl. Resist pork-barrel spending. Educate and persuade voters that their tax dollars support valuable projects with long-range benefits. Create funding policies that lead private investment to desired locations. Apply user fees, rather than subsidies, to guide behavior, reward smart choices, and discourage the waste of limited resources. Recognize the full cost of choices and be honest about who is paying for them.

8 **Keep score.** Reward municipalities that invest strategically in infrastructure, and keep local governments accountable. Use scorecards to level the competition for scarce public capital. Fund good projects that have strong smart growth and sustainability metrics.

Federal, state, and local public policies that follow these principles will encourage communities to make smart infrastructure decisions and connect to the region and the nation. Without such policies to guide infrastructure investment at the state and federal levels, local municipalities will have little technical ability or incentive to shift their investment strategies.

**SOURCE:** Adapted from ULI–the Urban Land Institute and Ernst & Young, *Infrastructure 2008: A Competitive Advantage* (Washington, D.C.: ULI–the Urban Land Institute, 2008), 55.

## What Can We Do?

What can we do to resolve America's infrastructure deficit? In 2005, ULI launched an infrastructure initiative in response to the belief—shared by many—that America's decision-making processes for infrastructure were flawed. The Institute's work since then has underscored the need to take a new approach—to inject new metrics into infrastructure decision making that encourage density, smart growth, and sustainability, and that reconnect infrastructure to land use and the built environment. Many of the elements of this new approach were described in the preceding chapter, in the context of transportation infrastructure; they are equally relevant to most other types of infrastructure. During the past few years, ULI trustees, members, staff, and outside experts have been asking, "What guiding principles or 'smart choices' can ULI promote to ensure that future new infrastructure is built intelligently?" The eight "first principles" outlined in the accompanying feature box are the product of their discussions.

### Finding the Money

The immediate question that comes to mind is, How on earth are we going to find the money? The answer is, we'll find some here, some there, and some somewhere else. Government budget deficits at the federal, state, and local levels; citizens' resistance to higher taxes; and increasing competition for government resources are the main culprits responsible for our nation's underinvestment in infrastructure. All three levels of government, as well as the private sector, need to share the burden of overcoming the infrastructure deficit. In New Orleans, for example, the levees are a federal responsibility; the interstate roads and bridges belong to the state; the pumps, streets, and alleys fall under the city's jurisdiction;[18] and the power company, Entergy, is privately owned and operated.

Perspectives on infrastructure funding are divided between traditionalists, who want to increase the fuel tax to fund the shortfall, and market-oriented innovators, who see "tolling, direct pricing of road use, private capital, private road concessions and public/private partnerships" as the central elements in infrastructure funding.[19] In Maryland, traditionalists such as Governor Martin O'Malley and Secretary of Transportation John D. Porcari advocate spending nearly $400 million more a year on transportation priorities—which would be supported by the addition of 12 cents to the 23.5-cent Maryland gas tax.[20]

Leaders in the "innovator" group include officials like U.S. Secretary of Transportation Mary Peters, Indiana governor Mitch Daniels, and Chicago mayor Richard M. Daley. Peters states the innovators' philosophy succinctly: "We're never going to solve congestion with higher federal gas taxes or additional earmarks; instead, we need fresh approaches like new technology, congestion pricing and greater private sector investment to get America moving again. . . . We must stop relying on yesterday's ideas to fight today's traffic jams."[21] Citing the reluctance of voters to accept gas tax increases in the face of already high gas prices, the Texas legislature's 122-19 vote against indexing the gas tax to inflation, and a poll showing that 62 percent of respondents in Minnesota oppose higher gas taxes to fix infrastructure, Ken Orski remarks: "Public opinion and the mood of the times seem to be on the side of the Innovators."[22]

But both sides are right. Closing the infrastructure gap will require both traditional sources of funds—including income, sales, and property taxes; water and sewer fees; general

## FIVE PRINCIPLES FOR SMART INFRASTRUCTURE INVESTMENT

Sunne Wright McPeak, former secretary of the California Business, Transportation and Housing Agency under Governor Arnold Schwarzenegger, is now CEO and president of the California Emerging Technology Fund, a statewide nonprofit organization dedicated to accelerating the deployment of broadband technology and closing the digital divide. In her keynote address to the 2007 ULI Forum on Infrastructure and Western Growth Patterns, she enumerated five principles for smart infrastructure investment:

1 **Begin with land use.** Fostering more efficient land use patterns will accommodate an expanded, adequate housing supply on less land than current sprawl trends forecast, provide consumers with more housing and transportation choices, reduce negative impacts on valuable habitat and productive farmland, decrease air pollution, and increase resource use efficiency.

2 **Make all infrastructure investments performance based and outcome oriented.** That is, use performance standards (such as reduced congestion and improved throughput, resource efficiency, increased walking and bicycling, at least a 50 percent fare-box return for public transit, and reduction of average trips generated per household by 20 to 40 percent) to evaluate proposed projects.

3 **Integrate strategies and investments.** The $12 billion in general-obligation bonds to be raised by the GoCalifornia program should be targeted toward the goals of improved air quality and transportation.

4 **Incorporate an ethic of stewardship for the future and the environment.** A cabinet-level climate action plan to reduce greenhouse gas emissions and require responsible energy use and generation needs to be enacted.

5 **Reform the way in which infrastructure is designed, financed, and constructed.** Infrastructure investments need to be coupled with land use planning to reverse sprawling, low-density development. Government agencies at all levels should identify planning funds over which they have control to put into a pot that can be used for developing an action plan to achieve the goals of a prosperous economy, a high-quality environment, and social equity. Infrastructure assistance from state and federal sources should be directed toward regions and jurisdictions that "accommodate within their boundaries enough housing for their natural population growth and workforce expansion."

Pointing out that "our usual discussions on infrastructure focus on what we are spending, not what we are getting," McPeak said that Governor Schwarzenegger asked her and other cabinet members what it would take to improve conditions in California, without concern for funding. The goal was not "to build our way out of congestion," but to drive congestion below today's levels while accommodating growth. The cost was estimated at more than $100 billion. California voters approved a state bond issue in December 2006, but more is always needed. The California efforts may or may not reduce congestion, but thanks to strong leadership, the state at least understands that it is actually possible to make improvements, and not simply allow roads, transit, and other infrastructure to deteriorate. As McPeak says, "Politics may be the art of the possible, but leadership is the art of the impossible."

**SOURCE:** Sunne Wright McPeak, keynote address, ULI Forum on Infrastructure and Western Growth Patterns, Los Angeles, 2007.

**1** Sunne Wright McPeak, speech presented at the ULI Center for Balanced Development in the West, Los Angeles, September 2007.

tax revenues; and bond issues—and more innovative, market-oriented sources such as public/private partnerships, user fees, tolls, transit fares, developer impact fees, tax increment financing, congestion pricing, and monetization of certain public facilities (assets).

Infrastructure funding is one area where public officials probably should take the lead, even though it is a tough sell politically. Stephen R. Blank, ULI senior resident fellow for finance, believes that private sources will remain interested in investing in infrastructure for the foreseeable future, but notes that suppliers of capital "cannot act as leaders because they are conflicted as to motives, objectives, and constituents (none of whom may reside in the city or county being financed)." He asserts that government—"local, municipal, regional, statewide, nationwide—needs to set its priorities, explain them to the public by quantifying the benefits and risks, accept responsibility for implementation, management and control, and then *get to it*, placing controls and measurable goals in plain sight."[23]

If the ASCE estimate that repairs to deficient bridges alone will cost $9.4 billion *a year* for 20 years is even close to the mark,[24] it seems appropriate to create a domestic "Marshall Plan for Infrastructure" to assist in funding the infrastructure deficit, as will be discussed later in the chapter. Hours before the 2007 Minneapolis bridge collapse, senators Christopher Dodd (D–CT) and Chuck Hagel (R–NB) announced a proposal for a national infrastructure bank that would use government bonds to finance capital investment. A few days later, James Hovland, mayor of Edina, Minnesota, asked:

> At the end of the day, do we, as voters in Minnesota, have the collective financial fortitude to demand that all our state elected officials finally make the transportation system infrastructure commitments necessary to keep us safe and competitive in the future? Let's hope that with this tragedy vividly in mind, our executive and legislative branches alike, in special session, create a financial strategy that assures a sound public infrastructure system for the future.[25]

## The Federal Role

There is no question that the federal government has a role to play in funding infrastructure. By doing three things, it could bring more efficiency to our country's logistical needs. First, it could place a higher priority on infrastructure funding. Second, it could create an integrated system in which airports, seaports, roads, highways, railways, and bridges fit into a cohesive whole. Europe, for example, is connecting its cities with a network of high-speed trains that travel at speeds of nearly 200 miles per hour (322 kilometers per hour).[26] In America, the Interstate Highway System created such a network for cars and trucks a couple of generations ago; now it's time for a next-generation plan that will coordinate and oversee establishment of "a transformative program linked to national competitiveness and sustainability."[27] This will involve decisions about transport corridors, global pathways, primary gateways, and coordination of state and local projects with the national plan. Third, the federal government could develop a mechanism for funding such a program. No small plans will suffice. In this instance, bigger *is* better. Why not enact and fund a domestic Marshall Plan for Infrastructure, at, say, $100 billion annually? That figure has been identified as today's equivalent of the $13 billion Marshall Plan, which helped finance Western Europe's recovery after World War II. If Congress really wants to think big, it could increase that figure to $740 billion—today's equivalent of the 5.4 percent of the gross national product that was directed to the Marshall Plan in 1947.[28] One is, of course, prompted to ask where the money will come from. This is not the place to advocate a particular funding source, but some that are being bruited about include a national bank backed by bonds, a national excise tax on automobiles and trucks, an increased gas tax, and a national lottery.

Politicians typically prefer to ignore infrastructure issues and let the next administration deal with them, because discussion of the subject inevitably leads to the no-no of raising taxes. Yet what has happened recently in New Orleans, New York City, and Minneapolis should have sounded a wake-up call that will produce some action. After all, there are historical precedents for massive federal support of infrastructure improvements—Thomas Jefferson and the Gallatin Plan, a federally financed network of roads, canals, and, later, railroads, named after Jefferson's Secretary of the Treasury, Albert Gallatin;[29] Abraham Lincoln and the transcontinental railroad; and Dwight D. Eisenhower and the Interstate Highway System.

The call for a national infrastructure plan comes from a variety of sources. In November 2004, ULI awarded Richard D. Baron, CEO of the St. Louis-based development firm McCormick Baron Salazar, its prestigious J.C. Nichols Prize for visionaries in urban development. Baron well understands the daunting challenge of funding these capital requirements if cities are left on their own, and in his acceptance speech he pointed to federal neglect as a prime reason for the decline of municipal infrastructure. Baron suggested that "some form of national urban development bank should be created to assist in financing the redevelopment of vacant land, abandoned plant sites, deteriorated commercial districts, empty schools, and closed shopping centers."[30] Partially as a result of Baron's call to arms, ULI launched its infrastructure initiative in 2005, which produced the highly regarded and widely read *Infrastructure 2007: A Global Perspective*, and, a year later, *Infrastructure 2008: A Competitive Advantage*. The first report asserts: "Let's accept as a given that funding U.S. infrastructure will cost big bucks—money for which federal, state, and local governments have not yet adequately planned or budgeted."[31] The second warns: "Ante up or fall behind."[32]

Professors Michael Pagano and David Perry, of the University of Illinois at Chicago, have suggested creating a new federal urban infrastructure bank and/or crafting an infrastructure restoration grant.[33] In the words of Pagano and Perry, "The imperatives of sound urban infrastructure are both so central to the health of cities and the nationstate, and, at times, so costly that they require a national fiscal response that is part grantor and part guarantor."[34] Felix Rohatyn, the well-known New York invest-

## COORDINATION IN MASSACHUSETTS

In 2003, under Governor Mitt Romney, Massachusetts established the umbrella Office for Commonwealth Development (OCD), with an environmentalist, Douglas Foy, as its first head. The OCD's purpose is to "promote sustainable development through the integration of energy, environmental, housing, and transportation policies, programs, and regulations." Anthony Flint, who worked under Foy, points out that "instead of operating in isolation, agencies that spend billions in capital and operating funds for critical infrastructure need to join forces."[1] Cabinet secretaries continued to run their own agencies and undertake new initiatives, but the OCD, as a standalone superagency, sent agency bureaucrats a strong message about coordinating their efforts and overcoming the silos in which they had been residing. As a result, says Flint, Massachusetts has been able to encourage dense residential development in town centers and downtowns; provide $30 million for transit-oriented development; set priorities by filtering $500 million in funds for local infrastructure; and help cities and towns create their own sustainable development initiatives.

The OCD worked because it was given the power of the purse strings. Previously, different agencies often worked at cross-purposes. The environmental agency, for example, might purchase land for open space, but then the department of transportation could build an arterial road next to it, which would spur development companies to lobby to get the land reopened for development. Foy was able to look at all the projects that required funds, and then rate them on the basis of long-term plans. Agencies were expected to take into account each project's environmental, transportation, housing, and energy impacts. Money was no longer being thrown at projects without an overarching vision; all projects were expected to work toward the same vision. The organizational structure proved to be effective. However, it takes strong central leadership to make such an organization work. The structure doesn't take power away from local municipalities (the agencies within the OCD were already statewide); it merely combines them and therefore forces them to act efficiently.

This model can work in many other states, particularly in northeastern states, where silos are entrenched. It is heartening to note that Connecticut governor Jodi Rell has already established the Office for Responsible Growth to coordinate housing, transportation, environmental, and economic development. The governors of New York and Virginia are considering their own versions of the OCD. In addition, California has pulled together business, housing, and transportation under one roof.

**1** Anthony Flint, "Agencies Working Together," *Boston Globe,* December 19, 2006.

ment banker, and Warren Rudman, the former senator from New Hampshire, have chimed in with a plan that might be eminently compatible with, and a vehicle for, a new Marshall Plan for infrastructure.[35] They argue that "the nation's infrastructure crisis is no less serious for being silent," and that a federal role is needed to fix it—a role reconceived, redrawn, and refinanced.

Rohatyn and Rudman recommend establishing a national investment corporation (NIC) along the lines of the European Investment Bank. The NIC would have the authority to issue bonds with maturities of up to 50 years to finance infrastructure projects. The bonds would be subject to due diligence and underwriting; they would be guaranteed by the federal government, and the NIC would be the "window" through which local and state applications for federal funding would pass. Over time, Rohatyn and Rudman foresee the NIC replacing the existing dedicated trust funds.

Fortunately, several pieces of pending congressional legislation would give higher priority to national planning for infrastructure maintenance and construction, through the creation of a national infrastructure bank that would be separate from the Highway Trust Fund. One can only hope that that such a plan will become the law of the land sooner rather than later.

## The Role of State and Local Governments

State and local governments have not ignored the infrastructure deficit. According to Rohatyn and Rudman, they are spending at least three times as much on infrastructure as the federal government.[36] The percentage of highway spending provided by the federal government since World War II, for example, has never exceeded 30 percent and currently stands at approximately 23 percent. According to the U.S. Conference of Mayors, in fiscal year 2005, local government expenditures on sewers and water supply totaled $82 billion—95 percent of all spending on sewers, and 99 percent of all spending on water.[37]

State governments usually control significant amounts of infrastructure funding. States such as Massachusetts recognize the role that infrastructure investment plays in growth policy, and channel such investments to support infill and urban reinvestment (see the accompanying feature box). Since 1971, the Minneapolis–St. Paul region has participated in a tax-sharing regime that spreads funds for schools and infrastructure throughout a seven-county area. While less prosperous counties typically receive more money than they contribute, the funds have helped the region as a whole by ensuring that every county has adequate infrastructure.

In 2005, the state of Washington, under the leadership of Governor Christine Gregoire, enacted a user fee in the form of a motor fuels tax that was phased in over time. The tax, which had reached 37.5 cents a gallon (9.9 cents a liter) as of July 1, 2008, is expected to raise $8.5 billion.[38] The legislature approved the tax to help fund nearly 300 projects over 16 years, including repairs of the state's dilapidated and congested roads and bridges, and improvements to highway safety and freight mobility.[39]

The California Infrastructure and Economic Development Bank (I-Bank) created the Infrastructure State Revolving Fund (ISRF) to provide low-interest loans to infrastructure projects ranging from highways and transit to defense conversion and sewage treatment. The ISRF uses a 200-point rating scale—which focuses on job creation and economic development, but also awards points for land use and environmental protection—to determine which projects are eligible for loans. Since June 2000, the I-Bank has approved more than $300 million in loans from the ISRF to finance a variety of infrastructure projects. And, in November 2006, California voters authorized $42.7 billion in bonded indebtedness for transportation, levees, water quality, open space, schools, and affordable housing. It is conceivable that other states could take similar steps. The problem with bonds, however, is that the burden of amortizing them falls on all taxpayers, whereas a motor fuels tax is paid primarily by users (car and truck drivers).

## Who Benefits? Who Pays?

As local officials have endeavored to adapt to the changing fiscal environment, traditional ways of funding infrastructure repairs and construction have been supplemented by other strategies. Municipalities sometimes capture sales tax and property tax revenues for capital projects. User fees—such as parking meter fees or wheel taxes, which charge for services enjoyed only by certain segments of the citizenry—have been enacted. Self-supporting enterprise funds, such as water utilities or city markets, have been set up. Special districts with their own taxing powers (water and sewer, insect and pest control, flood control and drainage, parks and open space, bridges and tollways, and so forth) have been created. Lease-back authorities have been created that enable cities to lease public infrastructure facilities to private entities and, in return, receive revenue that is considered nontax income. Tax increment financing has been used to raise money within a district. Even homeowners' associations have agreed to finance some infrastructure.

Perhaps most obviously, municipalities have floated industrial revenue bonds, regular revenue bonds, and general-obligation (GO) bonds. Municipalities have also entered into partnerships with the federal and state governments. When some highways and sewage treatment plants were constructed in the 1970s, for example, the percentage of participation was typically 75 percent federal, 15 percent state, and 10 percent local. For the Interstate Highway System, the ratio was 90/10/0. But those days are gone. The monies in the intergovernmental pipeline have largely dried up, and cities cannot float enough municipal bonds to get the job done.

Local budgets routinely reflect the issuance of bonds, and the revenues that are needed to pay them back in a timely fashion. When I was mayor of Indianapolis, we tried to make certain that no more than 10 percent of our budget would go to amortization of debt, and that no more than 50 percent of allowable bonding capacity in any district would be used: it seemed only prudent not to get overextended. As noted in the preceding chapter, voters in places like Denver and Austin have already made commitments to raise substantial funds for light-rail transportation. Phoenix has authorized new funds for roads and transit. In 2006, the citizens of Orange County, California, voted to extend an existing half-cent sales tax for an additional 30 years, a move that is expected to bring in almost $12 billion over 30 years to fund a host of transportation projects, including transit. The city of Santa Ana, to cite one example, has proposed a light-rail/streetcar project that appears to be eligible for funding under the program.[40]

Because local governments lack the authority to impose gas taxes, and since state politicians are usually loath to do so, bond issues—which have to be paid back and will thus burden the next generation—have become the funding vehicle of choice. The result, according to Dunphy, is that when bonds are issued, "drivers, truckers, transit riders, and water customers who will be the primary beneficiaries will not have to pay any more than nonusers."[41] He asks, "Does it make any sense for migrant workers to help rebuild California's infrastructure, while the guys who drive the big rigs and

Hummers take a pass?" When road users are charged, for example, those who drive more pay more. That seems to be fair. Some critics complain that such user charges are regressive, and they may indeed place a heavier burden on the poor than on the rich. But is there an alternative? If infrastructure is supported *only* by other funding sources—sales taxes, impact fees, and so forth—those who drive a lot typically end up paying the same as those who drive less. So any system that does not charge users gives them a pass.

The focus for funding infrastructure today must be on two issues: who benefits, and who pays. Like private developers, public transportation agencies prefer to finance projects with other people's money. Various units of government are therefore exploiting the fact that national and international investment funds are looking for investment opportunities. But involving the private sector in the financing or provision of infrastructure is not a new idea: toll roads date back to colonial days, and until the 1950s, public transit systems were created and run by private companies. Once the notion of "freeways" is replaced by the idea of toll roads, it is easier to imagine engaging the private sector in financing infrastructure. Making the transition to private sector financing will be challenging for transportation agencies, which will need to develop skills in evaluating deals and structuring private financing arrangements. But in any case, priva-

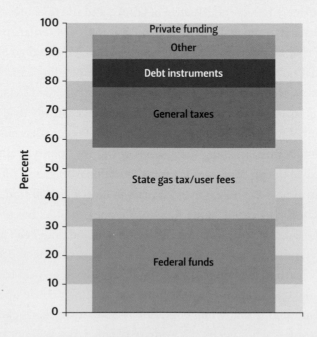

FIGURE 5-3 **Expected Funding Sources for Future Infrastructure Projects, 2008–2018.**

**SOURCE:** ULI and Ernst & Young, *Infrastructure 2008: A Competitive Advantage* (Washington, D.C.: ULI–the Urban Land Institute, 2008), 50.

tization and public/private partnerships, discussed later in this chapter, are likely to amount to a small share of a regional infrastructure network: experts peg the outer limit at around 10 percent.[42]

## User Fees

If you had stopped a group of New Yorkers on the street three years ago and offered them a chance to buy the Brooklyn Bridge, the response would have been "Fugheddaboutit"— or "What do you take us for, tourists?" Today, however, the response might be "Sure, once we finish conducting our traffic studies and line up some international lenders." It's a new world for those laboring in the field of infrastructure. What's changed?

As Figure 5-3 shows, people expect future funding for infrastructure projects to come mostly from familiar sources. But given the political reluctance to increase traditional taxes and fees, which provide a customary revenue stream for infrastructure maintenance and improvements, it seems clear that part of the solution to the infrastructure financing problem is to rely on the "user-pay" principle and on deeper involvement by the private sector. This was hinted at in Chapter 4, and needs to be explored in somewhat more detail.

Michael Pagano and David Perry have observed that there is a "historical movement" in the direction of market-based approaches to infrastructure financing—that is, away from debt and taxes and toward user fees.[43] Such a movement will increase user costs—not blatantly, as would occur through a gas tax, for example, but more subtly, through user fees and greater private sector involvement. For example, while I was mayor of Indianapolis, we enacted a wheel tax that was dedicated to funding street repairs. Only people who owned cars were affected. To cite another example, the city of Durham, North Carolina, imposes transportation impact fees on new development, and several local jurisdictions in the Triangle Area and on the Outer Banks have received authority from the North Carolina General Assembly to do the same. New residential developments can also be charged impact fees for parks, recreation, and open space; fees are typically based on square footage.

The rationale for user fees is to overcome the disconnect between those who use or benefit from certain infrastructure, like roads, and those who do not—but who still pay for such infrastructure if it is funded through general taxes. User fees link payment to the use of an asset—which, as Pagano and Perry point out, "cements the market-like relationship in the minds of the consumers, who can then adjust levels of consumption based on their preferences."[44]

Of course, asking developers to take more financial responsibility for the effects of growth increases their costs. As a result, the market-based approach to infrastructure funding does not always sit well with the private sector. In Clarksburg, Maryland, a new town being developed near Washington, D.C, developers agreed a decade or so ago to pay more than $60 million for needed infrastructure. In return, they received the right to begin to develop the town. In 2007, however, the Montgomery County Council gave preliminary approval to the creation of a special taxing district that would collect as much as $1,500 annually for 30 years from each homeowner in three Clarksburg communities to repay the developers, thus shifting the obligation from the developers back to the taxpayers.[45] While the council has yet to give final approval to the scheme, many residents objected because they rightly concluded that such a move would essentially be a gift to the developers, replacing their obligation to pay for the infrastructure with a new tax burden on the citizens of the affected communities.

## Public/Private Partnerships

Since the federal government does not provide adequate resources to help states and localities meet their infrastructure funding needs, these entities are coming up with devices of their own to fill the vacuum. One strategy is to enter into public/private partnerships (PPPs). In PPPs, the public and private sectors collaborate on a project, but government remains involved and retains a significant level of control, in order to ensure that the community receives the best value and that appropriate outcomes are achieved.[46] PPPs are useful "not only to bridge the gap between capital available and capital required for infrastructure investment," notes Ernst & Young's Dale Anne Reiss, "but also to transfer risk to the private sector and limit government's exposure."[47]

Consider two examples:

▸ Circle Centre is a $300 million, three-block downtown retail/entertainment complex in Indianapolis. The city put up about 60 percent of that amount by assembling the site and building the core, the shell, and the parking garages. It receives revenues from parking and rents, and a share of the project's net operating income. The Circle Centre Development Company investors (including one general and 19 limited partners) receive an 8 percent preferred rate of return as well as a share of the net operating income.

▸ In the Boston area, the Massachusetts Bay Transportation Authority (MBTA)—the public agency that is responsible for maintaining and expanding the regional transit system—owns 4,000 land parcels and 400 miles (644 kilometers) of right-of-way, but does not itself manage all that real estate. ULI Boston views the MBTA system as "a regional asset and critical piece of economic development infrastructure that anchors regional efforts to increase housing production, create jobs, grow smart and embrace diversity and inclusion."[48] To relieve MBTA's debt load of $8 billion, ULI Boston recommends that the commonwealth pay off bonds that were issued to fund transit projects undertaken before "forward funding" took effect in 2000.[49] But the private sector is also involved. For more than 12 years, Transit Realty Associates (TRA), a private real estate firm with a public focus, has produced more than $175 million in gross nonfare revenues and tripled the MBTA's recurring lease income. It has also helped finance the modernization of the agency's operations and fostered transit-oriented development in places such as Woodland Station, in Newton, where 180 apartments have been built by a private developer and a 548-unit parking garage is planned. "The debate [about PPPs] is over," says TRA, because results demonstrate what can be accomplished by "a dedicated program to maximize an agency's real estate holdings."[50] ULI Boston suggests that developers collaborate with the MBTA and with local citizens and agencies to change zoning regulations to permit higher densities around transit and build "more and better" transit-oriented development near existing and planned MBTA stations.[51]

Public/private partnerships don't always work out, for a number of reasons. Anticipated commitments may fall through. Either or both sides may be unable to put together the necessary financing. Community opposition can frighten off a potential participant. Irresolvable conflicts may erupt in the course of negotiations. A company could go broke. A change of public administration could kill a deal. Nevertheless, many communities have found that PPPs can be valuable tools for putting together projects that would be impossible under traditional approaches to economic development.

Each side brings important strengths to the table, and both sides can make money if the deal is properly structured. The government can raise public money, grant tax abatements, create tax increment financing districts, write down the cost of land it acquires, make grants or loans, and use eminent domain where appropriate. The private sector has design and marketing know-how, and can attract private capital and manage the project. The public sector has scant expertise in these areas, so it should avoid micromanaging and let the private sector do its thing. Successful PPPs involve a wide range of participants and stakeholders, including public agencies and officials, private for-profit companies, private nonprofit organizations, neighbors, businesses, schools, and community activists. The relationships among all these parties need to be built on a clear understanding of each participant's goals, a willingness to be flexible, consistent and coordinated leadership, fairness, and mutual trust.[52]

## Privatization

Public/private partnerships are often confused with privatization, but there is a difference. Privatization customarily involves the competitive outsourcing of some government activities to the private sector or the sale of a public asset to a private company. Local governments contract out large portions of their work in areas such as janitorial services, legal services, trash pickup, and snow removal. Sometimes large facilities, such as airports and wastewater treatment plants, are privatized. With privatization, a private entity essentially acquires and/or operates what has traditionally been public infrastructure.

Many local governments and states are selling off or leasing portions of their infrastructure to the private sector. This practice, which is believed to be bringing "dead capital" to life, is sometimes referred to as "asset monetization." If one were to propose buying the Brooklyn Bridge, it's likely that there would be sufficient interest—and money—for a "BB Investment Trust." The U.S. Department of Transportation has published model legislation to help local jurisdictions remove legal barriers to private sector investment in transportation infrastructure.[53]

Examples of privatization abound:

▸ Virginia has facilitated a 99-year lease of the nine-mile (14.5-kilometer) Pocahontas Parkway for $603 million.

▸ Pennsylvania is putting its turnpike out to bid, and 48 firms have submitted expressions of interest.

▸ New Jersey has asked the investment bank UBS to scour state government for assets or functions that could potentially be privatized.[54]

▸ Maryland and Delaware are considering leasing the toll segments of Interstate 95 to a private concession, although any such deal would require the assent of current bondholders.

▸ Chicago recently sold the Chicago Skyway Bridge to a Spanish-Australian consortium for $1.83 billion; it also sold four downtown parking garages to Morgan Stanley for $563 million.

▸ In Indiana, Governor Mitch Daniels spearheaded an initiative to lease the 157-mile (253-kilometer) Indiana Toll Road to Australia's Macquarie Infrastructure Group and Cintra SA for 75 years and $3.85 billion, in exchange for all toll and concession revenue. (Not incidentally, in the one year since it deposited the $3.85 billion check, Indiana earned more money than the toll road itself had generated in 50 years.)[55]

In a May 10, 2007, letter, the congressional leaders of the House Transportation and Infrastructure Committee, representatives James Oberstar (D-MN) and Peter DeFazio (D-OR), warned governors, state legislators, and state transportation officials against rushing into PPPs ("privatization arrangements" would have been more accurate) that may not "fully protect the public interest and the integrity of the national system." Oberstar and DeFazio stressed that PPPs can "supplement, but not provide a substitute for, public investments in transportation improvements." However, they offered no suggestions as to where these extra public funds would come from. The National Governors Association (NGA) responded, in a June 15 letter to the two congressmen, that fiscal pressures confronting the nation's transportation system, including burgeoning capacity needs and escalating operating and maintenance costs, are prompting states to look beyond traditional funding mechanisms.[56]

The upsides of privatization and the monetization of public assets seem both obvious and beguiling: immediate windfalls from the sale or lease of public assets, which can be used to address other needs; savings for taxpayers, because operation and maintenance costs are transferred to the private sector; more efficient service delivery; private sector job creation; and stable, long-term revenue streams for private investors, without the risk of investing in equities.

However, there are also drawbacks. As Bernard D. Rostker, former under secretary of the Army (1998 to 2000) pointed out recently, "The word *privatization* has gotten a black eye."[57] Selling an asset means that the governmental entity loses control of it. The public sector might not use the monies it receives in a responsible manner. Private companies could decide to defer maintenance—as, indeed, government already does—or to increase tolls above the contracted amount. They also could offer a lowball bid to get the job, then make their profit through change orders. Private entities are not accountable to the public; therefore the public could be shut out of opportunities for citizen input in the decision-making process. Political quid pro quos could be exacted (you get the contract, you make a campaign contribution, for example). Noncompete clauses in concession agreements could give private concessionaires an effective monopoly.[58] A private company could go broke. Interest rates could change abruptly. And private investors could incur substantial risks that would raise questions about liability and insurance coverage. For example, what if the Chicago Skyway—now privately owned by 12 pension funds—were to collapse like the Minneapolis bridge?

In July 2007, the Stockton (California) city council voted unanimously to scrap a $600 million deal with a multinational consortium to run its water treatment plant, even though 16 years were left on the contract. There were some legal issues involved, but more important to the citizens were noxious odors, sewage spills, fish kills, increased underground pipe leakage, high staff turnover, and, above all, escalating water rates after years of rate stability. The message from Stockton: privatization may work sometimes, but not always; some things are better left in the public domain.[59]

Privatization clearly has its plusses and minuses, but the current shifts from general-obligation bonds to revenue debt and from general tax financing to user-fee financing represent creative new efforts by state and local governments to reduce the infrastructure deficit. Privatization arrangements often look to be bargains on the surface, but it's really too early to tell whether or not they will work out, because there are so many unknown factors.

## Will the Money Be There?

In the middle of 2008—with the economy mired in a downturn that some are calling a recession, we must ask where the money for infrastructure is going to come from.[60] In the current quagmire of failing mortgage payments, heavy debt, defaults and foreclosures, and gigantic losses on Wall Street, nobody has the stomach to pay more for anything. Has the "Niagara of capital" that was flowing into real estate and some forms of infrastructure in the earliest years of the 21st century dried up? In mid-2006, Ernst & Young's Dale Ann Reiss noted that "private equity funds alone are estimated to have more than $100 billion available for investment globally, and in their search for investment opportunities, some funds are diversifying into infrastructure from real estate and other private market investments."[61] But a scant two years later, the contagion of the meltdown in the subprime market, caused in no small part by the cupidity and stupidity of the "masters of the universe" on Wall Street, has seeped into the nation's consciousness, and we are reading that a "collapse" has occurred—the result of troubles and loss of confidence in the credit and debt markets worldwide. In April 2008, *New York Times* chief financial correspondent Floyd Norris declared that "when all the losses are toted up, from mortgages to corporate loans to credit cards, the total could hit $1 trillion."[62] By the spring of 2008, the liquidity crisis had reached "epidemic proportions," according to ULI's Stephen R. Blank.[63] The question is, How long will this last?

As Floyd Norris has said, "No one—not investors, not managers, not regulators—is sure when this process will end."[64] One reason for the uncertainty is that so much depends on consumer confidence—which, as of June 2008, was still in decline.[65] In the long term, however, it is likely that confidence will be restored and that the economy will rebound, as it has after multiple economic slowdowns: 1987, 1929, 1907, 1893, 1857, and 1837, all the way back to the first crash on Wall Street in 1792.

One might be prompted to ask, given the financial stresses of 2008, whether there is any private equity floating around looking for a home. By 2006, Goldman Sachs had raised more than $6.5 billion to be invested in infrastructure. GE and Credit Suisse had announced that each would contribute $500 million to a global fund for investment in power plants, pipelines, airports, railroads, and toll roads.[66] How much institutional investors—such as pension funds, insurance companies, and investment banks—have been drained by the current collapse is difficult to determine. Nevertheless, As Ken Orski notes, "The U.S. private equity community does not intend to be left behind in exploiting investment opportunities in public infrastructure."[67] The *Financial Times* sees the infrastructure market as a hot one: "Private equity experts say infrastructure is one of the hottest asset classes at the moment because of investors' desire to buy into sectors unaffected by the credit crisis and the US economic slowdown."[68] U.S. Secretary of Transportation Mary E. Peters indicated at the end of April 2008 that "$400 billion in private sector capital . . . is available for infrastructure today."[69] Perhaps even more than that may be available. As Figure 5-4 shows, at the end of the second quarter of 2007, real estate capital sources alone amounted to some $4.6 trillion—and some of that, we can only hope, will be left after the collapse.

Steve Blank, ULI senior fellow for finance, sounds a much-needed note of optimism for the longer term:

> *Over time, assets held in inventory for sale will be reunderwritten, restructured, and repriced so that buyers will regain confidence in the process and the markets. The "fear of buying" will abate and trust will be reestablished. Losses will be taken and markets, suitably chastened, will re-open. And, it is hoped, a . . . page such as this will not be written a mere three years from today!*[70]

# An Idea Whose Time Has Come

As noted at the beginning of this chapter, America has two tasks: to properly maintain its aging infrastructure and to build additional infrastructure to support new development. We cannot simply assume that the next generation will solve the problem. "Business as usual"—meaning further deterioration—will result in economic decline and an unsustainable future. Yet maintaining existing infrastructure and building new infrastructure will be extremely expensive. We must therefore explore a broader range of financing mechanisms to help raise much-needed dollars. Because the entire nation—including the national economy—will benefit from strong, adequate infrastructure, financing through general taxation (gas taxes, highway trust funds, municipal bonds, and so on) should continue. In addition to the traditional public sources of funding, Congress should strengthen the federal role by establish an independent infrastructure bank, a national investment corporation, or a "Marshall Plan for Infrastructure."

ULI recommends the first option: funding a U.S. infrastructure bank that would issue 50-year, long-term bonds that would be aligned with the schedule for infrastructure paybacks. As the bonds are paid off, the bank would become self-sustaining.[71] The precise mechanism, however, is less important than the underlying principle: public policy should place a higher priority on infrastructure maintenance and funding: as Ken Orski has noted, "Good arguments can be made for streamlining agencies to break down funding silos and coordinate transport and land use policy, working with state and local governments.

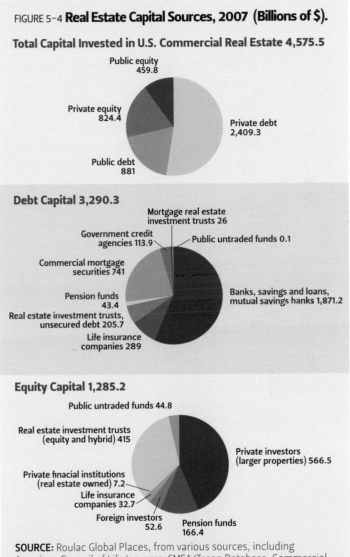

FIGURE 5-4 **Real Estate Capital Sources, 2007 (Billions of $).**

**Total Capital Invested in U.S. Commercial Real Estate 4,575.5**

- Public equity 459.8
- Private equity 824.4
- Public debt 881
- Private debt 2,409.3

**Debt Capital 3,290.3**

- Mortgage real estate investment trusts 26
- Government credit agencies 113.9
- Public untraded funds 0.1
- Commercial mortgage securities 741
- Pension funds 43.4
- Real estate investment trusts, unsecured debt 205.7
- Life insurance companies 289
- Banks, savings and loans, mutual savings banks 1,871.2

**Equity Capital 1,285.2**

- Public untraded funds 44.8
- Real estate investment trusts (equity and hybrid) 415
- Private finacial institutions (real estate owned) 7.2
- Life insurance companies 32.7
- Foreign investors 52.6
- Pension funds 166.4
- Private investors (larger properties) 566.5

**SOURCE:** Roulac Global Places, from various sources, including American Council of Life Insurers, CMSA/Trepp Database, Commercial Mortgage Alert, Federal Reserve, FannieMae.com, IREI, NAREIT, PricewaterhouseCoopers, and Real Capital Analytics, as cited in ULI–the Urban Land Institute and PricewaterhouseCoopers LLC, *Emerging Trends in Real Estate 2008* (Washington, D.C.: ULI–the Urban Land Institute, 2007), 23, with corrections.

**NOTE:** Excludes corporate, nonprofit, and government equity real estate holdings, as well as single-family and owner-occupied residences. Figures are as of second quarter of 2007, or in some cases projected through the second quarter of 2007.

At the very least, the 100-plus federal programs doling out money for transport projects need consolidation."[72]

Giving users a larger opportunity to participate in infrastructure financing is another idea whose time has come. The public sector ought not to bear the burden alone. One recent survey showed that a majority of respondents believe "total reliance on public resources and the fuel tax to fund investments in transportation infrastructure is no longer a realistic option. . . . Private capital and toll revenue financing will play a major role."[73] As painful as it may be, users also have a responsibility to support infrastructure. Just as people who want to be married have to pay a fee for a license, or those who want to travel from Buffalo to Albany on the New York State Thruway have to pay a toll, those who want and need to use the nation's public infrastructure should also pay.

Ken Orski has suggested that we should be working toward a gradual transition to a more market-oriented approach to building and managing infrastructure.[74] Orski's analysis is on target: government at all levels ought to develop mechanisms to capitalize on user-generated revenues. The market-oriented approach is based on the principle that "those who use, pay"—an idea whose time has come. Both this chapter and the preceding one have explored a few of the strategies that can be used to facilitate market-oriented funding: electronic toll collection, the imposition of road-user fees, developer fees, dynamic pricing, congestion zone pricing, private capital investment through the monetization of certain public assets, and public/private partnerships. No single strategy is perfect—but, used judiciously, each could help our various levels of government fund the infrastructure deficit and contribute to a better quality of life for all Americans.

### ENDNOTES

1   ULI–the Urban Land Institute and Ernst & Young, *Infrastructure 2007: A Global Perspective* (Washington, D.C.: ULI–the Urban Land Institute, 2007), 4.

2   Ibid., 30.

3   According to the *New York Times*, there is a distinction between *structurally deficient* and *functionally obsolete*. The first term does not mean that a bridge, for example, is dangerous or unsafe, but that it can no longer carry the load it was intended to support; the second term means that the bridge is too narrow or has inadequate clearance. Matthew L. Wald, "Deficient, but Not Necessarily Dangerous," August 5, 2007, section 4, 2.

4   *Opportunities in Private Infrastructure Investments in the US* (Deutsche Bank Group, May 2006), 4.

5   Quoted in William H. Hudnut III, *Cities on the Rebound* (Washington, D.C.: ULI–the Urban Land Institute, 1998), 110.

6   See Eloise Aguilar and Robbie Dingeman, "Sewer Work Nearly Done, Finally," *Honolulu Advertiser*, December 22, 2006, 1.

7   Pat Choate and Susan Walter, *America in Ruins: The Decaying Infrastructure* (Durham, N.C.: Duke University Press Paperbacks, 1983).

8   Dale Anne Reiss, "Infra-Investment," *Urban Land* (July 2006): 28.

9   National Petroleum Council, "Facing the Hard Truths about Energy," 2007; www.npchardtruthsreport.org/.

10  For a full discussion of this issue, see Michael A. Pagano and David Perry, "Financing Infrastructure in the 21st Century City: 'How Did I Get Stuck Holding the Bag?'" Great Cities Institute (GCI) Working Paper, Series GCP-06-02 (Chicago: GCI, College of Urban Planning and Public Affairs, University of Illinois at Chicago, May 12, 2006); available at www.uic.edu/cuppa/gci/publications/workingpaperseries/pdfs/GCP-06-02%20Michael%20Pagano&David%20Perry.pdf.

11  American Society of Civil Engineers (ASCE), *2005 Report Card for America's Infrastructure* (Washington, D.C., and Reston, Virginia: ASCE, 2005); available at www.asce.org/reportcard/2005/index.cfm.

12  Ibid., 34.

13  ULI–the Urban Land Institute and Ernst & Young, *Infrastructure 2008: A Competitive Advantage* (Washington, D.C.: ULI–the Urban Land Institute, 2008), 11.

14  Ibid.

15  Robert Dunphy, conversation with author, April 24, 2008.

16  *U.S. Mayor*, August 13, 2007, 7.

17  Sherry Appel, "NLC Tells Congress . . . ," *Nation's Cities Weekly*, September 10, 2007, 1.

18  Pagano and Perry, "Holding the Bag," 27.

19  C. Kenneth Orski, *Innovation NewsBriefs*, August 30, 2007.

20  See Phillip Rucker, "Study to Weigh Feasibility . . . ," Washington Post, September 27, 2007; and John Wagner, "Plan Falls Short . . . ," *Washington Post*, September 25, 2007.

21  Quoted in C. Kenneth Orski, *Innovation NewsBriefs*, September 18, 2007.

22  Ibid.

23  Stephen Blank, e-mail to author, August 17, 2007.

24  Leslie Wollack, "Congress and National Groups Examine . . . Infrastructure Needs . . . ," *Nation's Cities Weekly*, August 27, 2007, 1.

25  James B. Hovland, "A Conflict at the Helm of MnDOT?" *Minneapolis Star Tribune*, September 13, 2007, op-ed page.

26  ULI and Ernst & Young, *Infrastructure 2008*, 7.

27  Ibid.

28  Niall Ferguson, "Dollar Diplomacy," *New Yorker*, August 27, 2007, 81ff.

29  See Robert Fishman, "1808–1908–2008: National Planning for America," in *America 2050* (New York: Regional Plan Association, July 2007), 1.

30  Richard D. Baron, speech presented at the ULI fall meeting, New York, November 3, 2004.

31  ULI and Ernst & Young, *Infrastructure 2007*, 50.

32  ULI and Ernst & Young, *Infrastructure 2008*, 2, 11.

33  See Pagano and Perry, "Holding the Bag," 24.

34  Ibid., 23.

35  Felix Rohatyn and Warren Rudman, "It's Time to Rebuild America," *Washington Post*, December 13, 2005, A27.

36  Ibid.

37  "Infrastructure," *U.S. Mayor*, August 13, 2007, 7.

38  See Governor Gregoire's Web site, www.governor.wa.gov/priorities/transportation/default.asp.

39  "WA Gas Tax Up 1.5 Cents Tuesday to 37.5 Cents a Gallon," *Seattle Times*, June 30, 2008; available at http://seattletimes.nwsource.com/html/localnews/2008025506_webgastax30m.html.

**40** Ali Taghavi, Hobbs Institute, Chapman University, e-mail to author, May 6, 2008.

**41** ULI blog, November 13, 2006.

**42** ULI and Ernst & Young, *Infrastructure 2008*, 50.

**43** Pagano and Perry, "Holding the Bag," 1.

**44** Ibid., 28.

**45** Miranda Spivack, "Montgomery Tax Proposal Assailed," *Washington Post*, March 23, 2007, B1.

**46** Rick Norment, "Public-Private Partnerships for a Stronger Community," *Nation's Cities Weekly*, August 20, 2007, 6.

**47** Reiss, "Infra-Investment," 28.

**48** "On the Right Track: Meeting Greater Boston's Transit and Land Use Challenges," ULI Boston District Council Report, May 2006, 3.

**49** Ibid., 8.

**50** Joe Clements, "Transit Realty Starts Third MBTA Contract," GlobeSt.com, September 10, 2007.

**51** Ibid., 7.

**52** See Mary Beth Corrigan et al., *Ten Principles for Successful Public/Private Partnerships* (Washington, D.C.: ULI–the Urban Land Institute, 2005).

**53** See U.S. Department of Transportation, Federal Highway Administration Web site, www.fhwa.dot.gov/ppp/legislation.htm.

**54** See Christopher Swope, "Unloading Assets," *Governing* (January 2007): 36ff.

**55** Robert W. Poole, *Surface Transportation Innovations*, Issue #47 (September 2007); available at www.reason.org/surfacetransportation47.shtml.

**56** This exchange is well documented in C. Kenneth Orski's "News from the Transportation Front," reports 15 through 17, *Innovation NewsBriefs*, 2007.

**57** Bernard D. Rostker, speaking in a forum on privatization sponsored by ULI, the Woodrow Wilson International Center for Scholars, and Jones Lang LaSalle, April 30, 2008.

**58** C. Kenneth Orski, "The Debate on Public-Private Partnerships Has Been Joined," *Innovation NewsBriefs*, March–April, 2007.

**59** Adam Snitow and Deborah Kaufman, "Taking Back Our Water," *USA Today*, August 21, 2007, 11A.

**60** A recession is customarily defined as a decline in the nation's real gross domestic product, or negative real economic growth, for two or more successive quarters.

**61** Reiss, "Infra-Investment," 30.

**62** Floyd Norris, "Anatomy of a Collapse," *New York Times Book Review*, April 20, 2008; available at www.nytimes.com/2008/04/20/books/review/Norris-t.html.

**63** Stephen R. Blank, "A Simple Analogy," *Urban Land* (February 2008): 200.

**64** Norris, "Anatomy of a Collapse."

**65** Joshua Zumbrun, "Technically, No Recession (Feel Better?)," Forbes.com, April 30, 2008; www.forbes.com/businessinthebeltway/2008/04/30/economy-recession-fed-biz-wash-cx_jz_0430econ.html.

**66** Ryan Orr, "The Privatisation Paradigm: Jumping onto the Infrastructure Bandwagon," *Infrastructure Journal* (September–October 2006): 16.

**67** C. Kenneth Orski, "Beyond the Tipping Point IX," *Innovation NewsBriefs*, January–February, 2007.

**68** Francisco Guerrera, "Funds Get $10 Billion to Tap Global Expansion," *Financial Times*, May 12, 2008, 1.

**69** Mary E. Peters, "Opportunity 08: Transportation and the Economy," speech presented at the Brookings Institution, April 28, 2008.

**70** Blank, "Simple Analogy," 200.

**71** ULI and Ernst & Young, *Infrastructure 2008*, 52.

**72** Ibid.

**73** C. Kenneth Orski, "A Fresh Look at the Role of Private Investment in Transportation Infrastructure," *Innovation NewsBriefs*, May 15, 2008, 1.

**74** See C. Kenneth Orski, "A National Highway Program for the 21st Century—A Vision Scenario," *Innovation NewsBriefs*, March 14, 2007, for a more detailed analysis of this new philosophy of infrastructure funding.

# CHAPTER 6

# Get a CLUE: Climate, Land Use, and Energy

> Unless we abate the growing threat of global warming pollution, everything we do today to make a better world for tomorrow will be for naught.
>
> —ROBERT E. MINSKY, FORMER MAYOR, PORT ST. LUCIE, FLORIDA

*America's dependence on cars and roads has deconcentrated metropolitan settlements. But our migration away from the central city depended on the widespread availability—and afford-ability—of oil. Without this oil, and without alternative fuels and better transportation options, our suburbs will go into an irreversible decline. The more Americans drive, the more greenhouse gas emissions they generate, and the more they contribute to global warming. We are now beginning to understand the potential impact of two converging forces—decreasing oil supplies and increasing global warming—on the way that suburbia and exurbia are being built. As a nation, we must become more aware of the costs of low-density development, and of the need to reduce dependence on the automobile. Fortunately, the focus is shifting to greener and more compact development—specifically, transit-oriented and mixed-use development. In addition, Americans are beginning to attend to the risks of insuring coastal properties, and to develop a stronger ethic of conservation.*

**In the 1950s,** crude oil and gas prices were low, and inexpensive energy was readily available. Wartime rationing had ceased, and the family car provided the ticket to a freewheeling lifestyle. Since the postwar era, the nation's development patterns have relied on the automobile as the dominant—and often the only—mean s of transporta-tion, particularly for the vast majority of people who live, work, and play in the suburbs. The result? America is the world's primary source of the greenhouse gases (GHGs) that cause global warming. The carbon-based fuels—oil, coal, and natural gas—that supply the

U.S. economy with 85 percent of its energy also generate most greenhouse gases,[1] and transportation alone accounts for a full third of all carbon dioxide ($CO_2$) emissions in the United States.[2]

Sometime in the not-too-distant future, higher energy costs and global warming will coalesce into a "perfect storm" of forces that will drastically alter our way of life—unless we take steps *now*. Although most of us are not scientists, it is hard to escape three conclusions: First, because the world's supply of oil is finite, production and reserves will eventually peak and then decline—and, if demand continues to exceed supply, this will happen sooner rather than later. Second, there is a great deal of evidence to support the claims that global warming is taking place. And third, the combination of peak oil and global warming provide reason for serious concern.

## The Rising Cost of Energy

World oil demand in 2005 was approximately 82.5 million barrels per day, and total world oil production amounted to only about 81.1 million barrels per day—a difference that, over the course of a year, amounts to a 511-billion barrel discrepancy.[3] If demand continues to outstrip supply, prices will be driven upward. Yet for years, Americans have been buying more cars, driving more, and therefore using more fuel, remaining sulimely

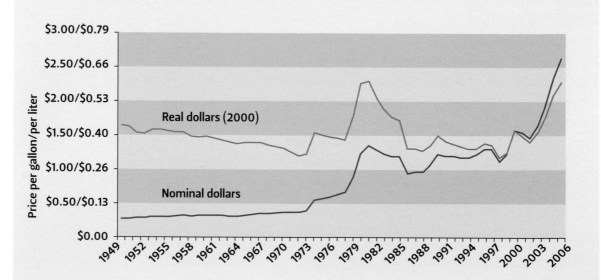

FIGURE 6-1 **U.S. Motor Fuel Prices, 1949–2006.**

**SOURCE:** Department of Energy (DOE), Energy Information Administration, *2006 Annual Energy Review* (Washington, D.C.: DOE, 2006).

**NOTE:** Prices for 1949–1977 are for regular leaded; prices for 1977–2006 are for all grades.

nonchalant about the possibility of running out of gas or not being able to afford it—although this attitude is beginning to change. Most Americans still rely on having a car to meet some of their transportation needs, but they can take two steps in the face of the high cost of energy: drive less and buy more fuel-efficient cars.

Although the number of vehicle-miles traveled (VMT) in the United States rose 2.7 percent a year from 1980 to 2005 and 1.9 percent from 2000 to 2005, it rose only 0.3 percent from 2005 to 2007—and actually dropped 4.4 percent between March 2007 and March 2008.[4] A combination of soaring gas prices (reaching more than $4 a gallon [$1.06 a liter] in the summer of 2008), demographic shifts (an aging population, younger people moving downtown, slower growth in the number of minority and women drivers), traffic congestion, and expanding public transportation choices seem to be putting a brake on people's driving. As illustrated in Figure 6-2, American drivers are cutting back—for the first time in 26 years. Anecdotal evidence suggests that high gas prices have forced many commuters to switch to mass transit, and that drivers are also cutting down on their driving for other purposes, including vacations, shopping trips, and chauffeuring kids to various activities. On June 2, 2008, "Ridership on Mass Transit Breaks Records," was one of the front-page headlines in *USAToday*; the accompanying article cited figures showing that from January to March of 2008, transit ridership had increased 3 percent over the same period in 2007—to 2.6 billion rides.[5]

In addition to driving less, many Americans are queuing up to buy more fuel-efficient cars. As oil and gasoline costs continue to climb—perhaps to as high as $500 a barrel for oil and $10 a gallon ($2.64 a liter) for gas—strong steps will have to be taken to develop such cars and trucks, and to unleash alternative sources of renewable energy. Rising energy prices are also having a serious impact on consumer confidence, and on the amount of money available for discretionary consumer spending. Changes in the price and availability of energy are likely to have more serious and transforming consequences for American culture and way of life than anything that's happened in decades.

## Global Warming

Within the scientific community, there is growing consensus that climate change is occurring, and that it is largely a result of GHGs emitted into the atmosphere by human consumption of fossil fuels. As early as December 2004, *Science* magazine stated that none of the 928 published peer-reviewed scientific articles on global warming disagreed with the consensus position that global warming is a fact.[6] In 2007, the Intergovernmental Panel on Climate Change (IPCC)—in a report written by more than 600 scientists, reviewed by another 600 experts, and edited by bureaucrats from 154 countries—made an "unequivocal" claim that the world faces serious consequences from climate change.[7] Even the president of Royal Dutch Shell, one of the world's largest oil companies, has warned that "easy oil is over. The debate over climate change is over. The only question is what we do about it."[8]

In the United States, average temperatures nationwide in 2006 were 2.2 degrees Fahrenheit higher than the mean temperatures nationwide for the entire 20th century. Globally speaking, the winter of 2006–2007 was the warmest on record: in the Northern Hemisphere, the combined land and ocean temperatures were, on average, 1.3 degrees Fahrenheit higher than they have been since record keeping began in 1880.[9] According to the IPCC, if the concentration of carbon dioxide ($CO_2$) in the atmosphere doubles from the pre-Industrial Age average of 280 parts per million (ppm), the average temperature is likely to increase between 4 and 8 degrees;[10] however, according to a 2007 article in the *Washington Post,* the globe "cannot sustain an additional temperature rise of more than two degrees Fahrenheit."[11] Currently, the concentration of $CO_2$ is 380 ppm—higher than at any time in the past 650,000 years—and is rising at the rate of 2 ppm a year.

The IPCC says that unless the world's spiraling growth in GHG emissions ends before 2015, the average global temperature will increase by 3.6 degrees, and there will be "extremely serious," even "terrifying," consequences, including "widespread extinctions of species, a slowing of the global currents, decreased food production, loss of 30 percent of global wetlands, flooding for millions of people and higher deaths from heat waves."[12] Princeton professors Robert Socolow and Stephen Pacala opine that "the boundary separating the truly dangerous consequences of emissions from the merely unwise is probably located near, but below," a doubling of the 18th-century concentration of $CO_2$. Business as usual may mean reaching 14 billion tons (12.7 billion metric tons) of carbon a year by mid-century, in contrast to the 7 billion tons (6.3 billion metric tons) we emit today.[13] This is simply not sustainable.

Let's consider just two aspects of the destabilizing impact of global warming. First, according to the Center for Research on the Epidemiology of Disasters, throughout the world, there have been "four times as many weather-related disasters in the last 30 years than in the previous 75," and the United State has suffered "more weather-related disasters than any other country."[14] Second, the current trends in the release of $CO_2$ and other GHGs into the atmosphere "threaten to raise sea levels as much as three feet [0.9 meters] by the end of the 21st century."[15] Worldwide, "a massive loss of ice, a long-predicted consequence of global warming, is now in progress, from Alaska to Patagonia, from the Rockies to the Alps."[16] If, for example, the Greenland ice sheet, which shrank by 50 cubic miles (208 cubic kilometers) in 2005, were to melt completely, sea levels would rise 20 feet (six meters), while a "mere" three-foot (0.9-meter) rise would flood prime real estate from San Francisco to New York and "turn at least 60 million people into refugees."[17]

As Carnegie Fellow David Rothkopf suggests, "We're not 'post-Cold War' anymore; we're pre- something totally new."[18] *New York Times* columnist Thomas L. Friedman takes a similar view: "I'd say we're in the 'pre-climate war era.' . . . Intensifying climate change, energy wars, and petroauthoritarianism will curtail our life choices and our children's opportunities every bit as much as Communism once did for half the planet."[19] As we plan for the future, we should sail between the Scylla of an apocalyptic vision of our future and the Charybdis of complacency. The earth is warming, and human beings are causing most of this warming. But that does not mean the world will come to an end tomorrow. We can—and must—plan for a sustainable future, by changing the ways we develop metropolitan America. Fortunately, Americans seem to be waking up to this challenge.

## What Does This Mean for How We Design Our Future?

ULI chairman Todd Mansfield has said that "climate change has added an important new dimension to land development issues we have been grappling with for a long time."[20] As the age of inexpensive energy ends, and global warming lurks in the shadows of our sunlit lives, we might well ask: What impacts will these forces have on metropolitan form? On land use patterns? And on the lives of our children and our grandchildren? It

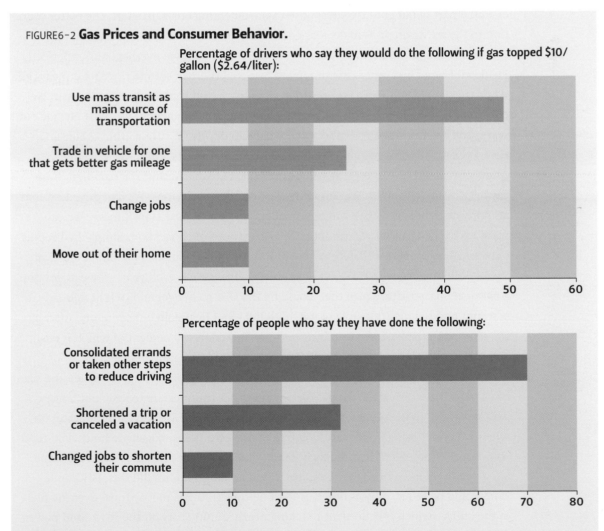

FIGURE6-2 **Gas Prices and Consumer Behavior.**

Percentage of drivers who say they would do the following if gas topped $10/gallon ($2.64/liter):

SOURCE: Paul Overberg and Larry Copeland, "Drivers Cut Back—a 1st in 26 Years," *USAToday*, May 18, 2007, A5; www.usatoday.com/news/nation/2007-05-17-gas-prices_N.htm.

is becoming clear that we must take action now to address rising energy costs, climate change, and other pressing environmental issues. Five actions can be taken as a starting point: develop an ethic of conservation; build green communities; develop compact communities; focus on transit-oriented development; and consider the impact of global warming on investment and insurance.

## An Ethic of Conservation

With the price of fuel climbing so rapidly, American attitudes are shifting from favoring conservation to calling for more production of domestic oil. That is understandable, and policy makers may decide to allow increased production, in order to achieve greater oil independence. In the long run, however, since fossil fuel is finite, since our appetite for oil does not seem to be abating, and since global warming appears to be caused mostly by GHGs generated by the burning of carbon-based fuels,[21] conservation should form an essential part of our country's response to the emerging crisis. In short, the better solution to the fix we are in is to decrease demand rather than to increase supply.

Americans waste so much energy! We leave lights on; we overheat our imperfectly insulated homes and offices in winter and overcool them in summer; we let our cars idle when they could be turned off; we drive when we could walk or use mass transit; we construct new buildings with scant attention to energy efficiency. We must change our ways, and the first—and essential—step will be to develop a strong ethic of conservation. Even small conservation efforts can have large impacts. There are so many ways Americans could save energy. It will be difficult, but we can shift the paradigm from capacity to sustainability. We can reorganize our daily activities. We can drive less, and at more efficient speeds. We can buy smaller cars. We can use transit more. We can wake up to the fact that we cannot build our way out of congestion. Simply by keeping our cars' tires properly inflated, we could save 1.2 billion gallons (4.5 billion liters) of the 130 billion gallons (492 billion liters) of gasoline we use each year.[22] We can develop a national infrastructure plan that would fix the U.S. passenger and freight railroad systems, and highlight the role of rail, both light and heavy, in our economy. After all, the railroads' core business is to transport raw materials (30 percent of which is coal), and in terms of tons moved per gallon of fuel, railroads are more efficient.[23]

We can build smaller houses. We can recycle. We can preserve green space and plant trees, which are the earth's lungs. We can jigger our thermostats to keep our homes a little warmer in the winter, a little cooler in the summer. We can turn the water off when we're not using it. We can switch to fluorescent bulbs: if a single household used six compact fluorescent light bulbs instead of incandescent ones, it would save some $72 a year (and use a third of the electricity); if a million homes did this, GHG emissions could be reduced by as much as 154,000 tons (139,706 metric tons) over the life of the bulbs—which is equivalent to taking nearly 30,000 cars off the road—and power demand would be reduced by about 24,400 kilowatts.[24] (In Australia, if a proposed requirement to use compact fluorescent bulbs is enacted, the country's carbon emissions will be reduced by 4 million tons [3.6 million metric tons] every year.)[25] Our religious traditions teach us the importance of being good stewards of the gifts we have received, and while this is not the place to go into the myriad ways we can practice conservation, it is important to point out that if each person does what he or she can to conserve energy, the combined efforts will have a significant impact.

Many cities are also doing what they can. Take Keene, New Hampshire, for example. Having experienced floods, high winds, ice storms, heavy rainfall, and damage to natural resources, the citizens of this small municipality (population 23,000) recognized that they could not just sit back and hope someone else would fix the problem. So they adopted a GHG emission-reduction action plan in 2004. Under this plan, the city

- Uses biodiesel fuel for municipally owned diesel vehicles and machinery
- Has installed a landfill methane-recovery system to provide energy to operate the city's recycling and solid waste transfer facility
- Uses a geothermal pump system to heat and cool its public works facility
- Uses energy-efficient light-emitting diode lights in its traffic signals
- Uses bicycles for downtown and neighborhood police patrols
- Has adopted an anti-idling policy for nonemergency city vehicles
- Has instituted a recycling program in all city buildings.[26]

## Green Communities

There can be no question that global warming and higher energy prices are having an impact on the nation's consciousness (and conscience) and influencing how we think about conservation and the built environment. As awareness of the need for greater environmental conservation, energy efficiency, and healthier places to live and work becomes more widespread, demand for green buildings, houses, and communities, which will be discussed in more detail in Chapter 9, will increase. Preserving green space will become more important as we consider the sustainability of the built environment.

The good news is that developers are making efforts to create green master-planned communities. One such community is Highlands' Garden Village, a mixed-use urban infill project situated between two historic neighborhoods in Denver, Colorado. Denver-based Perry Rose, an affiliate of the Katonah, New York–based Jonathan Rose Companies, undertook the transformation of the 27-acre (11-hectare) site, which was formerly occupied by an amusement park, theater, and display garden. Nature is woven throughout the community: a spine of parkland runs through the development; and residential, commercial, and retail uses are interspersed among gardens and public green spaces. The residences—including townhouses, single-family homes, live/work lofts, condominiums, and market-rate and affordable apartments—and 70,000 square feet (6,503 square meters) of office and retail space are set among pedestrian-friendly parks and walkways; the proximity of different uses encourages walking.[27] The site is located near downtown, and is situated on several bus lines, which helps reduce automobile use and transportation costs. Developer Jonathan Rose notes that the "green urbanism" of High-lands' Garden Village is an example of "biophilic design," which reflects "the essential human desire to live in community, while connected to nature."[28] It serves as a mean-ingful alternative to the "wanton environmental destruction and placeless character of post–World War II suburbanism"[29] and provides "a model for the reuse of vacated urban sites including declining malls, brownfields, and other abandoned urban areas."[30]

Mueller, a similar master-planned green community, is on the drawing boards in Austin. Under the ambitious plan, the Robert Mueller Municipal Airport would be redeveloped as a mixed-use urban village in the heart of the city. The hope is that the 711-acre (288-hectare) site will become a transit-oriented community with intercon-nected open space, pedestrian pathways, and five miles (eight kilometers) of hiking and biking trails. The vision calls for Mueller to become home to approximately 10,000 residents and 10,000 permanent employees. The award-winning master plan, designed according to new urbanist principles, will include a mixed-use town center; LEED- (Leadership in Energy and Environmental Design) certified buildings; some historic restoration (the old hangar and control tower); approximately 140 acres (57 hectares) of public open space; public art; and 4,600 residential units, 25 percent of which will be set aside for affordable housing. The Dell Children's Medical Center of Central Texas is already up and running in Mueller, and is on its way to becoming the first hospital in the world to achieve LEED platinum status. In the development of the hospital site, about 40 percent fly ash was substitute for traditional cement in the concrete mix; the result-ing drop in $CO_2$ emissions is equivalent to taking 450 cars off the road.[31] The community is being developed by a public/private partnership between the city of Austin and the Denver-based development company Catellus. The goal of both partners is to build a green community that decreases automobile use, increases energy efficiency, promotes environmental conservation, and fosters economic development.[32]

Greenlaw "Fritz" Grupe, chairman of the Stockton, California–based Grupe Company and a past chairman of ULI, is accomplishing a similar goal at Sanctuary, a master-planned community on the northwest edge of Stockton. At buildout, the development will contain 7,000 residential units and 250,00 square feet (23,226 square meters) of retail. Higher densities will be concentrated at the heart of the community, above and around the town center, and densities will taper off as one moves farther away. In contrast to the typical "sprawling" community, Sanctuary will have a pedestrian-friendly layout. The concentration of services in the town center will enable residents to walk more and drive less, and is anticipated to reduce the number of automobile trips by 10,000 per day—a notable accomplishment.[33]

## Compact Communities

City dwellers simply produce less carbon than suburbanites.[34] A recent Brookings Insti-tution study concludes that each resident of the nation's largest 100 metropolitan areas is responsible, on average, for 2.47 tons (2.24 metric tons) of carbon dioxide—14 percent below the national average of 2.87 tons (2.6 metric tons).[35] Why? Because development is more compact and densities are higher in cities, city dwellers make greater use of mass transit, walk more, and drive less. Several environmental and planning experts have warned that if local governments do not take active steps to limit sprawl now, the United States will find it nearly impossible to make deep cuts in GHG emissions in the decades to come.[36]

The goal of the Sacramento "blueprint" (mentioned in Chapter 3) is to limit sprawl by creating more compact neighborhoods and denser downtowns, and encouraging people to use bikes and light rail. The approach mandates an average of ten housing units per acre (25 per hectare). According to the *Wall Street Journal*, Sacramento has become "one of the nation's most-watched experiments in whether urban planning can help solve everything from high fuel prices to the housing bust to global warming."[37] The head of the Sacramento Council of Governments, Mike McKeever, points to some interesting facts to vindicate the initiative: "Between 2004 and 2007, the number of projects with apartments, condominiums and town houses for sale in the region increased by 533%, while the number of subdivisions with homes on lots bigger than 5,500 square feet [511 square meters] fell by 21%."[38]

Planning can help, but so can the market. It can do what government cannot: persuade people that density makes sense. David Mogavero, a Sacramento-based architect, predicts that "expensive oil is going to transform the American culture as radically as cheap oil did."[39] It is certainly making people take the blueprint more seriously. In a poll conducted in early 2008 by California State University, Sacramento, 12 percent of respondents indicated that they had changed jobs or moved in the past year "to shorten their commute to work."[40]

The authors of *Growing Cooler: The Evidence on Urban Development and Climate Change* make a compelling argument that compact development can and should be a key tool in offsetting the detrimental impacts of climate change. In fact, the book contends that compact development can be an even more powerful strategy than improved automobile fuel efficiency. *Growing Cooler* suggests that developing 60 percent of new growth in compact communities can prevent up to 85 million metric tons from reaching the atmosphere by 2030, just by getting more people out of cars. This would be equivalent to a 28 percent increase in federal vehicle efficiency standards, and would make a good start in reducing a decades-long trend of unsustainable development.[41]

VMT directly affects energy use and GHG emissions. Housing and commercial development clustered efficiently around transit—and in walkable communities and commercial centers—yields lower VMT and lower GHG emissions than housing in low-density communities on the distant suburban edge and sprawling retail and commercial campuses that can be reached only by automobile. Ed McMahon, ULI/Charles Fraser senior resident fellow for sustainable development, frames the issue simply: "We have two real choices for future development: we can grow more compactly, or we can continue to sprawl across the landscape at great economic, environmental, and social cost."[42]

We need a new pattern for future metropolitan development. We don't expect people to abandon their cars completely, but well-designed mixed-use communities could reduce both auto use and energy consumption, while at the same time meeting the needs of an increasingly diverse U.S. population. The sitcom suburbs no longer provide the kinds of places in which many of today's Americans want to live, work, and play. With today's high energy costs and credit crunches, the 6,000-square-foot (557-square-meter) house 30 miles (48 kilometers) from the center of town is the most obsolete product on the housing market—just as the large, gas-guzzling SUVs are the most obsolete products in the auto market. We need more choices and we need to grow smarter. And growing smarter means growing more compactly.

Higher densities are a necessity if we are to address the issues of sprawl and energy conservation. Noted urban writer Neal Peirce says unequivocally: "More compact development—mixed use, transit connected, democratic cities—is the *only* sustainable answer to global urban growth."[43] Yet the word *density* has so many negative connotations that perhaps we should dispense with it entirely and instead talk about intensifying land uses.

Three things are worth mentioning in the context of higher-density development. First, as noted earlier, densities in America have been decreasing since World War II, so increasing densities today can be seen as a return to more traditional development patterns rather than as a radical departure from them. Second, higher-density development can be designed in ways that are acceptable to most people. Third, 83 percent of Americans (more than four out of five) live in metropolitan areas.[44]

Many of America's most valuable and admired places—including Georgetown, in Washington, D.C.; Old Town Alexandria, Virginia; Lower Downtown (LoDo), Denver; and South Beach, Miami—are high-density communities. Middleton Hills, Wisconsin; Crawford Square, in Pittsburgh; Addison Circle, in Texas; and Courthouse Hill, in Arlington, Virginia, offer more recently developed examples of well-designed, intensive land uses that finesse many of the often-cited objections to higher-density development. They represent ways to artfully increase the intensity of land use through smaller lot sizes, narrower streets, more efficient parking, and accessory dwelling units over garages.[45] Converting single-family homes into duplexes—or even triplexes or quadriplexes—or converting a bedroom into a granny flat, can also help, as Jane Jacobs points out in the discussion of "sprawl densification" in her last book.[46]

Crawford Square, for example, snuggles 426 homes—including affordable and market-rate units, and rental and for-sale apartments, townhouses, and single-family homes—into an 18-acre (seven-hectare) site on the eastern edge of downtown Pittsburgh, in a badly deteriorated area. The development, which was master planned and designed by the Pittsburgh architectural firm Urban Design Associates, and developed by St. Louis-based McCormack Baron Associates, is designed in the Colonial Revival style, reflecting the character and scale of Pittsburgh's traditional urban neighborhoods. The street grid was modified to reconnect the neighborhood to downtown businesses, cultural attractions, and places of entertainment. Speed bumps are used to slow traffic, the entire community is pedestrian-friendly, and residents enjoy easy access to public transportation.[47]

The federal government defines a metropolitan area as "a dense cluster of 50,000 or more people, together with the surrounding jurisdictions from which it draws the bulk of its workers."[48] The nation contains 363 such areas. Ours is a much more urban— though less concentrated—America than that of the 1950s. Cities—with their cultural assets, their institutions of higher learning, their skilled labor, their ports of commerce and gateways for immigrants, their centralization of wealth-generating businesses that place a higher premium on brains than brawn—have become crucibles of creativity that cannot survive without density. That's where we find the innovation, human capital, infrastructure, and public and private institutions that essentially drive the American knowledge economy. As Bruce Katz, of the Brookings Institution, has pointed out, the American economy has evolved into a series of clusters, which he defines as "networks of firms that engage in the production of similar products and the provision of similar services." He adds, most tellingly, that firms within these clusters "crave proximity to pools of qualified workers" where face-to-face interaction, mobility of people and goods, and rapid sharing of ideas and innovations can occur. And that means higher densities—which are "the essence of urban places," and matter more in the knowledge economy than they did in the industrial economy.[49]

More compact communities, especially those served by transit, that incorporate smaller lot sizes; more efficient parking; integrated public open spaces and community facilities; and more intense land uses, such as live/work units, lofts, and accessory dwelling units, will produce higher densities—which, in turn, will reduce our dependence on the automobile. In areas that are not yet accessible by transit, the development of transit-ready communities may encourage local transit agencies or private companies to build new transit systems or to extend existing ones. As one ULI publication suggests, "Making these communities transit ready by establishing higher-density zones will create a built-in market that will make future transit viable."[50]

## Transit-Oriented Development

Transit-oriented development (TOD)— the creation of higher-density, well-designed communities that are well served by buses, subways, light rail, and/or commuter rail—will have to become more prevalent. Public opinion supports this point. In a 2007 survey sponsored by the National Association of Realtors and Smart Growth America, 75 percent of those polled said that improving public transportation and building communities that don't require as much driving were better long-term solutions for reducing traffic than building new roads, and 90 percent said that they believe new communities should be designed so that we can walk more and drive less, and that public transportation should be improved and accessible.[51] More availability does not necessarily mean people will choose to live in a transit-friendly neighborhood, but this option should be made available to those who are interested. As ULI's Robert Dunphy says, "We will have to get serious about providing transit options that truly compete with the convenience of the car."[52]

A rail transit station affords a marvelous opportunity to develop compactly and counteract the ever-widening gyre of land use. Arlington County, Virginia, supplies a case in point. Twenty-five years ago, Arlington planners made a conscious decision to encourage high-density development around five Metrorail stations situated along a single rail line. The compact and well-designed urban villages that resulted offer convenient automobile access and parking, a coordinated pedestrian system, revitalized neighborhoods, mixed-use properties, high-rise residential and office development, street-level shops and restaurants, and urban open space, and have greatly reduced the need for residents, office workers, shoppers, and others to travel by car. "We encourage the use of public transit and reduce the use of motor vehicles," says one Arlington County planner. Comments another: "Density makes transit work. Transit makes density possible. Cities need to be more aggressive, not just build a nice place to look at. Jane Jacobs was right: density and diversity do a city make."[53]

In Englewood, Colorado, a light-rail and multimodal transfer station has had a huge impact on the vitality of this first-tier suburban city. Near the station, which opened in July 2000 as part of Denver's Regional Transportation District, a public/private mixed-use TOD provides a model for intelligent regional design that directs development into established areas served by transit. CityCenter Englewood replaced a dead suburban shopping mall with a living, breathing downtown. The project focuses development on a central public place and includes upscale housing, a performing-arts plaza, a new city hall in a renovated department store, and extensive retail space, including a Wal-Mart that harmonizes with the surrounding context.[54]

In Arvada, at the other end of Denver's FasTracks system, mayor Ken Fellman says, "If you don't like sprawl, you had better like density. When land is limited, you have to grow vertically."[55] And that's what's happening. Although some people are resisting zoning changes that will allow taller buildings and greater density in mixed-use developments around FasTracks stops, the vertical use of land is gaining acceptance, particularly as communities come to understand that a critical mass will be necessary to support the new rail service.[56] The Denver Regional Council of Governments is advocating a 10 percent increase in the density of metro Denver communities by 2030. Metro Denver now averages four to 4.5 homes per acre (11 per hectare); increasing that to 6.5 or seven homes per acre (16 or 17 per hectare) will mean smaller lots, less water use, more compact development, shorter vehicle trips, and improved air quality—plus jobs closer to home. Concludes the *Denver Post*: "While there will always be a large audience for suburban homes with big backyards, a new audience is emerging for multi-family homes well located in the midst of thriving neighborhoods."

# The Impacts of Global Warming on Investment and Insurance

Global warming is beginning to give investors pause about where they will put their money, particularly when it comes to real estate. The title of a 2006 report by Lloyds of London says it all: "Climate Change: Adapt or Bust."[57] Mindy S. Lubber, president of Ceres, a coalition of public interest groups and institutional investors, has warned that "insurance as we know it is threatened by a perfect storm of rising weather losses, rising temperatures and more Americans living in harm's way."[58] Insurance companies are reacting by abandoning catastrophe-prone markets (including, for example, most barrier islands on the East Coast), jacking up rates, offering premium incentives for green construction and hybrid cars, investing in green companies, offering "pay per mile" car insurance, promoting markets for carbon-credit trading, and reducing their own carbon footprints.[59] To be fair to the insurance companies, while their reaction to catastrophe losses has been to withdraw from at-risk areas and raise prices, they also are working overtime to educate consumers about loss-prevention methods; to offer new products and services, such as pay-as-you-drive insurance and premium credits for owners of loss-resistant green buildings; to invest in the clean-technology sector; and to undertake in-house energy management programs.[60]

There's a lot we don't know about climate change, but we can be certain that global warming is occurring, that climate change can lead to more frequent severe weather conditions, and that insurance companies, investment managers, and other institutions charged with the pricing and mitigation of risk are paying close attention.[61] Lynn Thurber, CEO of LaSalle Investment Management, Inc., in Chicago, notes that Europe is way ahead of the United States in terms of thoughtful analysis of the impact of climate change on public policy and private investment, but she senses a growing awareness of the importance of the "greenhouse" debate in our country. She says that every time a request for proposal comes into her investment firm, a question comes up that wouldn't even have arisen just a few years ago: "What is your firm's expertise and experience in regard to energy-efficient buildings and investment in property assets in this era of global warming?"[62]

The commercial real estate industry in the United States has more than 4.6 million buildings and nearly 65 billion square feet (6 billion square meters) of space, and spends nearly $93 billion annually on energy. For the industry to remain competitive, which means keeping costs under control, proactive energy management strategies will have to be put in place, "from detailed energy audits and procurement strategies, to environmental sustainability programs and the latest technologies," according to a report developed by Jones Lang LaSalle IP, Inc. "It is clear," the report goes on, "that inaction, combined with current high prices and inevitable future price hikes, will have disastrous consequences for the corporate bottom line."[63]

It's also clear that the insurance world has focused on this problem. "The big buzz in the insurance industry today is climate change," we read in the *Washington Post*.[64] Forty-five billion dollars of insured losses from Hurricane Katrina certainly catalyzed the industry's concern. In October 2006, State Farm stopped writing new insurance on businesses within 2,500 feet (762 meters) of the ocean in Virginia Beach, Virginia. Hingham Mutual Group has canceled coverage on 9,000 homes on Cape Cod, and has withdrawn from coastal market coverage, which it considers too high risk. In Delaware, Westfield Insurance has canceled all coastal policies. In 2006, frightened by the risk of not having "the ability to manage" extreme weather events like hurricanes, ice storms, wildfires, drought, lightning strikes, soil subsidence, and wind and hail storms, Allstate Insurance stopped writing new homeowners' insurance policies for residents of New Jersey, Connecticut, Delaware, New York City, Long Island, and Westchester County—and in the most vulnerable parts of these markets, they are also not renewing existing insurance.[65] Where insurance companies continue to write policies, the premiums are skyrocketing. The *Boston Globe* warns that "global warming could soon hit homeowners in the pocketbook."[66] The long and the short of it is this: people who cannot find insurance cannot secure a mortgage—and therefore cannot purchase a house. Concludes *Newsweek:* "Regardless of who pays for the damages, climate change means tough economic choices for all Americans, 54 percent of whom now live within 50 miles [80 kilometers] of a coastline."[67]

Joseph F. Azrack, president and CEO of Citigroup Property Investors in New York, notes that people are still buying property in high-risk areas, and that while awareness of the impact of global warming is growing, the market has yet to take account of this exposure. "It's still too early to tell. Perhaps in five years, we will be clearer," he predicts. "But," he adds, "this is for sure. If the water rises even three feet [0.9 meters], cities like New York City and London will be severely affected. . . . We're beginning to think long term. Climate change will affect where and how we invest."[68] The concern from investors about how close a property is to the water, and how high it is in relation to it, is growing, advises Prudential's Charles Lowrey.[69]

On the bright side, climate change is creating tremendous opportunities to make a positive impact on global warming. The insurance industry is looking toward the development of "creative loss-prevention products and services that will reduce climate-related losses for consumers, governments and insurers, while trimming the emissions causing global warming," states Ceres, a network of investors, environmental groups, and public-interest advocates that enlists capital markets in the environmental fight. The group has published a report that identifies more than 190 concrete examples that are available or will soon be available from dozens of insurance providers in 16 countries.[70]

## How Can We Grow Smarter to Conserve Energy and Reduce Global Warming?

Surely there must be a better way for the public and private sectors to plan metropolitan America—a way that will make our cities, suburbs, and exurbs more connected and less autocentric. Of course, many Americans love living in large homes on big lots and

culs-de-sac, and are willing to put up with the long commutes that this lifestyle often
entails. But others believe that sprawl is hurting their quality of life, and these people
are looking for more choices—for something better.

Many of our current public policies have the undesirable impact of increasing sprawl,
auto dependence, GHG emissions and, consequently, global warming. Local zoning codes
require low-density, single-use development and often thwart compact development.
Public spending at the federal, state, and local levels often supports development at the
suburban fringe rather than in already developed areas. Transportation policies remain
focused on accommodating the automobile. An effective smart growth strategy to conserve energy and reduce global warming will mean rethinking these and other policies.[71]
Government need not continue to subsidize sprawl. The principles of smart growth—
mixing land uses; creating a range of housing and transportation choices; fostering walkable, close-knit, traditional neighborhoods with town centers; focusing on existing assets
like parks and transit systems; preserving open space; making development decisions
predictable, fair, and cost-effective; developing a strong sense of place; creating healthy

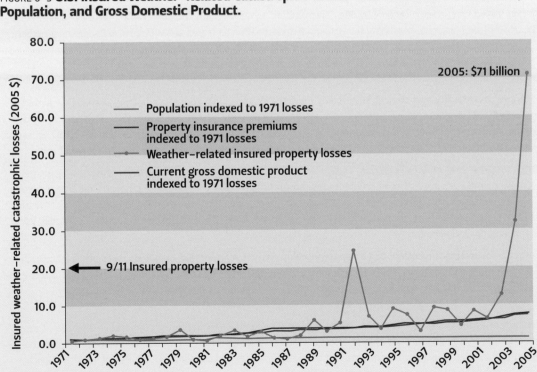

FIGURE 6-3 **U.S. Insured Weather–Related Catastrophic Losses versus Insurance Premiums,
Population, and Gross Domestic Product.**

**SOURCE:** Evan Mills and Eugene Lecomte, "From Risk to Opportunity: How Insurers Can Proactively and Profitably Manage
Climate Change," Ceres Report, August 2006: 1; http://216.235.201.250/NETCOMMUNITY/Document.Doc?id=75.

**NOTE:** To indicate relative growth rates, premiums, population, and gross domestic product are indexed to 1971 losses.

# ULI'S CLIMATE, LAND USE, AND ENERGY GUIDING PRINCIPLES

The Urban Land Institute recognizes that successful global reduction of greenhouse gas (GHG) emissions requires substantial investments in local communities. In 2007, the ULI Trustees formed the Climate, Land Use and Energy (CLUE) Advisory Group, which is made up of senior real estate professionals; together with ULI staff, the CLUE Advisory Group drafted the following principles:

1   **Foster a global response at the local level.** While the challenges are global in scope, impacts and actions will vary from region to region. Each community must adapt in unique ways and rise to the challenge of mitigating existing trends with bold and transformational long-term solutions. The effort to achieve a low-carbon global economy relies on local communities around the world.

2   **Empower strategic regional coordination.** Public and private investments made throughout our communities cumulatively determine a region's sustainability. Transportation, energy, industry, housing, and agriculture must be coordinated as part of an effective regional vision. Success depends on all levels of government being engaged in the effort to effect change.

3   **Reduce GHG emissions.** GHG emissions must be reduced in a verifiable manner, as communities and organizations make the transition to a low-carbon economy over time. The real estate sector should have the ability to participate in carbon markets by generating emissions reductions through investments in community revitalization and sustainability.

4   **Conserve natural resources by using land wisely.** Land use strategies should foster the conservation of water and energy in our communities, preserve ecological integrity, and minimize waste and pollution. Sustainable development should generally be compact, include a mix of uses, and conserve or restore land for its value as green infrastructure and to sustain biodiversity. New land use models should be pursued that allow communities and economies to grow without sacrificing the coherence, quality, or capacity of natural resource systems.

5   **Create mixed-use, mixed-income livable communities.** Employment is the cornerstone of community vitality, and housing choice is necessary to sustain a workforce. Concentrated areas of civic uses and employment can be organized with housing to form a land use framework for efficient regional transportation. Housing must include a diversity of types and a choice of locations providing easy access to employment and daily needs. Housing choice mitigates the forces of sprawl and reduces vehicle-miles traveled (VMT).

6   **Promote accessibility and choices in mobility.** Enhance ongoing innovations in automobile efficiency by reducing overall VMT. Encourage communities and regions to make moving people—rather than cars—a priority by promoting emissions-free and public modes of transportation and locating daily destinations in easily accessed places. Reducing VMT is the cornerstone of reducing GHG emissions and enhancing citizens' overall health.

7   **Track progress and explore feasibility.** Define the metrics of community sustainability, measure ongoing performance, and transparently communicate real progress with all stakeholders. Recognize that sustainable development relies on exploring feasible and practical opportunities that are grounded in reality and incorporate reasonable investment return. Sustainability grows from a culture of sound business practices, equitable fiscal management, and accountability.

8   **Cultivate leadership, invention, and entrepreneurship.** Growth is inevitable; sustainable growth is a community's choice. We can grow into a sustainable future through partnerships that transform markets and achieve the necessary economies of scale to mitigate existing impacts. Sustainable innovation is achieved through deliberate decisions made iteratively at every stage of projects and endeavors.

ULI recognizes that effective strategies to combat global climate change will require cooperative effort by all segments of the economy and all segments of society, around the globe. Given the multifaceted challenge and the many exemplary efforts by organizations around the world to meet this challenge, ULI does not seek to duplicate the effective efforts of others, such as those focused on transportation technologies or building technologies. By focusing on issues at the core of the ULI mission—the responsible use of land—ULI seeks to make an important contribution within the emerging chorus of collaboration and partnership.

**SOURCE:** ULI–the Urban Land Institute, Climate, Land Use, Energy Advisory Group, 2008.

communities for people of all ages; emphasizing historic preservation; and encouraging stakeholder participation in the decision-making process—can and should be put into practice in metro areas throughout the United States.

This is already happening. In Massachusetts, for example, the Smart Growth Fund, which is administered by the Office of Commonwealth Development, actually assists development in smart growth locations such as infill sites or suburban areas served by transit. (See the feature box "Coordination in Massachusetts" in Chapter 5.) In the Philadelphia metro area, the Delaware Valley Smart Growth Alliance reviews projects to determine whether they meet smart growth criteria, and certifies them if they do. Envision Utah is promoting smart growth as a way to save 171 square miles (443 square kilometers) of open space in the Greater Wasatch Valley. Maryland's Smart Growth and Neighborhood Conservation Act gives priority to existing, older communities for neighborhood improvements, public infrastructure, services, and schools. The point of all these programs is to foster compact development as an antidote to sprawl.

Smarter growth patterns can shape a new market profile by delivering compact, well-designed communities; mixed uses; and access to open space and transit, all of which will help reduce VMT and GHG emissions. Instances of successful compact development with well-designed, neotraditional densities abound; the following are just a few examples.

Issaquah Highlands is a high-density, new urbanist, master-planned community being developed through a public/private partnership in the foothills of the Cascade Mountains, 17 miles (27 kilometers) east of Seattle. Some 1,500 acres (607 hectares) of the 2,300-acre (931-hectare) community are being preserved as parks and open space. Plans call for a population of 8,000, to be housed in 3,290 dwellings—including single-family houses, townhouses, and for-sale and rental multifamily units, at densities of up to ten units per acre (24.7 units per hectare)—as well as 3.8 million square feet (353,031 square meters) of commercial and retail space. The developer, Issaquah-based Port Blakely Communities, negotiated agreements with the state, the city, and King County regarding zoning, vesting, transportation financing, annexation, environmental goals, and concurrency (timing development to match the construction of the infrastructure needed to service the project). This urban village is dedicated to "living green," and is constructed on principles of sustainability that encourage walking, biking, and transit use. Demonstrating how such design can create higher densities and reduce VMT, one resident says: "I was drawn to the density of the development and the sense of community that came from the sidewalks and porches and closeness of houses, the parks and common areas"; she walks to the Park-n-Ride (a 1,000-car garage) for a daily bus trip to downtown.[72]

In the central/southern part of the country, Plum Creek, a master-planned community being developed by Austin-based Benchmark Land Development, Inc., is taking shape in Kyle, Texas, approximately 20 miles (32 kilometers) south of Austin and 50 miles (80 kilometers) north of San Antonio, smack in the middle of the I-35 corridor, which promises to become one long megalopolis between the two large cities.

At buildout, the 2,200-acre (890-hectare) community will contain up to 8,700 homes, a mixed-use town center, employment districts, and a commuter rail station. Through pedestrian-friendly amenities such as narrow streets, rear-alley garages, hiking and biking trails, and sidewalks, the design places strong emphasis on reducing VMT. The commuter rail station, which is scheduled to open between 2010 and 2012, will be one of 14 stations connecting San Antonio and Austin, and thus will offer a viable alternative to the car as a means of getting to and from either city. Plans call for retail uses around the station, and for up to 1,000 units of dense multifamily housing nearby.[73]

Like Issaquah, Plum Creek can well serve as a model for a new metropolitan America. Both projects show how new development incorporating smart land use can help to conserve energy and reduce VMT while also providing more choices for more people; more attractive places for people to live, work, and play; and a better quality of life. The answer is not to reject suburbia, but to urbanize and humanize it.

Urban infill development also can accomplish the same result. Atlantic Station is a 138-acre (56-hectare) former steel mill and brownfield site in midtown Atlanta that has been redeveloped as a "new town in town," with a mix of residential and business uses. It will provide homes for some 10,000 people and employment opportunities for 30,000. Sidewalk cafés, restaurants, theaters and other places of entertainment, retail outlets, and expansive parks create a pedestrian-friendly, urban village atmosphere. A multi-modal bridge accommodating cars, pedestrians, bicycles, and mass transit spans Interstate 75/85, connecting Atlantic Station to a nearby Metropolitan Atlanta Rapid Transit Authority (MARTA) rail station as well as to ramps leading to the highway. Ironically, federal environmental regulations prohibited the use of federal funds for the bridge and ramps, because the Atlanta region was out of compliance with federal transportation conformity requirements. A U.S. Environmental Protection Agency (EPA) program, however, allows the EPA to waive environmental regulations when a superior environmental outcome can be achieved by some otherwise prohibited action. On the basis of an analysis that demonstrated that VMT and GHG emissions would be 34 percent lower at the Atlantic Station site than at three more remote greenfield sites, the EPA ultimately waived the conformity requirement for Atlantic Station.[74]

The challenges that high energy costs, GHG emissions, and climate change present for the U.S. development industry—and the housing industry, in particular—are formidable. But there is much that the housing industry, with the cooperation of public policy makers and the public, can do to address these challenges. Four of the best ways to respond to rising energy costs and GHG emissions are to build smaller single-family houses; build more multifamily housing units; invest more in historic preservation and the redevelopment of existing housing; and encourage infill development.

## Build Smaller Houses

Smaller houses—which clearly use less energy than larger ones—are growing in popularity. Small will be beautiful again. Reaction against "mansionization"—the demolition of smaller homes in order to build much larger homes on relatively small lots—is causing many jurisdictions to pass regulations to control the bulk of new houses. But the main drivers of the shift to smaller houses appear to be the downturn in the housing market and growing concerns about energy costs. For the past three decades, the average size of a new home increased by almost 50 percent—but suddenly, in 2007, the trend started to reverse, according to the American Institute of Architects (AIA). In AIA's 2007 annual survey, more residential architects reported home sizes decreasing than increasing; in the 2008 survey, architects who reported declines in the average size of homes outnumbered those reporting increases by two to one.[75] The *Washington Post* predicts that by 2015, the average single-family house will not be much larger than it is today (2,459 square feet [237 square meters]).[76]

ULI senior resident fellow and ULI/J. Ronald Terwilliger chair for housing John K. McIlwain points to the fact that "the median home size is about to decline for the first time since the early 1980s" as an encouraging sign.[77] He goes on to suggest the creation of "a residential cap-and-trade" program, since reducing home size is an effective way to reduce residential emissions. Such a program could offer credits for each home built at a size below a certain threshold—say, at first, today's median house size of 2,500 square feet (232 square meters). Those building homes larger than the threshold size would need to purchase the credits from those building smaller ones. Such a system would encourage homebuilders to construct smaller homes and would make those homes more affordable. Credits like this could be traded just as housing tax credits are today.

## Build More Multifamily Housing

The focus should not be on single-family housing alone. Multifamily dwellings use dramatically less energy than smaller single-family homes, and also help counteract sprawl. Common sense would lead to this conclusion, but some facts back it up. According to the U.S. Department of Energy's *2007 Buildings Energy Data Book*, in 2001, detached and attached single-family houses consumed 108.5 and 100.4 British thermal units (Btu), respectively, whereas multifamily units in buildings containing five or more units consumed only 41.0 Btu.[78] The rising cost of energy should encourage public officials and consumers to use a new affordability equation suggested by McIlwain: affordability = (housing cost + transportation cost) ÷ income.

## Invest More in Historic Preservation and Redevelopment

Another way to reduce residential energy use is to invest more in historic preservation, in the rehabilitation or redevelopment of existing residential structures, or in the conversion of commercial buildings to residential uses. Although some who are pursuing a green building agenda seem to think that achieving energy efficiency requires new construction, other green building advocates disagree, arguing that the greenest building is one that is already built. Michael Jackson, chief architect for preservation services at the Illinois Historic Preservation Agency, counters the notion that only new buildings can be green: "In order to realize life-cycle savings in a new building, compared with renovating an old building, the timeframes you need are longer than the predictable life of some of the buildings being built today."[79]

If a comprehensive sustainable development strategy is to be forged, it must also include the adaptive use of old sites, including historic, industrial, and residential structures. A functionally and economically obsolete building like a warehouse could be left in place or torn down. But adaptive use of the building—turning it into a museum, retrofitting it for condos or apartments, creating new office space—makes more sense. First, it preserves the urban fabric and context in terms of scale, materials, and design. Second, it enables the community to grow without having to extend water and sewer lines, roads, police and fire protection, and other services out into the country. Third, it saves energy because the existing structure contains a significant amount of "embodied energy"—"the total expenditure of energy involved in the creation of the building and its constituent materials."[80] Razing an old building means discarding this embodied energy. As real estate consultant Donovan Rypkema points out, tearing down an older building means failing to understand that "recurring embodied energy savings increase dramatically as a building life stretches over 50 years." Furthermore, tearing down and building anew involves replacing what disappears (typically brick, plaster, concrete, and timber) with materials "vastly more consumptive of energy" (typically steel, plastic, vinyl, and aluminum).[81] In short, renovating an older building simply requires less energy than building an entirely new structure.

## Encourage Infill Development

Constructing infill housing in developed areas is another answer to rising energy costs and sprawl. Most people still want to live in the suburbs, but the market for close-in housing is growing. The Brookings Institution has pointed out that about 15 percent of a city's land is vacant; this vacant land ranges from undeveloped open space to abandoned properties to polluted brownfields.[82] Not all of this land is buildable, but much of it is underused or filled with deteriorating structures, and is therefore ripe for infill development. In fact, in many cases, city liabilities can be turned into assets. If fallow urban sites such as abandoned rail yards, breweries, warehouses, or brownfields were inventoried—and if government offered developers and owners strong incentives to redevelop these properties—reasonably denser, well-designed housing could be achieved with no ill effects.

Each infill project is unique; it must be carefully planned, designed, and developed to fit the site and the context of the surrounding community. Such projects may be strictly residential, or they may include a mix of uses. But taken together, infill projects will have a cumulative benefit. Densities will be increased. A wider market will be created for those who want to move back to the city or to close-in suburbs. Infill development helps strengthen and preserve the historic character of the city and its urban neighborhoods. And these relatively small projects can create opportunities for locally oriented, small and medium-sized developers.

The obstacles to urban infill housing are considerable. Land assembly is more difficult. Environmental issues (polluted or toxic land, for example) must be overcome, and inadequate infrastructure (decrepit combined sewers, for example) has to be improved. Arranging the financing from public and private sources, and working with a city's bureaucracy, can be complicated and time-consuming. And there is always the potential for the not-in-my-backyard syndrome: neighbors who do not want anything to disturb the status quo. Nonetheless, a host of case studies assembled by ULI demonstrate how these obstacles can be overcome and financial success can be achieved.[83]

## Wake Up, America

We Americans have had it so good for so many generations that we have become complacent. Regrettably, America seems to be sleepwalking its way into the future. We seem to be coasting on our prosperity, hoping that things will not change. Our feelings of "American exceptionalism" have beguiled us into believing that we are insulated from the many problems the rest of the world faces.

But the warning bells are beginning to clang. We must wake up to the fact that the days of cheap and readily available oil are over, that the climate is changing, and that our addiction to a hydrocarbon economy is partly to blame. We cannot have lasting

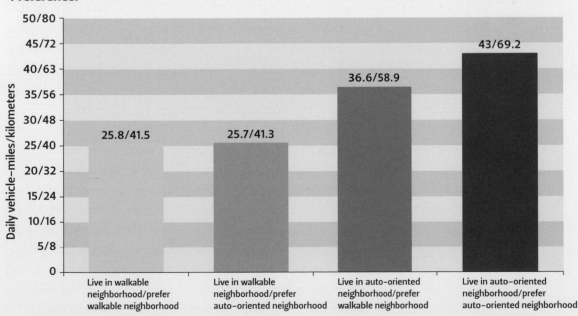

FIGURE 6-4 **Average Vehicle–Miles/Kilometers Traveled, by Neighborhood Type and Residential Preference.**

**SOURCE:** Reid Ewing, Keith Bartholomew, Steve Winkelman, Jerry Walters, and Don Chen, *Growing Cooler: The Evidence on Urban Development and Climate Change* (Washington, D.C.: ULI–the Urban Land Institute, 2008), 94.

environmental stability in a fossil-fuel-driven society. It should not take a megadisaster to persuade America (as well as India and China, which are copying America's carbon-dependent growth model) that we need to reduce our consumption of fossil fuels and decrease GHG emissions to halt global warming, or that more conclusive research and more advanced technological development of alternative energy sources are needed.

One wonders why the United States lags so far behind many European countries in moving beyond debate about whether global warming exists to implementing steps to alleviate it. The 27 countries in the European Union have invested tens of billions of euros in high-speed rail, transit, and bikeways; they have agreed upon and enacted binding green building requirements; and they have instituted a cap-and-trade system to control $CO_2$ emissions. Great Britain is taking strong steps to combat climate change through spatial planning. Under that nation's Planning Policy Statement 1,

> *regional planning bodies and local planning authorities should ensure that development plans contribute to global sustainability by addressing the causes and potential impacts of climate change—through policies which reduce energy use, reduce emissions . . . by encouraging patterns of development which reduce the need to travel by private car, or reduce the impact of moving freight, promote the development of renewable energy resources, and take climate change impacts into account in the location and design of development.*[84]

Notice that the word used is "ensure," not "encourage" or "suggest." As of July 2008, the British Parliament was considering legislation that would cut $CO_2$ emissions by at least 26 percent by 2020, and by at least 60 percent by 2050, in relation to 1990 levels.[85] There is a direct correlation between land use, VMT, and GHG emissions: the typical American suburb—low-density, disconnected, with single-use zoning and inadequate transit—encourages automobile use; but more compact, higher-density development, with a mix of land uses and a highly connected street network, leads directly to lower VMT—and to lower GHG emissions. Even if fuel efficiency improves fourfold, and even if we achieve transformational technological breakthroughs, we will still have to reduce our driving by 20 percent to achieve an 80 percent reduction in $CO_2$ emissions by 2050.[86] Reducing driving means giving people more transportation options and planning land to decrease the need for auto travel. That, in turn, means more compact development. Professor Lawrence Frank, of the University of British Columbia, has asserted that land use patterns that compel people to drive long distances just to work or to shop are "the root cause of transport emissions."[87] *Growing Cooler* estimates that a compact development strategy would reduce VMT by 12 to 18 percent by 2050, and $CO_2$ emissions from mobile sources some 7 to 10 percent.[88] The book also notes that people who live in walkable neighborhoods drive less than those who live in auto-oriented ones. And roughly one-third of current residents of automobile-oriented neighborhoods would prefer to live in a walkable neighborhood if they could find one, indicating "a ready-made market for compact development."[89]

In addition, *Growing Cooler* cites an analysis of 8,000 households in Atlanta, which concludes that "roughly one in three current residents of automobile-oriented neighborhoods would prefer to live in a walkable environment but were unable to find one, given current development patterns."[90] As Figure 6-5—drawn from a study of King County, Washington—illustrates, typical post–World War II development patterns in the U.S. yield higher $CO_2$ emissions.[91]

Living as we do, in a culture built on the availability of inexpensive gas, Americans as a nation have barely awakened to this perception, much less summoned the political will to address the issue or changed our habits. As will be seen later, mayors and some governors are moving in a positive direction, but one looks almost in vain for strong leadership from Washington, or from think tanks such as the Pacific Legal Foundation, which dismissed a draft version of *Growing Cooler* as "the latest anti-sprawl crusade based on global warming . . . no different from every other anti-sprawl campaign from Roman times to the present." Pacific Legal's spokesman James Burling then went on to say that "so long as people ardently desire to live and raise children in detached homes with a bit of lawn, there is virtually nothing that government bureaucrats can do that will thwart that."[92] To which one might add, "Perhaps so, but the price of gas may!"

Fortunately, America is adaptable, and has always been able to roll with the historical punches. The situation is not hopeless. After the mass production of automobiles began, a horse-and-buggy society disappeared. After oil was discovered, whale oil and candles were no longer needed. We can now expect new technologies to emerge that

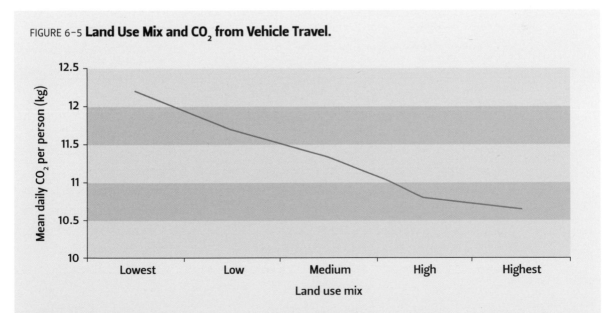

FIGURE 6-5 **Land Use Mix and CO₂ from Vehicle Travel.**

**SOURCE**: Bruce Appleyard, Lawrence D. Frank, and Sarah Kavage, "The Urban Form and Climate Change Gamble," *Planning* (August–September 2007): 19.

will help us adapt to the realities of a new global climate. New scenarios connecting land use and transportation planning will help those who work in the built environment to think and plan in terms of concurrency of infrastructure, transit-oriented development, and compact development. We can hope that our focus on these issues will become more intense. As a friend of mine puts it, "Somehow our current form of civilization has managed to solve the problems we have caused in spite of ourselves." Changing the way our society and our economy operate and summoning the political will to move in new directions will be like trying to turn a supertanker: it's tough to do, and slow to happen, but you can't wait until you run aground to figure out how to steer. Harvard professor John Holdren, a leading expert on energy and the environment, put the case well back in 2006: "If you want a different energy system in 2050, you really have to start changing it now."[93]

The message, then, is this: America, wake up! Change your ways, or you and your children will soon lose your quality of life. Begin planning now for a sustainable future, by accepting higher densities and more compact development. Build the communities of tomorrow in ways that will reduce your dependence on the car, or you will find yourselves stranded in exurbia, unable to afford the gas to fill your tank. Focus on developing new sources of renewable energy (a topic well beyond the scope of this book), or you will find yourselves victims of volatile international forces beyond your control. Fight climate warming on a global, federal, regional, and local basis, or you will be impoverished by high costs or drown in high water. Act now, or suffer later.

**ENDNOTES**

1 Robert Samuelson, "Just Call It 'Cap-and-Tax,'" *Washington Post,* June 2, 2008, A13.

2 Reid Ewing et al., *Growing Cooler: The Evidence on Urban Development and Climate Change* (Washington, D.C.: ULI–the Urban Land Institute, 2008), 2.

3 Department of Energy (DOE), Energy Information Administration, *2006 Annual Energy Review* (Washington, D.C.: DOE, 2006).

4 Federal Highway Administration, "Traffic Volume Trends," March 2008; www.fhwa.dot.gov/ohim/tvtw/08martvt/index.cfm.

5 *USAToday,* June 2, 2008, 1.

6 Naomi Oreskes, "The Scientific Consensus on Climate Change," *Science,* December 3, 2004, 1686ff.

7 Intergovernmental Panel on Climate Change (IPCC), *Climate Change 2007: Synthesis Report; Summary for Policymakers—Contribution of Working Groups I, II, and III to the Fourth Assessment Report of the IPCC* (Geneva, Switzerland: IPCC, 2007), 2; available at www.ipcc.ch/.

8 National Public Radio interview, March 15, 2007.

9 "Scientists: Winter of 2006–07 Was Earth's Warmest Ever Recorded," *USAToday,* March 15, 2007.

10 Neal Peirce, "Study Shows High Sea Rise Danger . . . ," syndicated column, September 9, 2007.

11 Juliet Eilperin, "Lawmakers on Hill Seek Consensus on Warming," *Washington Post,* January 31, 2007, A6.

12 Doug Struck, "Emissions Growth Must End in 7 Years, U.N. Warns," *Washington Post,* November 18, 2007, A10.

13 Robert Socolow and Stephen Pacala, "A Plan to Keep Carbon in Check," *Scientific American* (September 2006): 50.

14 Quoted in Charles Blow, "Farewell, Fair Weather," *New York Times,* May 31, 2008, A27.

15 Mark Hertsgaard, "While Washington Slept," *Vanity Fair,* May 2006, 200ff.

16 J. Madeleine Nash, "Chronicling the Ice," *Smithsonian,* July 2007, 72.

17 Juliet Eilperin, "Clues to Rising Seas," *Washington Post,* July 16, 2007, A6.

18 Thomas L. Friedman, "The Power of Green," *New York Times Magazine,* April 15, 2007; available at www.nytimes.com/2007/04/15/magazine/15green.t.html.

19 Ibid.

20 Todd Mansfield, remarks at ULI fall meeting, Las Vegas, Nev., October 25, 2007.

21 Samuelson, "Cap-and-Tax," A13.

22 George Will, "Same Old Soaring Gas Prices," *Washington Post,* April 5, 2007, A17.

23 J. Alex Tarquinio, "Do Railroad Stocks Have More Power to Burn?" *New York Times,* June 1, 2008, business section, 5.

24 Jenni Mintz, "Edison Has Plan to Give Away Fluorescent Bulbs," *Ventura* (California) *County Star,* April 13, 2007.

25 Michael Specter, "Branson's Luck," *New Yorker,* May 14, 2007, 123. Specter also points out that if the average American home used just one less light bulb, it "would be equivalent to removing nearly a million automobiles from the road."

26 Adam Millard-Ball, "Pollution Solutions," *Planning* (August–September 2007): 12.

27 Stephen R. Kellert, Judith H. Heerwagen, and Martin L. Mador, *Biophilic Design: The Theory, Science, and Practice of Bringing Buildings to Life* (Hoboken, N.J.: John Wiley & Sons, 2008), 302.

28 Ibid., 298.

29 Ibid.

30 Ibid., 302.

31 Mueller Web site, www.muelleraustin.com; Alan Bell, Dell Children's Medical Center, phone conversation with author.

32 Mueller Web site.

33 Greenlaw "Fritz" Grupe Jr., conversation with author.

34 "City Dwellers Produce Less Carbon, Report Suggests," cnn.com/US, May 29, 2008.

35 Andrea Sarzynski, Marilyn A. Brown, and Frank Southworth, "Shrinking the Carbon Footprint of Metropolitan America," Blueprint Policy Series, Brookings Institution, May 29, 2008; www.brookings.edu/~/media/Files/rc/reports/2008/05_carbon_footprint_sarzynski/carbonfootprint_report.pdf.

36 Juliet Eilperin, "Fighting Global Warming Block by Block," *Washington Post*, May 4, 2008, A3.

37 Ana Campoy, "With Gas Over $4, Cities Explore Whether It's Smart to Be Dense," *Wall Street Journal*, July 7, 2008, A1.

38 Ibid.

39 Ibid.

40 Ibid.

41 Richard M. Rosan, "Land Use and Climate Change," *Urban Land* (February 2008): 48–51.

42 Julie Campoli and Alex S. MacLean, *Visualizing Density* (Cambridge, Mass.: Lincoln Institute of Land Policy, 2007), back cover.

43 Neal Peirce, "'Endless' 21st-Century Cities: How Can We Make Them Livable?" syndicated column, April 6, 2008.

44 John L. Thornton, "Presidential Candidates Should Address Globalization's Challenges," *Charleston Post and Courier*, January 14, 2008; available at www.charleston.net/news/2008/jan/14/presidential_candidates_should_address_g27505/.

45 See Steven Fader, *Density by Design* (Washington, D.C.: ULI–the Urban Land Institute, 2000).

46 Jane Jacobs, *Dark Age Ahead* (New York: Random House, 2004), 215–217.

47 Urban Redevelopment Authority of Pittsburgh Web site, www.ura.org/showcaseProjects_crawfordSquare3.html.

48 Brookings Institution, "What Is a Metro Area?" Blueprint for American Prosperity: Unleashing the Power of a Metropolitan Nation; www.brookings.edu/projects/blueprint/whatis.aspx.

49 Bruce Katz, "A Much More Urban America," *Washington Post*, July 23, 2007, D3.

50 Mary Beth Corrigan et al., *Ten Principles for Smart Growth on the Suburban Fringe* (Washington, D.C.: ULI–the Urban Land Institute, 2004), 26.

51 See Smart Growth America Web site, www.smartgrowthamerica.org/narsgareport2007.

52 Robert Dunphy, conversation with author.

53 William H. Hudnut III, *Halfway to Everywhere* (Washington, D.C.: ULI–the Urban Land Institute, 2003), 330.

54 Hudnut, *Halfway to Everywhere*, 332; and City of Englewood Web site, www.englewoodgov.org/Index.aspx?page=468.

55 Ken Fellman, conversation with author.

56 The quotations and information in the rest of this paragraph are from Linda Castrone, "FasTracks Speeding Vertical Use of Land," *Denver Post*, May 29, 2007.

57 Lloyd's of London, "Climate Change: Adapt or Bust," 360 Risk Project Report, May 2006; www.lloyds.com/NR/rdonlyres/38782611-5ED3-4FDC-85A4-5DEAA88A2DA0/0/FINAL360climatechangereport.pdf.

58 Investor Network on Climate Risk, "New Ceres Report Warns of Rising Threat to U.S. Insurers and their Customers from Climate Change," news release, September 8, 2005; www.ceres. org/NETCOMMUNITY/Page.aspx?pid=322&srcid=601.

59 John Morrison and Alex Sink, "The Climate Change Peril That Insurers See," *Washington Post,* September 27, 2007, A25.

60 Evan Mills and Eugene Lecomte, "From Risk to Opportunity," *Ceres Report* (August 2006): Executive Summary, 2.

61 See L. James Valverde Jr. and Marcellus W. Andrews, *Global Climate Change and Extreme Weather: An Exploration of Scientific Uncertainty and the Economics of Insurance* (New York: Insurance Information Institute, June 23, 2006), 1, 36.

62 Lynn Thurber, conversation with author.

63 Dan Probst and John Schinter, "Energy Strategies for the 21st Century," Jones Lang LaSalle, 2006; www.propertyoz.com.au/library/06%20Energy%20Strategies.pdf.

64 Joel Garreau, "A Dream Blown Away: Climate Change Already Has a Chilling Impact on Where Americans Can Build Their Homes," *Washington Post,* December 2, 2006, C1–C2; available at www.washingtonpost.com/wp-dyn/content/article/2006/12/01/AR2006120101759_pf.html.

65 Karen Breslau, "The Insurance Climate Change: Coastal Homeowners in the East Are Losing Their Policies or Watching Premiums Skyrocket," *Newsweek,* January 29, 2007, 44; available at www.newsweek.com/id/70119?tid=relatedcl.

66 Beth Daley, "Homeowners May Feel Heat of Global Warming: Insurers Studying Impact on Rates," *Boston Globe,* August 6, 2006; available at www.boston.com/news/local/articles/2006/08/06.

67 Breslau, "Insurance Climate Change," 44–46.

68 Joseph F. Azrack, phone conversation with author.

69 Charles Lowrey, phone conversation with author.

70 Mills and Lecomte, "Risk to Opportunity."

71 Ewing et al., *Growing Cooler,* 13.

72 *Issaquah Highlands,* ULI Development Case Study C035024 (October–December 2005); Issaquah Highlands Web sites, issaquahhighlands.com/eNews/SeaMet-04.20.07. html; www.issaquahhighlands.com/; www.issaquahhighlands.com/whats_new. php?filter=events.

73 *Plum Creek,* ULI Development Case Study C036013 (July–September 2006).

74 Ewing et al., *Growing Cooler,* 86.

75 Kermit Baker, "As Housing Market Weakens, Homes Are Getting Smaller," *AIArchitect,* June 6, 2008, 1; www.aia.org/aiarchitect/thisweek08/0606/0606b_htdsq2.cfm.

76 "Survey Signals a Popularity Shift from Big Homes to Stylish Spaces," *Washington Post,* February 24, 2007, F6.

77 Quotations and information in this paragraph are from John McIlwain, "Greenhouse Gases and Green Housing," *Urban Land* (May 2007): 36–41.

78 U.S. Department of Energy, Office of Energy Efficiency and Renewable Energy, "2007 Buildings Energy Data Book," September 2007, 1–7; http://buildingsdatabook.eren.doe. gov/docs/2007-bedb-0921.pdf.

79 Tristan Roberts, "What's Green about Historic Buildings?" *Alliance Review* (January–February 2007): 6–7.

80 Donovan Rypkema, "New Life in Warehouse Districts," *Sustainable Urban Redevelopment* (Spring 2008): 8.

81  Ibid., 9.

82  See Myron Orfield and Robert Puentes, "Valuing America's First Suburbs," Brookings Institution, Center on Urban and Metropolitan Policy, 2002, 12; available at www.brookings.edu/es/urban/firstsuburbs/firstsuburbs1.pdf; Michael Pagano and Ann Bowman, "Vacant Land in Cities: An Urban Resource" (discussion paper, Brookings Institution, 2000), 3.

83  See Dian Suchman, *Developing Successful Infill Housing* (Washington, D.C.: ULI–the Urban Land Institute, 2002), 104–193.

84  Quoted in Jim Hecimovich, "Britain Goes into High Gear," *Planning* (August–September 2007): 53.

85  See the U.K. Parliament Web site, http://services.parliament.uk/bills/2007-08/climatechangehl.html. As of July 2008, the bill had been passed by the House of Lords and was being discussed and amended in the House of Commons.

86  An estimate by the Center for Clean Air Policy.

87  John Caulfield, "This Way," *Builder* (September 2007): 135.

88  Ewing et al., *Growing Cooler*, 88.

89  Ibid., 94.

90  Ibid.

91  Lawrence Frank, Sarah Kavage, and Bruce Appleyard, "The Urban Form and Climate Change Gamble," *Planning* (August–September 2007): 22.

92  Margot Roosevelt, "To Go Green, Live Closer to Work, Report Says," *Los Angeles Times*, September 21, 2007.

93  Jon Gertner, "A Nuclear Renaissance?" *New York Times Magazine*, July 16, 2006, 41.

# CHAPTER 7

# The Challenge for Housing:
# Stop Driving 'Til You Qualify

Normal is getting dressed in clothes that you buy for work and driving through traffic in a car that you are still paying for—in order to get to the job you need to pay for the clothes and the car, and the house that you leave vacant all day so you can afford to live in it.

—ELLEN GOODMAN

*Since the 1950s, middle-income families have flocked to the suburbs in search of affordable homeownership opportunities. But today's changing metropolitan form is presenting a difficult challenge: because housing costs have outstripped income, it has become impossible for many families to buy homes near their jobs, in first- or second-tier suburbs. So they drive farther and farther into exurbia, until they qualify for a mortgage. Housing in America ought to be more affordable and more available to low- and moderate-income families. We need to enact programs and policy changes—at all levels of government—to encourage the development of more affordable and more sustainable housing that is closer to workplaces. And we need to recognize that owning a single-family home in the suburbs is no longer the only ideal: many of today's and tomorrow's smaller and more diverse households will prefer other forms of housing in other locations.*

**MORE THAN ANYTHING ELSE,** owning a home has long represented the American Dream. The problem for many families today is affording one. Despite the recent downturn in the housing market—for the first time since the government began keeping records in

1950, the price of a typical U.S. house fell in 2007—many Americans still cannot afford to buy a home within a reasonable distance of their workplace.[1] This has created a workforce housing issue that must be addressed.

After World War II, homeownership took a big jump. (It has since leveled off.) The huge growth in homebuilding was accompanied—indeed, stimulated—by a tremendous increase in highway construction: in particular, by the 42,000-mile (67,592-kilometer) interstate system that was begun in the mid-1950s.[2] America's car culture exploded. Streetcars and trolleys pretty well disappeared, and automobile ownership rose dramatically. The number of cars on the road escalated from just under 26 million in 1945 to more than 52 million in 1955; by 1972, the number was 97 million.[3] The security of a single-family suburban home and the mobility of a family car was the very stuff of the American Dream, and appeared to meet the needs of our nation's workforce at the time.

But this is no longer the case. "A suitable living environment remains beyond the reach of many, many Americans. Homeownership now is just an impossible dream for many working families," says Ron Terwilliger, chairman and CEO of Trammell Crow Residential and a former chair of the Urban Land Institute. Terwilliger notes that in 2000, 90 percent of the average-income workers in Fairfax County, Virginia, just outside Washington, D.C., could afford to buy a median-priced home there; seven years later, that figure had dropped below 10 percent.[4] Although the amount of affordable housing varies from one U.S. metro area to another, the situation is tight almost everywhere.

Terwilliger—who is so concerned about the jobs/housing/transportation imbalance that in February 2007 he generously donated $5 million to ULI to establish the J. Ronald Terwilliger Center for Workforce Housing—adds that failure to address this problem "is going to continue to weaken this country in its global competition."[5] The Terwilliger Center's primary goal is to support the development of housing affordable to moderate-income workers, specifically by producing 3,500 workforce housing units—in Atlanta, southeast Florida, and Washington, D.C.—by 2012.[6]

Affordable housing has become a significant problem—and a touchy one. Everyone seems to be in favor of affordable housing, as long as it is located somewhere else: the not-in-my-backyard syndrome that surrounds affordable-housing projects can reach astounding levels of hostility. As a result, affordable housing gets a lot of talk, but far too little action. The key is to educate the public—to link affordable housing with the needs of America's police officers and firefighters, schoolteachers, auto mechanics, mail carriers, nurses, secretaries, dental assistants, custodians, and salesclerks—in short, those who make up the backbone of America's economy. These are the people who are being squeezed by the jobs/housing/transportation imbalance that permeates this country. They are paying a "time tax" because they have to spend so much time driving between their jobs and homes.[7]

The gap between income and housing prices has forced low- and middle-income homebuyers to move farther and farther away from the urban core and from the places where they work. This phenomenon may indeed be a matter of choice, reflecting the homebuyers' fundamental values about such things as time and quality of life. But for many of the 3.5 million commuters who travel 90 minutes or more each way (a number that has almost doubled since 1990), it is a necessity. These "extreme commuters" are "the fastest-growing category, the vanguard in a land of stagnant wages, low interest rates, and ever-radiating sprawl. They're the talk-radio listeners, billboard glimpsers, gas guzzlers, and swing voters, and they don't—can't—watch the evening news."[8]

Let's shift, for a moment, from homeownership to rental housing. In the early 2000s, rising home costs priced many prospective buyers out of the housing market, which made renting more attractive. Starting in 2007, the subprime mortgage crisis, coupled with tightening credit and a flood of foreclosures, again put home purchases out of reach, so renting still didn't seem like such a bad idea.[9] Long-term renters don't need a downpayment and needn't worry about future interest rates. That sounds pretty good—but let's look more closely. Among households with incomes under $10,600, 70 percent pay more than half of their incomes for housing, and among those with incomes ranging from $10,600 to $20,600, 71 percent are severely or moderately "cost burdened."[10] Thus, although renting may appear to be an affordable option in a difficult purchasing market, it is an option that will consume an inordinate portion of income in the nation's poorest households. In Montgomery County, Maryland, for example, which is by no stretch of the imagination a poor area, there are more than 5,000 names on waiting lists for public housing, and a family of four needs a household income of $67,000 a year to rent a two-bedroom apartment.[11]

According to the Joint Center for Housing Studies at Harvard University, as the larger housing market adjusts to an excess of supply and to the effects of foreclosures, rental markets will play an increasingly important role.[12] In particular, homeowners who have suffered foreclosure or lost their credit ratings will be moving into the rental market as time goes on. Rising rental costs will create substantial affordability problems for moderately and severely cost-burdened households. The income/housing-cost squeeze is also having an impact on some suburban communities, where single-family homes are being converted into eight- to ten-room boarding houses. Such arrangements lead to clogged streets and driveways, mounds of trash, and violations of health and safety standards.

## The Housing Market in Historical Perspective

In *Irrational Exuberance*, Yale economics professor Robert Shiller examined U.S. home prices between 1890 and 2004, and found that although home prices appear to be volatile, over the very long term they appreciate by less than 1 percent a year (in inflation-adjusted dollars).[13] That is not unexpected. Housing, as a concrete asset, is secure in comparison to other investments. Thus, despite recent experience, investments in housing should not be expected to provide a high rate of return.

FIGURE 7-1 **U.S. Home Prices, 1890–2004.**

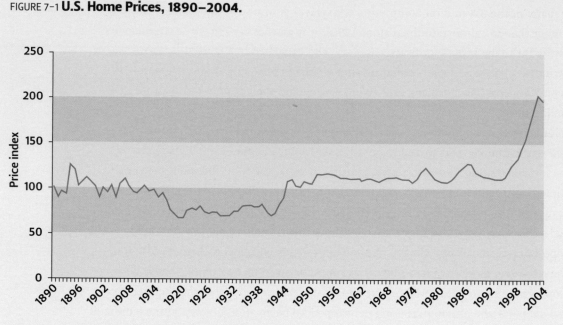

**SOURCE:** Robert J. Shiller, *Irrational Exuberance,* 2nd ed. (Princeton: Princeton University Press, 2005).

Between 1975 and 2000, the median price for an existing home increased by more than 50 percent, from less than $65,300 to $119,000 (in 2000 dollars),[14] while median income remained relatively unchanged in real dollar terms.[15] Between 1980 and 2000, the median house cost three times the median household income. Beginning in 2001, housing prices increased much faster than income—so that as of 2006, the median house cost 4.5 times the median household income.[16] The affordability problem has been further exacerbated by the fact that almost all income growth since 1975 has gone to people at the top of the income pyramid, while six in ten Americans experienced no increase in income.[17] Although the housing market rose to unprecedented heights during the early 21st century, 2005 appears to have marked the end of that exceptional expansion; since then, home prices seem to have returned to more normal rates of appreciation.

Of the factors affecting housing prices, interest rates have the most profound and complex effect. Interest rates have been volatile since 1975: from a high of 14 percent in 1981, they had fallen to a historic low of 4 percent by 2005. Moreover, in the early 2000s, banks and other lenders greatly loosened the terms for securing a mortgage, which resulted in a flood of money flowing into the housing market. This, in turn, drove up home prices. Although the median cost of a home rose substantially between 1999 and 2005, low interest rates kept monthly mortgage payments low. (The mortgage payment for a $300,000 dollar home at 5 percent interest, for example, is less than that for a $250,000 home at 7 percent interest.) Low interest rates allowed households to purchase more expensive homes without experiencing a substantial increase in their monthly mortgage payments.

The fall in interest rates created a housing bonanza: speculative buying was prevalent, baby boomers bought second homes, and many first-time buyers overreached themselves by using exotic mortgages (such as interest-only loans) to buy more expensive houses than they could afford. But in 2007 and 2008, defaults in the subprime lending markets, tighter credit, and stiffer requirements for securing a mortgage— including plenty of documentation and downpayments as high as 20 percent—led to a drop in the number of homebuyers. The facts are stark and bleak:

▸ The national homeownership rated peaked in 2004 and has been retreating ever since.
▸ By the end of 2007, foreclosure proceedings numbered nearly 1 million.
▸ Between 2005 and 2007, the median price for an existing home dropped by more than 6 percent—and between August 2007 and August 2008, by an additional 6.7 percent.[18]
▸ Between August 2007 and August 2008, the monthly sales volume dipped by 14.8 percent.[19]
▸ Between the end of 2005 and the start of 2008, total housing starts plummeted 35 percent.[20]

FIGURE 7-2 **Mean U.S. Income by Quintile, 1967–2006 (in 2006 \$).**

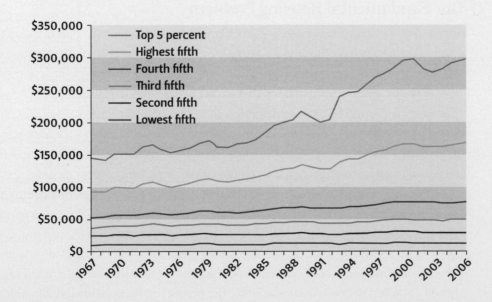

**SOURCE:** U.S. Census Bureau, "Income: Historical Tables—Households"; www.census.gov/hhes/www/income/histinc/h06ar.html.

FIGURE 7-3 **Interest Rates and Home Prices, 1976–2006.**

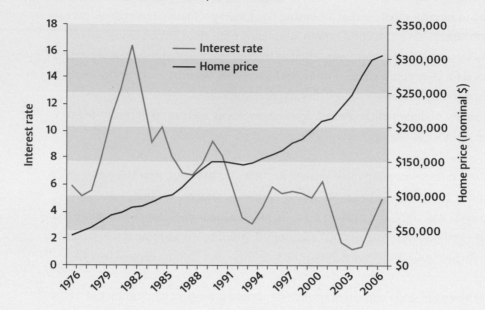

**SOURCE:** U.S. Census Bureau (home prices); Federal Reserve (federal interest rates).

However, even if housing prices continue to fall, housing will become even less afford-able for many low- to middle-income families until the housing market stabilizes.

## Our Fundamental Housing Problem

Simply put, the fundamental housing problem is this: all the elements that make up the cost of owning a home—the sales price, the mortgage, the cost of land, construction costs, and operating costs—have risen faster than people's incomes, except for those at the very peak of the income pyramid (the top 10 to 20 percent). Although affordable-housing advo-cates often argue over the precise definition of "affordable," the conventional wisdom is that prospective homebuyers should not spend more than three times their annual income on housing. Or, to put it another way, the Federal Housing Administration suggests that the payment on a mortgage should be no more than 29 percent of gross income.

Housing affordability is usually discussed in relation to area median income (AMI). Households earning below 50 percent of AMI are considered very poor; those earning between 50 and 80 percent of AMI are considered low income; and those earning between 80 and 120 percent of AMI are considered middle income. And affordability pressures are moving up the income scale.[21] According to the Harvard Joint Center for Housing Studies, between 2001 and 2006, the number of households spending more than half their income on housing increased to nearly 18 million, while 39 million were spending more than 30 percent of their income on housing.[22] This statistic is alarming because the lack of affordable housing is largely invisible: as a nation, the United States is fortunate enough not to be plagued by widespread homelessness or informal slum settlements. As our population increases to 400 million over the next several decades, however, we will be faced with the challenge of how to provide affordable housing for 100 million more Americans.

Although almost 70 percent of Americans own their own home, back-of-the-envelope calculations—to say nothing of the subprime mortgage crisis—suggest that many families are overreaching financially. In some areas, like Atlanta and Houston, it is possible to purchase a home for under $200,000; a household income of $65,000 brings such prices firmly within reach. Yet in places like Honolulu and New York City, median existing home prices easily top $500,000—so to own your own place, you need a salary of more $150,000. Woe to the young, or to the working-class family with two children, who are unlucky enough to be employed anywhere near Manhattan.[23]

Until now, many families have found affordable housing by moving farther and farther away from employment centers, to areas where the cost of land—and thus housing—is lower. Moving farther out saves money, if only direct housing costs are considered. Conversely, locations closer to the central city command a premium; people pay for the convenience of being closer to downtown. A study of land values and transit in Portland, Oregon, conducted by ULI's Robert Dunphy, suggests that the cost of a house drops between $5,000 and $7,000 for every mile (1.6 kilometers) of distance from the urban core.[24] But when the cost of transportation begins to rival that of housing, the "drive 'til you qualify" model starts to break down. A 2006 study by

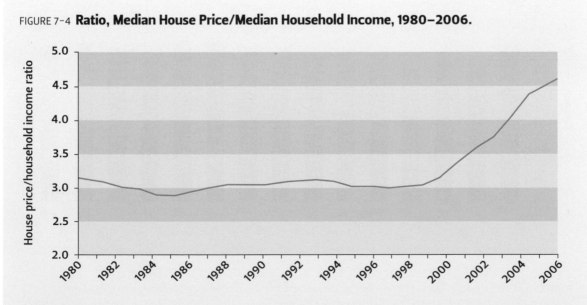

FIGURE 7-4 **Ratio, Median House Price/Median Household Income, 1980–2006.**

**SOURCE:** Joint Center for Housing Studies of Harvard University, "The State of the Nation's Housing: 2007," housing affordability index, www.jchs.harvard.edu/publications/markets/son2007/metro_affordability_index_2007.xls.

the National Housing Conference shows that a working family is forced to spend 77 cents more on transportation for every dollar saved on housing; basically, the cost of housing is exchanged for the cost of commuting.[25] As a result, combined housing and transportation costs become a better metric for affordability. Working families earning between $20,000 and $50,000 spend almost 60 percent of their income on transportation and housing, leaving very little for other expenditures such as food, education, health care, and leisure.[26]

FIGURE 7-5 **Average Percentage of Income Spent on Housing and Transportation by Working Families, Selected Cities.**

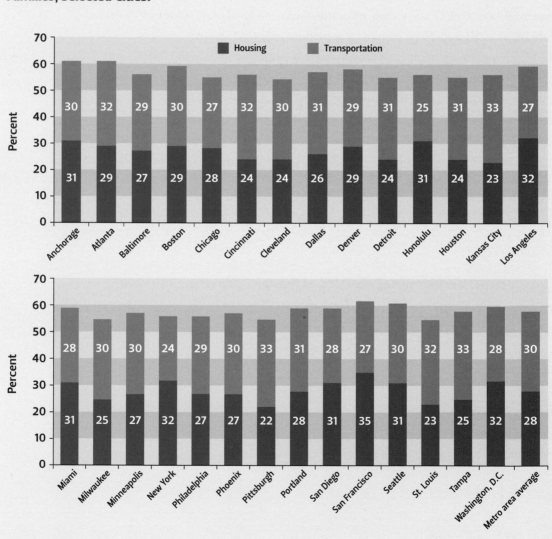

**SOURCE:** Barbara J. Lipman, "A Heavy Load: The Combined Housing and Transportation Burdens of Working Families," October 2006, 2–3; www.nhc.org/pdf/pub_heavy_load_10_06.pdf.

**NOTE:** Working families are defined here as those with combined incomes ranging from $20,000 to $50,000.

Figure 7-5 is revealing: in 17 of the 28 areas studied by the Center for Housing Policy, transportation costs are as high as or higher than housing costs. The average total transportation cost for working families is roughly $10,000 a year.[27] The cost of transportation combined with housing pushes working families to the margin, where even small increases in housing and transportation costs become very difficult to absorb. Rising home prices, coupled with increasing and volatile energy prices, operating costs, and transportation costs, could very well make the "drive 'til you qualify" model an unsustainable housing option for households earning 120 percent of AMI or less.

Because home prices in many U.S. housing markets have declined substantially, one might well ask if this dip will make homebuying easier and more affordable for the workforce. The answer is probably no, for three reasons. First, prices had risen so high before the housing bubble burst that the price of a home would have to go down at least 50 percent to be of much advantage to the middle-income homebuyer. Second, as lenders revert to more traditional lending criteria, credit becomes tighter—which means that most working households, whose incomes have remained flat, will have considerable difficulty obtaining a mortgage. Third, homebuilders' costs—financing, land acquisition, and construction materials—will not be going down.

## What Can Be Done?

Now we come to the big question: What can be done to solve America's affordable-housing problem? How can we ensure that America's workers and their families have access to safe and affordable housing? And how will the provision of such housing affect the changing metropolitan form?

As noted earlier, the fact that housing costs are rising more quickly than incomes creates a gloomy picture for housing affordability. This is a complex problem, and there is certainly no easy solution. However, government incentives can stimulate private sector development of affordable housing. Thus, policy makers and affordable-housing advocates should have, as their primary objective, the development of a toolbox of policies designed to dramatically increase the supply of affordable housing. The following actions are a starting point:

▸ Build more multifamily housing
▸ Build smaller homes
▸ Build affordable housing closer to the workplace
▸ Modify the low-income housing tax credit
▸ Enact a new homeownership tax credit
▸ Subsidize housing for low- and moderate-income workers
▸ Densify sprawl
▸ Create a national housing trust fund
▸ Provide more mixed-income housing
▸ Promote location efficient mortgages.

## Build More Multifamily Rental Housing

One hundred years ago, when America's cities were high-density, pedestrian-friendly areas, apartment living was considered chic. And after decades of suburban decentralization, the pendulum may be swinging back toward apartment living again, at least for some Americans. According to the National Multi-Housing Council (NMHC), 15 percent of American households rent an apartment in a building with five or more units, and the number of apartment dwellers is growing.[28] The NMHC lists a number of factors that are encouraging renewed interest in apartment living:

▸ Two of the fastest-growing demographic groups—young people in their 20s and retiring baby boomers—are among those most likely to select apartment living. Nontraditional households—including childless couples, people who live alone, and groups of unrelated individuals who share a home—are also growing in number and are likely to show a similar taste for apartments.

▸ Suburban jurisdictions are beginning to understand that apartments use existing infrastructure more efficiently than detached housing, and therefore reduce traffic and pollution and create pedestrian-friendly neighborhoods. As cities try to recruit middle- and upper-income households, they are finding that lifestyle renters (that is, high-end renters) are a key target market.

▸ Apartments offer time-pressed young professionals a hassle-free lifestyle.

▸ Financial constraints are making it smarter for many people—especially those who move frequently and do not want to be tied down—to rent than to buy.

▸ Better apartment amenity packages—including features such as attached garages; built-in, prewired entertainment centers; high-speed Internet access; private alarm systems; whirlpool baths; granite countertops; gas fireplaces; crown molding; on-site concierge services and fitness centers; billiard rooms; and cyber cafés—appeal to the growing numbers of young professionals, singles and mingles, single-parent households, and empty nesters who are looking for an easier lifestyle.[29]

For many, apartment living represents the realization of a new American Dream.

## Build Smaller Homes

Roger K. Lewis, a noted architect and a professor at the University of Maryland, asks whether we should be reducing greenhouse gas emissions and increasing affordability by building "artfully designed houses that are compact yet livable, that are reasonably priced and environmentally sustainable."[30] There's no question about it, American tastes do run to large, detached, single-family suburban homes. But sprawl is costly—so once again, we come home to the possibility that smaller is better. It is encouraging that the median home size has begun to decline for the first time since the early 1980s; from 2006 to 2007, the size of a median single-family house decreased two square feet (0.18 square meters).[31] Signs of downsizing are already apparent, according to ULI's John

McIlwain, "as aging baby boomers and young echo boomers seek smaller, high-quality homes in urban areas."[32]

## Build Affordable Housing Closer to the Workplace

Over the last ten years, only about 5 percent of the 17.3 million homes built in the United States were in urban or first-ring suburban areas, prompting Anthony Downs, of the Brookings Institution, to state that any analysis of population migrations must first ask, "Where are the jobs located?"[33] The response, then, should be to build afford-able housing closer to those jobs. In city after city, there is simply not enough affordable housing close to employment centers. This jobs/housing imbalance is forcing people to live farther and farther away from where they work. A survey conducted by ULI in cooperation with Harris Interactive, an independent polling firm, indicates that many people would prefer to live closer to their workplaces, and that their employers agree that this would be desirable.[34] The numbers speak for themselves. Of the 110 larger firms (those with at least 100 employees) surveyed, the findings were as follows:

- More than half (55 percent) report a lack of nearby affordable housing.
- The majority of companies surveyed indicated that the lack of affordable housing has a negative effect on the recruitment of entry- and mid-level staff (63 percent) and on retention as well (67 percent).
- Respondents reported that commute time increases stress (69 percent), negative emo-tions (63 percent), absenteeism (48 percent), attrition (46 percent), and high-risk behavior (27 percent).
- Almost six in ten companies (58 percent) report having lost employees because, at least in part, of long commute times.

What did the 1,215 U.S. workers surveyed say?

- Most workers earning less than $50,000 per year (67 percent) said that they would be more likely to move closer to work if more affordable housing were available, and 64 percent said that they would be at least somewhat likely to make a lateral employment move in exchange for a shorter commute.
- More than three-quarters of those in the 18- to 34-year-old age group (76 percent) would be at least somewhat likely to make a lateral employment move in exchange for a shorter commute.
- Eighty-five percent of workers who commute more than 90 minutes (round trip) would be likely to make a lateral employment move to cut their commute in half; 63 percent of *all* commuters would be likely to do the same.
- Finally, the majority of all commuters said that they would be at least somewhat likely to move closer to work if more affordable housing were available there.

This survey also revealed that people who do not perceive living closer to work as desirable may not be factoring in transportation costs as a rising expense. Nor are they necessarily aware that affordable housing close to their jobs may be an option for them. The reality is that moderate-income housing *can* be developed near employment centers in ways that provide a high quality of life while offering proximity to both amenities and work—to say nothing of the fact that a far-flung living environment is not sustainable in terms of conserving land or energy.

Building more housing in mixed-use developments would also help provide more affordable—and more compact—housing closer to workplaces. Such housing is being constructed, for example, in Stapleton, Colorado, a mixed-use, master-planned community being built by Forest City Stapleton, Inc., on the site of the former Stapleton International Airport. Located just ten minutes from downtown Denver, the 4,700-acre (1,902-hectare) community, which has been under development since 2001, will eventually house more than 30,000 residents and 35,000 workers. At buildout, in 2020, the community will contain 8,000 for-sale homes, 4,000 rental housing units (including a wide range of affordable units), 10 million square feet (929,000 square meters) of office space, 3 million square feet (278,700 square meters) of retail space, and two square miles (five square kilometers) of parks.[35]

Certainly one goal should be to expand the availability of sites for the development of affordable homes. Affordable housing can be developed on vacant or underutilized publicly owned property. In Woodinville, Washington, King County converted a surplus site slated to become a solid waste transfer station into Greenbrier Heights, a community of 170 affordable homes. In Indianapolis, the federal Urban Homesteading Program offered houses that had reverted to the U.S. Department of Housing and Urban Development (HUD) to would-be residents in a lottery; purchasers paid only $1 per home, but promised to upgrade their homes over a three-year period with sweat equity. In Fairfax County, Virginia, a low-density subdivision of 65 homes and five acres (two hectares) of surface parking was rezoned to make possible the development of Metro West—2,250 condominiums, apartments, and townhouses, at least 5 percent of them affordable— near a Metro station.[36] The project has been approved and is underway.

## Modify the Low-Income Housing Tax Credit

One policy change that would help many households whose incomes are being outstripped by rising rents would be to modify HUD's low-income housing tax credit (LIHTC) program, which is the nation's largest program to support the production of affordable housing. Under the LIHTC program, tax credits may be used only to construct rental housing, and income restrictions must remain in effect for at least 15 years. Currently, developers have two options: 40 percent of the units must be affordable to households earning 60 percent of AMI or less, or 20 percent of the units must be affordable to households earning 50 percent of AMI or less.[37] Raising the ceiling from 60 to 80 percent of AMI—and even higher, in high-cost cities—for a portion of the units, and changing the bottom limit to 40 percent for the rest of the units, would help to create new mixed-income communities and provide much-needed affordable housing for many members of the workforce who do not currently benefit from the LIHTC.

Throughout the nation's metropolitan areas, teachers, police officers, firefighters, salesclerks, municipal workers, and young people, among others, are being elbowed out of the housing market, and do not qualify for government assistance. For example, according to the Arlington (Virginia) Partnership for Affordable Housing, 25 percent of Arlington's police force, 9 percent of its firefighters, and fewer than half its school-teachers live in the county, a first-tier suburb of Washington, D.C. From 2000 to 2005, the county's supply of affordable housing declined by more than 50 percent, and 9,900 rental units became unattainable for households with incomes at or below 60 percent of AMI.[38] The proposed change in LIHTC policy would represent a boon for workforce members throughout the country.

## Enact a New Homeownership Tax Credit

A new federal homeownership tax credit for moderate-income households—a policy change recommended by the Millennial Housing Commission in 2002—would assist low-income homeowners and potential homebuyers, most of whom do not itemize their deductions and consequently cannot enjoy the deductibility of mortgage interest payments and real estate taxes. Such a tax credit could be structured like the LIHTC, which enables developers and builders to raise capital through the sale of tax credits to investors, which are then used to reduce rental costs.

For the past 40 years, state governments have become active players in the provision of affordable housing, and state housing finance agencies (HFAs) offer a variety of programs to support both rental and ownership housing. A homeownership tax credit program would be administered by state HFAs, which could use the credits to build or rehabilitate affordable for-sale housing in tight markets and to stimulate demand in weaker markets. The state HFAs would, either directly or through a local agency, use the credits to promote the production or rehabilitation of homes in eligible census tracts—that is, where production or rehabilitation costs exceed the ability of a working family to afford the property. The target market would be first-time buyers with incomes below 80 percent of AMI, although in high-cost cities the ceiling could be raised to 120 percent of AMI.

Developers would compete for the tax credits and could sell them to investors. The credits could also be used to achieve affordability for low-income homebuyers by lowering the primary barriers to homebuying—that is, insufficient savings to cover downpayment and closing costs, and/or the inability to make high mortgage payments. As the Millennial Housing Commission noted, "The advantage of the homeownership tax credit over direct subsidy programs is that it devolves authority to states and relies on private-sector partners to deliver allocated resources." Thus, the credit would become a valuable community development resource that would enhance the overall stability of neighborhoods.[39]

## Subsidize Housing for Low- and Moderate-Income Workers

Governments at all levels have programs designed to relieve low- and moderate-income households from the burden of high housing costs. Yet all these programs combined do not provide anywhere near the resources needed to meet the goal of the Housing Act of 1949: "a decent home and a suitable living environment" for all Americans.[40]

One obvious way to make housing more affordable is to provide government subsidies.[41] For the past 40 years, low-income households have been the major beneficiaries of federal housing programs. Although families with incomes below 60 percent of AMI, once the focus of federal programs, still have access to a limited (and inadequate) supply of housing vouchers, the federal government today subsidizes virtually no new housing production. Moreover, given a weak political constituency and ballooning federal deficits, the prospect for a new round of federal subsidy programs remains bleak. Nevertheless, in all likelihood, the housing needs of lower-income families will probably always require government subsidy programs.

Significant changes need to be made in the ways federal subsidies are structured and administered. Federal funding for subsidies must be markedly increased, not only to clear out the backlog of eligible low-income families, but also to enable programs to assist families from a mix of income levels. Assistance from programs like Section 8, HOPE VI, LIHTCs, and community development block grants (CDBGs) should be available to families earning up to 80 percent of AMI throughout the country, and to those earning up to 120 percent of AMI in metro areas with especially high housing costs.

Subsidies for moderate-income households would facilitate the creation of mixed-income developments and neighborhoods. Under a sliding system of benefits, families with higher incomes would receive a lower level of assistance. Strong management, good design, and well-located projects can help ensure that federal funds ultimately create decent, safe, and affordable housing for those who are unable—or struggling—to pay market rates.

## Modify Zoning and Building Codes

Because all zoning is local, local governments affect how their communities grow. Single-use zoning segregates residential, retail, and public spaces, while exclusionary zoning entices higher-income people to live on larger lots and forces out lower-income people. Local governments have become intensely interested in affordable housing, because this is the level of government at which the impact of the affordable-housing shortage is most immediately visible. Although many local governments are exploring ways to provide housing for low- and moderate-income families, most have few dollars to put behind the tools they develop. State and local governments can, however, make great strides through regulatory tools such as zoning and building codes.

Zoning and building codes may sound boring, but they often become the topic of hot debate. In fact, the regulatory regime is one of the single most important factors causing housing prices to exceed the reach of working families. Simply put, when the population continues to grow and the supply of housing is artificially restricted by zoning and building codes, the result is an unaffordable housing market. Changing zoning to permit and provide incentives for mixed-use development, more intense land uses, and higher-density development can help make housing more affordable.

In addition, making existing housing affordable is less expensive than building new affordable housing. Yet building codes often make rehabilitations and retrofits prohibitively expensive and time-consuming. The Ohio Alternative Building Code is an example of a code worth emulating. Adopted in 1986, the code establishes 18 criteria governing such things as height and area, smoke control, means of egress, and dwelling-unit separations. These guidelines, which keep buildings safe without incorporating all the complexities of state building codes, make it easier to rehabilitate older structures.

In general, older zoning policies need to be updated and made more flexible to permit a greater diversity of housing products, including multifamily homes, manufactured housing, and accessory dwelling units, and thus increase the availability of affordable homes—some of which, one hopes, would be built near workplaces. For example, under updated zoning regulations, Oakland (California) Community Housing, Inc., is using manufactured homes to provide affordable homes for working families in an infill setting. The city of Santa Cruz, California, has adopted zoning regulations that make accessory buildings legal, and has even hired architects to design prototypes, thus easing the permitting of projects for homebuilders who incorporate such designs.

Three types of zoning can be particularly useful: form-based codes, performance-based zoning, and inclusionary zoning.

## Form-Based Codes

Unlike conventional zoning regulations, which specify what type of use is permitted on a given piece of land, form-based codes address the mass, scale, features, facades, and functions of buildings, to make them appropriate to the context. Such codes also specify certain elements within the public realm, like a structure's proximity to the street, street furniture, trees, sidewalks, and travel lanes. According to the Form-Based Codes Institute, the codes "address the relationship between building facades and the public realm, the form and mass of buildings in relation to one another, and the scale and types of streets and blocks."[42] In other words, form is crucial. Yet form-based codes are not design guidelines; they are regulations. Form-based codes can be applied to all types of structures, including affordable housing. The goal is to create streets and buildings that work together, yielding an attractive public realm.[43]

## Performance-Based Zoning

Under performance-based zoning, which is closely allied to form-based codes, if a project meets certain performance requirements related to traffic congestion, parking space allotments, impervious surface ratios, protection of the environment, impact on infrastructure, or—most relevant in this case—workforce housing, the developer is awarded a certain amount of flexibility when it comes to density, use mix, and design. The use to which the property will be put is not as important as the impact of the project on the larger community. Thus, performance standards replace use standards: any use is permitted, as long as the development meets the measurable standards outlined in the zoning ordinance. The beauty of this strategy is that it imitates the way that cities developed before zoning. It allows developers to focus their time and resources on good development that meets community needs, such as affordable housing, rather than on fighting the regulatory regime.

In Chamblee, Georgia, northeast of Atlanta, city officials—recognizing that single-use zoning was blocking the redevelopment of 250 acres (101 hectares) around a MARTA transit station near the heart of the city—adopted performance-based zoning. Doing so made it possible to attract a developer who has launched a $20 million project on 80 of the acres (32 hectares). According to city development director Page Perkins, this "pro-market approach" worked much better than saying to the developer, "Our zoning requires you to do this project on this parcel," or "You can't put that over there because our zoning does not permit it."[44]

## Inclusionary Zoning

Inclusionary zoning is becoming increasingly popular as a tool for providing workforce housing, at least in some quarters. Ron Terwilliger has asserted that "local zoning is the number-one enemy of creating sufficient affordable workforce housing";[45] he has also suggested that inclusionary zoning, whether mandatory or voluntary, should be part of the answer (along with local land assemblage and affordable-housing trust funds). Inclusionary zoning requires that a modest portion of units in new developments (typically 10 to 15 percent) be priced at levels affordable to low- or moderate-income families. In return, the developer is awarded a "density bonus"—permission to build at a higher density than would otherwise have been allowed; alternatively, the developer may provide or fund affordable homes on another site.

Inclusionary zoning has worked very well for years in Montgomery County, Maryland. Massachusetts has implemented inclusionary zoning at the state level (see the accompanying feature box). California has a long history of inclusionary zoning, but it has not always been easy to implement.

The challenge is for the public and private sectors to continue to work together to make inclusionary zoning effective. Residents often cite the myth that inclusionary zoning will "bring the wrong people here to live next to us," and use this myth to get local officials all riled up to oppose such zoning. Nonetheless, the opportunity for innovation is ripe, and imaginative yet feasible ideas will be necessary to make inclusionary zoning work across the country.

## MASSACHUSETTS INCLUSIONARY ZONING LEGISLATION ADDRESSES AFFORDABILITY

Massachusetts has enacted legislation to address the problem of increasingly unaffordable housing for low- and moderate-income households. In the Boston region, where home prices have historically have been both volatile and expensive, the problem is especially acute. These high housing prices are caused, in part, by local land use regulations. To address this problem, the state has enacted two laws, Chapter 40B and Chapter 40R, that are designed to mitigate the negative effect of local zoning regulations on housing supply and simultaneously promote good development practices.

Under Chapter 40B, enacted in 1969, in communities where less than 10 percent of the housing stock is "affordable," new residential developments may be approved under flexible rules, as long as the proposed units include long-term affordability restrictions. To be eligible, at least 25 percent of a development's for-sale units must be set aside at prices that are affordable to families earning below 80 percent of area median income (AMI), and at least 20 percent of the units in a rental project must be affordable to families earning below 50 percent of AMI.[1] The statute has met with substantial opposition over the years because it effectively circumvents local control over the permitting process for new development. Nevertheless, according to the Citizens' Housing and Planning Association, as of 2006, Chapter 40B had been responsible for creating 43,000 housing units, of which approximately 23,000 were reserved for households earning below 80 percent of AMI.

In 2004, the state enacted Chapter 40R to provide financial incentives to encourage the development of new affordable and market-rate housing. This law aims to meet housing needs while promoting smart growth policies, including transit-oriented development and residential development near jobs and community centers. Under Chapter 40R, communities that establish smart growth zoning districts (SGZDs) receive a one-time incentive payment that can be as large as $600,000. Residential development within the SGZDs must meet minimum density requirements, and 20 percent of the units must be affordable to residents earning below 80 percent of AMI. As building permits are issued, a $3,000 one-time payment is awarded to the municipality. In addition, permitting inside of the SGZDs is streamlined to allow mixed-use and affordable housing development.[2]

**SOURCE:** Melissa Floca, former research associate, ULI.

**1** Citizens' Housing and Planning Association, "Fact Sheet on Chapter 40B: The State's Affordable Housing Zoning Law," January 2006; www.bos.frb.org/economic/neppc/briefs/2006/briefs061.pdf.

**2** Darcy Rollins, "An Overview of Chapters 40R and 40S: Massachusetts' Newest Housing Policies," Policy Brief 06-1, New England Public Policy Center at the Federal Reserve Bank of Boston, February 2006; www.bos.frb.org/economic/neppc/briefs/2006/briefs061.pdf.

## Densify Sprawl

The late Jane Jacobs coined the phrase *sprawl densification* in her final book, *Dark Age Ahead,* to describe efforts to modify residential dwellings in the suburbs. Jacobs recognized that large minimum-lot sizes; huge asphalt parking lots; long setbacks from the street; and single-use zoning, which separates residences, shops, and workplaces, have all increased sprawl.[46] Jacobs called for planning and zoning that would encourage higher residential densities in places that lie within easy walking or biking distance of basic amenities like shopping, cafés, banks, and recreational facilities or green space.

As empty nesters and retiring baby boomers no longer need large suburban homes but want to "age in place" in their communities, a whole new market for residential adaptation is opening up. Large single-family houses can be converted into duplexes, triplexes, and quadriplexes. Accessory buildings can be added at the rear of a lot, or alongside the main house. Small "granny flats" or "mother-in-law" apartments, common in the late 19th and early 20th centuries, can be built above garages. All of these changes can add up to increased residential densities within the existing metropolitan form. According to Neil Peirce, the benefits will include higher tax yields, flourishing local businesses, and livelier communities.[47]

## Create a National Housing Trust Fund

Local and state governments already use tools such as community land trusts and housing trust funds to preserve existing affordable housing or to construct new housing. Such funds are ordinarily supported by dedicated funding sources such as real estate transfer taxes, recording fees, or revenues from unclaimed property. As of July 2005, there were 293 city-operated housing trust funds; 76 county-operated ones; and 43 separate, state-operated housing trust funds in 37 states.[48] Where land trusts and housing trust funds already exist, affordability requirements should be extended to keep housing affordable over the long term. New programs should also be created to enable rehabbed affordable-housing projects to become as green and as energy efficient as possible.

A national affordable-housing trust fund, of course, would be even more useful. Past efforts to create one have failed, primarily because of concerns about increasing government spending and a ballooning federal deficit. The National Affordable Housing Trust Fund Act of 2007, introduced in the 2007–2008 congressional session under bipartisan support, would provide around $1 billion annually for the production, preservation, and rehabilitation of 1.5 million affordable homes over ten years, without requiring a large direct appropriation from the federal budget. The funding would come from nonbudgetary sources generated by Fannie Mae, Freddie Mac, and the Federal Housing Administration. For every $2 of trust fund monies, local jurisdictions would be required to provide a $1 match. After the House of Representatives passed the bill on October 10, 2007, it was received by the Senate, where it was read twice and referred to the Committee on Banking, Housing and Urban Affairs but has not been debated further.

## Provide More Mixed-Income Housing

Constructing affordable housing is said to be more difficult, and more costly, than conventional homebuilding. Developers certainly have to make a profit, or they will not stay in business. But the public and private sectors can cooperate to encourage the development of mixed-income housing projects, which contain both affordable and market-rate housing. The following examples of mixed-income housing make several lessons quite clear: it will work only where the number of market-rate units is high enough to create a critical mass, and where the units being offered are of the same nature and quality.[49]

Chatham Square is an urban infill redevelopment project that sits on a 4.16-acre (1.68-hectare) site near the historic district of Old Town Alexandria, Virginia, across the Potomac River from Washington, D.C. This HOPE VI project—which was completed in

2005 by a public/private partnership comprising Bethesda, Maryland–based developer EYA; the city of Alexandria; the Alexandria Redevelopment and Housing Authority; and Fannie Mae—replaced 100 distressed, 1940s-era public housing units on two city blocks with a higher-density, mixed-income community of 100 market-rate, for-sale luxury townhouses and 52 public housing rental units designed to be indistinguishable from the townhouse component. The project also contains attractive open space and structured parking. Chatham Square's townhouses sold out at an average cost of $870,000.[50]

Another HOPE VI project—High Point, in Seattle, Washington—is transforming a 716-unit post–World War II public housing project into an environmentally conscious, new urbanist mixed-income community of 1,600 new housing units, 45 percent of which are affordable and low-income rentals being constructed by the Seattle Housing Authority, and 55 percent of which are for-sale market-rate units or rental housing for seniors being built by for-profit and nonprofit developers. All housing units will be Energy Star–rated. Amenities include a public library branch, a health clinic, and a recreation center. The community, which is scheduled to be completed in 2009, received a ULI Award for Excellence in 2007.[51]

Atlanta developer Tom Cousins has made an extensive investment in the Villages of East Lake. Originally a posh Atlanta suburb, East Lake experienced a devastating turn for the worse when a 650-unit public housing project was built there, and the area deteriorated into a drug- and crime-infested war zone known to local police as "Little Vietnam." Shifting the property from government control to private hands has made a huge difference. Cousins—in partnership with the Atlanta Housing Authority, the East Lake Community Foundation, and others—demolished the complex in 1993 and rebuilt it as 542 high-quality, mixed-income townhouses, duplexes, and garden apartments, 50 percent of which are public housing and 50 percent of which are market-rate units. The community is anchored by a top-flight charter school, a YMCA, and an early-learning center, as well as a restored golf course, tennis courts, a pool, and play areas. The community also offers mentoring programs for kids and job- and life-skills training for adults. This holistic approach to urban revitalization has met with great success: crime rates are way down, school test scores are up, and property values have increased.[52] In 2003, the Villages of East Lake received a ULI Award for Excellence.

Built on a 1.74-acre (0.7-hectare) site—once home to the F&M Schaefer Brewery—in Brooklyn's diverse South Williamsburg neighborhood, Schaefer Landing offers a creative blend of 140 affordable rental apartments and 210 market-rate condominiums that has brought new life to the East River waterfront. Although all the affordable units are in one 15-story building and the market-rate ones are in two other structures (a second 15-story building and a 25-story tower), because the three structures feature the same exterior systems, it is not obvious which buildings contain which types of units. The project, which was completed in 2006, was developed by Kent Waterford Associates LLC, a partnership of three experienced developers and owners of affordable housing. Although the site lacked convenient access to public transit, the developer negotiated an agreement with a water- taxi service and agreed to subsidize the first year of the taxi's operations from Schaefer Landing, enabling residents to reach the foot of Wall Street in seven minutes.[53]

These examples—just a few of the nation's many successful mixed-income housing projects—should dispel certain myths that are prevalent about mixed-income housing: namely, that mixed-income housing will not work because high-income residents will not live near residents with much lower incomes; that mixed-income housing is not safe; that mixed-income housing brings down property values in the surrounding area; and that only nonprofit developers and public housing authorities can build it.[54] These projects demonstrate that higher-income residents need not be fearful of living alongside those of lesser means: the East Lake Foundation states emphatically that as a result of the redevelopment, "crime significantly decreased in both the immediate and surrounding areas."[55] The projects also show that the private sector can be creatively and profitably involved in building this kind of housing, and that well-designed mixed-income housing can become a neighborhood asset.[56] The development of the Villages of East Lake, for example, has raised property values in and around its boundaries, and has proven that affordable housing is not, by definition, an unattractive blight. The Villages of East Lake serves as a model example of urban revitalization and the provision of decent, affordable housing to low-income households.

As Ron Terwilliger points out, "The policies of the past, particularly the public housing policies of concentrating the poor, were a mistake for our society. What we need to do is find a way to have these families, whether they be minority or majority, dispersed throughout our society."[57]

## Promote Location–Efficient Mortgages

A location-efficient mortgage (LEM)—a registered trademark of the California-based nonprofit Institute for Location Efficiency—increases prospective homeowners' buying power by taking into account the amount of money people save when they live in location-efficient communities, defined as "neighborhoods where residents can walk from their homes to stores, schools, recreation and public transportation."[58] The idea is to offer households an incentive to live closer to transit. Homebuyers who obtain LEMs receive tangible benefits for living in homes that enable them to drive less. An LEM combines flexible criteria for financial eligibility, a low downpayment, and competitive, fixed interest rates on 15- to 30-year mortgages.[59] It requires a downpayment of at least 3 percent of a property's appraised value. By making location-efficient homes more affordable and easier to purchase, LEMs encourage people to live in more compact, transit-served neighborhoods. Although Fannie Mae has been promoting LEMs for several years, and has authorized lenders to issue LEMs in four metropolitan areas (Chicago, Los Angeles, Seattle, and the San Francisco Bay Area), these mortgages should be made more widely available.

# SIX ADDITIONAL STRATEGIES FOR INCREASING THE AVAILABILITY OF AFFORDABLE HOMES

**Strategy 1: Expand the Availability of Sites for the Development of Affordable Homes**
In most communities in which home prices are out of the reach of working families, land is quite expensive. Local governments can remove this obstacle by making publicly owned land and tax-delinquent properties available for the development of affordable homes. Governments also can expand the supply of sites for new homes through changes in zoning rules that make new areas available for residential development or increase the number of homes that can be built in existing residential areas.

**Strategy 2: Reduce Red Tape and Other Regulatory Barriers**
In the development world, time is money. The longer it takes to gain all the approvals necessary to build a home and the more uncertainty involved in the approval process, the higher the costs of newly built or renovated homes. By expediting the approval process for affordable homes and addressing other regulatory barriers that drive up costs—such as overly restrictive zoning rules and building codes, and regressive fees—state and local governments can cut through the red tape and expand the supply of affordable homes.

**Strategy 3: Harness the Power of Strong Housing Markets**
The greatest housing challenges are found in hot housing markets, where the costs of buying or renting a home are increasing much faster than incomes. Fortunately, state and local governments can take steps to capitalize on strong housing markets in order to expand the supply of affordable homes. These policies include strategies for tapping the increased tax revenue associated with increases in property values and an active real estate market, as well as providing incentives for or requiring the inclusion of a modest number of affordable homes within new residential developments.

**Strategy 4: Generate Additional Capital**
While successful efforts to reduce regulatory barriers can help expand the supply of affordable homes, in many communities additional resources are needed to bring the price of homes within reach of working families. Research indicates a range of promising approaches for generating revenue for this purpose, including leveraging additional federal funds through the LIHTC program, supporting the issuance of general-obligation bonds for affordable housing, and mobilizing employers to help their workers find affordable homes.

**Strategy 5: Preserve and Recycle Resources**
Given the limited availability of public funds for affordable homes, this funding must be used in a cost-effective manner designed to produce maximum benefits at minimal costs. Providing funds to help preserve existing affordable homes that might otherwise be lost to deterioration or gentrification is one particularly cost-effective strategy. Other cost-effective strategies include providing downpayment assistance in the form of loans rather than grants, and the use of "shared equity" strategies that help preserve the buying power of government subsidies for homeownership in markets with rapidly appreciating home prices.

**Strategy 6: Empower Residents to Purchase and Retain Market-Rate Homes**
The policies described above focus overwhelmingly on expanding the supply of homes. But the demand side of the equation also should be considered. When families have adequate incomes and credit to afford market-rate homes, the need for government intervention to provide affordable homes is greatly reduced. One demand-side strategy within the domain of housing policy is to invest in homeowner education and counseling, that help families navigate the complicated homebuying process and improve their credit and debt profile so they can access more private-market mortgage capital at reasonable rates. Given the rise of foreclosures in many markets, it is important to marry this "pre-purchase" strategy with a "post-purchase" strategy designed to help existing homeowners retain their homeownership status in the face of confusing mortgage products, rising interest rates, and rising property taxes.

**SOURCE:** Jeffrey Lubell, "Increasing the Availability of Affordable Homes: An Analysis of High-Impact State and Local Solutions," prepared for Homes for Working Families by the Center for Housing Policy, January 2007; www. homesforworkingfamilies.org/resources.dyn/Full_Policy_Report_1.10.07.pdf.

## An Impossible Possibility?

The affordable-housing crisis in this nation can be solved only through a combination of programs at all levels of government, and with the assistance of the private and nonprofit sectors. As our nation grows, providing affordable housing to more American families will require innovative solutions and sustained attention from public policy makers, to say nothing of more sympathetic understanding from the public. Existing federal programs need to be adequately funded and expanded to target households at a wide range of income levels. The federal government also needs to partner with state and local governments to facilitate the funding of local initiatives. At the local level, zoning and building codes need to be changed to encourage dense, mixed-use, mixed-income development. Communities should permit accessory units, while instituting strict controls on troublesome issues like design and parking. Incentives should be created to target growth near public transportation and existing infrastructure. Programs should also be devised to help homeowners reduce operating costs such as property taxes, insurance, and energy. In short, addressing the housing backlog that already exists and providing affordable housing for the next generation of American families will take a significant amount of political will, complemented by the assistance of the private and nonprofit sectors. Failing to make the required effort will mean an increasingly dire housing situation for low- and moderate-income households across the nation.

The changing shape of metropolitan America means that the single-family house in the suburbs is no longer the ideal home for everyone. Many Americans now prefer to live in denser, more diverse, walkable, transit-served communities. Yet the incomes of many working households are being outstripped by the still-rising costs of housing. Fewer and fewer Americans can afford to buy or rent a home within a reasonable commute of their jobs. The American Dream of "a decent home and a suitable living environment for every American family," as enunciated in the National Housing Act of 1949, is an impossible possibility; it is always out there to be achieved, but it is impossible to attain fully. However, if the dream is expanded to include affordable housing for Americans in our changing metro areas, it may become a reality for more people. Then will our pledge of "liberty and justice for all" come true, and then will the ideal enunciated some 60 years ago by Congress be realized.

**ENDNOTES**

1 David Leonhardt, "Holding On," New York Times, Key Magazine, April 4, 2008; www.nytimes.com/2008/04/06/realestate/keymagazine/406Lede-t.html?pagewanted=all.

2 U.S. Department of Transportation, Federal Highway Administration, "Interstate System"; www.fhwa.dot.gov/programadmin/interstate.cfm.

3 Paul Knox, "Schlock and Awe: The American Dream Bought and Sold," *American Interest*, March–April 2007, 60.

4 J. Ronald Terwilliger, speech presented to Arizona Multihousing Association, September 13, 2007.

5 Ibid.

6  The Terwilliger Center defines workforce housing units as those that are affordable to households earning between 60 and 120 percent of area median income.

7  The phrase is attributed to Arizona governor Janet Napolitano.

8  Nick Paumgarten, "There and Back Again: The Soul of the Commuter," *New Yorker*, April 16, 2007, 58.

9  Millennial Housing Commission, "Meeting Our Nation's Housing Challenges: Report of the Bipartisan Millennial Housing Commission," May 2002, 17; govinfo.library.unt.edu/mhc/MHCReport.pdf.

10  Joint Center for Housing Studies, Harvard University, "America's Rental Housing: Homes for a Diverse Nation," 2006, 17; www.jchs.harvard.edu/publications/rental/rh06_americas_rental_housing.pdf.

11  "Investing in Affordable Housing," *Montgomery County Gazette*, April 9, 2008, A-28.

12  Joint Center for Housing Studies, Harvard University, "The State of the Nation's Housing 2008," 26; www.jchs.harvard.edu/publications/markets/son2008/son2008.pdf.

13  Robert J. Shiller, *Irrational Exuberance*, 2nd ed. (Princeton: Princeton University Press, 2005).

14  U.S. Census Bureau, "Census of Housing: Historical Census of Housing Tables; Home Values"; www.census.gov/hhes/www/housing/census/historic/values.html.

15  National Association of Realtors data; U.S. Census Bureau, "Income: Historical Tables—Households"; www.census.gov/hhes/www/income/histinc/h06ar.html.

16  Joint Center for Housing Studies, Harvard University, "The State of the Nation's Housing 2007," housing affordability index; www.jchs.harvard.edu/publications/markets/son2007/metro_affordability_index_2007.xls.

17  U.S. Census Bureau, "Historical Income Tables—Households."

18  "Monthly Sales Volume" and "Median Home Price," *USAToday*, August 26, 2008, 7B, (graphs).

19  Ibid.

20  Joint Center for Housing Studies, "Nation's Housing 2008," 1–4.

21  Ibid., 27.

22  Ibid., 4. According to the U.S. Department of Housing and Urban Development, "100 Questions & Answers about Buying a New Home," housing should be no more than 29 percent of gross monthly income. See www.hud.gov/offices/hsg/sfh/buying/buyhm.cfm.

23  For a more complete analysis of issues relating to affordable housing, see the National Housing Conference Web site, www.nhc.org/housing/pubs-descriptions.

24  Robert Dunphy, "The Cost of Being Close: Land Values and Housing Prices in Portland's High-Tech Corridor," ULI Working Paper, Series #660 (October 1998).

25  See Barbara J. Lipman, "A Heavy Load: The Combined Housing and Transportation Burdens of Working Families," October 2006; www.nhc.org/pdf/pub_heavy_load_10_06.pdf.

26  Ibid., 3–5.

27  Ibid., 4.

28  National Multi Housing Council, "Apartments—The New American Dream?"; www.nmhc.org/Content/ServeContent.cfm?IssueID=10&ContentItemID=1828&siteArea=Topics.

29  Ibid.

30  Roger K. Lewis, "Shaping the City," *Washington Post*, April 12, 2008, F5.

31  U.S. Census Bureau, "Median and Average Square Feet of Floor Area in New One-Family Houses Sold by Location"; www.census.gov/const/C25Ann/soldmedavgsf.pdf.

32  Ibid.

33 Quoted in John Caulfield, "This Way," *Builder*, September 2007, 135.

34 William H. Hudnut III, "Workforce Housing: Filling an Unmet Need," presentation to the National Association of Real Estate Editors, Philadelphia, June 2007; based on the unpublished results of a May 2007 survey of consumers and employers conducted by Harris Interactive for ULI.

35 *Stapleton*, ULI Development Case Study C034004 (January–June 2004); and Stapleton Web site, www.stapletondenver.com.

36 See Fairfax County Web site, www.fairfaxcounty.gov/providence/vienna_mwest.htm.

37 Deborah Myerson, *The Business of Affordable Housing* (Washington, D.C.: ULI–the Urban Land Institute, 2007), 10.

38 See Kim A. O'Connell, "ISO: Affordable Housing for Public Workers," *Washington Post*, April 1, 2007, B8.

39 Millennial Housing Commission, "Meeting Our Nation's Housing Challenges," 29–31; http://govinfo.library.unt.edu/mhc/MHCReport.pdf.

40 National Housing Act of 1949.

41 There are many books, studies, and articles on subsidized housing programs. This is not the place to review them—or to review their recommendations about how to improve, supplement, or replace those programs.

42 Form-Based Code Institute (FBCI) Web site, www.formbasedcodes.org/.

43 Mary Madden and Bill Spikowski, "Place Making with Form-Based Codes," *Urban Land* (September 2006): 175; FBCI Web site.

44 See William H. Hudnut III, *Halfway to Everywhere* (Washington, D.C.: ULI–the Urban Land Institute, 2003), 385.

45 Ron Terwilliger, speech presented to the Arizona Multihousing Association, September 13, 2007.

46 Jane Jacobs, *Dark Age Ahead* (New York: Random House, 2004), 215.

47 Neal Peirce, "Aging of the Baby Boom: A Community 'Blueprint for Action,'" syndicated column, June 10, 2007.

48 Lipman, "Heavy Load," 10.

49 Paul C. Brophy and Rhonda N. Smith, "Mixed-Income Housing: Factors for Success," *Cityscape: A Journal of Policy Development and Research* 3, no. 2 (1997): 3, 25–26; available at www.huduser.org/periodicals/cityscpe/vol3num2/success.pdf.

50 *Chatham Square*, ULI Development Case Study C037008 (April–June 2007).

51 Julie D. Stern, *Urban Land Institute Award-Winning Projects 2007* (Washington, D.C.: ULI–the Urban Land Institute, 2007), 88–91.

52 Information based on materials provided as part of a presentation by Tom Cousins at the Woodrow Wilson Center, March 27, 2007.

53 Stern, *Award-Winning Projects*, 72–73.

54 See Deborah Meyerson, *Mixed-Income Housing: Myth and Fact* (Washington, D.C.: ULI–the Urban Land Institute, 2003).

55 East Lake Foundation, *East Lake—A Model for Successful Community Revitalization* (East Lake Foundation, August 4, 2006), 3.

56 Ibid, 12.

57 Quoted in *An American Challenge: Mixed-Income, Mixed-Use Neighborhoods* (Washington, D.C.: U.S. Department of Housing and Urban Development, 2000).

58 Institute for Location Efficiency Web site, www.locationefficiency.com/.

59 Ibid.

# CHAPTER 8

# Building Better Communities through Retail

## We've all entered the postmall era.

—PACO UNDERHILL

*Where and how retail space is developed is having an important impact on the changing metropolitan form. The age of the cookie-cutter mall is over. Retail is moving from strip shopping centers and enclosed malls to town centers—mixed-use, pedestrian-friendly areas that more closely resemble traditional downtowns. Neighborhood retail is being rebuilt. Suburban retail is becoming urbanized, and urban retail is becoming suburbanized. All of these trends are influencing—and being influenced by—other land uses in all parts of the changing metropolitan form.*

**IN THE SITCOM SUBURBS** of the 1950s and 1960s, shopping was designed to be different. Gone were the streetfront stores of city and small-town life—an eclectic mix of old and new, intimately connected with the life of the community. Family-owned businesses offering personalized service gave way to chain stores and mass-market appeal. Gone, too, were opportunities to walk from one's home or office to the corner store, the movies, the library, the town square, or the local café. In the suburbs, land uses were designed to be separate, and autos were required for every trip, every errand. This may have made sense at a time when noxious industrial uses dominated our cities, but it doesn't make sense today.

In the 1950s and 1960s, regional malls were the latest thing. These enclosed, inward-focused structures gradually replaced downtown retail in America, as the nation's department stores and other retailers followed their patrons to the greener pastures of suburbia. The malls offered plentiful parking; a pleasant, climate-controlled environment; and a broad variety of stores lined up along wide walkways. Just as important was what they enabled suburban shoppers to avoid: exposure to urban blight and crime. Yet regional malls could not avoid eventual obsolescence.

Beginning in 1956, some 2,000 regional malls were built across the country. By the early 21st century, however, the total had dwindled to around 1,500. The conditions that had originally led to the creation of the malls and had sustained them for decades changed dramatically, and are continuing to change. The market for malls has matured, and the stock is aging rapidly. Mall designs are too standardized to appeal to today's shoppers, who are looking for more authentic experiences and for a sense of connectedness to daily life. Traffic congestion inhibits the desire to go to the mall, and parking there is not as easy as it once was. Nontraditional households and demographic groups—singles, seniors, two-income families, racial and ethnic minorities, gen-Xers and gen-Yers—are ascendant, and often have different, more cosmopolitan shopping expectations than did the Ozzie-and-Harriet households of the 1960s.

That's not to say that malls are going the way of the dinosaurs, however. On the contrary, many stand-alone malls will remain at the pinnacle of the retail food chain. As Figure 8-1 demonstrates, there can be vast differences in how well the regional malls in a single metro area—most of them built during the 1970s—are doing today. Class A malls—like Tysons Corner Center, which is doing a phenomenal $689 in sales per square

FIGURE 8-1 **Sales Comparisons for Four Washington, D.C., Metro Area Regional Malls.**

| | Laurel Commons | White Flint |
|---|---|---|
| | Laurel, Maryland | North Bethesda, Maryland |
| Year opened | 1979 | 1977 |
| Gross leasable area (square feet/square meters) | 660,000/61,316 | 850,000/78,968 |
| Population of primary market | 254,646 | 450,000 |
| Average household income | $82,540 | $110,000 |
| Average number of shoppers annually | 5,000,000 | 10,000,000 |
| Sales per square foot/ per square meter (excluding anchors) | $235/$2,530 | $385/$4,144 |
| Food court | Yes; seats 500 | Yes; seats 600 |
| Number of stores | 100 | 125 |
| Number of parking spaces | 300 | 4,500 |
| Anchor stores | Macy's, Burlington Coat Factory, International Furniture Liquidators | Bloomingdale's, Borders Books & Music, Lord & Taylor |

**SOURCE:** *Directory of Major Malls* (Nyack, N.Y.: Directory of Major Malls, Inc.). **NOTE:** All data as of 2007.

foot ($7,416 per square meter), with 20 million customers walking through its doors annually—will continue to dominate their markets because they have the best sites, the best stores, and the largest selection of specialty goods that consumers want to buy.[1] Class B malls, however, are struggling to hold their own against a number of factors undermining their health: poor locations, the loss of anchors, demographic changes, and competition from other malls and shopping centers, big-box stores, category killers, power centers, and the Internet.[2]

## De-Malling the Mall

Malls can and will be reinvented. Because the shopping center industry is constantly changing, as retail products and consumer preferences change and physical structures age, shopping center owners must often decide whether to renovate—and if so, how. Once an owner determines that the return on investment will warrant a renovation, it is necessary to survey the market; borrow the capital for redevelopment; and design the improvements, paying particular attention to public open space, facades, signage, lighting, and parking—which must be safe, convenient, and ample.[3] Often, there will be four alternatives for a renovation: (1) leave the structure as is, but enlarge it by adding open-air components (it is unusual these days for expansions to include enclosed space); (2)

| Springfield Mall | Tysons Corner Center |
| --- | --- |
| Springfield, Virginia | McLean, Virginia |
| 1973 | 1968 |
| 1,485,810/138, 036 | 2,200,000/204,387 |
| | |
| 104,815 | 2,152,714 |
| $97,505 | $116,155 |
| 14,600,000 | 20,000,000 |
| | |
| $375/$4,036 | $689/$7,416 |
| | |
| | |
| Yes; seats 570 | Yes; seats 700 |
| 200 | 300 |
| 8,100 | 10,500 |
| JCPenney, Macy's, Target | AMC Theatres, Bloomingdale's, L.L. Bean, Lord & Taylor, Nordstrom, Macy's |

remove the roof, so that the mall is open to the air; (3) expand the mall by transforming parking lots into high-density retail; (4) demolish and begin anew.

To encourage such renovations, municipalities will need to change their attitudes toward—and regulations regarding—redevelopment. ULI's Michael Beyard emphasizes the importance of "fix it first"—a strategy that has already been discussed in the context of infrastructure: "It is far better for a community and for private investment to strengthen existing assets by encouraging reinvestment in them than to abandon them and build somewhere else, as has been the trend for the past 50 years."[4] In the past decade, the action has shifted from the construction of new malls on the metropolitan fringe to rehabilitation, repositioning, and intensification of uses at aging and underutilized mall sites that are deeply embedded in existing communities.[5] It's time to go back to the future!

To cite but one of many examples, Alderwood, an enclosed mall built in 1979, in Lynnwood, Washington, 15 miles (24 kilometers) north of downtown Seattle, has been transformed into "a multifaceted entertainment and retail center."[6] The mall was not failing—but the owner, General Growth Properties (GGP), believed that it was losing business to other centers in the region. To target a growing high-end market, GGP decided to renovate and expand Alderwood and to reposition it as a regional destination.[7] The reconfigured 1.5-million-square-foot (139,355-square-meter) space, which opened in November 2004, incorporates two intensively developed outdoor shopping areas; a 16-screen cineplex; attached and freestanding restaurants; attractively landscaped outdoor plazas; new retail tenants; an existing Nordstrom store that has been moved to a new building; parking decks; and lavish painting and outdoor artwork. Since the new Nordstrom's opening, its sales have doubled. As of 2005, annual rents had increased throughout the complex by ten to 20 percent (and were in the $45–$60 per square foot [$484–$646 per square meter] range); and overall sales averaged $480 per square foot ($5,167 per square meter). GGP anticipates recouping its development costs through higher rents, as leases roll over.[8]

As noted in the previous section, Class A malls are vibrant, and Class B malls are struggling. Class C malls, however, are a different story entirely. No longer competitive, worn down by age and obsolete formats, and unable to meet changing demographic needs, they are dead or dying. Because they offer much greater opportunities as other land uses, most of these malls probably need to be demolished rather than resuscitated. In 2001, PricewaterhouseCoopers suggested that almost 20 percent of all existing malls were crippled, nonproductive, and highly vulnerable to further deterioration.[9]

But demolition is only the first part of the answer. Dead malls can often be brought back to life as urban villages, with a mix of retail, residential, office, and/or other types of uses needed by the communities in which they are located. In *Ten Principles for Rethinking the Mall*, Michael Beyard and his coauthors make a salient observation when they say the question that needs to be asked when a mall falters is not "How can we save the mall?" but "How can we use this opportunity to create a higher-value, more sustainable real estate development that helps build a more livable community?"[10]

Belmar, an urban village in the Denver suburb of Lakewood, Colorado, provides a highly successful example. The development replaced a failed, 1.4-million-square-foot (130,064-square-meter) mall, Villa Italia, that was surrounded by a sea of asphalt big enough to park 5,000 cars. Built in the 1960s, Villa Italia had become obsolete 30 years later, and has now been replaced by 22 blocks of stores, office space, residences, and entertainment; nine acres (3.6 hectares) of parks, plazas, and green space; a contemporary arts center, and three public parking structures. As Tom Gougeon, of Continuum Partners, the project's developer, says, "Belmar is the downtown that Lakewood never had."[11] To which one might add one thing: it is a downtown without the city's chaos, grime, and crime—a fact that appeals to many homebuyers. (Belmar won a ULI Award for Excellence in 2006.)

Other examples of de-malled malls exist, but many more failed and declining malls throughout America offer ample opportunities for redevelopment. The conclusion is inevitable. As Beyard frames it, the changing metropolitan form has challenged mall developers to look for opportunities beyond the construction of new, enclosed centers on greenfield sites at the suburban fringe. Today's consumers are looking for more connectedness within their communities, more convenience, and more integration with their day-to-day lives as they shop. Since malls have not traditionally provided this type of environment, new types of shopping centers and more urban configurations are in demand, and "the age of the cookie-cutter mall is drawing to a close."[12] Creative destruction is at work.

One cannot ignore the positive effect of the "return on perception" as this new approach to retail emerges. Place matters. When people find places that they see as attractive and energized, they stay longer, come back more often, and spend more money. Such places elicit their affection. Many malls are being replaced by town centers and main streets because people are tired of the one-size-fits-all retail format. The design dividend is considerable.

Another positive effect of denser, mixed-use town centers is that they are more energy efficient than stand-alone centers. As the negative effects of global warming become more apparent, we as a society are beginning to recognize that we must reduce energy consumption and pollution—and that more compact, mixed-use development is one way to help achieve this goal. In other words, *how* we develop becomes as important as *how much* we develop. Shopping environments that are designed so that customers can multitask, and that can be reached by various forms of transportation, use less energy than centers that are accessible only by automobile. These denser, mixed-use developments require less energy because residents and employees can park their cars once and walk to many of their day-to-day activities—a very important consideration as the price of gasoline rises above $4 a gallon ($1.06 a liter). This doesn't result in a lower quality of life. On the contrary, it leads to higher-quality lifestyles in which convenience and livability are enhanced and consumer choices are maximized.

# Convenience and Experience

Retailing today is sharply divided between two types of shopping experience. The first is convenience- and value-oriented retail. One-stop big boxes like Wal-Mart, Home Depot, and Target attract people who want to get in and out of a store quickly, find everything they want in one location, and hope to save some money by paying discounted prices. In 2000, about 70 percent of all retail sales were at discounted or sale prices, according to retail consultant Bob Gibbs, president of Gibbs Planning Group, in Birmingham, Michigan.[13] On the other side of the divide is "aspirational" or "experience" retail, which blurs the line between retail, lifestyle, and entertainment. In this zone, shopping is not an isolated activity that takes place within a highly controlled, formulaic fortress. It's simply another aspect of life—one that occurs in an environment that more closely resembles a community center. People visit experience retail environments to enjoy themselves in the company of others, as well as to shop. Experience retailers engage customers in an inherently personal way, and attempt to compete with commoditization and standardization, which drive down the differentiation and price of goods and services.

Experience retailers include Crate & Barrel, Starbucks, and West Elm; more extreme examples of the concept include Hard Rock Café, Niketown, and ESPN Zone. These retailers are typically located in town centers in which people shop, but also take time to relax, eat, go to a movie, enjoy the ambience, visit with other folks, and be entertained. Today's town centers are more than just malls that have been turned inside out. They are places that connect to the street and to the surrounding neighborhoods—places that invite people in. These places seem to be what many people are looking for as they

FIGURE 8-2 **The Shifting Focus of Retailing.**

| Then | Now |
|---|---|
| Overbuilding/obsolescence | Reinvention/reuse |
| Utilitarian | Experiential and entertaining |
| Traditional | Value-oriented or specialty shopping, or Internet shopping |
| Independent stores | Chains |
| Private realm | Public environment |
| Separate | Integrated into the community |
| Single use | Mixed use |
| Indoor | Outdoor |
| Parking lots | Parking structures |
| Malls | Town centers |
| Strips | Lifestyle centers |
| Food courts | Food |
| Throwaway buildings | Sustainable design |
| Drab | Green |
| Follows suburbanization | Follows (re)urbanization |

strive to connect with their community. They present themselves as more authentic and better attuned to the lifestyles and aspirations of their customers than traditional suburban shopping centers. They add, in the words of Christopher Leinberger, of the Brookings Institution, "walkable urbanity" to the place. Walkable retail centers also make clustered development nearby more attractive, since people will be able to park once and walk to various destinations.

Chapter 4 discussed the need to create more walkable environments. After more than a half-century of auto-dependence, Pasadena, California, has undertaken a coordinated effort to return to its walkable roots.[14] Paseo Colorado, a three-block urban village, replaced an enclosed mall, transforming an inward-focused shopping experience into a walkable, mixed-use environment that reintroduces streetfront shops, provides interior retail, and reconnects the urban block pattern. Two light-rail stations are within a ten-minute or so walk. Paseo Colorado is a key element in the city's effort to "transform Colorado Boulevard into an inviting pedestrian link."[15]

## The Urbanizing of Suburbia

Because it is the most public of all land uses, retail is typically the focus of commercial districts around the world. Retail adds energy, excitement, and activity to the public realm, drawing people in as they go about their daily business. America's suburbs, however, were built largely without commercial districts, relying instead on single-use, auto-oriented shopping centers. This situation is now beginning to change, as America's suburbs age and take on many of the characteristics of the nation's older cities. Suburbs are beginning to evolve just as cities have evolved for millennia—where we have allowed them to do so. Walkable environments are being created; housing choices broadened; mobility options planned for; land uses mixed; and, in urbanized suburban commercial districts, densities selectively increased. In many of America's metropolitan areas, diversity and civic and cultural presences are being enhanced, and obsolete and underutilized properties are being redeveloped to provide more cosmopolitan environments and amenities. Downtowns—the places that many suburbanites have avoided for decades, and one of the last missing pieces of the suburban development puzzle—are now being added in suburbs from coast to coast, although they are euphemistically being called town centers. The irony is inescapable. It seems that "Americans want to spend time in places that look like cities but feel like suburbs."[16]

The need for more sustainable retail-anchored town centers is becoming more apparent. Valencia, California, was one of the first places to build a shopping district that evoked an old-fashioned town center, and such town centers have since become very popular, even though they have been growing older. The Valencia center offers just about everything one's heart could desire in shopping and entertainment: from name-brand stores to a carousel for kids; from a popular Japanese restaurant to a Colonial Williamsburg store.[17] As suburban populations have soared, along with jobs and shopping opportunities, many suburbanites have chosen to live independently from the older cities that form the core of their metro areas. Many people never "go downtown," except for an occasional symphony concert, sporting event, or night on the town. At the same time, however, suburbanites are becoming increasingly aware of their own communities' shortcomings. They don't like the inconvenience and dysfunction that are slowly eating away at their vaunted quality of life. Immature and inefficient development patterns, monumental traffic jams, ugly commercial strips, obsolete shopping malls, an aging monoculture of single-family homes, environmental degradation, and the lack of a strong civic presence and urban amenities are all evidence that the Ozzie-and-Harriet suburbs have failed to meet all of their residents' needs.

The most important anchors of today's retail-driven suburban town centers and commercial districts are the public spaces around which they are organized and designed. Unfortunately, traditional suburbia offers few public places that are suitable for retail development or accommodating to all segments of society—places where people can get together to interact with each other, to celebrate, to stroll, to protest, to sit and watch the world go by, or just to enjoy day-to-day living. The reason is that these types of places are typically found in and around downtowns, and downtowns were never part of the suburban dream. From the beginning, suburbs revolved around private places like backyards, swim clubs, country clubs, and malls. At best, downtowns were considered anachronisms; at worst, they were places to avoid—filled, as they were, with crime, deterioration, poverty, and people who were "different." So suburban downtowns were never built.

Today's suburban communities have a once-in-a-generation opportunity to create energized suburban commercial districts anchored by retail and mixed with other uses, including dining and entertainment. The marketability and sustainability of the world's great metropolitan areas—including both the cities and their suburbs—is and will be determined, to a large extent, by the success or failure of their public realms. Suburbs in the new metropolitan form must learn from older cities, but should not mimic them. The hierarchy of public spaces, places, and corridors that characterizes great public realms creates frameworks for shaping metro areas as they grow, and reflects and reinforces their lifestyle, character, and livability. The best mix creates integrated public networks that optimize choices for moving around, observing, relaxing, interacting with others, engaging in life's daily pleasures and pursuits, and building a harmonious sense of community. But the public realm does not create itself; it is not space that is left over after the buildings are built. The public realm must be planned, designed, paid for, and maintained as an integral part of the never-ending city-building process carried on by both the public and private sectors.

Numerous trends—many of which result from the changing metropolitan form—are driving a sea change in suburban attitudes toward cities, downtowns, and public gathering places. These trends include the following:

▸ First, and most importantly, the typical suburbanite has changed. Suburbia is no longer dominated by white middle-class married couples with children. Today's suburbs are as diverse as the cities they surround in terms of race, culture, income, age, sexual preference, and lifestyle. This implies that different development solutions—such as a range of housing types to accommodate all lifestyles at different life-cycle stages—are needed to meet contemporary needs.

▸ Many of the problems once associated with downtowns—especially crime, deterioration, and visual blight—have largely dissipated. Today, downtowns are cool again.

▸ Relentless, low-density suburban development patterns that require a car to go anywhere are unsustainable, given the projected scale of suburban growth.

▸ There is a powerful desire in suburbia to recreate the sense of community and connectedness that was lost to the rapid metropolitan growth of the past few decades. Traditional town development is increasingly regarded as a solution to this feeling of placelessness.

▸ Suburbanites, along with everyone else, harbor a simple desire for more convenience in their busy lives.

▸ Smart growth is growing in popularity as voters begin to realize the hidden costs of current suburban development practices.

▸ Finally, suburbanites may not want to live downtown, but that doesn't mean they don't want the amenities of a sophisticated urban lifestyle.

If suburban retailing is going to adjust to these new trends, we will have to think about the regulations that govern it. U.S. retail square footage per capita has been growing faster than the population. In 1980, there were 13 square feet (1.2 square meters) per person; by 2007, this number had risen to 20.3 square feet (1.9 square meters) per person.[18] Most retail markets are saturated, and competition is ferocious. Many suburban communities have designated all the land along their highways for commercial uses, and then waited for developers and retailers to fill in the individual parcels. According to a ULI study, this practice has led to too much retail zoning and sprawl, because it has had the effect of "extending strips prematurely in discontinuous and inefficient ways" and rendering much retail space obsolete. The answer lies in pruning back the amount of land zoned for retail—which, paradoxically, will foster retail growth, support revitalization, and improve the quality of existing retail strips.[19] Retail zoning will also need to become more mixed use and form based in order to encourage the types of pedestrian-oriented environments in which contemporary retailing thrives.

## Big-Box Transformations

As traditional suburban and exurban markets become saturated with Targets, Wal-Marts, and Best Buys, a major transformation is occurring in the big-box world. To maintain their growth and please Wall Street, big-box chains are considering urban locations and constructing innovative urban configurations on infill sites. Big-box stores are also looking longingly at dense older communities for new sites because these locations are among the last frontiers available to them. But appropriate urban sites are difficult to secure and even more difficult to get approval to build on, since communities don't want to undermine the competitiveness of existing stores—even though they may want the big-box tax dollars.

This emerging trend has enormous and complex implications for the metropolitan form and the revitalization of existing communities. Big-box stores are difficult to integrate into traditional, pedestrian-oriented retail environments because of their enormous size and the large parking fields that they typically require. And because low prices are the *raison d'etre* for big-box stores, multilevel configurations, higher design standards, and expensive structured or underground parking may not be options unless public subsidies are provided. But residents are often unsupportive of such subsidies—and, in fact, may oppose big-box stores—because of their concerns about traffic congestion and parking, as well as their supposition that their favorite local stores will not be able to compete. Although it may be sound public policy in the abstract to bring value-oriented shopping to urban customers, the reality is difficult to achieve without creative public/private partnerships. Nevertheless, as land values rise; as suitable exurban sites become more scarce; as customers become more demanding about value, choice, and convenience; and as opportunities for growth on greenfield sites become more limited because of governmental interest in encouraging sustainable development, the urbanization of the big box is becoming an inexorable trend.

## Modern Retail Centers

The newest iterations of the shopping mall have been popping up everywhere in recent years. Often referred to as "lifestyle centers," these projects are typically positioned at the upscale, upper-middle end of retail, and are designed to appeal to customers' aspirations. The first shopping center in the nation developed as a lifestyle center was the Shops of Saddle Creek, in Germantown, Tennessee, near Memphis. With its landscaped pedestrian environment, variety of national specialty shops, good restaurants, fountains, and accessibility, it is an experience in itself.

Two main forces are driving the creation of these centers: the need to give customers more than they get at a typical shopping mall (more shopping, dining, and entertainment choices; a more pleasant environment; more connections with the community), and the desire to position shopping centers closer to where affluent professionals live, in order to take advantage of the booming luxury-goods market. In the seven-mile (11-kilometer) ring around Saddle Creek, for example, the average household income is $86,270. "They are the fastest growing retail format today," says Terry McEwen, president of Tennessee-based Poag & McEwen, the development firm that industry experts credit with pioneering lifestyle center development.[20]

In contrast to the value offered by the big-box format, lifestyle centers offer comfortable, experiential environments in every size, from neighborhood to regional. They typically feature stores like Pottery Barn, Williams-Sonoma, and Barnes & Noble; open-air formats with comfortable outdoor furniture where one can sit in the sunshine and watch the world go by; lush landscaping and stress-relieving fountains; fitness and health centers, spas, and other leisure activities; special services and amenities targeted to aspirational customers; and a generally nurturing atmosphere.

Calling a lifestyle center a mall "is like calling Secretariat a horse—technically correct, but somehow insufficient."[21] In 2002, these centers numbered just 30; today they are impossible to count because the characteristics once associated exclusively with lifestyle centers have been incorporated into all types of contemporary retail and mixed-use environments. In fact, Beyard argues that "what is being called lifestyle is really just modern retailing. . . . Virtually all new retail centers have environments that reflect so-called lifestyle characteristics."[22]

Moreover, characteristics of lifestyle centers are being integrated into urban or semiurban revitalizations. The Americana at Brand, in Glendale, California; downtown Silver Spring, in Maryland; Atlantic Station, in Atlanta, Georgia; and the Market Commons at Clarendon, in Arlington, Virginia, are all examples of this trend. Thus, the likely successor to the lifestyle center will be its predecessor: a traditional main street. If this happens, and these centers continue to morph into mixed-use redevelopment projects, significant neighborhood revitalization will be the happy result.

## Urban Neighborhoods: The Forgotten Frontier

There is only one place in America with more spending power than stores to spend it in: the traditional downtowns and inner-city neighborhoods of our older cities. Over the past five decades, retailing in urban neighborhoods has hollowed out, leaving most cities

---

### FIVE METROPOLITAN RETAIL DEVELOPMENT STRATEGIES

1  Reduce the overall amount of retail-zoned land.

2  Plan for commercial districts, not retail strips.

3  Explore ways to share tax revenues from retail development.

4  Update regulations to require urban mixed- and multiuse, form-based, and pedestrian-oriented commercial development.

5  Offer incentives for the redevelopment of obsolete shopping centers and deteriorated suburban strips.

**SOURCE:** Michael Beyard, ULI senior resident fellow and ULI/Martin Bucksbaum chair for retail and entertainment.

and many inner-ring suburbs with too few shopping opportunities to support healthy neighborhoods and strong communities. Despite years of publicity and effort—and recent development successes—the shameful reality is that America's inner-city neighborhoods are still the forgotten frontier of retailing.

Many inner-city neighborhoods remain blighted by mile after mile of desolate commercial streets and retail strips, and millions of residents are forced to travel outside their communities just to shop for basic needs. While this situation is slowly changing in some communities—as gentrification occurs, or where forward-thinking retailers and public and private sector developers bring services to inner-city markets—any drive through vast swaths of American cities shows that much more needs to be done. No other developed country would tolerate the situation that exists in today's American inner-city neighborhoods, and we've tolerated it for far too long. The results are apparent to anyone living in or visiting a U.S. city today: commercial streets with deteriorating buildings; storefronts that are empty or occupied by marginal, month-to-month tenants; an undersupply of essential goods and services; poor pedestrian environments and amenities; and untended streets and sidewalks.

The decline of neighborhood retail has had a profound effect on the desirability of many urban neighborhoods and communities. The convenient availability of goods and services is a key factor that people consider when choosing where to live. Thus, neighborhoods are dramatically weakened by a lack of suitable retail. Residents who can afford to leave such neighborhoods do so, and potential new residents choose to live elsewhere. Communities without neighborhood retail options cannot be sustained over the long term.

As gentrification takes hold in many urban and close-in suburban neighborhoods, retailers are taking notice for the first time in a generation. Neighborhood retail is no longer viewed as "for poor people" only. Retail pioneers—both chains and mom-and-pop stores—are beginning to meet the largely untapped market for urban retail by locating in neighborhoods that have been woefully underserved for years. Because these retailers have been encouraged by their initial success in these areas, it is reasonable to expect that this trend will expand into even poorer neighborhoods in future years, as retailers continue to look for promising new markets. Retail still follows rooftops, but today this is as likely to occur in cities as in suburbs.

With much of the retail industry focused on glitzy, innovative projects, from the latest lifestyle centers to new suburban town centers, it's easy to lose track of the reality that many communities have virtually no retail at all, and little hope of getting any—none of the chain stores, none of the restaurants, none of the specialty outlets, none of the entertainment, and none of the services that we take for granted in our day-to-day lives. And it's important for us to remember that no neighborhood can be truly livable without retail services, and that no metropolitan area can be truly sustainable with rot at its core.

But there's good news on this front: urban retail is not disappearing. As a matter of fact, according to the Brookings Institution, some $3 trillion in public and private funds will be invested in U.S. urban communities during the next decade.[23] Michael Rubinger,

## EIGHT STEPS TO RESHAPE THE STRIP

Communities can begin to improve existing commercial strips by undertaking long-term efforts that will gradually transform these strips into mixed-use town centers. The following actions can help.

1  **Put a firm limit on the length of any commercial district.** Wherever possible, focus on depth rather than length: a four-square-block district offers as much potential commercial space as one that is spread along 16 blocks of a single street, while concentrating commercial uses and encouraging shared parking and walking among stores.

2  **Limit curb cuts.** Consolidate entrances from the roadway to a few main driveways, with internal service streets based on a block system to connect businesses and parking areas. This will relieve traffic backups, accidents, and the need to widen main roads.

3  **Unify the streetscape.** Use continuous trees and high-quality parking lot landscaping to create a unified streetscape and, where possible, planted medians in the main roadway to limit left-hand turns.

4  **Provide attractive sidewalks and safe crosswalks.** The ability to walk to and within retail districts will encourage shared parking and use of public transportation.

5  **Build continuous, form-based street frontage in denser pulses of commercial development.** Hide large parking lots and structures with small, closely spaced storefronts and parking behind or on the side. Intersperse lower-density development or open space between the higher-density pulses.

6  **Require contextual architecture.** Ensure that ground floors are designed for retail uses, with higher ceiling heights, a mix of floor plates, and individualized shopfronts. Multistory buildings with offices and/or residences above the stores can diminish the "big box" feel of traditional strip malls.

7  **Encourage a mix of other uses.** Including residential or office space is a step toward building a convenient and walkable neighborhood rather than a driving-only strip district.

8  **Eradicate ugliness.** Encourage appropriate facades and signs, underground utility wires, street trees, and improved design of new buildings.

**SOURCE:** Adapted from Michael D. Beyard and Michael Pawlukiewicz, *Ten Principles for Reinventing America's Suburban Strips* (Washington, D.C.; ULI–the Urban Land Institute, 2001).

president and CEO of the New York City–based Local Initiatives Support Corporation (LISC)—an intermediary organization devoted to promoting urban revitalization— is encouraging in his assessment of future opportunities for redevelopment: "These markets are being rebuilt to the point where retailers are starting to look at them in a serious way."[24] Bay Street, in Emoryville, California, for example, has been transformed from a deteriorated urban commercial street into a vibrant streetfront retail destination.

For years, residents of Congress Heights, an inner-city neighborhood in Washington, D.C., had been forced to cross the Maryland state line to find a full-service grocery store. After a five-year search, the William C. Smith Company—which was already at work renovating and replacing housing stock and building a recreation center in the neighbor- hood—recruited Landover, Maryland–based Giant Foods to build a 65,000-square-foot (6,039-square-meter) grocery, its largest in the metro area. The Giant store created 300 full- and part-time jobs in the neighborhood and helped bring in other retailers, including

Staples and Starbucks, says Oramenta Newsome, director of the LISC Washington office.[25] LISC helped jump-start the project with $18.6 million in tax credits.

On the other side of the country, in the Diamond Neighborhood of San Diego, a $25 million commercial/cultural project known as Market Creek Plaza came into being in the early years of the new century, on the ten-acre (four-hectare) site of a long-abandoned factory bordered by barbed wire. The project was the result of a partnership between the nonprofit Jacobs Center for Neighborhood Innovation (JCNI) and more than 3,000 residents, who came together in teams, working with JCNI on every aspect of the development: planning, design, construction, leasing, and operation.[26] The retail space includes a bank, restaurants, multicultural shops, and the first major chain grocery store in the community in 30 years. Broad community participation and the leverage supplied by JCNI and the federal new markets tax credit were the keys to the success of this project, which received a ULI Award for Excellence in 2007. The development, begun in 1998 and completed in 2005, created more than 360 temporary construction jobs and more than 170 permanent jobs; more importantly, it "recaptured nearly $24.4 million in annual economic leakage from the neighborhood."[27]

The challenges of rebuilding persist not only in low-income neighborhoods, but also in many other urban and urbanized locations where retailing never recovered from the shift to suburban shopping centers. Even in some of the most affluent suburban communities, where first-generation auto-oriented shopping streets have begun to urbanize and take on characteristics of urban shopping districts, redevelopment efforts are often stymied by residents who object to the transition, as well as to the changes in character, diversity, and density that the transition requires.

In addition, the changing physical and environmental requirements for successful retailing have altered the competitive positions of many neighborhood retail streets. Existing store spaces, especially in older urban areas, are often too small to accommodate the large and growing floor plates of most modern chain retailers. The lack of convenient parking and the lack of adequate governmental attention to the area's problems also tend to discourage retail development. Redeveloping these streets can be problematic without a carefully thought out public/private strategy that permits development flexibility, encourages retailer innovation, and improves the public realm.

In all cases, rebuilding neighborhood retail is a difficult, lengthy, and complicated process. It differs significantly from developing a suburban shopping center on a greenfield site or reestablishing a downtown shopping district. Innovative strategies must be employed to restore the neighborhood's vitality and competitiveness. Neighborhood retail streets are betwixt and between most communities' established retail locations, and they have been largely forgotten or purposefully avoided for years by retailers, developers, and shoppers. The reasons are clear: widespread misperceptions about the extent of urban buying power, the belief that greater retail opportunities lie elsewhere, and the fact that many of the social problems faced by urban neighborhoods have proved difficult to solve.

Even before Hurricane Katrina struck, the situation in inner-city New Orleans was particularly illustrative of the problems of underserved neighborhoods. While the tourist's image of New Orleans was one of commercial vibrancy and fun, as exemplified by the French Quarter, the nearby Lower Ninth Ward had no grocery store, no bank, and few other stores or services. Many of the city's other poor neighborhoods faced similar retail deficiencies. Of course, the lack of retail services was just a symptom of deeper community problems: the poor were largely warehoused in isolated and dilapidated public housing with little hope of bettering their lives. Unemployment was above 30 percent, public education was deficient, health care was poor, the crime rate was high, and racism was a part of everyday life. While this situation was extreme, similar situations exist today in cities around the country, and retail simply cannot flourish in this type of environment.

Post-Katrina, the rebirth of lost neighborhoods in New Orleans could provide a golden opportunity to create mixed-income neighborhoods that can support retail services and serve as a model of sustainable, retail-served urban communities for the rest of the country. But to accomplish this will require more than simply building stores and finding tenants willing to lease space. It will require building healthy neighborhoods where retail can flourish.

The opportunities for reestablishing retail along urban neighborhood commercial streets are great. Through careful planning, these streets can be given new roles to fill in today's marketplace that will better serve neighborhood residents. Visibility is still extremely important for retail success, but there are different types of visibility. The Barnes & Noble store in downtown Bethesda, Maryland, is hidden on a secondary street. Yet it is highly successful. Why? Although the Bethesda Barnes & Noble lacks a large parking lot and has no frontage on a major roadway, it is located in an attractive, walkable, bikeable, mixed-use environment, with lots of higher-end residential development nearby. It is a place where people stay longer, spend more money, and come back more often—in short, a place worthy of affection. But we must offer a word of caution here: attempts to recreate past glories, a commonly voiced goal, rarely succeed, because most urban neighborhoods have changed dramatically over the past few decades, and their position in the regional hierarchy of retail destinations has been marginalized by newer concentrations of retail in wealthier neighborhoods with better access, visibility, parking, security, and retail environments.

The large trade areas that many neighborhood retail streets once enjoyed have been shrunk by newer retail centers; changes in retail merchandising have rendered obsolete much of the retail space along neighborhood streets; demographic shifts have reduced population densities and buying power; and a critical mass of retailers no longer exists along many of these streets. The result has been lower demand, high vacancies, a poor retail environment, and a failure to adapt to changed competitive circumstances. To achieve long-term sustainability, plans for rebuilding neighborhood shopping streets must recognize these changes and embrace solutions that are realistically market based.

It is not enough to base plans solely on enlightened public policy goals, no matter how well intentioned, or on the community's wish list.

In spite of the challenges faced by neighborhood retail streets, their future is turning much brighter. The timing is right to rebuild these places. Numerous metropolitan trends are redirecting growth back into existing communities, and this has positive implications for the rebirth of neighborhood retail. Urban living is becoming more popular among empty nesters, singles, seniors, and nontraditional households. Immigrants are flocking to neighborhood streets as low-cost places to open small businesses, stores, and restaurants. Retailers are again interested in urban locations, because their traditional suburban markets are saturated. States are increasingly concerned about the effects of sprawl and are instituting smart growth policies. Pedestrian-oriented streetfront retail environments are gaining favor with today's consumers. Inner-city crime has declined dramatically in the past ten years. And local governments are using increasingly sophisticated planning, regulatory, and financial incentives to encourage market-based real estate investments targeted to distressed urban neighborhoods.

But these positive trends alone are not enough to ensure that rebuilding will occur on its own, even in affluent locations, and it is important to realize that it will take far more time and effort to rebuild neighborhood retail than it took to destroy it. The challenge for the public and private sectors is to work together aggressively to create an environment in which retail can thrive. If this doesn't happen, retailers will continue to shun neighborhood streetfront locations and to choose what they believe to be more competitive sites. Gaining the public sector's commitment is a difficult challenge because cities and states are faced with increasingly limited resources and many new and competing obligations. Nevertheless, ways must be found, as part of a long-term strategy, to get started today on the task of rebuilding retail services, because the future prosperity of our metropolitan areas depends on it.

## Creating Real Places

People change. Tastes change. Habits change. Markets change. Retail industry experts believe that malls need to change every seven years to remain relevant. And the cycle of change is accelerating. As the metropolitan form has morphed from city and suburb to a complex, interrelated, regional mosaic of development nodes and edgeless cities, shopping has also evolved, and it is continuing to evolve. Some malls and older-format shopping centers are still relevant. But big boxes, category killers, and online shopping are deeply entrenched in the retail mainstream, and they have rendered many older retail formats irrelevant forever. For the affluent, urban shopping streets, lifestyle centers, and "fortress malls"—like Costa Mesa's South Coast Plaza or northern Virginia's Tysons Corner Center—have become the specialty shopping environments of choice. More moderate-income families shop at suburban town centers, regional malls, and strip centers. The poor travel great distances to shop—or they do without. And everyone frequents the big boxes.

A new form of retail—one that is very different from the cookie-cutter malls and strip retail centers of the 1960s and 1970s—can provide a key to the revitalization of older urban and inner-ring suburban areas. If it is to remain competitive and meet the needs of today's and tomorrow's consumers, retailing in 21st-century America must evolve in ways that will support our maturing and densifying metro areas and neighborhoods. As Beyard notes,

*The really important goals of modern retailing . . . should be to create real places that reflect deeper community values such as sustainability, adaptability to changing consumer demands, denser mixed-use environments that offer convenience, and true community focus and connections with surrounding neighborhoods. And they should be put in locations that make sense from a regional perspective, that serve overlooked customers, and where transit can be accommodated now or in the future.*[28]

**ENDNOTES**

1 *Directory of Major Malls* (Nyack, N.Y.: Directory of Major Malls, Inc.).

2 ULI defines a power center as a shopping center that contains at least one super anchor (perhaps a discount department store or a warehouse club); multiple off-price, category-specific anchors; and a minimal number of small, side-space tenants that together constitute no more than 15 percent of the total gross leasable area. See W. Paul O'Mara, Michael D. Beyard, and Dougal M. Casey, *Developing Power Centers* (Washington, D.C.: ULI-the Urban Land Institute, 1996). According to Michael Beyard, a category killer is an off-price, category-specific retail anchor tenant, like TJ Maxx (apparel), Circuit City (electronics), Bed, Bath and Beyond (housewares and linens), and so forth. These stores are designed to "kill" their competition by offering a deep selection of goods in one retail category at the lowest prices.

3 See Anita Kramer et al., *Retail Development*, 4th ed. (Washington, D.C.: ULI-the Urban Land Institute, 2008), Ch. 8.

4 Michael Beyard, "Rebalancing the Retail Ratio," *Urban Land* (January 2007): 40.

5 Michael D. Beyard et al., *Ten Principles for Rethinking the Mall* (Washington, D.C.: ULI-the Urban Land Institute, 2006), iv-viii.

6 Kramer, *Retail Development*, 189ff.

7 Ibid.

8 Ibid., 209, 211.

9 William H. Hudnut III, *Halfway to Everywhere* (Washington, D.C.: ULI-the Urban Land Institute, 2003), 353.

10 Beyard et al., *Ten Principles*, 32.

11 Jamie Reno, "Scenes from a New Mall," *Newsweek*, December 4, 2006, 60; available at www.newsweek.com/id/43924.

12 Michael Beyard, conversation with author, August 2008.

13 Bob Gibbs, conversation with author, June 2007.

14 Adrienne Schmitz and Jason Scully, *Creating Walkable Places: Compact Mixed-Use Solutions* (Washington, D.C.: ULI-the Urban Land Institute, 2006), 140ff.

15 Ibid., 141.

16 Joel Kotkin, "An Age of Transformation," *Economist*, May 29, 2008; available at www.joelkotkin.com/Commentary/Economist%20An%20Age%20of%20Transformation.htm.

17 Kotkin, "Age of Transformation"; and Westfield Valencia Town Center Web site, http://losangeles.citysearch.com/profile/283666/valencia_ca/westfield_valencia_town_center.html.

18 Data from Cushman & Wakefield Healy & Baker.

19 Michael D. Beyard and Michael Pawlukiewicz, *Ten Principles for Reinventing America's Suburban Strips* (Washington, D.C.: ULI–the Urban Land Institute, 2001), 8.

20 Parija Bhatnagar, "Not a Mall, It's a Lifestyle Center," CNN/Money, January 12, 2005; http://money.cnn.com/2005/01/11/news/fortune500/retail_lifestylecenter/.

21 Ibid.

22 Michael Beyard, "Beyond Lifestyle," *Urban Land* (January 2008): 38.

23 Steve McLinden, "Worth a Second Look: Nonprofits Reveal Urban Opportunities Missed by the U.S. Census," *Shopping Centers Today*, July 2006; available at www.metro-edge.com/download/Shopping_Centers_Today_072006.pdf.

24 Ibid.

25 Ibid.

26 Julie D. Stern, *Urban Land Institute Award-Winning Projects 2007* (Washington, D.C.: ULI–the Urban Land Institute, 2007), 12.

27 Ibid., 13.

28 Beyard, "Beyond Lifestyle," 38.

# CHAPTER 9

# Green Is Neither Red nor Blue

**We do not inherit the land from our ancestors; we borrow it from our children.**

—NATIVE AMERICAN PROVERB

*Infill and compact development can serve as helpful antidotes to sprawl, but with America's population growing by 100 million in the next 40 years or so, continued greenfield development is inevitable. But it must take a different form than it has in the past. It must be planned, designed, and developed to create sustainable, environmentally sensitive places where residents can live, work, and play in harmony with nature and with each other. Thinking "green" can carry Americans beyond the political divide of "red" and "blue." Green infrastructure and green building can promote connectivity in urbanizing pods of development and help conserve energy. These and other 21st-century strategies need to be implemented throughout the nation. A greener metropolitan America will be a better, more livable America.*

**IMAGINE HOMES, BUSINESSES,** schools, and even entire communities, all built in harmony with nature. Instead of degraded resources, wasted energy, and toxic materials, there would be abundant green space; energy-efficient and environmentally friendly buildings; and places that are beautiful, walkable, health-enhancing, and built to last. That's what sustainability is all about.

The sitcom suburbs of the mid-20th century were made up of isolated pods of look-alike houses, all of similar sizes, shapes, and prices. Most of these suburbs were built on greenfields, with no thought of preserving wildlife or native plant habitat. Energy was cheap, so there was no need to make the houses energy efficient. And because construction materials were also relatively inexpensive, no effort was made to use sustainably produced materials, or to recycle or reuse materials. The houses in these suburbs were separated from most other land uses; anyone who wanted to buy a loaf of bread or a quart of milk had to climb into the family car and drive to a "convenience store" on the nearest commercial strip. Inside the development, residents might have big yards, but there were few, if any, parks or public gathering places—except the cul-de-sac. Streets were wide, houses were dominated by garages, and parents were forced to drive their children everywhere for everything, from soccer games to dancing school.

But things have changed. During the past two decades, environmentalists, developers, and homebuyers have become more concerned about the impact of development and the way we live in the natural environment. A new style of development—known as *sustainable, green,* or *environmentally friendly*—has emerged, and is becoming increasingly marketable. Two complementary ideas—smart conservation and smart development—represent the next generation of smart growth. This two-pronged approach recognizes that development can be a powerful tool for conservation, and can be used to promote more efficient growth patterns wherever development takes place. Smart conservation and smart development are two of the most important planks in a new environmentalist platform that focuses on protecting and restoring land, but also concentrates on the pace, shape, and location of development.

Our goal should be to plan, design, and build places that last. As economist Herbert Stein has said, "If something is 'unsustainable,' that means it won't be sustained."[1] Sustainable communities will not wear out after a generation of use. They are environmentally sound, economically viable, culturally appropriate, and socially equitable. To create such communities, we must implement responsible land use planning that will mitigate rather than exacerbate the impact of development on the natural environment.

Where and how will we build these sustainable places? Greenfield development offers "the most practical, affordable, and achievable chance to build without sprawl, given its potential to create large-scale, conserved open lands and sustainable modern infrastructure."[2] But the greenfield development of today and tomorrow must take a very different form than that of the past. Likewise, those who invest in these communities must take a very different attitude toward their investments.

At ULI's 2008 Developing and Investing Green Conference, keynote speaker Peter Calthorpe, founder and president of Calthorpe Associates, in Berkeley, California, stressed that sustainable development must take a holistic approach and encompass a range of goals, including energy conservation, land preservation, workforce housing close to jobs, and transportation choices. "Where you choose to develop is more important than what you develop," said Calthorpe, pointing out the substantial energy savings—in terms of energy consumed by homes and transportation—offered by a denser urban setting as opposed to a sprawling, isolated suburban area. Well-designed density, in conjunction with mixed-income, mixed-use, transit-oriented development, can be "fighting territory," in terms of battling restrictive zoning and other land use regulations, but it is the "right territory," according to Calthorpe.[3]

Responsible property investment involves the conscious decision to conduct all business operations in ways that contribute to the long-term well-being of the community and the environment. The good news is that this is happening in broader and broader development circles each year. South Carolina- and Colorado-based Chaffin/Light Associates, for example, states that its primary focus is "the development of sustainable communities that provide built and social environments that reflect the culture of the surrounding area."[4] Portland, Oregon-based Gerding Edlen Development's goal is "creating sustainable and inspiring places to work, live, and learn."[5] The mission of the New York-based Jonathan Rose Companies is to

*repair the fabric of cities, towns and villages, while preserving the land around them. To do this, we plan and develop diverse, mixed-use, transit-accessible, mixed-income communities or components focused on nodes of transportation. At the same time, we develop plans to preserve surrounding farms and open spaces. The result is equitable, and supports the cultural, environmental and biological health of the bioregions we work in.[6]*

In yet another example, Charlotte, North Carolina-based developer Crosland states in its corporate philosophy, "We take our role very seriously in shaping the future of the communities we build. Whether we enhance an urban environment and promote a pedestrian environment by mixing uses, or preserve valuable wildlife and tree canopy, we are committed to creating a sustainable future."[7]

Crosland's Terrazzo development, in Nashville, Tennessee, is the Southeast's first Leadership in Environmental and Energy Design (LEED) precertified building. The 14-story mixed-use development, which is expected to be completed in spring 2009, contains 20,000 square feet (1,858 square meters) of retail space and 75,000 square feet (6,967 square meters) of office space, topped by ten floors of residential space featuring 109 luxury condominiums. Terrazzo is incorporating double-flush toilets that will reduce water use by 40 percent, a vegetated roof that will reduce urban heat island effects, and additional features that will reduce energy consumption. More than 50 percent of the project's construction waste is being recycled. Its urban location places it within walking distance of public transit, shopping, dining, and entertainment.[8] Another Crosland project, Biltmore Park Town Square, in Asheville, North Carolina, will be a high-density, mixed-use community that conserves land, reduces driving, encourages walking, and better manages stormwater runoff, thereby achieving a number of sustainable development goals.

Sustainable development employs, conserves, and enhances the community's resources so that ecological processes are maintained and the quality of life, now and

# THE SANBORN PRINCIPLES FOR SUSTAINABLE DEVELOPMENT

In 1994, the National Renewable Energy Laboratory gathered a group of nationally known experts in every field related to sustainability. This group developed the following set of seven principles, which have been used by cities, towns, and groups around the world to move toward a more sustainable future.

1  **Ecologically responsive.** The design of human habitat shall recognize that all resources are limited, and will respond to the patterns of natural ecology. Land plans and building designs will include only those with the least disruptive impact upon the natural ecology of the earth. Density must be most intense near neighborhood centers where facilities are most accessible.

2  **Healthy and sensible buildings.** The design of human habitat must create a living environment that will be healthy for all occupants. Buildings should be of appropriate human scale in a nonsterile, aesthetically pleasing environment. Building design must respond to toxicity of materials, electromagnetic fields, lighting efficiency and quality, comfort requirements, and resource efficiency. Buildings should be organic, and should integrate art, natural materials, sunlight, green plants, energy efficiency, low noise levels, and water. They should not cost more than current conventional buildings.

3  **Socially just.** Habitats shall be equally accessible across economic classes. Small spaces, charmingly designed, can be solutions for quality, sustainable, low-cost housing.

4  **Culturally creative.** Habitats will allow ethnic groups to maintain individual cultural identities and neighbor- hoods.

5  **Beautiful.** Intimacy with the beauty and numinous mystery of nature must be available to enliven our sense of the sacred.

6  **Physically and economically accessible.** All sites within the habitat shall be accessible and rich in resources to those living within walkable distance. Accessible characteristics include clean, accessible, economical mass transit; bicycle paths; small neighborhood service businesses; radical traffic-calming strategies; and places to go where chances of accidental meetings are high.

7  **Evolutionary.** Designs shall include continuous re-evaluation of premises and values, shall be responsive to demographic changes and flexible enough to change over time to support future user needs. Initial designs should reflect our society's heterogeneity and have a feedback system.

**SOURCE:** Donald Aitken Associates Web site, www.donaldaitkenassociates.com/sanborn_daa.html.

in the future, is enhanced. In North Charleston, South Carolina, the Noisette Company is creating Noisette, a sustainable community in the city's 3,000-acre (1,214-hectare) historic center, which includes a 350-acre (142-hectare) closed naval base. According to founder John Knott, this "new American city" is being developed on the basis of the Sanborn Principles (see the accompanying feature box), which were created in 1994 by a diverse group of visionaries who came together to describe the essential attributes of a sustainable community. These characteristics, says Knott, "balance social, economic and environmental well-being, while recognizing the importance of beauty and the need for continuous evolution in a changing world."[9] As our homes, offices, and com- munity facilities become reflections of our new green values, the "green movement" has to do not only with the car we drive and the energy we use, but also with how we live and work in a post-McMansion age.

## What Can We Do?

How, then, are we to create a green metropolitan America? Doing so will require a commitment to conserving green infrastructure, implementing green regionalism, promoting green building, and providing incentives for—or even mandating—sustainable development.

### Green Infrastructure

Across the country, land is being developed faster than ever before: more than 2 million acres (809,371 hectares) of open space is converted each year. This decentralization began at the beginning of the 20th century, and expanded exponentially in the 1950s and beyond, as more and more Americans moved into suburban subdivisions on former farmland. Land is being developed faster than ever—at a rate of nearly two acres (0.8 hectares) every minute, according to the American Farmland Trust.[10] In addition, land is being consumed at a rate that far exceeds population growth. A July 2001 report published by the Center on Urban and Metropolitan Policy at the Brookings Institution stated that "between 1982 and 1997, the amount of urbanized land in the United States increased by 47 percent. . . . During this same period, the nation's population grew by only 17 percent" (see Figure 9-1).[11] Today, there is no longer a clear and simple distinction between the urban and rural landscapes. Our metropolitan areas are expanding at an ever-increasing rate into our forests, farmlands, and green space. This accelerated consumption of land, with its resulting fragmentation of open space, is one of the most pressing conservation challenges facing our nation in the 21st century.

Some argue that land in America is still plentiful, and that only 5.4 percent of American land is developed. But much of our undeveloped land is either is unsuitable for development (that is, it is in deserts, muntains, or wetlands), or is protected from development (that is, it is in national forests and other public land holdings). With 53 percent of the population living on 17 percent of our nation's land area, the real challenge is finding open space reasonably close to home and work. Los Angeles is a good example. It has reached its natural boundaries—the mountains and the ocean—but the county's population is projected to grow by over 3.5 million by 2050.[12] Undeveloped land in the desert beyond the city offers scant relief. Given that a majority of the growth demand will be for relatively affordable housing, the answer is not greenfield development anywhere and everywhere; instead, it is infill, redevelopment, and smart growth on the fringe.

FIGURE 9-1 **U.S. Population Growth versus Growth in Urbanized Land, 1982–1997.**

| | Percent Change in Population | Percent Change in Urbanized Land |
|---|---|---|
| Midwest | 7.06 | 32.23 |
| Northeast | 6.91 | 39.10 |
| South | 22.23 | 59.61 |
| West | 32.21 | 48.94 |
| United States | 17.02 | 47.14 |

**SOURCE:** William Fulton, Rolf Pendall, Mai Nguyen, and Alicia Harrison, "Who Sprawls Most? How Growth Patterns Differ across the U.S.," Brookings Institution, Center on Urban and Metropolitan Policy, July 2001, 19; www.brookings.edu/es/urban/publications/fulton.pdf.

The first step in accommodating growth in the right settings is to identify those places that must be protected from development. Communities that have a blueprint for conservation usually do a better job of accommodating growth in appropriate areas. One of the key issues for development is the concept of predictability and certainty: developers want to be certain that the approvals process will go smoothly, and citizens want assurance that treasured open space or cultural resources will be there forever. It is this shared need for predictability and certainty that should bring both groups together. When communities identify where development should go and what resources should be protected, both sides can have more confidence in the process. On the other hand, when citizens think all land is up for grabs, they often oppose development everywhere.

One of the world's preeminent biologists, Edward O. Wilson, has remarked that "it is quite possible by the end of the century that we could destroy the rest of the natural world and with it as many as half the species of plants and animals on Earth."[13] This would be an immeasurable loss. One effect of our sprawling development patterns is what author Richard Louv calls "nature-deficit disorder." In *Last Child in the Woods,* Louv points out that schools may teach students about the Amazon rain forest or endangered species, but conventional development patterns do little to encourage children's direct interaction with the natural terrain outside their own doors.[14] How children understand and experience nature has been turned upside down: instead of touching, feeling, and smelling the natural world as they play in it, today's children are immersed in a synthetic version of nature cultivated in malls and displayed on TV. Louv argues that to fully comprehend global threats to the environment and to flourish as healthy citizens of the planet, children need to have a stronger connection to the natural world. Indeed, contact with, and awareness of, nature appears to be a fundamental human need. Tomorrow's sustainable communities must meet this need by providing natural places near homes, schools, and workplaces.

Hence, it seems only prudent that we plan in such a way that a community's "green infrastructure" is identified and sustained. When we use the word *infrastructure,* we usually think only of built infrastructure such as roads, power lines, and water systems, and of social infrastructure such as schools, hospitals, and libraries. The concept of green infrastructure, however, puts air, land, and water on an equal footing with built and social infrastructure, and transforms open space from "nice to have" to "must have." Thus, green infrastructure, like other infrastructure, would form an integral part of government budgets and programs.

What gives the term *green infrastructure* staying power is the evocative image it brings to mind: planned networks of green spaces that benefit wildlife and people, and link urban settings to rural ones. In *Green Infrastructure: Linking Landscapes and Communities,* Mark A. Benedict and Edward T. McMahon define green infrastructure as "a community's natural life-support system—a strategically planned and managed network of habitat, parks, greenways, conservation easements, and working lands with conservation value that support native species, maintain natural ecological processes, sustain air and water resources, and contribute to the health and quality of the community's life."[15] Green infrastructure networks encompass a wide range of landscape elements, including natural areas such as wetlands, woodlands, waterways, and habitat; public and private conservation lands such as nature preserves, wildlife corridors, greenways, outdoor recreation and trail networks, and parks; cultural and historic resources that provide community character; and public and private working lands, such as forests, farms, and ranches, that have conservation value.

When planned as part of a system of green infrastructure, open space can meet a community's need for parkland and outdoor recreation space while also helping to shape the urban form and buffer incompatible uses. Green infrastructure can even reduce public costs for stormwater management, flood control, and other forms of built infrastructure. Green space can also increase property values and make development more attractive. Perhaps these benefits explain why, between 2000 and 2005, the total acreage of land put into trust nearly doubled, to almost 11.9 million acres (4.8 million hectares), as did the acreage under conservation easements.[16]

Most current efforts to protect open space on the fringe are reactive, site specific, narrowly focused, and not well integrated with land use planning or other public policies. The conservation of green infrastructure, however, represents a dramatic shift in the way local and state governments think about green space. Green infrastructure planning is proactive, systematic, large scale, and well integrated with growth management, transportation planning, and other public policies. One option for the design of green space is the CEDAR approach, which assesses all possible types of open space: cultural, ecological, developmental, agricultural, and recreational. According to the Salt Lake City–based Center for Green Space Design, the CEDAR model "defines, designs, protects and networks a community's open spaces," creating a green infrastructure system that is comprehensive, based on local knowledge, and suited to regional needs.[17] When a community evaluates its open space needs according to the CEDAR principles, it gains valuable insight into the legacy it wants to preserve for future generations.

Another option is "greenprinting," a strategy devised by the Trust for Public Land. Greenprinting is a four-step regional process designed to identify and protect open space and to create a long-term blueprint for the public conservation process. The steps include visioning by government and private organizations; extensive public conversations to discuss priorities such as recreation, watershed protection, flood control, and habitat preservation; identification of the targeted land; and development of a game plan to pay for and acquire land. The end result is a geographic information systems computer model showing which green infrastructure should be protected from development.

Green infrastructure is being created at all scales: local, metropolitan, regional, and state. Consider the following examples:

▸ Under Florida's statewide greenways plan, an integrated approach is used to identify an ecological network of natural hubs, linkages, river corridors, and coastlines—as well as a recreational/trail system connecting parks, urban areas, and cultural sites.

## SEVEN PRINCIPLES FOR BUILDING GREEN INFRASTRUCTURE

The following seven principles can help developers, public policy makers, environmentalists, and concerned citizens plan and build green infrastructure in their communities.

**1  Green infrastructure functions as a framework for both conservation and development.** By making green infrastructure the framework for conservation, communities can plan for interconnected, green, open-space systems. Where isolated islands of nature exist, green infrastructure planning can help identify opportunities to restore the vital ecological connections that will maintain and protect those areas.

**2  Design and plan green infrastructure before development begins.** Restoring natural systems is far more expensive than protecting undeveloped land. Constructed wetlands and other restoration projects often fail to function as well as their natural counterparts over the long term, so it is essential to identify and protect critical ecological hubs and linkages in the early stages of planning.

**3  Linkage is key.** A strategic connection of system components—parks, preserves, riparian areas, wetlands, and other green spaces—is critical to maintaining vital ecological processes and the health of wildlife populations.

**4  Green infrastructure functions across community boundaries and at different scales.** Green infrastructure systems should connect urban, suburban, rural, and wilderness landscapes and incorporate green-space elements at state, regional, community, and parcel scales.

**5  Green infrastructure is grounded in sound science and land use planning theories and practices.** Experts in conservation biology, landscape ecology, urban and regional planning, landscape architecture, geography, and civil engineering are critical to the successful planning and design of green infrastructure systems.

**6  Green infrastructure is a critical investment.** Strategic placement of green infrastructure can reduce the need for gray infrastructure, freeing funds for other community investments. Green infrastructure also reduces a community's susceptibility to floods, fires, and other natural disasters.

**7  Green infrastructure engages key partners and can involve diverse stakeholders.** Successful master plans forge alliances and relationships between public and private organizations. Such plans can potentially assuage opposition to new development by ensuring stakeholders that growth will occur only within a framework of conservation and open-space lands.

**SOURCE:** Jo Allen Gause, ed., *Developing Sustainable Planned Communities* (Washington, D.C.: ULI–the Urban Land Institute, 2007), 49.

Harmony, a new town being developed in central Florida, is going beyond state and federal requirements with a strategy to preserve 70 percent of its 11,000 acres (4,452 hectares) as ecologically functional open space—including wetlands, lakes, woodlands, and pasture—that is integral to the town's design.[18]

▸ In Miami, mayor Manny Diaz has advanced a green agenda that includes the establishment of a green space utility program and a dedicated fund to maintain and protect Miami's urban forests and green space.[19]

▸ Through a program designed to preserve the foothills and open space around Boulder, Colorado, city government has succeeding in protecting from development more than 43,000 acres (17,401 hectares) surrounding the city. The city most often purchases land outright at fair market value, but it has also used conservation easements and other methods. The result is a true greenbelt that surrounds the perimeter of the city and encourages more efficient development in the city center.

▶ The mission of MillionTreesNYC, a public/private partnership between the New York City Department of Parks and Recreation and the New York Restoration Project, is to plant and care for 1 million new trees in New York City by 2017. The public and private partners of MillionTreesNYC, including citizen volunteers, are planting trees in school-yards and playgrounds; on public housing campuses; in business districts; in commercial and residential developments; and in front yards and on other private lands. The program will expand New York City's urban forest by 20 percent.

▶ To address concerns about the loss of agricultural and green space resources, the town of Pittsford, New York, has implemented a green infrastructure plan. Pittsford's Greenprint began with a community visioning process that identified the working agricultural and natural landscapes that were an essential part of the town's character. Pittsford then commissioned a fiscal analysis of the revenues and expenses associated with existing and potential land uses. The analysis demonstrated that it would be less expensive to implement a new land use plan than to continue the current zoning policy. Pittsford's plan targeted 2,000 acres (809 hectares) of land for permanent protection and created several enhanced economic development sites for commercial and light-industrial development. Because taxpayers understood that protection of open space, including the purchase of development rights, would cost less per year than full buildout of the town, they supported the plan. Landowners supported the plan because they were fairly compensated for the loss of their development rights.

▶ Baltimore plans to double its tree canopy through its Urban Forestry Initiative. Under the Green Canopy program in Sarasota, Florida, the city will buy and plant a tree in a neighborhood if two-thirds of the property owners pledge to water it.

▶ After going through a greenprinting process, voters in Jacksonville, Florida—a city that "used to smell like pulpwood and Puppy Chow"[20]—approved a half-cent sales tax to fund $2 billion worth of new projects, including $50 million to preserve open space. As of mid-2008, Preservation Project Jacksonville had preserved some 53,000 acres (21,448 hectares) through a combination of sales taxes, bonds, and matching federal and state funds.[21]

▶ Bellevue, Washington, has reclaimed its natural systems through the coordinated design of a citywide park system and a stormwater management program. In the early 1970s, the local government decided to change its stormwater system from underground pipes to a less expensive surface drainage system. Today, two city agencies, the Storm and Surface Water Utility and the Parks and Recreation Department, use the same land to accomplish multiple objectives. The utility bears responsibility for water resources and has a budget for land acquisition. The parks department manages much of the utility's land for parks, ball fields, playgrounds, interpretive areas, and trails. Many of these open-space assets are also elements of the stormwater system. As a result of their partnership, both agencies have reduced costs while achieving their diverse objectives.

▶ Neighboring Seattle and King County, Washington, support the Puget Sound region's Cascade Agenda—a long-term plan that, under the greenprinting model, has preserved 2.6 million acres (1.05 million hectares) of green space and water. King County is anticipating a population increase of 100 percent (from 3.5 to 7 million) in the next 60 years, a fact that worries many forward-thinking residents who are concerned about loss of open space and natural systems, overcrowding in parks and on roads and trails, and sprawling growth. "We're dying a death of a thousand cuts," says Cascade Land Conservancy president Gene Duvernoy, "with a little development here, a shopping center there." King County recently bought an entire forest and the development rights to 90,000 acres (36,422 hectares) in order to preserve the green space, create bikeways and walkways, and, perhaps most importantly, absorb carbon emissions.[22]

Green infrastructure facilitates the development of what Rutherford Platt, professor emeritus at the University of Massachusetts at Amherst, calls "the humane metropolis"— a community that can be described as green, healthy, sociable, civic, and inclusive, where people can connect with one another and enjoy a shared urban experience.[23] The humane metropolis is the opposite of a gated community, with its walls or fences and guards shutting out the world.[24]

## Green Regionalism

Site-specific environmental impact statements and the control of stormwater runoff, soil erosion, vegetation removal, and steep-slope construction on a site-by-site basis perpetuate a segmented mitigation system that violates the way natural systems actually function. America needs broad, regional strategies to overcome its fragmented, piecemeal approach to green infrastructure and development, and to link environmental sustainability and local land use planning. Growth typically occurs through a series of incremental decisions, but growth on the fringe provides an opportunity to connect the increments into a meaningful whole. Responsible land use requires vital partnerships based not on confrontation but on a shared vision and mutual goals. To establish a framework that will guide both conservation and development in ways that will benefit the community, the environment, and the economy, developers, environmentalists, local governments, and regional planning organizations must all work together.

Sustainable Cascadia exemplifies green regionalism. The organization, which is allied with the Cascade Agenda, fosters collaboration, education, and collective action to achieve bioregional sustainability. It helps individual communities in the region to identify and develop strategies that meet the challenges of sustainability. Sustainable Cascadia also encourages communities to work together to address shared economic, social, and ecological concerns. Nongovernmental organizations, governmental agencies, corporations, and citizens participate in such efforts in ways that enable them to overcome fragmented and competing ways of operating.[25]

The question is not *whether* we will grow but *how* and *where* we will grow. Few would argue against the benefits of development in urban infill and brownfield sites, but limiting development to these settings is unrealistic if we are to meet the needs of our growing nation. Over the past two decades, urbanized land in the United States has increased by nearly 50 percent, and today the majority of development occurs 25 to 35 miles (40 to 56 kilometers) from urban centers.[26] To address this rapid growth on the fringe will require new regional partnerships, innovative ideas, and proactive approaches. Developers, environmentalists, planners, municipal and county governments, councils of government, and metropolitan planning organizations will all have to be involved if sprawl is to be avoided and sustainable development achieved. Our country cannot go on building one subdivision, one shopping center, one office park, one asphalt parking lot at a time forever. That is not good planning in the 21st century; it is only granting a series of permits that gobble land, increase dependence on the car, and fail to conserve green space.

## Green Building

Once viewed as a fringe movement, the green building movement is gathering strong momentum. Forecasts by Arthur C. Nelson, of Virginia Tech, indicate that two-thirds of the development on the ground by 2050 will have been built between 2007 and 2050, including 89 million new or replacement homes and 190 billion square feet (17.7 billion square meters) of new offices, institutions, stores, and other nonresidential buildings.[27] This transformation represents a historic opportunity to dramatically reduce the environmental impacts of the building sector, including $CO_2$ emissions. Commitments have been made to build 1 billion square feet (92,903,040 square meters) of green construction between 2007 and 2009—which is encouraging, in view of the fact that buildings consume 40 to 45 percent of America's energy output and produce 60 percent of $CO_2$ emissions.[28] Those who built and lived in the suburbs of the 1950s and 1960s didn't worry about whether their homes were sustainable; the mantra back then was "a couple of rooftops and out," and no thought was given to using renewable resources to promote energy efficiency. But now, according to ULI, "it is clear that the real estate industry is on the cusp of a tremendous change that will affect our places of work and daily life in the coming decades."[29]

Green building is emerging as a new way of constructing housing. New approaches are important because, according to U.S. Department of Energy calculations, the residential sector is responsible for 21 percent of all U.S. carbon emissions.[30] Building green—whether a home or an office building, a school or a master-planned community—involves conscious and close attention to a wide range of features. These include the following:

▸ Orienting a structure to maximize solar exposure in winter and to maximize shade in summer; solar exposure not only reduces the need for heating, but may also support the use of photovoltaic (PV) panels to generate electricity.
▸ Conserving natural features such as wetlands and vegetation.
▸ Maximizing natural daylight.
▸ Minimizing stormwater runoff.

**PLANNING FOR AGRICULTURE ON THE URBAN FRINGE**

We plan for housing, commerce, infrastructure, recreation, and the environment. But planning has ignored agriculture. As growth spreads on the fringe, it eventually comes up against productive agricultural land. Without planning, farmland on the urban edge is regarded as vacant land awaiting a higher and better use, not as a resource that accounts for more than half the nation's food production, including well over three-quarters of its fruits and vegetables. To the untrained eye, farmland appears to be ubiquitous, and one farm is indistinguishable from another. That makes the land difficult to protect. Moreover, those who oppose development like to use the preservation of farmland—regardless of its quality, extent, or location—as an argument against development. In the absence of planning to address the inevitable clashes between development and agricultural uses, is it any wonder that farmland remains up for grabs, and that it is the main point of contention between developers and those who want to stop growth?

A number of forward-looking communities are now planning for agriculture. They begin by identifying the most productive farmland, then set aside large enough areas, with farms of sufficient size and productivity to be sustainable, and direct and expedite development elsewhere. It is just as important to plan for agriculture's other needs—for example, through zoning codes that give farmers freedom to do what they must to be successful—and to provide the economic support and infrastructure to sustain agricultural viability. Without these measures, farmland will not remain farmland, even if it is off limits to development.

For some excellent examples of planning for agriculture, see the American Farmland Trust's Web site, www.farmland.org.

- Incorporating technologies that minimize water consumption, such as low-flush toilets and low-flow faucets.
- Using energy-efficient heating, ventilating, and air-conditioning (HVAC) systems (such as natural-gas-fired chillers instead of electric ones).
- Installing high-quality wall insulation, insulated glass windows, and occupancy and light-level sensors.
- Incorporating recycled and recyclable materials.
- Installing cool or green roofs.
- Using low-VOC (volatile organic compounds) products for floor and wall coverings, furniture, carpets, paints, adhesives, and sealants.
- Occupying the least amount of land possible.

Green buildings must be planned, designed, constructed, and managed differently from conventional buildings. They require a highly integrated approach, involving the developer, project manager, architect, engineer, landscape architect, contractor, and others, all of whom must collaborate to conserve materials and resources. As San Francisco mayor Gavin Newsom observed in setting up his city's Green Building Task Force, "We must create more energy and resource efficient buildings in San Francisco to meet our aggressive greenhouse gas reduction targets."[31] Which is to say, urban and suburban planning need to be based on energy efficiency and environmental considerations, higher densities, preservation of open space, and better use of transit.

Solara, an affordable multifamily housing development in San Diego, offers one example of how green building can reduce energy costs and carbon emissions. The 56-unit project, which also contains a community center, was developed by the nonprofit Community Housing Works and is fully powered by PV cells. Incorporating the PV cells added $1.1 million to the development budget, but the owners expect to recover the cost within seven years, through reductions in their electric bills. The PV cells produce sufficient energy for lighting, heating, cooling, and all other residential energy needs, and they even feed daytime surplus energy into California's electric grid. As a result, the project's operating carbon footprint has been reduced by 95 percent. ULI/J. Ronald Terwilliger chair for housing John K. McIlwain says that "Solara shows it is possible to all but eliminate carbon emissions from newly built residential buildings by a combination of design and construction techniques that cost much the same as conventional construction today."[32]

## Green Retail

As is the case with other building types, the greening of retail is underway. Nevertheless, retailing lags behind, and is striving to catch up as the costs and benefits of sustainability become more apparent.

Greening has two meanings for retail development. On the one hand, retailers can use a number of innovative techniques to conserve energy and achieve more sustainable designs; examples include planting the enormous roofs of both shopping centers and big-box stores; recycling runoff from roofs and parking lots; using indigenous plantings that require little irrigation; substituting energy-conserving lighting, heating, and cooling equipment; installing solar paneling; and using local, energy-efficient building materials. On the other hand, sustainability for retailing also involves the location and configuration of the stores and shopping centers themselves. The goal should be to encourage customers to take care of a number of different tasks on a single trip; to reduce automobile trips by increasing access from transit, and for bikers and pedestrians; to increase convenience by mixing uses; and to build closer to where consumers live and work. The increasing urbanization of retailing in both cities and suburbs will be an important emerging aspect of the greening of retail and the development of a stronger nationwide commitment to the conservation of energy and resources.

## Incentives for Green Development

Fortunately, the federal government is encouraging energy efficiency and waste reduction by offering tax incentives to commercial building owners and leaseholders. In the Energy Policy Act of 2005, a deduction of up to $1.80 per square foot [$19.38 per square meter] is allowed for the installation of energy-efficient heating, cooling, ventilation, lighting, and hot water systems, and for part of the building envelope, as long as all the energy-efficiency measures combined "reduce the total annual energy and power costs by 50 percent or more."[33] Another step in the right direction was the enactment of the

Energy Independence and Security Act of 2007, which includes a new initiative known as the Energy Efficiency and Conservation Block Grant Program. Under this program, which is similar to the community development block grant program, Congress established a $10 billion ($2 billion a year for five years) funding authorization (but not an

## THE LEED GREEN BUILDING RATING SYSTEM

While many different green building rating systems have been established since the 1990s at the local, national, and international levels, the U.S. Green Building Council's (USGBC's) Leadership in Energy and Environmental Design (LEED) Green Building Rating System has become the gold standard for rating green buildings. According to the USGBC, LEED "encourages and accelerates global adoption of sustainable green building and development practices through the creation and implementation of universally understood and accepted tools and performance criteria."[1]

LEED is a third-party certification program that has become the nationally accepted benchmark for the design, construction, and operation of high-performance green buildings. Under this performance-oriented rating system, buildings earn points for satisfying criteria designed to address specific environmental impacts inherent in the design, construction, operation, and management of a structure. By earning the required number of points, buildings qualify for one of four levels of LEED certification (certified, silver, gold, and platinum, in that order). The program gives building owners and operators the tools they need to have an immediate and measurable impact on their buildings' performance. LEED promotes a whole-building approach to sustainability by recognizing performance in five key areas of human and environmental health: sustainable site development, water savings, energy efficiency, materials selection, and indoor environmental quality. LEED rating systems currently exist for new construction, existing buildings, commercial interiors, core and shell construction, schools, retail, healthcare, and homes.

A new LEED rating system, currently in its pilot period, will integrate the principles of smart growth, new urbanism, and green building into the first national rating system for neighborhood design. LEED for Neighborhood Development (LEED-ND) is a collaboration among USGBC, the Congress for New Urbanism, and the Natural Resources Defense Council. The post-pilot version of the rating system, which will be available to the public, is projected to launch in 2009. LEED-ND certification is expected to provide independent, third-party verification that a development's location and design meet high standards for environmentally responsible, sustainable development.

Whereas other LEED rating systems focus primarily on green building practices, with only a few credits regarding site selection, LEED-ND will provide an objective basis on which to certify developments as smart growth, while still incorporating green building practices. In short, LEED-ND will create a label, as well as a set of guidelines for decision making, which could serve as a concrete signal of, and incentive for, better location, design, and construction of neighborhoods and buildings.

The existing LEED rating system has a proven track record of encouraging builders to use green building practices; future versions will set the bar for green building leadership.[2] LEED-ND can be expected to have a similarly positive effect on development trends to revitalize existing urban areas, decrease land consumption, decrease vehicle-miles traveled, improve air quality, decrease runoff of polluted stormwater, and build communities where people of a variety of income levels can coexist, and where jobs and services are accessible by foot or transit.

**SOURCE:** U.S. Green Building Council Web site, www.usgbc.org/DisplayPage.aspx?CategoryID=19; Anuradha Kher, "LEED 2009 Opens for Public Comment," *Multi-Housing News,* May 19, 2008; www.multihousingnews.com/multihousing/content_display/industry-news/e3i166e2aeceb59a4e1596da87247d0bab1.

**1.** U.S. Green Building Council, "LEED Rating Systems"; www.usgbc.org/displaypage.aspx?cmspageid=222.

**2.** The USGBC board of directors released details of LEED 2009 for public comment in May 2008; the new version includes several key advances, including a predictable development cycle, transparent weighting of credits for environmental and human impacts, and regionalization.

appropriation) for a new federal partnership to assist municipalities, counties, and states to increase energy efficiency.[34] In addition, both the Warner-Lieberman Carbon Cap and Trade Bill and the reauthorization of the Federal Highway Trust Fund are expected to include requirements to reduce carbon and vehicle miles traveled, putting more pressure on state and local governments to encourage more efficient land use.[35]

At the state level, a proposal pending in Pennsylvania's House of Representatives would provide a tax credit for new construction and renovation of existing multifamily, commercial, and industrial buildings—again, to promote efficiency and reduce waste—if the buildings contain at least 10,000 square feet (929 square meters) and comply with high-performance building standards.[36] The bottom line is to exercise environmental responsibility in the selection of materials, in the choice of construction techniques, and in the design and installation of building operating systems, which will not only improve the environment, but also the health of the occupants.

A number of cities now offer incentives—including financial assistance, tax breaks, expedited permit reviews and density bonuses—to encourage green building, and some have even begun to mandate it, as the following examples illustrate:

- In Pasadena, California, a Green Building Practices Ordinance that went into effect on April 15, 2007, requires private and public buildings to be designed, rehabilitated, and constructed according to the LEED rating system. The city is conducting free "going green" seminars for residents and developers to "learn how to incorporate techniques, maintenance and management into their homes, offices and daily lives," according to Mayor Bill Bogaard.[37]
- Under the District of Columbia's Green Building Act of 2006, which went into effect on March 8, 2007, beginning in 2012, privately owned, nonresidential projects of 50,000 square feet (4,645 square meters) or more that involve new construction or substantial improvements must be LEED certified. Some public projects must comply with the new standards even earlier. The act also contains an incentive program designed to encourage early adoption of LEED standards.[38]
- Boston mandates green building guidelines for private developments. In addition to the standard LEED points, the city has implemented several green building credits, including the Modern Grid Credit, for the use of on-site electrical power and heat generation; a historic preservation credit for adaptive use of historic buildings; and the Modern Mobility Credit, for transit-oriented developments (TODs). Mayor Thomas Menino has announced plans to plant 100,000 trees by 2020, and Solar Boston has announced a $500,000 initiative to bring solar energy to as many rooftops as possible.[39]
- On Earth Day (April 22) 2008, the Los Angeles City Council voted to approve the city's Green Building Program. Based on LEED compliance, the initiative will require new developments of more than 50,000 square feet (4,645 square meters) to be 15 percent more energy efficient than current California codes require. Los Angeles is the largest city in the United States to adopt a mandatory sustainability program of this magnitude.[40]

▸ Stamford, Connecticut, and the Connecticut Housing Finance Authority helped to finance the 238-unit Metro Green Residential project. Groundbreaking for this mixed-use, mixed-income TOD, which is located one block from a major transit center and within walking distance of thousands of jobs, was held in June 2008. New York–based Jonathan Rose Companies is developing the LEED-ND (LEED for Neighborhood Developments) pilot project, which is expected to serve as a model for smart growth in Connecticut and beyond.[41]

▸ Under innovative legislation approved by the county council in April 2008, new homes built in Montgomery County, Maryland, would have to meet federal energy efficiency standards. The measure, which is meant to reduce residential energy consumption by 15 to 30 percent, is just part of a far-reaching environmental initiative that also includes property tax credits for residents who switch to renewable energy sources.[42]

▸ The city of Dallas has implemented strong green building initiatives. A city ordinance requires that city facilities of more than 10,000 square feet (929 square meters) be designed and built to meet—at a minimum—the LEED silver standard. The city is "the number one municipal purchaser of renewable green power in the United States," and boasts one of the largest clean vehicle fleets in the country.[43] The city is also retrofitting existing buildings with high-efficiency HVAC and lighting systems. Dallas is the only city that has been chosen to partner with the Environmental Protection Agency on a pilot program for its Sustainable Skylines Initiative (designed to improve air quality), which, if successful, will likely be used as a model for other cities. Upon recommendation of its Green Building Task Force, in early April, 2008, the Dallas City Council unanimously adopted an ordinance designed to reduce energy and water consumption in all new houses and commercial buildings.[44]

FIGURE 9-2 **Financial Benefits of Green Buildings.**

| | 20-Year NPV (per Square Foot/ Square Meter) |
|---|---|
| Energy value | $5.79/$62.32 |
| Emissions value | $1.18/$12.70 |
| Water value | $0.51/$5.49 |
| Waste value (obtained during construction only, which is estimated at one year) | $0.03/$0.32 |
| Value of commissioning operations and management (i.e., monitoring and adjusting building systems) | $8.47/$91.17 |
| Productivity and health value, LEED certified and silver | $36.89/$397.08 |
| Productivity and health value, LEED gold and platinum | $55.33/$595.56 |
| Less green cost premium | ($4.00)/($43.05) |
| Total 20-year net present value (NPV), certified and silver | $50.00/$538.20 |
| Total 20-year NPV, gold and platinum | $65.00/$699.65 |

**SOURCE:** Anne Frej, *Green Office Buildings: A Practical Guide to Development* (Washington, D.C.: ULI–the Urban Land Institute, 2005), 47; CapitalE analysis.

# The Benefits of Going Green

Building green has its benefits. It conserves materials and resources, uses materials and resources more efficiently, fosters greater respect for the environment, minimizes waste, creates a healthy and comfortable setting for inhabitants, produces positive publicity, and is more sustainable than conventional construction. The Herman Miller Market-Place in Zeeland, Michigan, for example, has earned an Energy Star rating because it has decreased the amount of energy needed for indoor lighting by making 62 percent of its wall space out of glass.

Some critics assert that building green is more expensive—and that may indeed be the case in terms of upfront costs; in the long run, however, accumulated energy savings will more than offset additional costs. And many studies indicate that building green actually reduces capital and operating costs.[45] These cost savings come from reduced energy and water use, more economical treatment of waste, and lower maintenance costs. Figure 9-2 shows that the net financial benefits of green building are about $50 to $65 per square foot ($538 to $700 per square meter), depending on the degree of certification. As McIlwain says, if it costs little—if any—more to build green, "there is absolutely no reason why all building codes should not require all new construction to meet at least the basic LEED standards."[46]

The following are just a few of the "down home" examples that illustrate the benefits of green development:

▸ Treasure Island, a redeveloped former U.S. Navy base in San Diego Bay, is on track to become a sustainable community, thanks in part to a 150-page sustainability plan that establishes metrics for measuring progress in terms of various goals. At buildout, in 2018, the 450-acre (182-hectare) community will contain 6,000 residential units (30 percent of which will be affordable to low-income residents), shops, hotels, entertainment facilities, and a 300-acre (121-hectare) park and organic demonstration farm. Every home will be within a 15-minute walk of a transit hub.[47]

▸ In January 2006, Clara Vista Townhomes, in Portland, Oregon, became the first LEED silver-certified affordable-housing project in the nation. The project's sustainable features include whole-house ventilation systems, on-site rainwater filtration, efficient hydronic space heating, rooftop solar water-heating systems, natural drainage swales for stormwater management, and low-flow plumbing fixtures. The commitment of the developer—Hacienda Community Development Corporation, a nonprofit group dedicated to improving the quality of life for the state's low-income Hispanic families—to green development practices stems from a desire to build homes that decrease the long-term burden of utility costs and create a safe, healthy environment for residents.[48]

▸ Del Sur, a master-planned, mixed-use community being developed 20 minutes from downtown San Diego, will include 2,500 market-rate homes, 469 low-income homes, business and commercial space, a transit center, a fire station, two schools, and more than 1,900 acres (769 hectares) of dedicated open space shared with its sister community,

# FT ULI SUSTAINABLE CITIES AWARDS RECOGNIZE INNOVATION

Beginning in 2008, the Urban Land Institute and the *Financial Times* began partnering to present the FT ULI Sustainable Cities Awards. These awards recognize outstanding and innovative programs that have been implemented to advance the application of sustainability principles to land use and thereby promote their incorporation in cities and throughout the real estate industry. The nine programs that received awards in 2008 all demonstrate global relevance, add strategic value to companies and communities, and enhance the environment while serving as examples of best practices and innovative thinking in the area of sustainable land use.

**Cascade Land Conservancy, for the Cascade Agenda**
The Cascade Agenda is a 100-year visioning exercise that seeks to preserve more than 1.3 million acres (526,091 hectares) of forest and farmland by using market-based tools—primarily the transfer of development rights—to create incentives for smart growth practices across Washington's Puget Sound region. The program exhibits a sophisticated understanding of sustainability issues.

**City of Chicago**
The city of Chicago is a true leader in incorporating preservation and sustainability practices into its own operations and in the delivery of services to its constituents. Chicago is comprehensively involved in green practices, which are integrated into city ordinances. Both the size and scale of the city's influence are impressive.

**City of Greensburg, Kansas**
After a 2007 tornado destroyed 90 percent of the building stock of Greensburg, a small Kansas farming town (population 1,389), the citizens voted to rebuild for a sustainable future. Less than a year later, the city had adopted a master plan that incorporated sustainable goals and standards, and resolved that every municipal building will be constructed to LEED platinum standards. Greensburg's model for the reconstruction of rural communities after natural disasters is applicable globally.

**Enterprise Community Partners, for its Green Communities Program**
Since 2004, the Green Communities program of Enterprise Community Partners has invested more than $570 million to create more than 11,000 units of green affordable housing in 100 U.S. cities. Major capital investment, coupled with technical assistance, has allowed Enterprise Community Partners to integrate sustainable building practices into the affordable-housing sector on a large scale.

**Jones Lang LaSalle, for its Portfolio Sustainability Management Program**
Jones Lang LaSalle is setting influential standards for its own portfolio and those of its clients. The company's Portfolio Sustainability Management Program helped clients save $38 million in energy costs, reduce energy use by 210 million kilowatt-hours, and avoid producing 133,000 metric tons of greenhouse gases in a single year.

**Kennedy Associates, for Responsible Property Investing**
Kennedy Associates believes that buildings developed and managed according to sustainability principles possess a competitive advantage over traditional structures, and it applies this commitment across the entirety of its billion-dollar portfolio. All the firm's newly constructed developments are built to achieve LEED silver certification; Kennedy also strives to achieve Energy Star standards for all its existing buildings.

**New Songdo City Master Plan**
The master plan for Songdo, a new city in South Korea designed by Kohn Pedersen Fox, is complete, and construction, by Gale International with POSCO E&C, is underway. This private enterprise plan, which is a pilot project in the LEED-ND program, features a strong emphasis on reducing carbon use. The master plan applies state-of-the-art green practices in urban design, engineering, construction, infrastructure, and energy systems.

**PNC Bank, for Its Greening PNC Program**
Since 2000, when PNC's corporate headquarters was the nation's largest green building and the first financial building to be LEED certified, the firm has led all U.S. companies in LEED certifications. PNC has incorporated this commitment into a corporate policy that now includes 41 Green Branch locations. The company also has a substantial influence on the sustainability of its supply chain.

**Vulcan, for Creating a New Model for Sustainable, Mixed-Use Urban Communities**
Vulcan's strategic approach to the redevelopment of 60 acres (24 hectares) it owns in Seattle's South Lake Union neighborhood has revitalized the former industrial district, attracting new employers and creative-class tenants. The real estate organization's civic responsibility and social inclusion are admirable, and its strategy for urban infill is exemplary.

**SOURCE:** Compiled from ULI news releases, 2000–2008.

Santaluz. More than 90 percent of the community's construction waste is being recycled, and nearly every home will incorporate a core set of sustainable features that include drought-tolerant landscaping, tankless water heaters, and hot-water-on-demand systems. The community's LEED platinum-certified information center was built with materials recycled from the construction site and from dismantled structures.[49]

▸ A study released in May 2008 by Bethesda, Maryland-based mutual fund company Calvert, which promotes socially responsible investing, ranked KB Home of Los Angeles as the nation's number-one green homebuilder on the basis of four factors: energy, building materials, land, and water. The company "leads the pack because of its comprehensive approach to sustainability at the policy, program and performance levels," said the study, which also noted that homebuyers are willing to pay, on average, $18,500 more for "greener and cleaner" homes.[50]

▸ IBM is inaugurating a $1 billion per year program with the goal of doubling the energy efficiency of its computer data centers and those of its corporate customers.[51]

▸ Lerner Enterprises, a private real estate developer in the Washington, D.C., area, has implemented the Green Initiative Program, which is purchasing wind power for Dulles 28 Centre, a new 300,000-square-foot (27,871-square-meter) retail center.[52]

Putting the issue in a larger, longer-term perspective, the former president of the U.S. Conference of Mayors, Douglas Palmer, of Trenton, New Jersey, recently noted that Americans will build 40 million new homes and 20 billion square feet (1.9 billion square meters) of commercial office space over the next 25 years, which could result in a staggering amount of greenhouse gas emissions. But "by building intelligently through the use of energy efficient design and technology, we can realize over $50 billion and significant pollution reductions over that time."[53]

## Green Is Here to Stay

ULI Chairman Todd Mansfield opened the Institute's fourth annual Developing and Investing Green Conference with the observation that sustainable development has "entered the mainstream" of the land use industry, and is no longer viewed as a "passing fad."[54] As a result of the convergence of high energy costs and climate change, responsible people have awoken to the need for sustainable development. ULI President Richard M. Rosan tells a story that demonstrates how "green has hit." In November 2006, he was talking with a New York City real estate broker, who told him, "I don't think our tenants care about green. They just want to get into space ASAP." But six months later, the same broker said to him, "You won't believe what's happened. Today, none of the leading companies will look at a space in New York unless it's green."[55]

We've come a long way since the 1950s, when the United States seemed to have a limitless supply of land, energy, and building materials. Americans in general and the development industry in particular have become much more aware of the fact that these resources are *not* limitless, that we must learn to value, conserve, and protect them, as well as to use them wisely. Going green means more than conserving open space and constructing energy-efficient buildings. It means building for people and nature, not cars; building in a way that reduces $CO_2$ emissions; and building in ways that promote healthier lifestyles.

To meet the needs of our growing population, America's changing metropolitan form needs to grow in greener, smarter ways. We need to think in terms of saving open space, avoiding sprawl, conserving finite resources, and improving people's health through how we plan, design, and develop the built environment. Sustainability means building green, and building green creates sustainability. This should not be a political issue. Green is not red, nor is it blue. If anything, it is red, white, and blue. All Americans, regardless of their political leanings, can—and should—be concerned about sustainability, energy efficiency, compact development, health, and environmental responsibility. We owe it to our children and our grandchildren.

**ENDNOTES**

1   Quoted in David Ignatius, "Markets' World of Worry," *Washington Post*, September 27, 2007, A25.

2   Jim Heid, *Greenfield Development without Sprawl: The Role of Planned Communities* (Washington, D.C.: ULI–the Urban Land Institute, 1999), 1.

3   Peter Calthorpe, keynote speech, ULI's Fourth Annual Developing and Investing Green Conference, April 7, 2008.

4   Chaffin/Light Associates Web site, www.chaffinlight.com/partnership_history.html.

5   Gerding Edlen Development Web site, www.gerdingedlen.com/index.php.

6   Rose Companies LLC Web site, www.rosecompanies.com/whoweare/index.html.

7   Crosland Web site, www.crosland.com/about_us/sustainability/35361.shtml.

8   Crosland Web site, www.crosland.com/apartments/under_development/19323.shtml; Terrazzo Web site, www.terrazzonashville.net/pdfs/green.pdf.

9   Noisette Company, *The New American City: City of North Charleston; Noisette Community Master Plan* (North Charleston, S.C.: Noisette Company, 2003), 1.2.

10  *American Farmland Trust 2007 Annual Report* (Washington, D.C.: American Farmland Trust, 2007), 4.

11  William Fulton, Rolf Pendall, Mai Nguyen, and Alicia Harrison, "Who Sprawls Most? How Growth Patterns Differ across the U.S.," Brookings Institution, Center on Urban and Metropolitan Policy, July 2001, 19; www.brookings.edu/es/urban/publications/fulton.pdf.

12  California Green Solutions, "California Growth Projections Are +25 Million by 2050~!" July 7, 2007; www.californiagreensolutions.com/cgi-bin/gt/tpl.h,content=625.

13  Bret Schulte, "A Plea for Preservation," *U.S. News & World Report*, September 5, 2006, 24; available at www.usnews.com/usnews/news/articles/060827/4qa.htm.

14  Richard Louv, *Last Child in the Woods: Saving Our Children from Nature-Deficit Disorder* (Chapel Hill, N.C.: Algonquin Books of Chapel Hill, 2006).

15  Mark A. Benedict and Edward T. McMahon, *Green Infrastructure: Linking Landscapes and Communities* (Washington, D.C.: Island Press, 2006), 1.

16  Land Trust Alliance, "Private Land Conservation in U.S. Soars," news release, November 30, 2006; Trust for Public Land, "Americans Invest in Parks & Conservation: LandVote 2006." A conservation easement is "a voluntary private agreement that restricts future development,

while often allowing continued traditional uses such as farming or forestry.

17 Center for Green Space Design Web site, www.greenspacedesign.org. For more information about CEDAR and CEDAR workshops, contact the Center for Green Space Design, 311 South 900 East, Suite 201, Salt Lake City, Utah 84102.

18 Jennifer Wolch, "Two by Two," *Planning* (August–September 2003): 31–35.

19 "Miami Mayor Diaz Advances," *U.S. Mayor*, May 7, 2007, 4.

20 *Orlando Sentinel Tribune*, quoted in Louv, *Last Child in the Woods*, 259.

21 Nathan Rezeay, e-mail to author, June 11, 2008.

22 Neal Peirce, "Global Warming Challenge: Think Like It's 2050," syndicated column, September 3, 2006.

23 Rutherford Platt, ed., *The Humane Metropolis: People and Nature in the 21st Century* (Amherst, Mass.: University of Massachusetts Press, 2006).

24 Neal Peirce, "The Humane Metropolis: Are We Ready?" syndicated column, April 1, 2007.

25 Sustainable Cascadia Web site, www.sustainablecascadia.org/mission.php.

26 Stella Tarnay, "Green Neighborhoods," *Urban Land* (May 2005); Lawrence A. Selzer, *Ten Principles for Smart Growth on the Fringe* (Washington, D.C.: ULI–the Urban Land Institute, 2004), foreword.

27 Reid Ewing, Keith Bartholomew, Steve Winkelman, Jerry Walters, and Don Chen, *Growing Cooler: The Evidence on Urban Development and Climate Change* (Washington, D.C.: ULI–the Urban Land Institute, 2008), 6.

28 John Caulfield, "This Way," *Builder*, September 2007, 136.

29 Anne Frej, *Green Office Buildings: A Practical Guide to Development* (Washington, D.C.: ULI–the Urban Land Institute, 2005), 2.

30 U.S. Department of Energy, Energy Information Agency Web site, www.eia.doe.gov/emeu/aer/pdf/pages/sec2_4.pdf.

31 "San Francisco Mayor Newsom's Green Building Task Force Calls for Mandatory Environmental Standards for Private Sector Buildings," *U.S. Mayor*, July 30, 2007, 6.

32 "How Green Should Green Be?" The Ground Floor (ULI blog), October 8, 2007; http://thegroundfloor.typepad.com/the_ground_floor/2007/10/how-green-shoul.html#more.

33 Duane Morris, "Making It Easier to Be Green: Financial Incentives for Energy-Efficient Buildings," *Alert*, March 21, 2007; available at www.duanemorris.com/alerts/alert2450.html.

34 "New USCM Energy Block Grant Program Comes Online Just in Time," *U.S. Mayor*, January 14, 2008, 16.

35 Tom Murphy, John Miller, and Uwe S. Brandes, "On the Front Lines of Positive Change," *Urban Land Green* (Spring 2008): 39.

36 "New USCM Energy Block Grant."

37 Mayor Bill Bogaard, Pasadena, California, report to the community, fall 2007.

38 Emily A. Jones, "Washington, D.C., Enacts Green Building Requirements for Private Projects," Construction WebLinks, April 16, 2007; www.constructionweblinks.com/Resources/Industry_Reports__Newsletters/Apr_16_2007/wash.html; Green Building Act of 2006 (B-16-0515); www.dccouncil.washington.dc.us/lims/getleg1.asp?legno=b16-0515.

39 Erika Schnitzer, "Special Report: Boston 'LEEDs by Example' with Green Building Initiatives," *Multi-Housing News*, May 16, 2008; available at www.multihousingnews.com/multihousing/content_display/industry-news/e3ia6bfab03d267bc8a3b6db9279216ece1.

40 Anuradha Kher, "L.A. to Have Mandatory Green Building Measures," *Multi-Housing News*, April 22, 2008; available at www.multihousingnews.com/multihousing/content_display/industry-news/e3ib126be14e01ab768d8e184a9140f6e1a.

41 Alex Padalka, "Rose Companies' Metro Green Breaks Ground in Stamford," greenbuildingsNYC.com, June 9, 2008; www.greenbuildingsnyc.com/2008/06/09/ml-rose-companies-metro-green-breaks-ground-in-stamford/.

42 Ann E. Marimow, "Montgomery Aims to Make Green Homes Mandatory," *Washington Post*, April 23, 2008, A1.

43 City of Dallas, "'Green' Is New Building Standard in Dallas," news release, April 9, 2008.

44 Tom Leppert, "Sustainable Skylines," *Urban Land* (April 2008): 40.

45 See, for example, Frej, *Green Office Buildings*, 14.

46 John McIlwain, conversation with author, June 2008.

47 Jo Allen Gause, ed., *Developing Sustainable Planned Communities* (Washington, D.C.: ULI–the Urban Land Institute, 2007), 26.

48 Ibid., 85.

49 Denise Meyer, "San Diego–Area Green Development Recognized by National Building Industry," *Commercial Property News*, May 12, 2008; available at www.commercialpropertynews.com/cpn/content_display/property-types/multi-family/e3i595 b48df06c95e2ec0435c1ffb44255c.

50 Allan Lengel, "In Green-Building Study, NVR Lands at the Bottom," *Washington Post*, May 7, 2008, D4.

51 Steve Lohr, "I.B.M. Effort to Focus on Saving Energy," *New York Times*, May 10, 2007, C11.

52 Mark Heshmeyer, "CoStar Green Report: Making Climate Relevant to Investment," CoStar Group News, February 14, 2007; www.costar.com/News/Article.aspx?id=B9C3CE14AA2BD3 F5EF79980CEE410666&ref=100.

53 Quoted in Brett Rosenberg, "Mayors Continue to Lead Climate Change Battle," *U.S. Mayor*, February 12, 2007, 25; available at http://usmayors.org/usmayornewspaper/documents/02_12_07/pg25_climate_change.asp.

54 "Build Green or Build Obsolete," The Ground Floor (ULI blog), April 8, 2008; http://thegroundfloor.typepad.com/the_ground_floor/2008/04/build-green-or.html.

55 Charles Lockwood, "Why Commercial Green Is Growing," *Wall Street Journal*, October 29, 2007.

# CHAPTER 10

# Leadership Creates Positive Change

Be engaged; be involved in what goes on around you. Be present in your own life. Find something you believe in passionately and get into it. Get outraged. Take a stand.

—TOM WALES, FORMER ASSISTANT U.S. ATTORNEY, SEATTLE

*As has been discussed throughout this volume, if responsible land use is to be achieved, the changed—and still changing—metropolitan form requires a new paradigm for planning and development. The situation is urgent. We cannot wait until tomorrow; we must act now. As developers work to build vital, sustainable communities, they must exhibit creative leadership. Visionary, innovative, and responsible leadership cannot accommodate business as usual. It must recognize the issues identified in the foregoing pages and take constructive steps to address them. Leaders must believe that these problems can be solved, and that new strategies can be crafted that will enable our nation's metropolitan areas to compete effectively in the global economy. Leaders must plan and work now for a more sustainable America tomorrow. In what follows, a few characteristics of land use leadership will be discussed—because leadership, like love, is a many-splendored thing. Hold its prism to the light, and it refracts in many different ways.*

**THE URBAN LAND INSTITUTE'S** mission is "to provide leadership in the responsible use of land and in creating and sustaining thriving communities worldwide." To support this mission, ULI member Daniel Rose, a legendary figure in the real estate industry, has committed $5 million to fund the creation of the ULI Daniel Rose Center for Public

Leadership. "Success for large-scale developments invariably reflects effective working relationships between the public and private sectors," says Rose. "I hope that this new center, through education and training, will be a significant factor in facilitating such relationships."[1] The center's programs will emphasize leadership in a regional context, integrated problem solving, public/private cooperation, and experiential and peer-to-peer learning. Well over 800 mayors, for example, have committed to reducing the carbon footprints of their communities, and ULI hopes that the center can help them to understand the relationship between local land use policies and efforts to combat global warming—and thereby make them more effective leaders. The center will also facilitate deeper understanding on the part of private sector leaders of the particular problems public sector officials confront in their work.

Given this commitment by ULI to enhancing leadership among real estate developers and public officials, it might be well to turn, in this final chapter, to the topic of leadership. After visiting seven states, a group of academics from Cleveland State and George Washington universities concluded that successful community building requires vision and leadership:

> *Time and again we found that in cities that had successfully transformed their economic and residential base, vigorous leadership was present and was driven by a well-articulated vision. At times, that vision was seated in the state house; other times, it was located at city hall and/or in the community. In city after city where progress had occurred, vision and leadership, sustained over time and backed by resources, played a decisive role.*[2]

While this book has dealt with many complex and difficult issues, it must end with the upbeat notion that creative transformation can be achieved through strong leadership. Americans used to smoke on airplanes, but they don't anymore. Not long ago, few people wore seat belts; now practically everyone does. Restaurants, schools, and buses used to be racially segregated; they are no longer. Attitudes and modes of thinking and acting can—and must—change. Such change requires the kind of leadership that will fight the complacency of those who are comfortable with business as usual. It forsakes the "come weal, come woe, my status is quo" attitude in favor of George Bernard Shaw's words, as paraphrased by John F. Kennedy: "Some look at things that are, and ask why; I dream of things that never were and ask why not."

So let's take a closer look at some characteristics of the leadership that is transforming—and must continue to transform—land use in America, in order to bring about a more sustainable future.

## Leadership Is Passionately Engaged

As the epigraph at the beginning of this chapter suggests, a leader shows passion for his or her cause, and becomes deeply involved in making a dream come true. Leaders don't dabble, nor do they give up. They "keep on keepin' on." Certainly this was true of Wales, who was murdered—possibly for a stand he had taken on a hot issue.

Leaders "get into it." They feel "outraged" by one or more of the issues we have been looking at, and want to do something positive to address them. They analyze a situation and then take decisive action. They believe in what they are doing and are not afraid of innovation. Leaders come from all walks of life—from the public sector, the private sector, nonprofit organizations, and grass-roots America—and they engage, both professionally and personally, in the following activities:

- Meeting the market demand for new and different kinds of housing, neighborhoods, and development types to create and/or restore a sense of community in the built environment
- Forging ahead with new regional governance mechanisms and alliances that have authority as well as responsibility
- Creating compact, well-designed communities that have a sense of place, instead of constructing sprawling, low-density development at the fringe
- Taking bold steps to help address the infrastructure deficit, while concentrating on maintaining existing infrastructure investments before building new infrastructure
- Bringing affordable housing for America's workforce closer to job locations in urban and suburban centers
- Establishing a milieu in which retailing can thrive, particularly in urban neighborhoods and town centers
- Understanding the implications of global warming and rising energy costs for land use, and the importance of greener infrastructure, greener buildings, and a greener environment.

Lincoln Heights, Ohio—an extremely poor first-tier suburb on the north side of Cincinnati, with a 99 percent minority population—offers a vibrant example of creative residential infill development in an at-risk neighborhood. This development is being spearheaded by Cincinnati Housing Partners, Inc. (CHP), a nonprofit organization that rehabilitates neglected houses and builds new ones on infill sites to provide high-quality, for-sale housing for lower-income households (those earning less than 80 percent of the area median income). CHP believes that neighborhoods are renewed one house at a time, block by block, and has built or rehabilitated some 165 homes in the Cincinnati area, many of them in Lincoln Heights. During her time at CHP's helm, Sister Ann Rene McConn was full of vision, vim, and vigor—as well as a little vinegar. She was passionately engaged in helping poor neighborhoods develop better housing, and gave her professional life to this cause. She was realistic, yet optimistic. She never gave up. She once told me, without grandiosity but with admirable grit, "If I can get a sewer and water tap, I can buy a place, tear down the old dwelling, and put up a new house!"[3] Her sense of urgency and unstinting resolve underlay the rebuilding of these 165 homes. That's leadership.

## Leadership Requires Vision

The academics cited earlier pointedly connect leadership with vision. Leaders have a dream, like Sister Ann's dream of rehabbed homes in poor neighborhoods. Leaders look toward the future. They take the long view, and ask, Where do we want to be as a community 25 years from now? What do we want our community to look like? What policies and strategies for developing the built environment today will help us achieve our vision for tomorrow?

Arlington County, Virginia, illustrates how land use planning can guide transportation decisions. No single person was responsible for the decisions; they were a collective triumph. Ideally, a regional land use plan should be in place before transportation infrastructure is planned. But in practice, development plans based on a clearly articulated vision for the community are the exception. The Arlington experience stands out as a rare example of how to do things right: local leaders developed a vision for land use surrounding a new rail transit line, and have sustained that vision for more than 30 years. Arlington County board member Christopher Zimmerman states the case clearly:

> Arlington's success is based on the application of transit with supporting land use. It isn't enough just to build stations and ask people to ride. And if the station is surrounded by parking, a great asset is wasted. To reap the full benefits of the investment in rail (including environmental, fiscal, and quality of life), development must be transit-oriented, and not just transit-adjacent.[4]

In 1960, when the Metrorail transit system was being planned for the Washington, D.C., region, land was acquired along the Interstate-66 corridor to facilitate a cost-effective route for the rail system through Arlington County. However, because the county was home to an emerging market for government office space, a strong single-family residential market, and a large number of garden apartments, Arlington planners—recognizing that the proposed route would be inconvenient for residents and that it offered scant development potential—turned to community-based groups, citizen committees, and the county board for advice about a potential alternative. The upshot was the development of a smarter plan that has allowed the rail stations to contribute to the county's commercial and residential core. This proved to be a prescient vision that led to a land use plan which, in turn, caused Metrorail's Orange Line to be relocated through the center of Arlington, underneath a failing commercial corridor known as Wilson Boulevard. Today, five of the Orange Line stations in Arlington are hubs of activity featuring pedestrian-oriented, high-density residential, retail, and office development. In 1970, the Rosslyn/Ballston corridor had 5.6 million square feet (520,257 square meters) of office space and 7,000 residential units. By 2002, it had 21 million square feet (1,950,963 square meters) of office space and almost 25,000 residential units.[5] This is a real success story for transit-oriented development.

"The results in Arlington show that transit can be a powerful tool to reduce vehicle miles traveled, and the resulting congestion and air quality problems—but only if it is combined with supportive land use policies," observes Zimmerman. "These include concentrating densities within the first quarter-mile [0.40-kilometer] of a station; providing a mix of uses in the station sector; and creating a truly walkable environment."[6] In a study of the corridor, ULI concluded that through "a strong vision, smart planning, and the political will to sustain the vision over time, Arlington has leveraged Metrorail to nourish strong office, retail, and residential growth and to determine the direction of development."[7]

## Leadership Sees the Big Picture

During political campaigns, I frequently visited factories to shake hands. Invariably, I was impressed by the boss's explanation of how the various assembly lines fit together. He had a macroscopic view of the operation, and understood how the parts added up to more than the whole. That's leadership. It sees the big picture. It does not allow itself to be distracted by minutiae or small-picture thinking.

In 2000, the National Association of Regional Councils proclaimed the 21st century "the century of the region."[8] Regions have become the basic building blocks of the global economy. They embrace the central city and its contiguous suburbs. They include municipalities and unincorporated land. In a region, people read the same newspapers, listen to the same radio stations, and root for the same sports teams. Even where it appears that residents are widely scattered, regions share the same basic commuter shed for work, shopping, and play.

As suggested in Chapter 3, regional thinking has become essential for governance in the 21st century; it is therefore illuminating to look at the many efforts to overcome the parochialism and balkanization that characterize many metro areas. Leaders who think and act in regional terms are on the right track.

The Citistates Group, headed by journalists Neal Peirce and Curtis Johnson, has been extraordinarily active in advocating collaboration across traditional boundary lines. According to its Web site, the group is "focused first and foremost on metropolitan regions and how they position themselves to cope with the demanding economic, environmental, and social challenges of the 21st century."[9] During the past 20 years, in an attempt to encourage local communities to see the big picture, Peirce and Johnson have written Citistates Reports on strategic issues facing 24 metropolitan regions. These reports—including, most recently, a series on critical issues facing the six-state New England region—have been published by more than 50 newspapers.

In a January 2007 executive order, Arizona governor Janet Napolitano formally created the Governor's Growth Cabinet, which consists of representatives from 15 state agencies, to coordinate agency initiatives in the areas of growth and infrastructure.[10] The cabinet collaborates with towns, cities, and tribal communities to develop and implement a smart growth process that integrates land and water use planning with the planning of existing and future state infrastructure. In addition, the governor directed state agencies to channel future discretionary funding to communities that agree to participate in and abide by a smart growth process. One of the Growth Cabinet's major projects involves working collaboratively with public and private sector partners to create a vision and plan for development of the Superstition Vistas area, which encompasses 275 square miles (712 square kilometers) south and east of Mesa and Queen Creek and is owned by the state and managed by the state land department. This project exemplifies Napolitano's commitment to taking a wide look at the structures of governance in order to overcome duplication of function and forge a more collaborative and regional approach to sustainable development.

In the Cascadia Region, King County executive Ron King has set up a climate-response planning team to help Seattle and its neighbors reduce the county's greenhouse gas emissions and prepare for the effects of climate change. This leader understands that a region's carbon footprint includes the footprints of local jurisdictions, and that individual municipal efforts to combat global warming must be coordinated in a larger effort.

Jerry Abramson, the mayor of Louisville/Jefferson County, Kentucky, recently engineered the consolidation of these two units of government. The city/county merger is not complete, of course, but it represents the fruit of Abramson's vision and leadership over a long period of time, beginning when he was elected mayor of the city, to eliminate some of the overlapping functions of local government. Abramson understands that a regional approach to governance will enhance the competitive advantages of both city and county. He sees the big picture.

Finally, throughout the country, more than 40 ULI district councils are pressing for more regional approaches to land use and transportation. The ULI North Texas District Council has joined with the Greater Dallas Planning Council in sponsoring symposia on first-tier suburbs and other regional issues. In the Austin region, ULI's Austin District Council has worked with Envision Central Texas (ECT) to develop a regional (five-county) agenda for land use, transportation, and the environment. Former district council chair Jay Hailey has been a strong proponent of ECT's work, and served on its board for several years. In the Sacramento, California, region, substantial leadership has been provided by Joe Coomes, an active ULI member who, in the late 1990s, recognized a need for more regional collaboration in the Sacramento Valley. As the president of Valley Vision from 1997 to 2000, Coomes spearheaded the effort through which the local ULI district council vigorously supported an outreach program to convene meetings at which mayors and other public leaders could discuss regional issues. Some 24 municipalities and six counties ultimately became involved, leading to the creation of a "blueprint"—a 50-year regional growth strategy for the Sacramento Valley. ULI sponsored programs on topics such as "The Role of Smart Growth in Meeting Demand for Development in the Sacramento Region," "Air Quality in the Sacramento Region," "Implementing the Blueprint: The Image of the Future or Just Another Pretty Picture?" and "Flood Control and Land Use."

## Leadership Takes Prudent Risks

Politicians don't like to raise taxes. It's risky—and I know, because I once lost an election on the tax issue when I was running statewide in Indiana. I tried to defend myself by differentiating between wise spending and wild spending, and I reminded the voters of a comment by Oliver Wendell Holmes to the effect that taxes are the price we pay for civilization. But alas, to no avail.

So what a handful of leaders in San Diego did resonates as an example of the willingness to take a prudent risk. San Diego is known in transit circles as "the city that started the 'light rail craze' in the United States." Planning for the San Diego Trolley began in 1976. Planners considered various alternatives, including a heavy-rail system similar to San Francisco's, restoration of a 1949 streetcar system, an elevated system, express bus routes on freeways, and light rail. The goal was to design and build a system that would reduce congestion and air pollution while promoting retail, commercial, and residential development around transit stops. In 1976, tropical storm Kathleen destroyed parts of the Southern Pacific Railroad's San Diego & Arizona Eastern line, making its right-of-way from downtown San Diego to Tijuana immediately available, so the Metropolitan Transit Development Board purchased this "minimum operable segment" for $18.1 million. The San Diego Trolley opened in 1981, and has grown incrementally to three lines. With 53 stations and 51.1 miles (82 kilometers) of track, the system has a daily ridership of more than 100,000. The federal government declined to help fund the project, so a sales tax was instituted—under the leadership of state senator Jim Mills, mayor Pete Wilson, and planning principal Mike Stepner—to help pay for the trolley construction. Says Stepner: "The Trolley has helped shape development in San Diego. The Mission Valley Line and the East Line have created urban nodes in walkable, mixed-use communities where none had existed before."[11]

Every developer takes risks. It's part of the game. There are no guarantees that when money is borrowed to do a project, things will turn out well. The public sector can help minimize the risk for the private sector, however, as the revitalization of downtown Silver Spring, Maryland, suggests (see the feature box in Chapter 4, "Transportation and Place Making: Downtown Silver Spring, Maryland"). In Silver Spring, because private developers—with support from the county and state—were willing to invest in the project, decline was reversed, and the area's assessed value more than doubled.

This mixed-use redevelopment could not have happened without public and private sector leadership that was willing to take some big risks. The state provided $36 million for the redevelopment, while Montgomery County, under the leadership of county executive Douglas M. Duncan, invested $151 million in the project, assembled the land, made infrastructure and streetscape improvements, funded the construction of two parking garages, and restored a historic 1930s theater for the American Film Institute. The public investment of $187 million leveraged more than $200 million of private sector development that was spearheaded by Jim Todd, president of the Peterson Companies, of

Fairfax, Virginia, and his associates. The initial redevelopment has led, in turn, to more than $2 billion in new construction and renovation. Todd's mantra has been "Public money for public purposes, private money for private purposes," and he credits the county with "giving us incentives instead of punishment," which made the private development possible.[12]

## Leadership Collaborates

Leaders persuade people to work together. They don't go it alone. They partner. And they help each partner "play their 'A' game," as famed Indianapolis Colts quarterback Peyton Manning says in the motivational speech he gives to business groups.[13] Leaders accomplish their objectives because they don't care who gets the credit. They understand that there is strength in numbers. They avoid the "I" words—*individual, isolate, island, I*—in favor of "C" words like *collaborate, cooperate, collegial,* and *consensus.*

A case from the Charlotte, North Carolina, metro area illustrates the point. In Huntersville, on the city's northern edge, Crosland and Pappas Properties has made a stunning effort to reshape suburbia, transforming a single-use, automobile-oriented place into an upscale, mixed-use development—what ULI chairman Todd Mansfield describes as "a fortress against sprawl."[14] When Crosland designed this product in 1999, it was a novel idea, and a major rezoning was required to achieve the necessary use designations and density to support the economics of the project. "The notion of a lifestyle center with retail, office, and residential uses integrated in a suburban setting (now known as main street or town center development) was quite new," says Mansfield. "It was a real education process to get retailers and construction lenders to embrace the product. Very few professional firms had expertise across multiple product disciplines."[15]

The developers faced multiple risks:

- Selling a new product that was poorly understood
- Maintaining integrity—that is, ensuring that all the mixed uses of the project would be functional
- Meeting a tight schedule
- Introducing a strong fashion element that was not in the initial plans
- Introducing multiple product types, each of which was in a different phase of the economic cycle (including what was at the time a weak apartment market).

"The challenges seem less in retrospect," Mansfield comments, "but when we started, we were experimenting with new forms that are now considered almost standard, but were not so then."[16] The result? Birkdale Village, a 52-acre (21-hectare) town center, built on the site of a former horse farm. Patterned after New England seacoast towns, the project contains 320 luxury apartments, 285,280 square feet (26,503 square meters) of retail space, and 52,502 square feet (4,878 square meters) of Class A office space. Mansfield points out that while this suburban area already had a growing housing market and appealing neighborhoods that were underserved by retail, it lacked a sense of place. Crosland and Pappas's intent was to create a place that would draw people together through an appealing product mix, a human scale, and high-quality open spaces and gathering places. According to Mansfield, because its grid street pattern links it to the surrounding neighborhood, which includes 491 single-family homes and townhouses, Birkdale Village has become "the de facto main street for the area."[17]

To make Birkdale Village possible, the developers worked with elected officials, planning commission members, and neighborhood groups to rezone the greenfield site. Developers persuaded the lending community that "something new that they did not understand could nonetheless be successful," comments Mansfield. Retailers had to be "pushed to accept the design format that now they readily embrace." Mansfield adds that "the only effective partnerships are those in which the public and private sectors share a common vision for a community's future, and are committed to seeing it through." The cooperation of local government was needed because Birkdale Village represented "a new product that did not fit readily into existing building and zoning codes." Crosland limited the government's role to review and approval, choosing not to ask for financial assistance.[18]

What insight does this project provide into the nature of leadership? A leader is a coordinator, a consensus builder, a coach (notice those "C" words again)—someone who makes sure that details are taken care of and that the right stakeholders are always at the table. Mansfield puts it this way: "Large-scale mixed-use projects require a quarterback to coordinate and balance interests. We learned this lesson at Birkdale, where we didn't have a designated point person for the first part of the project."[19]

James J. Chaffin Jr., chairman of South Carolina–based Chaffin/Light Associates, is another leader who understands the importance of working with stakeholders and giving them a sense of ownership in a development. His is a partnership philosophy. Widely hailed as a leader in sustainable development, Chaffin/Light began, in the late 1970s, to develop low-density communities focused on preserving nature and open space. The firm's first such project, located near Beaufort, South Carolina, was Spring Island, a 3,000-acre (1,214-hectare) community that demonstrates how developers can permanently dedicate a substantial portion of land for open space and trails, then protect that land through conservation easements and/or deed covenants. Each of Chaffin/Light's communities has a fully staffed nature center that not only manages the conservation easement on the property, but also provides environmental education for residents. "It's clear that government and nonprofits cannot by themselves conserve and manage all the open space they would like to preserve," says Chaffin. "If we can do more private-public partnerships where homeowners begin to feel they are the stewards of their environments, then there might be a formula here to conserve more land."[20]

## Leadership Perseveres

Notre Dame football coach Knute Rockne once said, "When the going gets tough, the tough get going." Leaders do not give up. They keep at it, no matter the difficulty. To borrow from Peyton Manning again, "It's easy to be a leader when things are great. But when times are tough, when it's gut-check time, those are the times when real leaders need to step up."[21]

This brings us to Marty Jones, president of Boston-based Corcoran Jennison Companies, which has been a leader in building mixed-income housing that is workforce-friendly, as the following examples indicate. In the 1970s, Corcoran Jennison—then known as Corcoran Mullins Jennison, Inc. (CMJ)—forged a 50/50 partnership with residents of the 58-acre (23-hectare) America Park—one of the worst public housing projects in Massachusetts—that transformed the project into King's Lynne, a mixed-income property in which one-third of the units are reserved for moderate-income households and one-third for very low-income households, and one-third are rented at market rates. According to Jones, King's Lynne was the first public housing to be converted to private, mixed-income housing. Today it is fully leased, in top condition, and a financial success. Says Jones: "The practices at King's Lynne serve as the blueprint for redeveloping troubled public housing . . . nationwide."[22] In 2007, the project received a ULI Heritage Award for Excellence, in recognition of its having established new concepts and standards that have been emulated elsewhere in the more than 25 years since it was developed.

The firm's Harbor Point project is another example of the transformation of public housing into private, mixed-income housing. In the 1980s, CMJ—building on its experiences at King's Lynne, and again through a partnership with residents—converted Columbia Point, a mostly vacant, boarded-up public housing project that was plagued by drugs and violence, into a revitalized, fully occupied, mixed-income neighborhood on Boston's waterfront. Harbor Point—which won a ULI Award for Excellence in 1992—is widely cited as a national model for HUD's HOPE VI program. Jones says her company's core business is "mixed-income rental deals that have some measure of affordability for low-income people. Sometimes we use tax credits. Sometimes we comply with local inclusionary zoning requirements. We are pleased and proud that many of the people living in even the deeply affordable units today are in the workforce in some way."[23]

Jones adds that "persistence is key." She likens development work to putting a jigsaw puzzle together—layering in different levels of financing, wending one's way through the bureaucracy, coping with neighborhood and political leaders, building support for a project. Mixed-income development is not easy. Worries abound about property values deteriorating, crime encroaching, renters defaulting. But strong leadership perseveres.

Such was the case with Randy Nichols, CEO of the Denver-based Nichols Partnership. Every day, in the Cherry Creek neighborhood of suburban Denver, Nichols would drive past the site of a Sears department store and automotive center with a large, mostly empty surface parking lot. Nichols kept thinking, "It could be a lot more than it is." Out of that thinking came the vision of a much higher and better use for the unde-rutilized site. His master plan for what came to be known as Clayton Lane was based on the "big idea" that if existing zoning could be modified, the site could be transformed from suburban to urban in character, with a new urbanist mixed-use retail district that would increase building heights and densities.

But having a vision doesn't mean that others will buy into it. Nichols and his team attended some 50 meetings before Denver's city council unanimously approved the rezoning. They met with city officials, the local business improvement district, the design review board, and seven powerful neighborhood groups to allay concerns that the project would be too tall and too dense, that it would have a negative impact on traffic and parking, and that it would destroy the eclectic identity of Cherry Creek's independently owned businesses. Eventually, they won over the neighborhood, which gave its approval, as did the public entities.

Completed in March 2005, the $163 million Clayton Lane is a 704,000-square-foot (65,403-square-meter) pedestrian-oriented mixed-use infill project that combines retail, commercial, and residential development. It contains a corporate headquar-ters, a luxury JW Marriott hotel, 1,647 parking spaces, and 25 upscale condominiums. (Affordable housing is a ten-minute drive away.) Every building contains ground-floor retail space. Structures are oriented toward a main street (also named Clayton Lane), and the project incorporates narrow, pedestrian-friendly streets and wide sidewalks. Through a partnership with a local nonprofit group, Transportation Solutions, bicycle lanes connect to a local bike path, to a bike-commuter facility, and to a bike shop. In 2004, the project won the U.S. Environmental Protection Agency's Clean Air Excellence Award.[24] The average return on investment for the equity investors has been 40 percent, demonstrating that mixed-use infill, while posing challenges and risks, can be highly rewarding when done well. In addition, Clayton Lane has catalyzed the development of new mixed-use infill projects on neighboring blocks.

Nichols didn't just have a vision: he had the tenacity to stick with it through thick and thin. The development of Clayton Lane illustrates the essence of leadership: creat-ing a vision, communicating it, and then cultivating it—that is, bringing it to fruition. Nichols persevered until he accomplished his goal.

The experience of Randy Nichols and his team demonstrates that a leader/developer must possess almost infinite patience, a willingness to bear the brunt of criticism, steady perseverance, and a wily knowledge of local politics. Nichols says the project took "three or four years of concentrated effort . . . persistence every day . . . a willingness to focus and not be distracted."[25]

## Leadership Discerns Signs of the Times

"A willingness to plan and build for change" in the ever-changing, ever-evolving metropolitan form is "critical," says Todd Mansfield, "because cities are about people, not buildings; and people are constantly changing the way they use their cities."[26] Leadership not only embraces change; it encourages it, promotes it, nurtures it. It discerns the signs of the times, and acts accordingly. Mansfield has written an entire book on the subject, founded on his belief that America "really craves . . . a brand new day of community." He points out that this craving is "like a vein of gold to marketers" who recognize that "the creation of an organized system to get people instantly involved in their new neighborhood" will satisfy the new American Dream of community, of people "coming back together."[27] That's a wave of the future, and discerning leaders like Mansfield are riding it.

Two other signs of the times are the shortcomings in our nation's infrastructure and the need to become more energy efficient. Both areas present plenty of opportunities for leadership. Prescient leaders today are talking and writing about the silent crisis of the deterioration of America's infrastructure. Because of the huge sums needed, this is an area in which government will have to take the lead. Of course, private sector companies have joined the battle by purchasing public assets and partnering with the public sector. Unlike most Americans, who have a blasé attitude toward infrastructure and are sleepwalking their way into the future, developer Richard Baron understands the deterioration that threatens our municipal infrastructure. As noted in Chapter 5, Baron identifies federal neglect as a prime reason, and recommends "some form of national urban development bank" as a solution. In November 2004, when Baron was awarded ULI's J.C. Nichols Prize for visionaries in urban development, he concluded his acceptance speech with a ringing cry for leadership: "The development community must exert its leadership to force a reexamination of national priorities in such a way that the politics of urban transformation is viewed as a critical strategy in stimulating our economy. . . . Let us agree that cities are worth saving. . . . It is time to end the silence about the condition of our cities."[28]

And, of course, nonprofit organizations like ULI and the American Society of Civil Engineers (ASCE) are chiming in by warning about the crisis. The Center for Strategic and International Studies has formed the Commission on Public Infrastructure to "raise public awareness and dialogue on the subject of America's mounting infrastructure problems, and to help lead the country towards making more innovative investments in public infrastructure."[29] The poor grades awarded in ASCE's 2005 Report Card and ULI's 2007 and 2008 publications about infrastructure have sounded the cry of "Wake up, America!" Nonetheless, the main burden of leadership falls on the federal government, which must accept responsibility for funding the necessary maintenance, operation, and construction of the nation's infrastructure, with a modicum of help from state, county, and municipal government.

The nation can be grateful for a few efforts being made in Washington to deal with this crisis. Momentum is gathering for renewal, in 2009, of the Highway Trust Fund authorization; more immediately—and thanks to discerning bipartisan leadership—as of summer 2008, several bills are pending in the Senate that would authorize the creation of a national infrastructure bank. Christopher Dodd (D-CT) and Chuck Hagel (R-NE) have introduced a bill to create a national infrastructure bank, funded by a $60 billion bond issue. Another bill, proposed by Ron Wyden (D-OR) and John Thune (R-SD), calls for $50 billion worth of Build America Bonds to pay for transportation infrastructure.[30] The hope behind both these proposals is that public investment will leverage private investment. As Senator Dodd said in a March 11, 2008, hearing on the Dodd-Hagel bill, "Using limited federal resources, it would leverage the significant resources and innovation of the private sector. It would tap the private sector's financial and intellectual power to meet our nation's critical structural needs." To which Senator Hagel added, "The federal government does not and will not have the resources to meet our future national infrastructure needs."[31]

To look at another example, today people are thinking "green" and expecting development to become more energy efficient and environmentally friendly. The mission of Katonah, New York–based Jonathan Rose Companies—a leader in sustainable development—is "to repair the fabric of cities, towns and villages, while preserving the land around them."[32] Rose understands the importance of counteracting global warming by reducing vehicle-miles traveled, so he has committed his network of affiliated companies to planning, developing, and managing "diverse, mixed-use, transit-accessible, mixed-income communities,"[33] often in collaboration with nonprofit partners and local governments. One of Rose's best-known communities is Highlands' Garden Village. Located three miles (4.8 kilometers) from downtown Denver, the project has won praise—and a 2007 ULI Award for Excellence—for its sustainable design principles, pedestrian walkways, water-conserving grasses, and easy access to public transportation. It also demonstrates that an extraordinary range of uses, housing types, and incomes can not only be accommodated on smaller sites, but may actually enhance their economic and social viability.

Because "green buildings in smart growth locations have lower operating costs and higher market appeal (thus higher rental rates) than non-green buildings and therefore tend to be more profitable," Rose believes that "over the next ten years, an all green, cash-flowing, transit-based or walkable portfolio will outperform a portfolio of sprawl-located buildings." Rose has started the Rose Smart Growth Investment Fund I, L.P., the first national smart growth real estate investment fund to focus exclusively on providing economic and environmental returns."[34] The fund is investing in green real estate assets—primarily office, retail, and multifamily properties in urban or village settings within convenient walking distance of amenities, mass transit, public services, schools, and other existing infrastructure. If the fund acquires properties that are not green, Rose's company will generate a "greening plan" for such assets to improve their environmental performance. For example, the fund has purchased two adjacent buildings in downtown Seattle that are located close to a light-rail transit stop and within walking distance of prime cultural, commercial, and tourist destinations. Built in the 1920s, the structures contain offices above ground-floor retail space. Rose is making capital investments to improve energy efficiency and environmental performance, and billing the buildings as the "greenest and healthiest" historic buildings in the marketplace.[35]

Fortunately, some of our country's leaders in the energy-supplying field understand the critical need to become more energy efficient and to reduce greenhouse gas emissions. Charlotte, North Carolina–based Duke Energy Corporation is the nation's third-largest producer of carbon emissions, but James E. Rogers, the firm's chairman and CEO, supports regulations on carbon emissions, which he says will trigger the development of more efficient uses of a variety of energy sources, including coal; natural gas; and nuclear, wind, and solar power. "I can envision a world in which we [power companies] get paid not by kilowatt usage, but based on how we help you optimize energy," Rogers told the more than 700 attendees at ULI's Fourth Annual Developing and Investing Green Conference. Decarbonizing the nation's energy supply means radically lowering the emissions generated by power and transportation, Rogers said, noting that such an achievement could be spurred by development that is more concentrated and less auto dependent. Climate change, he added, can be mitigated only by "entertaining the politics of possibilities of innovation" rather than "the politics of limitations."[36]

Rogers is leading the charge for "a Manhattan or Apollo project"—that is, for "more dollars and more focused effort," to develop cleaner technologies, although he recognizes that it may take as long as 20 years to achieve the goal of greater energy efficiency. He calls this "cathedral thinking"—thinking that looks far down the road, rather than at immediate returns. His phrase is reminiscent of one of the inscriptions on the door of a 16th-century cathedral in Seville, Spain: "Let us build a cathedral so great that those who follow will think us mad for having made the attempt." Leaders think no small thoughts![37]

As noted earlier, American mayors have locked into the green movement in important ways. More than 850 U.S. mayors—whose cities represent more than 25 percent of the nation's population—have signed the U.S. Conference of Mayors' Climate Protection Agreement, which was initiated by Seattle mayor Greg Nickels. In singing, these mayors have pledged that by 2012, $CO_2$ emissions in their cities will be 7 percent below 1990 levels.[38]

Of course, persuading voters that green is good and that their energy-wasting habits need to be changed—and winning public support for the pledges—will be a struggle, as will the shifts in land use patterns required to achieve more compact and transit-oriented development. But mayors throughout the country have awakened to the fact that walkable, workable, livable cities are sustainable. If cities focus on public transit rather than cars, and on building to high standards of energy efficiency, they will develop a more sustainable way of life that will save money, create new jobs, and help rescue the environment from the perils of climate change. Hence, in Seattle, Mayor Nickels proposed a new streetcar line in 2005, the city council approved the project in 2005, and streetcar operations began in December 2007.

Without Nickels's leadership, the mayors of the country might not have been galvanized into action. Nevertheless, the approximately 850 mayors who signed the Climate Protection Agreement are a reminder that leadership can be collective as well as individual. Collective leadership is also exemplified in Palo Alto, in California's Silicon Valley, where city planners and elected officials have realized that older communities can be transformed—that is, rebuilt—so that new ones do not have to be built on the edge.

Palo Alto is more than 100 years old. The city encompasses about 26 square miles (67 square kilometers), and has a population of 61,200, excluding Stanford University students. It has some 35 identifiable residential neighborhoods, each with a distinct character. Half of these neighborhoods have been developed since World War II. Palo Alto's updated comprehensive plan aims to transform conventional suburban, auto-oriented areas into pedestrian-friendly, mixed-use environments. The plan allows multifamily housing and accessory dwelling units in single-family neighborhoods, but controls architecture and scale to maintain each neighborhood's traditional character. It is designed to "discourage sprawl in the face of serious growth pressures, by focusing development within a defined 'urban service area,' encouraging compact development, and directing growth toward transit corridors and existing activity centers."[39]

Palo Alto has developed design standards and performance requirements for its mixed-use districts that regulate scale, parking, and building setbacks and orientation. The city also encourages the reuse of existing buildings and surface parking lots; the redevelopment of underused parcels; the introduction of support services in office parks; higher densities around transit stations; and the development of transit, pedestrian, and bicycle facilities to reduce automobile dependence.[40] In addition, the plan focuses on the acquisition of open space that will link existing habitats and create continuous regional wildlife corridors.

Palo Alto's leaders could have resigned themselves to urban sprawl and made no effort to reverse the centrifugal trends of post–World War II suburbanization. Instead, they understood that today, people yearn for community. They want to belong, to be reconnected, to "re-village" themselves. In *Better Together,* a sequel to the well-known *Bowling Alone,* Robert Putnam sounds a pessimistic note. He insists we are "no longer building the dense webs of encounter and participation so vital to the health of ourselves, our families, and our polities."[41] Putnam is about half right. Sprawling development has destroyed many "dense webs" and isolated us from one another. But a countertrend is occurring, because developers have discerned the signs of the times: "Today, a new sort of revolution quietly brews. . . . we are craving the community we lost along the way and searching out different sorts of dwelling places. From ocean to ocean, Americans are rejecting the isolation of the suburban century and rediscovering the pleasures of connectivity."[42] And the good news is that many planners and developers are addressing that demand.[43]

## Leadership Makes a Visible Difference

New Orleans–based developer Joseph C. Canizaro loves to describe leadership as "making a visible difference." Leaders create positive change. Their impact on the built environment is transforming. One can see results on the ground of their willingness to make their vision come true.

## ULI J.C. NICHOLS PRIZE RECOGNIZES RESPONSIBLE LEADERSHIP

First awarded in 2000, the annual Urban Land Institute J.C. Nichols Prize for Visionaries in Urban Development was established to recognize an individual, or a person representing an institution, whose career demonstrates a commitment to the highest standards of responsible development. The $100,000 prize honors the legacy of legendary Kansas City developer J.C. Nichols, a founding ULI member who is widely regarded as one of America's most influential entrepreneurs in the field of land use. "The purpose of this prize is to recognize land use leaders who use innovative processes, techniques, and insights to obtain the highest-quality development practices and policies," says Richard M. Rosan, president, ULI Worldwide.

The broad spectrum of professions represented by the eight recipients of this prize demonstrates that visionary land use decisions are made by leaders from all walks of life. The common trait shared by all of these winners is their innovative and responsible leadership in the use of land. All of them share a love of urban environments and an appreciation for the impact that physical places can have on the community. They do not see land use as an end in itself, but as a means to create better cities and communities, a new and improved metropolitan form.

### 2000: Joseph P. Riley Jr., Mayor of Charleston, South Carolina

Joseph P. Riley Jr., the inaugural award winner, received the award for his innovative approach to public housing and urban redevelopment. One of Riley's earliest efforts to revive Charleston involved the redesign of public housing. The mayor shunned proposals for "fenced-in" housing projects and instead opted for scattered-site housing designed to blend in with the surrounding neighborhood. Riley's belief—"If you build it, make it beautiful"—led the city to create affordable housing that was aesthetically pleasing and that, in the end, actually increased neighborhood property values.

### 2001: Daniel Patrick Moynihan, Former U.S. Senator

Daniel Patrick Moynihan, who represented the state of New York in the U.S. Senate from 1977 until 2001, spent more than four decades in public service. He believed that buildings—particularly public buildings—should serve a greater purpose than simply providing shelter; they should instill pride among the citizens who use them. As the Senate sponsor of the landmark Inter-

modal Surface Transportation Efficiency Act of 1991, Moynihan helped change federal rules to allow funding to be spent on a wide range of projects—including transit and other alternatives to automobile use—according to local needs. He also worked to preserve much of downtown Washington, D.C., by revitalizing blighted areas with parks and government offices; Moynihan's goal was to keep residents in the city by creating appealing public spaces that the entire community could enjoy.

### 2002: Gerald D. Hines, Urban Developer

"The greatest achievement in development is the development of a community," said Gerald D. Hines, founder and chairman of the Hines real estate organization. Hines saw the opportunity to define cities by their places and buildings, and is widely regarded as an industry visionary who raised the bar for commercial real estate in the last half of the 20th century by commissioning top architects to design structures that would leave a distinctive imprint on the skyline. The unique and prominent buildings and mixed-use communities he has created have instilled a sense of identity in urban and suburban centers throughout the world.

### 2003: Vincent Scully, Architectural Historian and Professor

Vincent Scully, the nation's preeminent architectural expert, taught several generations of architects, planners, art historians, developers, Yale students, and politicians that architecture is a "continuing dialog between generations that creates environment across time." Over the course of his almost 60 years as an architectural historian, Scully focused increasingly on the role of architecture and design in creating a strong sense of place, something he referred to as the "architecture of community."

### 2004: Richard D. Baron, Urban and Affordable-Housing Developer

Since 1973, Richard D. Baron and his company, McCormack Baron Salazar, Inc.—a for-profit firm that specializes in the development of economically integrated urban neighborhoods—have developed thousands of affordable- and market-rate housing units in cities throughout the United States, making the firm one of the nation's most successful developers of inner-city mixed-income communities. McCormack Baron Salazar takes a holistic approach to community development that stems from its mission "to rebuild neighborhoods in central cities that have deteriorated through decades of neglect and disinvestment." Baron has demonstrated that developing affordable housing can be both the right thing to do and good business.

**2005: Albert B. Ratner and Forest City Enterprises, Inc.**
Founded in 1921 by Albert B. Ratner's father, two uncles, and an aunt, Forest City got its start building and selling two-car garages. Since then, the company has grown exponentially into a highly respected, multi-unit national real estate development organization. According to James Ratner, Albert's cousin and partner, the company's willingness to develop in "iffy" locations can be attributed to Albert's contrarian nature. "When everyone else said the urban markets of America were places you didn't want to be, and that the only place to be was in the suburbs, Albert took exactly the opposite tack," he said. "The trick is to have the foresight to understand where people will go if you can create the place." Creating long-lasting, mutually beneficial partnerships with the public sector and other private companies is another long-standing tradition at Forest City.

**2006: Peter Calthorpe, Architect and Urban Planner**
A cofounder of the Congress for New Urbanism, Peter Calthorpe has long understood the importance of design in creating socially responsible developments. What began as a teenager's passion to "save the environment" evolved into a more than 30-year career in urban planning and design that has been devoted to the creation of communities that are as easily negotiated on foot as by car, and that significantly improve the balance between land development and land preservation. Today, Calthorpe, principal of the architecture, urban design, and urban planning firm Calthorpe Associates, is widely regarded as one of the nation's most influential urban designers. His work has improved the growth patterns of communities from coast to coast and overseas, and he has pioneered the emerging field of regional design.

**2007: Sir Stuart Lipton, Urban Developer**
The first person outside the United States to be chosen as a Nichols Prize laureate, Lipton is widely considered to be one of London's most visionary, creative, and committed developers. He began reshaping the city's landscape in 1983, when he founded Stanhope

Properties LC. Under his guidance, the Stanhope team developed—both on its own, and in partnership with others—a wide range of office buildings in a variety of settings throughout London and the surrounding area. Lipton, now deputy chairman of Chelsfield Partners, believes that the "greatest places are those that generate civic pride," and therefore strives to use engaging public spaces as the focal point of his developments.

**2008: F. Barton "Bart" Harvey III, Affordable-Housing Developer**
Former chairman of the board and chief executive officer of Columbia, Maryland–based Enterprise Community Partners, Bart Harvey is widely respected within the housing and greater real estate community, not just for successfully carrying on the legacy of Enterprise founder and industry legend James Rouse, but for expanding the organization's focus to ensure its continued success in the 21st century. During Harvey's 13-year tenure as chairman and CEO, Enterprise's investment in affordable homes grew from $200 million to more than $1 billion, and from 5,000 affordable homes per year to more than 20,000 units annually. In 2004, Harvey further advanced the organization's mission by spearheading the launch of the Green Communities Initiative, an unprecedented commitment to bring the economic and environmental benefits of sustainable development to low-income communities. Overall, Enterprise has raised and invested more than $8 billion to create more than 215,000 affordable homes and strengthen low-income communities nationwide. This extraordinary achievement reflects an unwavering commitment by Harvey and the entire organization to building economic and social stability through inclusive communities.

**SOURCE:** Compiled from ULI news releases, 2000–2008.

In Indianapolis, Myron D. (Mike) Higbee, CEO of Development Concepts, is revitalizing a tired, brownfield-laden industrial neighborhood. Called Martindale on the Monon, this mixed-income development is bringing new life to a lackluster section of town (Martindale) along an abandoned railroad line (the Monon). Says Higbee:

> The landscapes of older urban areas must be reconfigured to compete with the redefined suburban lifestyle. Cities and towns must now determine how to create urban neighborhoods that offer a true mix of land uses, ranging from residential to commercial. The opportunity to live within walking distance or a short drive from work, shopping, entertainment, and services is the new gold standard for a quality neighborhood.[44]

Old single-family infill housing is already in place at Martindale on the Monon, and the company is now working on a six-city-block live/work district anchored by a 280,000-square-foot (26,013-square-meter) redeveloped warehouse known as the National Design Center. (The name refers to the National automobile, which was built there in the early 20th century, when Indiana was the leading location for automobile manufacturing. Henry Ford and Thomas Edison are said to have once walked the floors of the warehouse.) Higbee is putting a $3 million charter school in the center, as well as a 30,000-square-foot (2,787-square-meter) home for what he calls "creative class businesses"—in this case, artists who specialize in digital fabrication. A dispenser for cotton swabs has been designed in the center, as have signs for the new *New York Times* building. The center will also feature a furniture outlet and stores that will make and sell office and residential accessories and outdoor art objects. Additional plans for the neighborhood call for a convenience store and restaurants, as well as other traditional urban amenities.

"Nobody thought we would make it," says Higbee.

> Time had forgotten this neighborhood. There had been no investment. We took the position that this neighborhood could not be brought back by simply doing PUFU ["paint up/fix up"] and a few homes at a time. We wanted to test a more macro approach. So we got the land under control by buying it up quietly for a couple of years, and remediating it. Then we brought back the market forces that had left (the only time property ever changed hands until we came in was at a tax sale), partnering with the city and the Martindale/Brightwood CDC [Community Development Corporation]. We put together a program to flip the neighborhood and make it attractive to market forces, while at same time we made sure existing homeowners were not moved out. Our risk, of course, was that the market forces would not come back. We had to overcome drug and blight problems and, at the same time, put $200,000 to $300,000 homes in a section of town where the average home value was $50,000 to $60,000.
>
> We aimed at single-family, market-rate homebuyers to invest in the neighborhood, and have sold 35 homes to date. A second thing we had to do was establish an environment that was conducive for services and businesses, so we created a live/work district with lots of

*affordable apartments. Now, young professionals are bringing in new income levels and restoring property values. One lady told me her $30,000 home had gone up to $100,000, and she thanked me for that instant equity![45]*

Mike Higbee is a leader. He has made a visible difference.

## Leadership Communicates Believable Hope

John L. Knott Jr., president and CEO of the Noisette Company, in North Charleston, South Carolina, and his associates are in the process of building the 3,000-acre (1,214-hectare) new community of Noisette.[46] Knott is a leader whose heart is filled with hope, which he communicates to others. In a time when so many Americans are fearful, worried, and pessimistic about the future, it is bracing to encounter someone who has such a positive outlook on life and believes in the future. John Knott is someone who says "We can," not "We can't."

The North Charleston City Council adopted Knott's master plan for the Noisette community in 2004. The plan—which was developed in the wake of the 1996 Charleston Naval Base closure—calls for a diverse, sustainable, mixed-use community with 5,000 to 7,000 residences and 6 to 8 million square feet (557,418 to 743,224 square meters) of nonresidential development in one of the most heavily industrialized cities in South Carolina. Forty percent of the community will be open space. Noisette—which has been cited as a national model for municipal revitalization efforts—is the largest urban reclamation project in the nation.[47] This "city within a city" will transform a blighted, crime-ridden older suburb and empty shipyard into a new sustainable community through the rehabilitation of established neighborhoods, new construction, adaptive use, preservation of open space, mixed-use residential development, and commercial revitalization. The development is a public/private partnership that is expected to cost about $2 billion and require 20 years to accomplish. Knott is calling it "the New American City." Talk about hope! Yet this is realistic, not foolish, hope.

A hallmark of the Noisette project is its commitment to sustainability, green infrastructure, and energy-saving buildings. For example, the design for the reuse of 10 Storehouse Row—an abandoned naval warehouse that has been converted for use by small, entrepreneurial start-up businesses, with artists' studios, office space, and a building-arts school—makes heavy use of transparent and translucent materials, and revolves around natural light coming in from the clerestory level. To conserve water, waterless urinals and low-flow faucets have been installed. Knott says, "It isn't about the green buildings or structures—it's about the culture of sustainability. We're not in the building business; we're in the human habitat business."

When asked what he felt were the essential ingredients of leadership in promoting this sustainable redevelopment, Knott listed the following:

▸ Do it yourself first, personally and corporately.

▸ Have the courage to change.

▸ Have the courage to lead.

▸ Be a lifelong learner about our world and become a systems thinker with a triple-bottom-line focus.

▸ Realize that air and water are essential for human life and that we are jeopardizing our own species' future for short-term economic gain.

▸ Understand that our actions are about our children and grandchildren's future, not our own.

▸ Have a sense of responsibility, in what we create, to the long-term spiritual, social, psychological, economic, and physical health of those we serve and our larger community.

Ultimately, Knott's assessment of the current situation is upbeat: "The development community has some of the most creative and effective leaders in this country. We are the solution to many of our country's economic, social, environmental and human health problems."[48]

## Leading the Way

On that optimistic note, this volume comes to a conclusion. America must foster the leadership needed to plan for a sustainable future. Nothing that has been said in the foregoing pages should be construed as invalidating the hope of achieving the traditional American Dream. The ideal pursued since the dawn of suburbanization still resonates with a majority of Americans. But the metropolitan form has changed dramatically during the past 50 years. So, too, has the American Dream. Achieving the American Dream no longer means *only* owning a single-family suburban house with a nice lawn and a two-car garage. Today, there are many different versions of the American Dream. Some people still want to live in the suburbs, while others prefer exurban or urban living. Some like to rent; others like to buy. Some choose single-family homes, while others prefer apartment living. Overall, the dream today is more urbanized and more oriented toward connecting people.

Our leaders—in both the public and private sectors—must understand these new American dreams in the context of the new polynuclear metropolitan area, which looks more like a spiderweb than a bicycle wheel. Sustainability has become a touchstone for the new American dreams. As our population grows, our leaders will have to embrace more compact development and higher densities. They will have to take greater care to ensure that land use and transportation planning, along with infrastructure repair and construction, go hand in hand, leading to smarter growth rather than greater sprawl. This will result in denser, more walkable, more diverse and, ultimately, more livable communities than those built in the 1950s. The suburbs of the future, reflecting the new demographics of our metro areas, will need to become more urbanized, to feature a greater mix of uses, and to provide housing that is affordable to our country's work-force. Places will have to be linked to each other by more than the automobile; they must be walkable, bikeable, and transit accessible.

Is changing metropolitan America to plan for a sustainable future impossible? No. All that is required is a broad horizon in one's mind, an unflagging spirit in one's heart, an ability to discern the signs of the times, and a willingness to work with passion and perseverance. With these tools, positive change will occur, problems will be solved, and leadership will bear much fruit as the new metropolitan American form unfolds.

**ENDNOTES**

1   "Real Estate Industry Legend Daniel Rose Provides $5 Million to Fund ULI Daniel Rose Center for Public Leadership in Land Use," ULI press release, May 8, 2008.

2   Harold L. Wolman et al., *States and Their Cities: Partnerships for the Future* (Washington, D.C.: Fannie Mae Foundation, 2007), 1.

3   Sister Ann Rene McConn, personal communication with author.

4   Christopher Zimmerman, conversation and e-mail exchanges with author.

5   See the Arlington County Web site, www.co.arlington.va.us/Departments/CPHD/planning/docs/CPHDPlanningDocsGLUP_metrocorridors.aspx.

6   Christopher Zimmerman, conversation and e-mail exchanges with author, March 2008.

7   Robert Dunphy, Deborah Myerson, and Michael Pawlukiewicz, *Ten Principles for Successful Development around Transit* (Washington, D.C.: ULI–the Urban Land Institute, 2003), 3.

8   National Association of Regional Councils (NARC), *State of the Regions 2000: A Baseline for the Century of the Region*, Report #3 (Washington, D.C.: NARC).

9   Citistates Group Web site, http://citistates.com/.

10   Janet Napolitano, "Executive Order 2007-05: Promoting Smarter Growth"; available at www.azcommerce.com/doclib/smartgrowth/eo_2007-05.pdf.

11   Mike Stepner, phone conversation with author, March 2008.

12   Jim Todd, conversation with author, March 2008.

13   Vincent Mallozzi, "Two Quarterbacks, All Business on the Field, Share Wisdom," *New York Times*, June 24, 2008, C18; available at www.nytimes.com/2008/06/24/sports/football/24manning.html?_r=1&oref=slogin.

14   Todd Mansfield, Ross P. Yockey, and L. Beth Yockey, *Craving Community: The New American Dream* (Seattle, Wash.: Abecedary Press, 2007), 232.

15   Todd Mansfield, e-mail to author, July 2008.

16   Ibid.

17   Prema Katari Gupta, Kathryn Terzano, Dorothy Verdon, and Nora Yoo, *Creating Great Town Centers and Urban Villages* (Washington, D.C.: ULI–the Urban Land Institute, 2008), 79.

18   Tom Mansfield, e-mails and conversations with author, July 2008; Crosland Web site, www.crosland.com/properties_services/mixed-use_development/; and *Birkdale Village*, ULI Development Case Study C034002 (January–March 2004).

19   Todd Mansfield, e-mails and conversations with author.

20   Chaffin/Light Associates Web site, www.chaffinlight.com/enviornmentalstewardship.html.

21 Mallozzi, "Two Quarterbacks."

22 Marty Jones, phone conversation with author, March 2008.

23 Ibid.

24 *Clayton Lane,* ULI Development Case Study C036019 (October–December 2006).

25 Randy Nichols, conversation with author, March 2008.

26 Todd Mansfield, speech presented to ULI Nashville District Council, Nashville, Tennessee, June 2007.

27 Mansfield, Yockey, and Yockey, *Craving Community,* 123, 193.

28 Richard D. Baron, speech presented at ULI fall meeting, New York, November 3, 2004.

29 Center for Strategic and International Studies Web site, www.csis.org/component/ option,com_csis_progj/task,view/id,568/.

30 ULI and Ernst & Young, *Infrastructure 2008: A Competitive Advantage* (Washington, D.C.: ULI– the Urban Land Institute, 2008), 50. See also Mary E. Peters, "Opportunity 08: Transportation and the Economy," speech presented at the Brookings Institution, April 28, 2008.

31 As quoted in C. Kenneth Orski, *Innovation NewsBriefs,* May 1, 2008, 2.

32 Jonathan Rose Companies LLC Web site, www.rose-network.com/whoweare/index.html.

33 Ibid.

34 Jonathan Rose Companies LLC, "Rose Smart Growth Investment Fund I, L.P."; www.rosecompanies.com/resources/RSGIF_brochure_070911.pdf.

35 Ibid.

36 James E. Rogers, keynote speech, ULI's Fourth Annual Developing and Investing Green Conference, April 7, 2008.

37 Fareed Zakaria, "Cathedral Thinking," *Newsweek,* August 20–27, 2007, 48.

38 Mayors Climate Protection Center, "List of Participating Mayors," 2007; http://usmayors. org/climateprotection/list.asp.

39 Adrienne Schmitz, *The New Shape of Suburbia* (Washington, D.C.: ULI–the Urban Land Institute, 2003), 48–49.

40 Ibid.

41 Quoted in Mansfield, Yockey, and Yockey, *Craving Community,* 11.

42 Ibid., Introduction.

43 Ibid.

44 Myron D. Higbee, phone conversation with author, March 2008.

45 Ibid.

46 The Noisette Company is already internationally known for its ecologically conscious developments, including Dewees Island, which won a ULI Award for Excellence in 2001.

47 Catherine Fahey and John H. Tibbetts, "From Base Closure to New Urbanism," *Landscape Architecture* (June 2006): 86.

48 John L. Knott Jr., e-mail to author, March 2008.

# Related ULI Publications

*Affordable Housing: Designing an American Asset* (2005).

*Best Practices in the Production of Affordable Housing*, ULI Community Catalyst Report 3 (2005).

*The Business of Affordable Housing* (2007).

*The Case for Multifamily Housing*, 2nd ed. (2003).

*Compact Development: Changing the Rules to Make It Happen*, ULI Community Catalyst Report 6 (2007).

*Creating Great Town Centers and Urban Villages* (2008).

*Creating Value: Smart Development and Green Design* (2007).

*Creating Walkable Places: Compact Mixed-Use Solutions* (2006).

*Developing Around Transit: Strategies and Solutions That Work* (2004).

*Developing Housing for the Workforce: A Toolkit* (2007).

*Developing Successful Infill Housing* (2002).

*Developing Sustainable Planned Communities* (2007).

*Environmentally Sustainable Affordable Housing*, ULI Community Catalyst Report 7 (2008).

*Getting Density Right: Tools for Creating Vibrant Compact Development* (2008).

*Great Planned Communities* (2002).

*Greenfield Development without Sprawl: The Role of Planned Communities* (2004).

*Growing Cooler: The Evidence on Urban Development and Climate Change* (2008).

*Higher-Density Development: Myth and Fact* (2005).

*Infrastructure 2007: A Global Perspective* (2007).

*Infrastructure 2008: A Competitive Advantage* (2008).

*Making Smart Growth Work* (2003).

*Mixed-Income Housing: Myth and Fact* (2003).

*Mixed-Use Development Handbook* (2003).

*The New Shape of Suburbia: Trends in Residential Development* (2003).

*Place Making: Developing Town Centers, Main Streets, and Urban Villages* (2003).

*Regenerating Older Suburbs* (2007).

*Smart Growth Transportation for Suburban Greenfields* (2003).

*Ten Principles for Developing Successful Town Centers* (2007).

*Ten Principles for Rebuilding Neighborhood Retail* (2003).

*Ten Principles for Reinventing America's Suburban Strips* (2001).

*Ten Principles for Reinventing Suburban Business Districts* (2002).

*Ten Principles for Smart Growth on the Suburban Fringe* (2004).

*Ten Principles for Successful Public/Private Partnerships* (2005).

*Transforming Suburban Business Districts* (2001).

*Translating a Regional Vision into Action*, ULI Community Catalyst Report 2 (2005).

*Urban Infill Housing: Myth and Fact* (2001).

*Workforce Housing: Barriers, Solutions, and Model Programs* (2003).